**Upper Austria**
Pages 190–213

**Lower Austria
and Burgenland**
Pages 132–159

- Hollabrunn
- Krems
- Linz
- Wels
- Melk
- St Pölten
- Vienna
- Steyr
UPPER
AUSTRIA
LOWER AUSTRIA
AND BURGENLAND
- Eisenstadt
- Wiener Neustadt
- Oberpullendorf
- Leoben
STYRIA
- Tamsweg
- Graz
- St Veit an
der Glan
- Gamlitz
- Villach
- Klagenfurt

0 kilometres          50

0 miles                    50

**Styria**
Pages 160–189

EYEWITNESS TRAVEL

# Austria

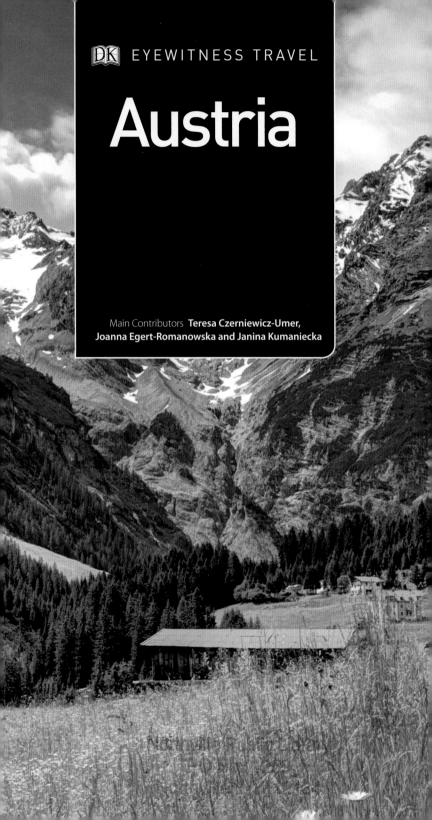

# DK EYEWITNESS TRAVEL

# Austria

Main Contributors **Teresa Czerniewicz-Umer, Joanna Egert-Romanowska and Janina Kumaniecka**

Penguin
Random
House

Produced by Wydawnictwo
Wiedza i Życie S.A., Warsaw

**Art Editor** Paweł Pasternak
**Consultant** Małgorzata Omilanowska
**Cartographers** Magdalena Polak, Olaf
Rodowald, Dariusz Romanowski
**Photographers** Wojciech and Katarzyna
Mędrzakowie
**Illustrators** Michał Burkiewicz,
Paweł Marczak, Bohdan Wróblewski
**DTP Designer** Paweł Pasternak
**Editors** Teresa Czerniewicz-Umer,
Joanna Egert-Romanowska
**Designers** Elżbieta Dudzińska,
Ewa Roguska, Piotr Kiedrowski
**Contributors**
Janina Kumianiecka, Ewa Dan, Marianna
Dudek, Konrad Gruda, Małgorzata
Omilanowska, Marek Pernal, Jakub Sito,
Barbara Sudnik-Wójcikowska, Roman
Taborski, Zuzanna Umer

Dorling Kindersley Limited

**Editor** Sylvia Goulding / Silva Editions Ltd.
**Translator** Magda Hannay
**DTP Designers** Jason Little, Conrad van Dyk
**Production Controller** Bethan Blase

Printed and bound in China

First American edition 2003

17 18 19 20 10 9 8 7 6 5 4 3 2 1

Published in the United States by
DK Publishing, 345 Hudson Street, New York,
New York, 10014

**Reprinted with revisions 2006, 2008,
2010, 2012, 2014, 2016, 2018**

Copyright © 2003, 2018 Dorling
Kindersley Limited, London
A Penguin Random House Company

A CIP catalog record is available from the
Library of Congress.

Published in the UK by Dorling Kindersley
Limited.

ISSN 1542-1554
ISBN 978-1-4654-6789-8

MIX
Paper from
responsible sources
FSC™ C018179
www.fsc.org

# Introducing Austria

# Vienna Area by Area

The enchanting lakeside village of Hallstatt

**The information in this
DK Eyewitness Travel Guide is checked regularly.**

Every effort has been made to ensure that this book is as up-to-date as possible
at the time of going to press. Some details, however, such as telephone numbers,
opening hours, prices, gallery hanging arrangements and travel information are
liable to change. The publishers cannot accept responsibility for any consequences
arising from the use of this book, nor for any material on third party websites, and
cannot guarantee that any website address in this book will be a suitable source of
travel information. We value the views and suggestions of our readers very highly.
Please write to: Publisher, DK Eyewitness Travel Guides, Dorling Kindersley,
80 Strand, London, WC2R ORL, UK, or email: travelguides@dk.com.

◀ **Title page** Beautiful Alpine mountain view, Tyrol   **Front cover image** Hallstatt village in the Salzkammergut region of Austria
**Back cover image** Colourful houses lining the Inn river, Innsbruck

# Contents

The colourful façade of Hundertwasser-Haus in Vienna

Statue of Mozart in
Mozartplatz, Salzburg

Burgtheater in Vienna

# HOW TO USE THIS GUIDE

This guide will help you to get the most out of a visit to Austria. The first section, *Introducing Austria*, locates the country geographically, and provides historical and cultural context. Subsequent sections describe the main sights and attractions of the capital, Vienna, and the different regions. Information on shopping, entertainment, accommodation, restaurants and sports can be found in the *Travellers' Needs* section, while the *Survival Guide* provides many useful tips on everything you need to know when visiting Austria.

## Vienna

The city is divided into three areas: Inner City, North of Mariahilfer Strasse and South of the Ring. Sights outside the centre are described in the *Further Afield* section. All sights are numbered and plotted on the area map. Detailed information for each sight is given in numerical order.

**Sights at a Glance** lists the sights in an area by category: Historic Streets and Buildings, Museums and Galleries, Churches, Parks and Gardens.

**Pages** referring to Vienna are marked with a pink thumb tab.

**A locator map** shows where you are in relation to other areas of the city.

**1 Area Map**
For easy reference the sights are numbered and located on the area map. They can also be found on the maps of Vienna, on pp121–5.

**2 Practical Information**
All the sights of Vienna are described individually. The practical information includes addresses, telephone numbers, opening hours, admission charges, transport links and disabled access. The key to the symbols used is on the back cover flap.

**A suggested route** for sightseeing is indicated with a dotted red line.

**3 Street-by-Street Map**
This gives a bird's-eye view of the most interesting area of each sightseeing section.

**1 Introduction**
The landscape, history and character of each region are described, and the most interesting sights for visitors are highlighted.

## Austria Region by Region

In this guide Austria is divided into six regions, each of which is explored in a separate section. The most interesting cities, towns, villages and sights are shown on each Regional Map.

**2 Regional Map**
The regional maps show the main roads and the topography. All the important sights are numbered and details on how to get to and around the region are given.

**Boxes** give further details about interesting sights.

**Colour coding** on each page makes it easy to find a region; the colours are explained on the inside front cover.

**3 Detailed Information**
Major towns, villages and other tourist sights are numbered and listed in the order they appear on the Regional Maps. Each entry contains detailed information on the main places of interest.

**The Visitors' Checklist** for each major sight provides practical information to help you plan your visit.

**4 Austria's Major Sights**
At least two pages are devoted to each major sight. Historic buildings are dissected to reveal their interiors. For interesting towns or town centres, street maps are provided, with the main sights located and described.

# INTRODUCING AUSTRIA

# DISCOVERING AUSTRIA

The following tours have been designed to take in as many of the country's highlights as possible, while keeping long-distance travel manageable. The first tour outlined on the pages that follow is a 2-day tour of Austria's fascinating capital, Vienna, a city packed with monuments, family attractions and cultural diversions. This itinerary can be done as a stand-alone tour or combined with any of the regional itineraries that follow. There are four tours, each lasting a week, which cover the forests and vineyards of Eastern Austria, the historic treasures and sub-Alpine hills of Southern Austria, Salzburg and the lakes-and-mountains wonderland of Salzkammergut, and the stunning highland scenery of the Austrian Alps. Choose and combine tours or dip in and out and be inspired.

**Wolfgangsee, the Salzkammergut**
Set against an impressive mountain backdrop, this 15-km- (9-mile-) long lake, with its emerald green waters, is one of the most charming lakes in the Salzkammergut region.

| 0 kilometres | 50 |
| 0 miles | 50 |

## A Week in the Austrian Alps

- Spend a day sightseeing in **Innsbruck**, the historic capital of the Austrian Tyrol.

- Feast on the scenic beauty of **Seefeld**, an idyllic village set amid cow-grazed pastures.

- Venture into the most dramatic of Austria's Alpine valleys, the **Ötztal**.

- Explore the Arlberg Pass region, home to the chic mountain resorts of **St Anton** and **Lech**.

- Spend a day hiking in the hills around **Kitzbühel**, surrounded by some of Tyrol's most spectacular peaks.

- Stroll through the meadows and barns of **Pinzgau** before visiting the foaming **Krimmler Wasserfälle**.

- Take a ride on a steam train and marvel at the all-year glaciers in **Zillertal**.

**Melk Abbey, Eastern Austria**
Perched spectacularly on a rocky outcrop overlooking the Danube, the magnificent Baroque Melk Abbey is one of the country's most stunning attractions.

◄ Watercolour of the area around the Neo-Gothic town hall, Neues Rathaus, Vienna

## A Week in Salzburg and the Salzkammergut

- Admire the splendid Baroque architecture and pay tribute to the city's most famous inhabitant, Mozart, in the lovely city of **Salzburg**.

- Tour the stately home of **Schloss Hellbrunn** before heading for the ice caves at **Werfen**.

- Marvel at the Gothic art and beautiful lakes-and-mountains landscapes around **Wolfgangsee**.

- Spend a day discovering the enchanting, historic town of **Hallstatt**.

- Venture into the world of Emperor Franz Josef I by visiting his favourite spa resort, **Bad Ischl**.

- Visit the pretty lakeside communities of the **Traunsee**.

- Explore Salzkammergut's quieter corners around **Bad Aussee**.

## A Week in Eastern Austria

- Spend a couple of days exploring **Vienna**, Austria's compelling capital.

- Head south towards the **Neusiedler See**, a reed-fringed habitat for rare birds.

- Explore the provincial capital **St Pölten** and the sumptuously decorated abbey at **Melk**.

- Follow the Danube riverbank through the historic towns of **Wachau**.

- Enjoy a lazy tour of the low hills and scramble through the dense woods of **Waldviertel**.

- Stroll through the leafy pathways of the **Vienna Woods (Wienerwald)**.

## A Week in Southern Austria

- See the rich collections of antiquities and contemporary art in museum-filled **Graz**.

- Head to the hills east of Graz to **Riegersburg**, one of Styria's greatest castles.

- Follow the Mur river to **Murau**, a historic town nestled in the shadow of the Niedere Tauern mountains.

- Explore the valleys of northern Carinthia, home to medieval **Friesach** and the fine Romanesque cathedral at **Gurk**.

- Visit the dramatic fortress of **Hochosterwitz**. End the day in the Carinthian capital of **Klagenfurt**.

- Take to the road or the water to tour **Wörthersee**, Austria's glitziest summer-holiday lake.

- Continue the Carinthian lake tour and discover the charming **Millstätter See**.

**Key**

— Eastern Austria

— Salzburg and the Salzkammergut

— Southern Austria

— The Austrian Alps

## Two Days in Vienna

*Exploring Vienna's cobbled streets, lavish churches and grand architecture is a fascinating journey through centuries of history.*

- **Arriving** Vienna's Schwechat Airport is located 19 km (12 miles) southeast of the city centre. The CAT (City Airport Train) takes around 20 minutes to reach the city centre.

- **Getting Around** Vienna has an extensive, reliable public transport system and it is possible to explore a great deal of the city in a short period of time.

### Day 1

Begin your exploration of Vienna's Innere Stadt or "Inner City" with a visit to the Gothic cathedral **Stephansdom** *(p62)*. Its spire dominates the busy square of Stephansplatz. The **Mozarthaus Vienna** *(p61)*, where Mozart composed the *Marriage of Figaro*, is just a few steps away. Next, head to the south of Stephansplatz, where the pedestrianized Kärntnerstrasse sweeps past boutiques and cafés. Venture to the western end of the Innere Stadt to see the **Hofburg** *(pp68–9)*, a vast complex of palaces and offices that was once the symbolic heart of the Habsburg Empire. Visit the **Reichskanzleitrakt**, the former apartments of Franz Josef, *(p73)* and the **Schatzkammer**, or treasury *(p73)* for a taste of former imperial splendour.

Striking façade of the Spanish Riding School in Vienna

Opposite the Hofburg is the famous **Spanish Riding School** *(p71)*, where white Lipizzaner stallions peer at passers-by from their street-side stables. Head west across the monument-lined Ringstrasse to the **Kunsthistorisches Museum** *(pp88–91)*, one of the world's leading collections of antique treasures and old masters.

### Day 2

Start by exploring the cluster of sights that are within easy walking distance of the Innere Stadt. Just west of the Ringstrasse is the vibrant **MuseumsQuartier** *(pp86–7)*, home to the Leopold Museum, the modern art gallery MUMOK and a growing number of cafés and theatres. Take a short eastward stroll from here to Karlsplatz, site of the late-Baroque masterpiece, the **Karlskirche** *(pp98–9)*. Continue on to the **Belvedere** *(pp102–3)* to explore its beautiful gardens and art museum. Next, board the U4 metro line from Karlsplatz station to **Schönbrunn** *(pp114–15)*,

The giant Riesenrad, or Ferris wheel, at Prater

another former imperial residence with formal gardens. End the day by taking the metro once again to **Prater** *(p108)*, north of the Danube. This park is a huge expanse of lawns and trees. It is an ideal spot for a stroll or a bicycle ride. Look out for the Prater's iconic Riesenrad (Ferris wheel), which attracts visitors until late in the evening.

## A Week in Eastern Austria

- **Airports** Arrive at Vienna's Schwechat Airport, which is the best entry point to access Eastern Austria.

- **Transport** There are good rail connections between Vienna and Eastern Austria's main towns. A car is essential for exploring areas such as the Neusiedler See, the Waldviertel and Vienna Woods.

### Days 1 & 2
*See the Vienna itinerary.*

### Day 3: Eisenstadt and the Neusiedler See

Head southeast from Vienna to explore the town of **Eisenstadt** *(pp158–9)*. Visit the Baroque chateau **Schloss Esterházy** *(p158)*. Next, pay a visit to **Haydn-Haus** *(p159)*, now a museum dedicated to composer Josef Haydn. From here it is a short distance to the **Neusiedler See** *(pp156–7)*, ringed by fishing villages and grassy plains. The town of **Rust** *(p156)*, with its seasonally nesting storks, is the most picturesque of the lakeside settlements. Round the day off with a drive around the northern end of the lake to the reedbeds and marshes of the eastern shore, a landscape best enjoyed in the **Seewinkel National Park** *(p157)*.

### Day 4: St Pölten and Melk

Visit **St Pölten** *(pp136–7)*, a lively market town with a well-preserved Baroque centre. Reserve most of the day for the stunning abbey at **Melk** *(pp146–7)*, located 30 km (19 miles) west. The abbey contains a host of artworks, a historic library and a dizzyingly decorated Baroque church.

## Day 5: The Wachau

Stretching between Melk and Vienna is the Wachau, where a stretch of the Danube loops its way between vineyard-covered hills. Enjoy an excellent day-long tour here, starting with the ruins of the medieval castle at **Dürnstein** *(p142)*. Stop off at the delightful town of **Krems** *(p142)* and finally, tour the **Egon-Schiele-Museum** *(p138)* at Tulln.

## Day 6: The Waldviertel Tour

North of the Wachau is the **Waldviertel** *(pp144–5)*, a rustic region of low hills and forests that stretches to the Czech border. Take a clockwise circuit of the area through the lovely old towns of **Zwettl** *(p144)* and **Gmünd** *(p144)* and past the impressively turreted **Schloss Rosenburg** *(p145)*.

## Day 7: The Vienna Woods

To the southwest of Vienna are the forested hills known as the **Vienna Woods** *(pp141–2)*, which are perfect for walking or cycling. Stop at the Seegrotte underground lake at Hinterbrühl before ending the day at a *Heuriger* wine bar in **Gumpoldskirchen** *(p141)*.

### A Week in Southern Austria

- **Airports** Arrive at Graz Thalerhof and depart from Klagenfurt.
- **Transport** Train transport from Vienna to Graz is swift, comfortable and scenic, taking you over the 965 m (3,166 ft) Semmering Pass. Trains are a good way to explore the main towns of the region, although a car is needed to reach the smaller towns.

## Day 1: Graz

Full of fine architecture and parks, the Styrian capital of **Graz** *(pp164–7)* is one of Austria's most elegant cities. Explore a clutch of outstanding art museums here and take time out to see the weaponry collections of the **Landeszeughaus** *(pp168–9)*. Consider a half-day trip to the Austrian Open-Air Museum at **Stübing** *(pp170–71)*, which provides fascinating insights into rural life.

Pretty view of the Wörthersee, Austria's warmest lake

## Day 2: Riegersburg and Bad Blumau

Head through the countryside east of Graz to **Schloss Riegersburg** *(p174–5)*, an imposing hilltop fortress with an absorbing museum. Continue on to the spa resort **Bad Blumau** *(p174)* to see the wacky buildings designed by Friedensreich Hundertwasser.

## Day 3: Bruck an der Mur to Murau

Head to the north of Graz and spend the morning in the historic market towns of **Bruck an der Mur** *(p172)* and **Leoben** *(p187)*. Next, follow the Mur valley west past the foothills of the Niedere Tauern. Take a side-trip to the historic silver-mining village of **Oberwölz** *(p179)* before arriving at **Murau** *(p179)*, the prettiest of Styria's well-preserved medieval towns.

## Day 4: Friesach and Gurk

Venture out to the green hills of northern Carinthia with a stop in

Rooftops of Graz's Old Town, a UNESCO World Heritage Site

the perfectly preserved medieval town of **Friesach** *(p278)*, before heading up the Gurk valley to admire the **cathedral** *(p273)*, which is a masterpiece of Alpine Romanesque architecture.

## Day 5: Hochosterwitz and Klagenfurt

Spend half a day seeing the famously dramatic medieval castle of **Hochosterwitz** *(pp272–3)*, before moving on to explore the Renaissance squares of the Carinthian capital, **Klagenfurt** *(pp274–7)*. Packed with good hotels and restaurants, Klagenfurt is the ideal base for the last few days of this tour.

## Day 6: The Wörthersee

Experience Riviera chic, Carinthian style, with a trip round the **Wörthersee** *(pp280–81)*, stopping off at the lake resort of Pörtschach. End the day in swanky bustling **Velden** *(p280)*, with its casino and glitzy café-bars.

## Day 7: Villach and the Millstätter See

Wander through the well-preserved historical centre of **Villach** *(p278)* before taking a scenic drive round the **Millstätter See** *(p278)*. If it's too cold for a dip in the lake, then head to Schloss Porcia in nearby **Spittal an der Drau** *(p278)*. Explore the excellent local museum here.

> **To extend your trip…**
> Just north of Spittal an der Drau, the turreted medieval town of **Gmünd** *(p279)* is the site of the Porsche Museum.

## A Week in Salzburg and the Salzkammergut

- **Airports** Arrive at Salzburg's W A Mozart Airport, which has good connections with other European cities.

- **Transport** Salzburg is only 2 and a half hours from Vienna by train. Little of the Salzkammergut region is covered by the Austrian rail network, although there is a good public bus service based in the regional centre, Salzburg.

Bad Ischl, a popular health resort in the Salzkammergut region

### Day 1: Salzburg

Spend the day exploring one of the most stunning Baroque towns in Europe, **Salzburg** (pp218–27), which features churches and palaces framed by distant snowy Alps. Wander through the lovely Old Town before stepping into the cathedral, or **Dom** (p224), or the **Kollegienkirche** (p223) to get a taste of 18th-century architecture at its best. Devote an hour each to the **Mozarts Geburtshaus** (p223), the house where he was born, and the art collections of the **Residenzgalerie** (p223), before strolling up to **Hohensalzburg** (pp226–7), the hilltop fortress that overlooks the town centre. In the afternoon, relax among the flower- and rosebeds of the famous **gardens** at Schloss Mirabell (p219).

### Day 2: Schloss Hellbrunn and Werfen

No visit to Salzburg is complete without a trip to **Schloss Hellbrun** (p228). Explore the 17th-century retreat, built by Archbishop Marcus Sitticus, is located 4 km (2 miles) south of the town. Its well-preserved interiors are surrounded by pleasure gardens. Consider extending your trip to **Werfen** (p229), 40 km (25 miles) south of Salzburg, where you can see the Eisriesenwelt show caves that contain spectacular ice formations. If time allows, break your journey in **Hallein** (pp228–9), midway between Werfen and Salzburg, to visit its museum devoted to Celtic archaeology.

### Day 3: Around the Wolfgangsee

Travel to one of the most picturesque lakes in the Salzkammergut region, the Wolfgangsee, fringed by the pretty villages of Strobl, St Gilgen and **St Wolfgang** (p209). The last is famous for its pilgrimage church, home to a stunning Gothic altarpiece by Michael Pacher. Allow time for a cup of coffee and cake at **Weisses Rössl** (p209), the historic resort hotel that inspired a famous operetta in the 1920s.

---

**To extend your trip…**

North of the Wolfgangsee is the **Attersee** (p211), a magnet for boating and sailing enthusiasts. Detour westwards to the **Mondsee** (p210). The lake's main settlement (also called Mondsee) is home to a historic Benedictine Abbey.

---

Splendid interiors of the Dom, the first cathedral church in Salzburg

### Day 4: Hallstatt

Reserve an entire day for **Hallstatt** (p212), arguably the most breathtaking of the Salzkammergut settlements. With Bronze Age artifacts in the local museum, a historic graveyard, and a salt mine high above town, there's a great deal to see. Next, visit the spectacular **Dachstein Caves**, Dachsteinhöhlen (p213), high above the southern end of the Hallstätter See.

### Day 5: Bad Ischl

Situated midway between the Wolfgangsee and the Traunsee, the historic spa town of **Bad Ischl** (p209) oozes with Habsburg tradition. Take a tour of Emperor Franz Josef's summer retreat, the **Kaiservilla** (p209), and follow it up with a trip to one of the town's traditional patisseries for coffee and delicious cake.

### Day 6: The Traunsee

Surrounded by craggy peaks, the Traunsee represents the Salzkammergut at its most picturesque. Tour the delightful historic towns of **Traunkirchen** (p208), Altmünster and **Gmunden** (p208), each of which serves as a bathing resort in summer.

### Day 7: Bad Aussee and the Nearby Lakes

Head to the historic salt-mining town of **Bad Aussee** (p184), the jumping-off point for two of the Salzkammergut's lesser-known lakes, **Altausseer See** (p184) and Grundlsee. Enjoy the charming views from these lakes, which are surrounded by green meadows and forest.

## A Week in the Austrian Alps

- **Airports** Arrive at and depart from Innsbruck Kranebitten Airport.

- **Transport** Innsbruck, Kitzbühel and the Arlberg are all connected to Austria's train network. You will need to rely on a private car or public bus to explore Austria's Alpine valleys.

### Day 1: Innsbruck

Begin a day in Tyrol's vibrant capital with a stroll around the compact medieval centre, pausing to admire its many highly decorative façades – of which the Renaissance-era **Goldenes Dachl** (p244) is the most celebrated. Get a taste of Innsbruck's imperial heritage with a visit to the **Hofkirche** (pp246–7), where a monument to Maximilian I presides over a flamboyant collection of statues. Stroll along the elegant boulevard of Maria-Theresien-Strasse, with its famous views of the Alps, or take the cable car to **Bergisel** (p247). The hill is popular for its easy walking trails and extensive mountain panoramas. Next, visit **Schloss Ambras** (p245), a Renaissance chateau filled with artistic treasures and curiosities collected by Archduke Ferdinand II.

### Day 2: Seefeld

Spend a day in the pretty mountain village of **Seefeld** (pp256–7), northwest of Innsbruck. Take a leisurely hike over the Alpine meadows and enjoy the awe-inspiring views. Return to Innsbruck for an evening in one of its folksy restaurants.

### Day 3: The Ötztal

Head west from Innsbruck to Imst before turning south into the **Ötztal** (p256), one of Austria's longest, deepest and most majestic Alpine valleys. Head to the village of Obergurgl, at the head of the valley, which is surrounded by high peaks. Return to the hiking and skiing resort of **Sölden** (p256), in the middle of the valley, which offers plenty in the way of refreshment and accommodation.

### Day 4: The Arlberg and Vorarlberg

Continue west by road or rail over the **Arlberg Pass** (pp260–61), the stark mountain barrier that divides Tyrol from Austria's westernmost province, Vorarlberg. If you are travelling by car, opt to take a detour to the world-famous mountain resorts of **St Anton** (p261) and **Lech** (p258), busy with skiers and après-ski life in winter, and blissfully fresh and invigorating during the summer hiking season.

### Day 5: Kitzbühel and Kufstein

Head to the main mountain resort of eastern Tyrol, **Kitzbühel** (p251), a pretty medieval town, and once the winter sports capital of the country. Spend the entire day outdoors hiking in the local mountains. There are several cable cars taking tourists up onto the high Alpine meadows: ride the Hahnenkammbahn for a superb panorama of the surrounding Alps, or take the Hornbahn to reach the Alpine Flower Garden. Afterwards, take a side-trip to **Kufstein** (p251), in the shadow of the Kaisergebirge, site of a historic fortress and an absorbing regional museum.

### Day 6: The Pinzgau

Begin the morning south of Kitzbühel in the green pastures of Pinzgau. Follow the rustic road west towards the spectacular foaming waters of the **Krimmler Wasserfälle** (p237), then head east towards the lakeside centre of **Zell am See** (p236), the starting point for the breathtaking mountain road over the Grossglockner Pass.

### Day 7: The Zillertal

Before heading back to Innsbruck, be sure to explore at least part of the **Zillertal** (pp252–3), a picture-postcard valley of pretty villages squeezed between the lofty Alps. Don't forget to take time out for a ride on the Zillertal's famous narrow-gauge railway, or take a side-trip up the Tux valley to enjoy year-round skiing on the Hintertux glacier.

Houses on the banks of the river in Innsbruck

# Putting Austria on the Map

Located in the southeastern part of Central Europe, Austria covers an area of 83,858 sq km (32,378 sq miles), and spans five major geological formations: the Eastern Alps, the Alpine and Carpathian Foreland, the Pannonian Basin, the Vienna Valley and the Czech Massif. Its longest river is the Danube, which flows from west to east. Landlocked, Austria borders Germany, the Czech Republic, Slovakia, Hungary, Slovenia, Italy, Switzerland and Liechtenstein. It has over 8.5 million inhabitants, 1.8 million of whom live in Vienna.

Weiden

Cham

Regensburg

Deggen

Aalen

Ingolstadt

Donauwörth

Landshut

A8   10

Ulm

**GERMANY**

Augsburg

Munich

Braunau

Landsberg am Lech

München

Memmingen

Ammersee

Rosenheim

Chiemsee

Salzburg

Starnberger See

Salzburg

Hallein

Bodensee

Füssen

Kufstein

Gol

Bregenz

Reutte

Garmisch-Partenkirchen

Wörgl

St Johann in Tirol

Dornbirn

Ehrwald

Brixlegg

Feldkirch

Seefeld

Schwaz

Zell am See

Vaduz

Schröcken

Innsbruck Kranebitten

Innsbruck

Bludenz

Landeck

Brunico

Lienz

**Europe**

NORWAY

SWEDEN

North Sea

DENMARK

N. IRELAND

IRELAND

UNITED KINGDOM

NETHERLANDS

POLAND

**ITALY**

Cortina d'Ampezzo

Tolmezzo

BELGIUM

GERMANY

CZECH REPUBLIC

SLOVAKIA

HUNGARY

Belluno

FRANCE

SWITZ.

AUSTRIA

Vienna

SLOV.

CROATIA

Feltre

Pordenone

BOSNIA HERZ.

SERBIA

MONTEN.

KOZ.

Treviso

Lignar

SPAIN

ITALY

ALBANIA

MAC.

Mestre

Venice Marco Polo

Bay of Triest

PORTUGAL

GREECE

Venezia

**Key**

National border
Motorway
Major road
Railway
Minor road

CZECH REPUBLIC

Plzeň

Vltava

Havlíčkův Brod

Tábor

Jihlava

Strakonice

Třebíč

Brno

Brno-Tuřany

České Budějovice

Znojmo

Gmünd

Zbiornik Lipieński

Horn

Mistelbach

Hollabrunn

Rastenfeld

Rastenfeld

Krems

Stockerau

SLOVAKIA

Morava

Passau

Freistadt

Tulln

VIENNA

Bratislava

Schärding

Linz

Melk

St Pölten

Vienna

Bratislava

Ried in Innkries

Wels

Donau

Amstetten

Haag

Bruck an der Leitha

Innsbruck

Steyr

Neusiedl am See

Waidhofen

Eisenstadt

Traunkirchen

Mittersee

Windischgarsten

Mitterbach

Wiener Neustadt

Neusiedler See

Bad Ischl

Neuenkirchen

Bad Aussee

Enns

Hieflau

Bromberg

Oberpullendorf

Irdning

Radstadt

Bruck an der Mur

AUSTRIA

Leoben

Szombathely

Mauterndorf

Murau

Judenburg

Mur

Graz

Graz

HUNGARY

Friesach

Wolfsberg

Zalaegerszeg

Spittal an der Drau

Leibnitz

Feistritz

Villach

Klagenfurt

Drau

Maribor

Mura

Ptuj

Nagykanizsa

Kranj

Ljubljana

Celje

Čakovec

Varaždin

Koprivnica

Ljubljana

SLOVENIA

Drau

Novo Mesto

Sava

Vrbovec

Zagreb

CROATIA

0 kilometres 50
0 miles 50

# A PORTRAIT OF AUSTRIA

Magnificent mountains span two-thirds of present-day Austria, gathering in a massif at the centre of the country. The breathtaking scenery of Alpine peaks, lakes and enchanting valleys, together with excellent year-round facilities for a variety of sports, attracts many visitors. Innumerable cultural events and fascinating historical sights make every visit unforgettable.

Austria grew at a crossroads, with the main routes between northern Europe and Italy, and from western to eastern Europe, meeting at Vienna. The Habsburg kings and emperors, who ruled the country for almost seven centuries, pursued expansion via matrimonial alliances rather than sending troops into battle. Although not entirely avoiding bloodshed, they managed to incorporate several provinces into central Austria through a series of arranged marriages, beginning with the duchy of Tyrol, followed by the powerful Czech kingdom, the equally strong Hungary and a sizeable chunk of Italy. Austrian culture, while traditionally linked with that of Germany, became an eclectic mix of Italian, Slav and Hungarian influences.

Austria's contemporary political structure is similar to that of most other states in the European Union (EU). The country is a federal state, consisting of nine provinces

(Bundesländer), each with a provincial capital. The head of state is the president, elected for a term of six years; the most important political figure is the head of the federal government, or chancellor (as in Germany). The government consists of a legislative branch, comprising a two-house parliament, and an executive branch. Parliamentary elections are held every four years, when votes are cast for candidates put up by the political parties. Although there are a number of political parties, including a strong coalition of environmental groups, since 1949 the conservative Austrian People's Party (ÖVP) and the centre-left Social Democratic Party of Austria (SPÖ) have dominated parliament. Voter participation is high, with as much as 75 per cent turnout in federal elections. The minimum voting age is 16.

Like Switzerland, Austria is officially a neutral state, a status established by the

View over the Hohe Tauern mountain range, from Heiligenblut in Carinthia

◀ Riding a motorcycle on the high Grossglockner Alpine road, Austrian Alps

Europabrücke, connecting northern and southern Europe

production. Organic produce is usually indicated on restaurant menus and in the shops as "bio". Genetically modified (GM) farming is highly contentious, with the government in dispute with the EU over a total ban on the practice. Politically, the coalition of green parties that represent the ecology movement is ever powerful.

Austrian State Treaty of 1955. Due to its location at the centre of Europe, Austria played a pivotal intermediary role in East–West negotiations during the Cold War. It is home to many international organizations, among them a dozen United Nations bodies, the International Atomic Energy Agency (IAEA) and the Organization of Petroleum Exporting Countries (OPEC). Although it is a member of the European Union and part of the Schengen Area, Austria does not belong to NATO. Its soldiers, however, do participate in UN peacekeeping and other humanitarian missions.

## Environment

Roads once trodden by foreign armies are today busy with visitors travelling from northern Europe to warmer climes in the south. The Brenner Pass, which leads to Italy, with its spectacular Europabrücke (Europe Bridge), has become one of Europe's busiest transit points, causing a major problem for Austria, where protecting the natural environment is a primary concern.

By constitutional amendment, nuclear power is banned entirely in Austria. Emphasis is instead placed on renewable energy: only 30 per cent of electricity across the nation is generated by fossil fuels; hydroelectric power and renewable energy sources make up the rest.

Organic farming is widespread, accounting for 19 per cent of all food

## Tourism

The country has much to offer: winter sports on snow-covered slopes, and beautiful mountains and lakes in summer all attract large numbers of visitors. The impressive infrastructure offers superb conditions for rest and recreation. Ski (or mountain) resorts feature funicular railways and cable cars, chair and drag lifts, and magnificent pistes and toboggan runs. Elsewhere, river banks and lakes are well maintained. There are plenty of places to eat, and overnight accommodation ranges from small pensions and private homes to luxury hotels, all guaranteeing a very pleasant visit.

Festivals take place throughout the year. Among the most famous are the Viennale, or the Vienna International Film Festival, and the Schubertiade, a world-renowned concert series dedicated to Schubert that attracts as many as 30,000 classical music

Guests enjoying a dip in the thermal pool at a hotel in Lutzmannsburg

Skiing at Mooserwirt, Tyrol, in winter

fans to the small town of Hohenems in Vorarlberg. There are a plethora of local and regional events, too. During Honigfest (Honeyfest), in Hermagor in Carinthia, girls dress up as bees, while costumed young men snap bullwhips to "wake up" the earth for spring during Aperschnalzen. Another seasonal festival is the New Year's Day salute (Neujahrsschiessen), where local squads dressed in traditional costumes raise antique musket rifles. The regional authorities also organize sports events and art exhibitions, and local theatre and music festivals.

A traditional horse-drawn carriage

### Language and Religion

Modern Austria has very little linguistic or ethnic diversity despite being a haven for refugees fleeing from the former Yugoslavia in the 1990s, as well as for people from other regions of the Balkan peninsula. A small number of citizens are ethnic Slovenes, Croats and Hungarians. Around 90 per cent of the country's population speaks German, although not every German-speaker will find it easy to communicate with every Austrian. While the Vienna Burgtheater is regarded as one of the foremost German-language theatres in the world, many Austrians speak a pronounced local dialect, though this is easier to understand for those with a basic command of German than Swiss-German. Some things have different names than they do in Germany. A bread roll, for instance, is called a Semmel instead of a Brötchen, a tomato is a Paradeiser and not a Tomate, and the hospital is the Spital, rather than a Krankenhaus. English is understood far more widely here than in France or Italy.

Nominally, 74 per cent of Austrians claim to be Roman Catholic, but church attendance is one-third of this figure.

A typical Alpine pension in Kartitsch, East Tyrol

The annual church festival in Villach in Carinthia, a weekend of folk music and parades

## Culture and Media

Austria's considerable influence in music is renowned the world over. Music aside, however, the country has produced works and talents that have reached acclaim and importance far beyond its borders. Perhaps the best-known Austrian is Arnold Schwarzenegger, body builder, action-movie star and former governor of California. Hollywood has also benefited from gifted directors Fritz Lang, Otto Preminger and Billy Wilder, as well as actors Christoph Waltz, Erich von Stroheim and Hedy Lamarr. Sporting heroes include Formula One legend Niki Lauda, and skiing champions Franz Klammer and Toni Sailer, who is the only person to win gold at all three Alpine events at the Winter Olympics.

Austria has also produced many Nobel Prize winners. Perhaps the most famous among them are Konrad Lorenz, a researcher into animal and human behaviour, who was awarded the Nobel Prize for Medicine in 1973, and Erwin Schrödinger, who won the prize for his work on quantum theory. The work of Sigmund Freud, the Viennese psychiatrist who became the founding father of psychoanalysis, has heavily influenced modern psychology, as well as other domains of science and culture. Other notable names include Gaston Glock, founder of the firearms company; Ferdinand Porsche, famed car engineer; and Hans Asperger, known for his work on mental disorders.

Tying in with its café culture, Austria has more newspaper readers than most other EU nations. The state-owned *Wiener Zeitung* claims to be the oldest paper in the world, while the conservative tabloid *Neue Kronen Zeitung* is the country's bestseller. *Die Presse* and *Der Standard* sell some 800,000 copies a day.

View of the impressive Millenium Tower and Brigittenauer Bridge across the Danube

The traditional parade of Tyrolean hunters in Götzens

Austria was the last country in Europe to allow private radio and television broadcasting. Now, in addition to the state ORF network, there are independent stations, as well as online services such as Netflix and Amazon.

## Traditions

Austria is one of the most modern and efficiently run countries in Europe, but its people are still fiercely protective of their traditions. Local and regional festivals abound *(see pp20–21)*, and traditional folk costume, the *Tracht*, is still worn as formal wear. The costumes, made of high-quality wool and natural linen, can be worn anywhere, even to an elegant ball at the Viennese Opera. An entire branch of the textile industry is devoted to their design and manufacture. Men wear green loden jackets and *Lederhosen* (leather breeches), while women wear a *Dirndl*, a dress comprising a bodice, puffed sleeves, a full skirt and apron.

Another Austrian speciality are the *Heurigen*. These are wine taverns serving the year's new-vintage wines. Mostly found in and around Vienna, these taverns were

Child in folk costume

originally attached to vineyards whose owners had a licence to sell beverages but not food. Secretly, though, they also offered home-produced meats, especially when a pig had been slaughtered. Today, they serve grilled pork knuckles – delicious, but very filling – as well as roast hams, grilled ribs and other specialities. In keeping with tradition, the wine is brought to the tables by waiters who also take payment; the food is available from self-service buffet counters. The *Heurigen* are characterized by a uniquely sociable ambience, with all the guests joining in the merriment. Many a dedicated beer-drinker has become a devotee of young wine at a *Heuriger* evening.

One of the many wine taverns *(Heurigen)* around Vienna

# The Formation of the Alps

About 70 million years ago, during the Cretaceous period, the African plate and the Adriatic microplate both began to move north. The Alpine range was thrown up when the latter collided with the European plate. The Tethys Sea that lay between them was almost entirely obliterated, and sediment deposited at its bottom over millions of years was carried far to the north, and tossed as vast nappes over the rigid block of indigenous rocks of the Central Alps. The formation of the present Alps ended in the Miocene period, some two million years ago, and subsequent erosion gave them their final shape.

**The Krimmler Falls** in the Hohe Tauern National Park are the highest waterfalls in the Alps and the fifth highest in the world, dropping almost 400 m (1,312 ft).

**The Northern Limestone Alps** are formed of soft carbonate rock. The mountains, such as the Dachstein Group (2,995 m/9,826 ft), have characteristically steep slopes, yet their summits are rounded domes rather than sharp peaks.

Northern Limestone Alps

European Plate

Mantle, between crust and core

Downward flow of magma (molten rock)

**The central part of the Austrian Alps** consists of hard crystalline rock (gneiss, shale). The oldest and the hardest among these mountains form the steep fells of the Hohe Tauern.

**The Alps** possess the right conditions for the formation of glaciers. Largest in the Eastern Alps is the Pasterze; together with 40 others it forms a thick mantle on the Grossglockner massif, covering 40 sq km (15 sq miles).

**The end of the Ice Age** marked the beginning of a new type of erosion. The Northern Limestone Alps have Europe's largest cave systems and underground streams, typical features in limestone regions.

## Mountain Scenery

*The current shape of the Alps was created during the Ice Age (between 600,000 and 10,000 years ago). It is characterized by distinctive post-glacial cirques, suspended valleys, moraines, thaw lakes and vast U-shaped valleys filled with material carried down the mountains.*

## The Austrian Alps

The Austrian Alps are part of the European section of the Alpide belt, which rose between 70 million and two million years ago. In geological terms they form an entity known as the Eastern Alps. They occupy an area about 500 km (310 miles) long and 150 km (95 miles) wide. One of Europe's most fascinating regions, the Austrian Alps enchant visitors with their beautiful high peaks and the unique idyllic atmosphere of the mountain villages and small towns that nestle in vast, cultivated valleys. The most valuable ecological areas have been made into national parks, including the Hohe Tauern – the largest in the Alps and one of the largest in Europe, featuring Austria's highest mountain range with some 266 peaks of over 3,000 m (9,800 ft) in height. In summer, the Alps are a magnificent area to explore on foot or bike, while in winter they provide an excellent base for winter sports.

Central Alps

Southern Limestone Alps

Plate movement

Adriatic Plate

Mantle

**Key**

- Northern Limestone Alps
- Central Alps
- Hohe Tauern
- Southern Limestone Alps
- Alpine Foreland

**The majority of Alpine lakes** were created by retreating glaciers. Some of the most beautiful can be found in the Salzkammergut region, in the Northern Limestone Alps.

# The Landscape of Austria

Austria has a highly diverse landscape because of its location at the junction of four regions. The north of the country is part of the Central European natural region, originally dominated by deciduous and mixed forests, while the southern part belongs to the Alpine region. The southeast lies in the Illyrian region, which benefits from a Mediterranean climate, resulting in a rich flora and fauna including edible chestnuts and rare species of lizards and snakes. The northeastern part of the country belongs to the Pontian-Pannonian region, with surviving species of steppe flora and characteristic fauna including the suslik (a ground squirrel), hamster and great bustard.

**The Alpine belt** stretches from the zone of the mountain pine up to the ice and snow fields. At altitudes of 2,500–3,200 m (8,200–10,500 ft), snow is present all year. This snow-line is called the "nival belt".

**The transition zone** between forest and Alpine grassland is covered in scrub (dwarf mountain pine, rhododendron and alder). Here, the growing season lasts only 70–100 days.

**Alpine high mountain grasslands** and low meadows contain a wide variety of species and plant communities. Mountain arnica (in the foreground) avoids limestone soils and is a highly regarded medicinal plant.

**In gulleys** and hollows, in valleys and along the banks of the streams, Austrian flora is at its most magnificent.

**Traditional grazing** in the forest belt has preserved the natural fauna and flora of the Alpine meadows and pastures.

## Austria's Mountainscapes

*The climate and flora change with altitude, as is typical of mountain environments. The lower regions are covered with mixed forests (including beech). The upper parts have coniferous trees (Arolla pine, spruce and larch) up to about 1,800 m (5,900 ft), above which are brush thickets and colourful Alpine meadows.*

**Humid**, cool valleys are the perfect habitat to encourage the growth of herbaceous plants.

**Lakes** situated at higher altitudes are poor in nutrients and hence their surrounding flora and fauna are extremely sparse.

## Austrian Fauna

Austrian fauna is typical of that of Central Europe. Along with invertebrates (primarily insects: beetles and butterflies), it features a rich avifauna, small numbers of amphibians (newts, salamanders, fire-bellied toads and frogs) and reptiles (Aesculapian snakes, grass snakes, lizards), and mammals, including rodents, marten, fox, weasels and hoofed animals. Mountain animals – insects, rodents (marmots) and deer (red deer, chamois) – are particularly fascinating.

Upper forest region, mainly spruce

**The marmot**, a rodent, burrows deep into mountain meadows and Alpine pastures. When disturbed, it emits a high-pitched whistle.

**Chamois** are ideally adapted for moving over steep rocks.

**Red deer** *(above)* live in the deciduous and mixed forests in the high mountains. They have a fawn-coloured coat. The male sheds its antlers in spring.

**The Alpine ibex** *(right, a female)* came close to extinction towards the end of the 20th century, but is now being successfully reintroduced.

## Austrian Flora

Some 60 per cent of Austria's territory is mountainous, which determines the country's key flora. Forests occupy as much as 39 per cent of the country's entire area, occurring mainly in the Alps and in the Czech Massif. Many areas of special environmental interest enjoy some form of legal protection as nature reserves, nature monuments and national parks. One of the first was the Hohe Tauern National Park.

**The Arolla pine** *(Pinus cembra)*, along with the larch, forms large tree populations in the upper forest regions.

**Swiss Rock Jasmin** *(Andro-sace helvetica)*, with its rounded clusters, is typical on limestone soil.

**Bitterwort** *(Gentiana lutea)* is common in meadows, clusters of herbaceous plants and forest verges. Bitterwort liqueur has long been used in folk medicine.

# The Music of Austria

Austria was – and remains to this day – a world-renowned centre for music. Musical life in present-day Austria has typically been closely linked with that of Germany, as well as the Habsburg Empire. Composers belonging to the First Viennese School contributed to the emergence of the Viennese Classical style, with Joseph Haydn, Wolfgang Amadeus Mozart and the German composer Ludwig van Beethoven its main proponents. Their work inspired 19th-century composers such as Franz Schubert, Johann Strauss, Anton Bruckner, Hugo Wolf and Gustav Mahler.

**Franz Schubert**, one of the earliest exponents of the Romantic style, is best-known for his *Lieder*, or songs. He also composed piano music, chamber music and symphonies.

**Arnold Schönberg**, together with his students, Alban Berg and Anton Webern, developed the Viennese dodecaphonic school after 1918. His best-known work is the sextet *Verklärte Nacht*.

Wolfgang Amadeus Mozart

Mozart's sister, Maria Anna, known as Nannerl

**Joseph Haydn**, one of the Viennese Classicists, was a court composer to Count Esterházy. In 1790 he moved to Vienna. His works include over 100 symphonies, 83 string quartets, 52 piano sonatas, 14 masses and many other compositions.

## Wolfgang Amadeus Mozart

*A child prodigy, Mozart had the gift of perfect pitch and an unrivalled memory. He achieved musical perfection with his symphonies, operas (The Marriage of Figaro, Don Giovanni, The Magic Flute) and his masses, including the unfinished Requiem, which is shrouded in mystery.*

| | | | | | |
|---|---|---|---|---|---|
| **1715–77** Georg Christoph Wagenseil | **1756–91** Wolfgang Amadeus Mozart | *Wolfgang Amadeus Mozart* | | **1824–96** Anton Bruckner | **1860–191** Gustav Mahle |
| | | | **1819–95** Franz von Suppé | **1825–99** Johann Strauss (the Younger) | |
| **1700** | **1725** | **1750** | **1775** | **1800** | **1825** | **1850** |
| | **1739–99** Karl Ditters von Dittersdorf | | **1791–1857** Carl Czerny | **1804–49** Johann Strauss (the Elder) | **1852–95** Josef Schrammel |
| | **1732–1809** Joseph Haydn | | | | **1860–1903** Hugo Wolf |
| *Joseph Haydn* | | **1797–1828** Franz Schubert | **1801–43** Joseph Lanner | |

**Johann Strauss (the Younger)** has been proclaimed "the king of the waltz", thanks to compositions including *The Blue Danube* and *Tales from the Vienna Woods*.

## Foreign Musicians in Austria

Vienna, an important cultural centre on the European map, has always attracted musicians and composers from other countries. The Renaissance brought Flemish artists, and the Baroque period attracted Italians. Vienna was home to Christoph Gluck, Ludwig van Beethoven, Johannes Brahms and others. The main exponent of the New Viennese operetta was the Hungarian Franz Lehár.

**Johannes Brahms** (1833–97), German composer and outstanding creator of traditional symphonies, piano and chamber music, was unsympathetic towards progressive trends.

Portrait of Anna Maria, Mozart's mother

Leopold, Mozart's father

**Anton Bruckner** is probably best known for his nine symphonies, but he also wrote church music, in particular choral works.

**Ludwig van Beethoven** (1770–1827), German composer and one of the Viennese Classicists, battled from 1798 with his progressive deafness. His best-known work is perhaps the *Ninth Symphony*, with the Ode to Joy in its finale.

**Gustav Mahler** started his career as a conductor and only in later years devoted himself to composing music. His most important work is a cycle of ten monumental symphonies.

| | | | | | | | |
|---|---|---|---|---|---|---|---|
| | **1900–1991** Ernst Křenek | **1935** b. Kurt Schwertsik | **1941** b. Dieter Kaufmann | | **1971** b. Michael F P Huber | | **2009** Haydn Year |
| **4–1951** Arnold önberg | | **1926** b. Friedrich Cerha | | **1956** b. Herbert Willi | | **2006** Mozart Year | |
| **75** | **1900** | **1925** | **1950** | | **1975** | **2000** | **2025** |
| **4–1949** mund Eysler | **1885–1935** Alban Berg | | | **1960** b. Karlheinz Essl | | | **1998** Arnold Schönberg Center opened in Vienna |
| **3–1945** Anton von Webern | | | | **1943** b. H K (Heinz Karl) Gruber | **1971** b. Bernhard Gál | | |
| | | *Edmund Eysler* | | | | | |

# The Architecture of Austria

Since the Middle Ages, Austria has been at the forefront in the development of architecture. Particularly typical of the Austrian architectural landscape are the vast abbeys built in medieval times and modernized during the late Baroque period, as well as the multi-storey town palaces and large country residences built for the aristocracy in the 17th and 18th centuries. The late 1800s and early 1900s marked the birth of modern town architecture, in public buildings such as theatres, banks and government offices. These and other buildings displayed typical Habsburg-era features – monumentality and a distinctly ornamental character.

**Cupolas** crowned with openwork lanterns, inspired by Renaissance domes in Italy.

**Pediment** with an early-Renaissance statue of Christ blessing the people.

**Heiligenkreuz Abbey** *(see p140)* was built in the 12th to 13th centuries, but only the Romanesque church remains from that period. The abbey itself is a magnificent Baroque structure erected in the 17th century. The courtyard has an imposing St Mary's column.

**Schwaz church**, dating from the 15th century, with its opulent star vaulting resting on slender columns, and its interior illuminated by vast windows, typifies the lightness of Baroque architecture *(see p249)*.

**Windows** with grab-frames, typical of the early Baroque period.

**Statues of saints** by Michael Bernhard Mandl

**The decorative railings** of the famous staircase at Mirabell Palace in Salzburg *(see p219)* are the masterpiece of architect Johann Lukas von Hildebrandt and sculptor Georg Raphael Donner.

**The octagonal** layout of the top storey of the tower is a typical feature of the Lombardy style.

**The Vienna State Opera House** *(see p96)*, conceived by August von Sicardsburg and Eduard van der Nüll, was completed in 1869. Its façade and interior, particularly the auditorium, the foyer and the grand staircase, are examples of the opulence, ornamentation and pomposity typical of 19th-century Austrian architecture.

**Statues of Moses and Elijah**

**Oval tower windows** serve to amplify the sound of the bells.

**Melk** is one of the most famous Benedictine abbeys and the largest surviving abbey complex in Europe. The spectacular Baroque abbey was designed by Jakob Prandtauer *(see pp146–7)*.

**Vast clock faces**

## Salzburger Dom

*The cathedral, begun in 1614 to a design by Santino Solari and finished in 1657, is one of the earliest twin-towered churches of the modern era found anywhere north of the Alps. It is also the earliest and most magnificent example of the Early Baroque style in the entire Danube region (see p224).*

## Friedensreich Hundertwasser

Hundertwasser (1928–2000) was a highly successful painter, graphic designer and architect. He was born Friedrich Stowasser, but adopted a new name while studying at the Academy of Fine Arts in Vienna. His decorative style of painting was close to that of abstract artists, with subject matter often associated with the natural environment. His buildings *(see pp108–9)* are distinguished by their highly experimental, extravagant shapes, combining colourful new architectural ideas with the artist's vision of structures that blend with the natural environment. Irregular in shape, they employ a variety of unusual materials, including ceramics.

The Bad Blumau resort complex *(see p174)*

# Austrian Art

Austrian painting, like the country's literature, cannot be considered in isolation from artistic movements in neighbouring countries. Art in Austria developed in close relationship with German art, but it was also influenced by the Italian, Hungarian and Czech cultures. Over many centuries, the imperial court in Vienna acted as a strong magnet for artists from all over Europe. In the 19th century, the artists of the Viennese Secession produced outstanding works of art. Some of Austria's painters have gained international acclaim, but it is well worth becoming acquainted with its lesser artists, too.

*The Entombment*, by Albrecht Altdorfer

## Medieval

The earliest examples of pictorial art in Austria include illuminations and wall paintings. The late-8th-century *Codex Millenarius (maior)*, kept in Kremsmünster Abbey, is regarded as the oldest illuminated manuscript. The Austrian art of illumination flourished during the 11th and 12th centuries, particularly thanks to the Salzburg monastery scriptoria which, among other works, produced the famous Admont Bible (c.1130–40).

The oldest wall paintings in Austria, dating from the first half of the 11th century, are found in the Church of St Ulrich in Wieselburg. The Benedictine abbey church in Lambach has original wall paintings of Old Testament scenes, created in the last quarter of the 11th century. Paintings dating from the 12th century can be seen in St John's Chapel in Pürgg, the Benedictine abbey church in Nonnberg and in the castle chapel of Burg Ottenstein, near Zwettl.

From the 14th century, panel painting flourished, particularly in Vienna under Rudolph IV. The 15th century is notable for the works of Jakob Kaschauer and Thomas von Villach. At the turn of the 16th century, Austrian painting was influenced by Italian *Quattrocento* art, especially the works of Michael Pacher and his students. The Danube School, influential in the early 1500s, was represented by Wolf Huber and Albrecht Altdorfer of Regensburg, who painted the altar in the abbey of St Florian, near Linz.

## Renaissance

The Renaissance style entered Austrian painting around 1530. Interesting wall paintings, created soon after that date, include the secular decoration of the Knights' Room in Goldegg Castle near St Johann (1536), and the paintings devoted to Reformation themes in Pölling church, near Wolfsberg. Hans Bocksberger, one of the most outstanding Renaissance artists, decorated Freisaal Castle and the castle chapel in Burg Strechau.

Until the 16th century, Austrian painting was strongly influenced by Italian artists such as Giulio Licinio, Teodoro Ghisi and Martino Rota, who worked at the court in Graz, and Donato Arsenio Mascagni in Salzburg. Local artists, such as Anton Blumenthal, whose paintings adorn the presbytery of Gurk Cathedral, and Jakob Seisenegger, a portrait-painter, were also influenced by Italian art.

## Baroque

In the 17th century, Italian art continued to influence Austrian painting. One of the most important painters of the Baroque period was Pietro de Pomis.

The Austrian victory in the Battle of Vienna in 1683 was a historic event that proved very influential in the development of art. It brought about political and economic stability and with it many new artistic initiatives. The capital, Vienna, began to attract foreign artists, such as Andrea Pozzo, the Italian master of illusionist painting. Vast interior compositions were created to complement the magnificent architectural works by Johann Bernhard Fischer von Erlach and Johann Lukas von Hildebrandt. This particular style of fresco painting flourished thanks to artists such as Johann Michael Rottmayr, Martino Altomonte and, in the following generation, Paul Troger, Daniel Gran and Bartolomeo Altomonte. Great portrait-painters of the 18th-century included Johann Kupetzky, Martin van Meytens and Johann Baptist von Lampi.

*The Holy Family with St Joachim and St Anna*, by Franz Anton Maulbertsch

A prominent representative of late Baroque painting, Franz Anton Maulbertsch created frescoes as well as numerous works on religious and secular themes. The last great artist of the Baroque era was Martin Johann Schmidt, who produced magnificent wall paintings, for example for Melk Abbey.

*Portrait of Hanna Klinkosch,* by Hans Makart

### 19th Century

The most important Neo-Classical painters in Austria were Heinrich Friedrich Füger and Joseph Anton Koch. In 1809, the Brotherhood of St Luke was formed at the Vienna Academy of Fine Arts. Its members, the Nazarenes, mostly German painters (including Julius Schnorr von Carolsfeld, and only a few Austrians) set out to revise religious art.

An important figure during the Biedermeier and Realism periods in Austria was Ferdinand Georg Waldmüller, creator of small-scale genre paintings. The most outstanding academic painter was undoubtedly Hans Makart, who created vast compositions on allegorical or historic themes, as well as brilliant portraits. In the town of Szolnok, in today's Hungary, an artists' colony was established by a group of landscape painters inspired by the French Barbizon School.

Probably the best-known of all Austrian painters was Gustav Klimt, the founding member and main representative of the Vienna Secession. He used gold in his paintings and embellished them with striking "mosaics". The subject matter was often allegorical, infused with a subtle eroticism.

*Time of the Rose Blossom,* by F G Waldmüller

### Modern

Expressionism played a major role in early-20th-century Austrian art. The foremost artists associated with this movement included Egon Schiele, Richard Gerstl and Oskar Kokoschka, and, in Upper Austria, Alfred Kubin. An important figure of the 1930s and the period following World War II was Herbert Boeckl. A versatile artist (he also produced wall paintings), Boeckl drew his inspiration from fantasy realism, popular in post-war Vienna. Ernst Fuchs, Anton Lehmden and Wolfgang Hutter were members of the Vienna

School of Fantastic Realism, which was inspired by surrealism. Abstract art was represented by Max Weiler and Josef Mikl. An unusual late-20th-century figure who escapes easy classification was Friedensreich Hundertwasser *(see p31),* who became famous with his architectural project of unusual buildings erected in and around Vienna.

The artists of Viennese Actionism achieved considerable notoriety in the 1960s. "Happenings" organized by the group revolved around the use of the body as a sculptural medium. Their fascination with self-mutilation and sadomasochism culminated in the death of one of the group's members, Rudolf Schwarzkogler.

Gustav Klimt's *Danaë* (1907), one of his famous erotic paintings

# Sport in Austria

Austria is a sport-loving nation, a fact reflected in the great popularity of recreational sports as well as in the country's success in international competitions. For a nation with a relatively small population, the number of European and world champions, as well as Olympic medallists, in Austria is very high. Some three million people – members of 27,500 sports clubs – participate in various sports and sports contests. The most popular and widely pursued sport is downhill skiing, followed by other winter pursuits such as Nordic (or cross-country) skiing and snowboarding. In the warmer months, Austrians turn to soccer, tennis, swimming, golf, cycling and windsurfing.

### Alpine Skiing

Alpine or downhill skiing has been the number one national sport in Austria for over 100 years. Mathias Zdarsky (1856–1940) is known as the "father of alpine skiing". He wrote one of the first instructional books, designed the first steel ski bindings and organized, in 1905, the first slalom race. Most importantly, however, he urged Austrians to get off the gentle flats and head up into the mountains.

Austria is a go-to destination for professional as well as recreational skiers. The Winter Olympics have twice been held in Innsbruck (1964 and 1976) and World Cup races are hosted at a number of resorts around the country. The very first race of the season is always held on the Rettenbach glacier above Sölden. The international Hahnenkamm races in Kitzbühel are famous the world over, in part due to their inclusion of the dangerous downhill race, the Streif.

Lauded ski racers include Franz Klammer, often cited as the greatest downhill skiier of all time, and Hermann Maier. Top of the pack is Toni Sailer, considered the greatest champion of all – he won gold at every single Alpine event at the 1956 Winter Olympics.

### Nordic Skiing

Generally, Nordic skiing encompasses cross-country skiing and ski jumping. Austria's glaciers are ideal locations for both training and competitions; in 2017, Seefeld hosted the Nordic Combined World Cup championships, an event previously held on the Dachstein glacier in Styria. Austrians flock to cross-country trails, which are generally free or of very modest cost. One highlight of the cross-country calendar is the 4 km (2.5 mile) trail in Obertaun dedicated exclusively to nude skiers.

Ski jumping is also very popular. Austria won gold, silver and bronze medals at the 1976 Winter Olympics in Innsbruck, and two of the prestigious Four Hills ski jump tournaments take place in Innsbruck and Bischofshofen.

Record-breaking ski jumper, Andreas Goldberg

### Luge

Luge or bobsleigh racing is another popular winter pastime. Each autumn, the World Cup luge season starts in Innsbruck, on the track built there for the 1976 Winter Olympics. Lying prone on the sled, lugers achieve speeds of over 100 kph (62 mph) as they hurtle down the ice. Austrian competitors have won several medals in this discipline at the Olympic Games, as well as at various World Championships and World Cup events.

Amateurs can experience a ride on the Olympic bobsleigh, luge and skeleton tracks in Innsbruck-Igls, with a professional brakeman and driver keeping control.

Hermann Maier on his final slalom run in Hinterstoder

Johann Wolfmayr and team in the World Championship in pair driving

## Soccer

Austria's national soccer (or football) team may struggle to compete with the world's best, but the sport remains one of the country's most popular – for spectators and participants.

The national team has an unenviable record of failing to qualify for world and European championships. It has competed in the World Cup only seven times, most recently in 1998. In 2008, Austria co-hosted the UEFA European Championships (more commonly known as the Euros) with Switzerland. The team automatically qualified for the event as a result but was knocked out at the group stages. After qualifying for the 2016 Euros, the team faced a similar fate: it lost to its bitterest historical rival, Hungary, and crashed out at the group stages once again.

Austria's top competitive soccer league is the Bundesliga, with ten teams battling to claim the league title. Vienna is home to two of the most successful teams: Rapid Wien has won the national championship 32 times while its rival Austria Wien has claimed the crown 23 times.

Despite playing for Germany's Bayern Munich, the country's most famous footballer is David Alaba. Making his international debut in 2009 at just 17, he holds the record for the youngest player to play for Austria.

Stefan Schwab of Rapid Wien, playing against Ajax

## Horse Riding

Founded in 1872, the first sports riding club in Austria, the Campagnereiter-Gesellschaft, had the Emperor Franz Joseph I, himself a keen rider, as a patron. It consisted mainly of military personnel, and is considered to be the predecessor of the Bundesfachverband für Reiten und Fahren (Federal League for Riding and Driving), which was established in 1962.

Austrian riders have achieved many international successes. Two of its legends include the pre-war master of horse dressage, Alois Podhajsky, and showjumping champion Hugo Simon, a big character among Austrian riders during the 1980s and 1990s. In the 1980s, Austrian competitors began to achieve considerable success in harness racing, involving one- and two-horse carts.

Rodeos – known as *Westernreiten* (wild west riding) – have been introduced from America, and are very popular across the country.

## Canoeing and Mountain Biking

With its many rivers and lakes and its superb mountain scenery, Austria boasts the perfect natural conditions, along with a well-developed infrastructure, for both canoeing and mountain biking. Though this does not always translate into international medals, the huge popularity of summer mountain sports among Austrians and visitors is nevertheless very noticeable.

Mountain canoeing is practised on turbulent mountain streams. In 2012, the mountain biking World Championship was held in Saalfelden.

Helmut Oblinger competing in the individual slalom in Sydney

# AUSTRIA THROUGH THE YEAR

Austria is a conservative country and Austrians value their traditions highly. In many regions the population maintains such ancient customs as the rites of spring and ritual re-enactments of death and resurrection, as well as various festivals associated with the grape harvest. Carnival festivities and parades are also big crowd-pullers, and many festivals are associated with the main religious holidays, such as Easter, Corpus Christi and Christmas.

Labour Day (1 May) is the traditional day for workers' processions. These national festivities, plus scores of regional and local cultural events catering for the arts, fill the Austrian events calendar almost every day of the year. Many festivals enjoy an international reputation, including the Salzburg Festival, the Bregenz Festival and the Vienna Viennale. Information on the full range of events is available from tourist offices or the Internet.

## Spring

Spring sees the re-opening of regional museums that were closed for the winter. The Viennese Prater funfair starts up at full steam. Traditionally, Lent is a period of abstinence, but the shops are already full of Easter specialities, their shelves laden with chocolate bunnies, Easter eggs and other sweet delicacies.

### March

**Palmprozessionen** Palm Sunday processions, held around Austria, are based on ancient traditions, yet are highly imaginative.
**Frühlingsfestival** Vienna. Classical music festival.
**Easter carols** During Holy Week and the run up to Easter, singers carol through the streets of some towns. The most famous carolers are the Leiden-Christi-Singen in Grossarl (Salzburger Land) and the Antlasssingen in Traunkirchen (Upper Austria).

**Osterfestspiele** *(Holy Week and Easter)* Salzburg. Easter Festival with opera and classical music concerts.

### April

**Easter** On Easter night, mountain slopes are lit with Easter bonfires called **Osterfeuer**. Easter Sunday begins with the traditional chocolate Easter egg hunt, **Eiersuchen**. A pastry in the shape of a lamb *(Osterlamm)* is traditionally given to children at Easter by their godparents.
**Donaufestival** *(mid-April–mid-May)* Krems. Festival of contemporary theatre and music.

### May

**Wiener Festwochen** *(early May–early June)* Vienna. The country's biggest arts festival.

Narzissenfest on Altausseer See

**Labour Day** *(1 May)*. Day of workers' marches and demonstrations; also of numerous shows and sporting events.
**Passionsspiele** Erl in Tirol. Passion plays organized every six years (the next event is in 2019). Following the May première, the plays are then performed every Saturday and Sunday until early October.
**Pfingstfestspiele Salzburg** *(Whitsun weekend)* Salzburg. Opera and classical music concerts.
**Musikwochen Millstadt** *(mid-May–early October)* Millstadt, in Carinthia. International music festival.
**Gauderfest** *(1st weekend in May)* Zell am Ziller, in Tyrol. Festival of strong beer, with animal fights and wrestling.
**Kufenstechen** *(Whit Sunday/Monday)* Gailtal, in Carinthia. Jousting tournament.
**Internationale Barocktage** *(Whit Friday–Monday)* Melk Abbey. Baroque music days.
**Narzissenfest** *(late May–early June)* on the banks of the Altausseer See in Salzkammergut. Narcissus flower festival, music and processions.

Palm Sunday procession, Thaur

## Average daily hours of sunshine

**Sunshine Chart**
The largest number of sunny days occurs in July, but May, June and August are also sunny. The cloudiest month is December.

## Summer

Summer is the height of the tourist season. Theatres close for the summer, but the most important arts festivals, including the Salzburg and Bregenz Festivals, take place during this season. There are also numerous popular entertainment events and traditional village festivals.

Corpus Christi procession in Hallstatt, Salzkammergut

## June

**Corpus Christi** Processions throughout Austria; the best take place in Salzkammergut, in Gmunden, Hallstatt and Traunkirchen.

**St Pauler Kulturersommer** *(June–mid-August)* St Paul's Abbey, in Carinthia. Festival of classical music.

**Schubertiade** *(June, August, September)* Schwarzenberg, in Vorarlberg. Festival of Schubert's music.

**Styriarte** *(end June–end August)* Graz. Festival of early and contemporary music.

**Donauinselfest** *(late June)* Danube Island, Vienna. A three-day pop music event.

**Internationale Konzerttage Stift Zwettl** *(late June–late July)* Zwettl, in Lower Austria. Festival of organ music.

## July

**Oper Klosterneuburg** *(July)* Klosterneuburg, north of Vienna. Throughout the month, a programme of opera performances is held in the courtyard of the palatial Kaiserhof.

**Jazzfestival** *(mid-July)* Wiesen, Burgenland. Jazz festival.

**Salzburger Festspiele** *(July– late August)* Salzburg. Festival of music, opera and theatre; most important event of the summer.

**Bregenzer Festspiele** *(end July– late Aug)* Bregenz. Performances of theatre, opera and music on the stage on Lake Constance.

**Rathaus Film Festival** *(July– August)* Vienna. Opera and music films, shown on a big screen in front of the town hall.

**Kammermusikfest Lockenhaus** Schloss Lockenhaus, in Burgenland. Chamber music.

**Samsonumzug** *(late July)* Tamsweg, Salzburger Land. Samson's procession; saints' statues are paraded in town.

**Operettenfestival Baden** *(late July–early September)* Baden, near Vienna. Festival of operetta.

**Operettenfestspiele** Mörbisch, on Neusiedler See. Festival of operetta.

## Carinthischer Sommer
Ossiach, Villach, in Carinthia. Carinthian summer festival.

**Operettenfestival** *(July–August)* Bad Ischl, Salzkammergut. Festival of operetta.

**Innsbrucker Festwochen der Alten Musik** *(July–August)* In and around Innsbruck. World-renowned festival of early music and Baroque opera.

## August

**Jazzfestival** Saalfelden. Jazz concerts, performed by several hundred artists.

**Piratenschlacht** *(early August)* Oberndorf. Pirates fight it out on the Salzach river.

**Chopin Festival** *(mid-August)* Gaming Abbey. Musicians perform in a series of concerts celebrating the work of Chopin.

**Assumption of the Virgin Mary** *(15 August)*. Colourful processions all over Austria. The most interesting is the **Schiffsprozession** (ship procession) on Wörthersee.

**Internationaler Johannes Brahms Wettbewerb** Velden and Pörtschach on Wörthersee. An annual international Brahms competition featuring string and piano soloists.

Fire dance during the Salzburg Festival

## Average monthly rainfall

**Rainfall Chart**
The summer months are not only the hottest but also the wettest time of the year. Western regions tend to be wetter than central areas of Austria.

## Autumn

In the towns, autumn marks the start of the theatre and opera season. In the mountains, the sheep and cows are rounded up and brought back down from their summer pastures, accompanied by various festivities. Grape harvest festivals are held in the wine-producing areas, mainly in Lower Austria and Burgenland. The lightly fizzing *Sturm* appears on the tables, quickly followed by new-vintage wines. Numerous music events attract music lovers throughout the country.

### September

**Ars Electronica** *(early September)* Linz. Technology exhibition accompanied by concerts of electronic music.
**Haydntage** *(early September)* Eisenstadt. Festival of music by Haydn.
**Festlicher Almabtrieb** *(mid-September–mid-October)*. Flocks return from the mountains.

Various festivities take place, and the mountains echo to the sound of cows' bells.
**Brucknerfest Linz** *(September)* Linz. The Bruckner Festival starts with **Klangwolken** (sound clouds), a series of concerts on the banks of the Danube with laser light shows.
**Badener Beethoventage** *(September–October)* Baden. Festival of Beethoven's music.
**Internationale Woche der Alten Musik** *(early September)* Krieglach, in Styria. International Week of Early Music.
**Internationales Brahmsfest** *(mid-September)* Mürzzuschlag. International Brahms festival.

### October

**Winzerumzüge** *(mid-October)* Weinviertel and Wachau Valley, Lower Austria; wine-producing regions of Burgenland. Grape harvest festivals.
**Niederösterreichischer Weinherbst** Lower Austria. The "Wine Autumn" is a time of increased eating and drinking in the old inns of ancient wine-producing villages, often regarded as historic architectural treasures.
**Steirischer Herbst** Graz. The Styrian Autumn is an avant-garde arts festival, one of the most prestigious events of the season, taking place over four weeks. Festival-goers are mainly young people, and the events include theatre and opera productions,

performance arts, films, music concerts, talks and art exhibitions.
**National Day** *(26 October)*. Celebration of the Declaration of Neutrality in 1955.
**Viennale** *(late October)* Vienna. Two-week international film festival.
**Wien Modern** *(end October–end November)* Vienna. Contemporary music festival, initiated by Claudio Abbado.

Krampus Devil and St Nicholas at a St Nicholas party

### November

**Salzburger Jazz-Herbst** *(early November)* Salzburg. Ten days of traditional jazz concerts and films.
**St Martin's Day** *(11 November)*. This is the day when all Austria feasts on *Martinigans* – roast St Martin's goose.
**Voice Mania** *(November–December)* Vienna. A capella festival in unusual venues.
**Weihnachtsmärkte** *(late November–December)*. Start of the Christmas market season. On offer: tree decorations, gifts, food and drink; best in Vienna, Salzburg, Klagenfurt, Spittal an der Drau and Villach.

Start of Bruckner Festival, Linz

## Average monthly temperature

**Temperature Chart**
The hottest month is July, with August and June being only slightly cooler. Winters are cold, particularly in January, when temperatures often drop below freezing point.

## Winter

Winter begins with the pre-Christmas shopping rush. Christmas figures and decorations adorn every shop window. The main shopping streets in the towns and villages sparkle with lights. As soon as Christmas is over, fresh festivities get under way. New Year's Eve marks the beginning of the Carnival season, celebrated in Austria with numerous balls.

The famous Vienna Opera Ball held in February

### December

**St Nicholas parties** *(early December)* Tyrol. The most interesting of these include **Klaubaufgehen**, a masquerade in Matrei, and **Nikolospiel** in Bad Mitterndorf. In Thaur (Tyrol), people traditionally display cribs in their homes.

**Adventsingen**. Advent concerts held in Salzburg.

**Steyrer Kripperl**, Steyr. One of the last stick-puppet theatres, performs nativity plays using the various crib displays. The crib display in Bad Ischl is also worth seeing. Nativity plays are staged throughout the country.

**St Stephen's Day (Stephanitag)** *(26 December)*. Colourful festival (**Stefaniritt**) in the Lavanttal Valley in Carinthia.

Christmas decorations in Kohlmarkt, Vienna

### January

**New Year's Day** *(1 January)*. Austria welcomes the New Year with champagne and fireworks; people dance in the streets and squares, regardless of the weather.

**Neujahrskonzert** *(1 January)*. Traditional New Year's concert of the Vienna Philharmonic Orchestra transmitted throughout the world from the Golden Hall of the Wiener Musikverein.

**Epiphany** *(6 January)*. *Dreikönigssingen* (singing for the Three Kings) – Austria bursts into song on the Day of the Three Magi.

**Perchtenlauf** Carnival procession to mark the start of the party season. It rotates between four towns in Pongau: St Johann, Altenmarkt, Bischofshofen and Bad Gastein.

**Salzburger Mozartwoche** *(late January)* Salzburg. Mozart Week.

**Resonanzen**. A festival of early music held at Vienna's Konzerthaus.

### February

February is the main Carnival season.

Masquerades and magnificent balls are held throughout the country.

**Opernball** *(last Thursday of Carnival)* Vienna Opera Ball.

**Villacher Fasching** *(end of Carnival)* Villach.

**Maschkerertanz** *(end of Carnival)* Steinfeld, Carinthia. Colourful festivities mark the end of the Carnival season.

### Public Holidays

**Neujahr** New Year (1 Jan)

**Dreikönigsfest** Epiphany (6 Jan)

**Ostern** Easter

**Tag der Arbeit** Labour Day (1 May)

**Fronleichnam** Corpus Christi

**Pfingsten** Pentecost

**Mariä Himmelfahrt** Assumption of the Virgin Mary (15 Aug)

**Nationalfeiertag** (26 Oct)

**Allerheiligen** All Saints (1 Nov)

**Mariä Empfängnis** (8 Dec) Immaculate Conception

**Weihnachten/Stephanitag** Christmas (25/26 Dec)

# THE HISTORY OF AUSTRIA

In the Middle Ages, Austria was only one of several small duchies within the Holy Roman Empire, but during 600 years of Habsburg rule it rose to the rank of a world power and was influential in determining Europe's fate. The Austro-Hungarian Empire ended with World War I. Since the end of World War II, Austria has played a key role in European politics and democracy.

## Prehistory and Early Middle Ages

The geographic nature of Austria's territory, opening up towards the Bohemian-Moravian Valley and the Hungarian Plains, meant that, from the 7th century BC, this area was regularly raided and populated by belligerent Scythians, Celts and Germanic tribes. At the end of the 1st century BC, the land south of the Danube was occupied by the Romans, who in the middle of the 1st century AD, during the reign of the Emperor Claudius, founded the Province of Noricum here, with its main centres in Carnuntum (near Hainburg) and Vindobona (Vienna).

The influence of the dominant Roman culture and civilization over the entire region began to wane in the 2nd century AD, during a period of increased German raids. In AD 180, Emperor Marcus Aurelius died in Vindobona, in the war against the Marcomanni and Quadi tribes.

From the 4th century onwards, during the Great Migration of Nations, the territories of present-day Austria saw successive waves of invading Huns, Goths and Avars. Later arrivals included Slav and Bavarian settlers. The Bavarian tribal state, established and consolidated during the 7th and 8th centuries, was crushed in 787 when Charlemagne deposed his vassal Tassilo III, the last Prince of Bavaria, and annexed his territories. In 803, Charlemagne also defeated the Avars and established a margravate (territory) on the banks of the Danube, between the Enns River and the Vienna Woods, which became the nucleus of the Austrian state. Its existence was cut short by Magyars, who raided it in the early 10th century.

## Babenberg Austria

Following the defeat of the Magyars in 995, on the banks of the Lech river near Augsburg, the German King Otto I restored the margravate; his successor, Otto II, handed it as a fief to Leopold I of the Babenberg dynasty (976–94). The centre of the margravate was Melk, on the Danube river. Having defeated the Magyars, Leopold extended the frontiers of his province up to the Vienna Woods. In 1156, Henry II Jasomirgott was given the title of duke, and Austria became a hereditary fief of the Holy Roman Empire. Vienna began to assume its role as capital city.

**170** Raid by the Germanic tribes of Marcomanni and Quadi

**493** Raid by Theodoric, king of the Ostrogoths

**739** Founding of the bishopric of Salzburg

*The "Ostarrichi Urkunde" document of 996*

**803** Charlemagne founds the eastern margravate

AD 1    500    650    800    950    1100

**AD 4th–7th century** The Great Migration of Nations. Raids by Huns, Goths, Avars, Slavs and Bavarians

**45** Foundation of the Roman province Noricum

**787** Charlemagne deposes the last independent Bavarian prince, Tassilo III

**976** Leopold I Babenberg becomes the first Margrave of the margravate

*Tassilo's chalice of 777*

◀ Emperor Franz Joseph I, who ruled 1848–1916

## Bohemian Austria

In 1246, the Babenberg line died out and Austria fell into the hands of the Bohemian kings Vaclav I and Ottokar II. The latter, having annexed Carinthia and Carniola (1269), became the most powerful duke in the empire. He had his eyes on the German crown, but in the 1273 election a more modest feudal lord rose to the German throne, the landgrave (count) of Upper Alsace, Rudolf von Habsburg (1273–91). He defeated Ottokar II in 1278, took the Austrian territories and handed them to his sons as hereditary fiefs. From then on, for the next 640 years, the fate of Austria became tied to that of the Habsburg dynasty.

**Death of Frederick II Babenberg**

The double-seated Carinthian ducal throne, joined by pieces of Roman stone, Maria Saal

## The Habsburg Rise to Power

Rudolf I and his successors pursued a very successful policy of acquiring new territories. During the 14th century, in addition to Austria, Styria, Carinthia and Carniola, the Habsburgs gained control of Tyrol (1363) and Trieste (1382). An important contribution to the strengthening of the dynasty was made by Rudolf IV, called "the Founder" (1358–65), who founded Vienna University and laid the foundation stone for St Stephen's Cathedral, the church that to this day remains one of the symbols of the Austrian capital. Rudolf signed a treaty with the Emperor Charles IV – Bohemian king of the Luxemburg dynasty – stating that in the event of one of the dynasties (Habsburgs or Luxemburgs) dying out, the other would reign over both territories. This situation arose in 1438 when, following the death of Emperor Sigismund of Luxemburg, both the imperial crown of Germany and the throne of Hungary and Bohemia passed to the Austrian Duke Albrecht II of Habsburg, and on his death to his cousin Frederick III (1440–93), who was regarded as the last emperor of the Middle Ages. His motto was written as the five vowels – AEIOU – which were variously interpreted, for example as "Austriae Est Imperare Orbi Universo" (The Entire World is Austria's Empire).

## The Empire of Charles V

This maxim appeared close to becoming true during the reign of Maximilian I (1486–1519), who by his marriage to Maria of

**1156** Thanks to privileges granted by Frederick Barbarossa, Austria is elevated to the status of a Duchy of the Reich. Margrave Henry II Jasomirgott becomes its first duke

**1251** Austria ruled by Ottokar II

**1358** Rudolph IV, the Founder, ascends to the throne

| 1100 | 1150 | 1200 | 1250 | 1300 | 1350 |

**1246** End of the Babenberg line. Vienna occupied by the Bohemian King Vaclav I

*Detail of the medieval altarpiece at the Abbey Church of Klosterneuburg by Nicolas of Verdun, 1185*

**1278** Rudolf von Habsburg defeats Ottokar II in the Battle of Dürnkrut. Austria becomes a hereditary fief of the Habsburgs

Gothic altar in Zwettl Abbey

younger line of Habsburgs, taking control of Austria – Styria, Carniola, Carinthia and Tyrol – and the Jagiellon inheritance – Bohemia, Moravia, Silesia and western Hungary.

## Reformation and Turkish Threat

During the Reformation, the state, now with a population of seven million, became the scene of fierce religious conflicts. Ferdinand and his successor, Maximilian II (1564–76), pursued a policy of tolerance towards the Protestants, but Rudolf II (1576–1612), brought up in the staunchly Catholic Spanish court, declared himself in favour of the Counter-Reformation. The growing religious conflict led to the Thirty Years' War (1618–48), which ravaged large areas (51 castles, 23 towns and 313 villages in Austrian-ruled countries alone).

Burgundy in 1477 gained control of Alsace, Lorraine and the Netherlands, one of the richest countries in Europe. He also entered into a treaty with the Jagiellons – thus reviving his claims to the Bohemian and Hungarian crowns – and, by arranging the betrothal of his son Philip to the Spanish Infanta Joan, extended Habsburg rule over the Iberian Peninsula and the South American dominions. In 1519, Maximilian's successor, his grandson Charles V (1519–56), heir to the Spanish and Austrian territories, succeeded to the throne of an empire over which, it could be said, "the sun never set".

Turkish banner, captured in 1683

Even greater destruction was caused by the wars fought in the 16th and 17th centuries against the Turks, who twice tried to conquer Vienna (1529, 1683). The crushing defeat suffered by the Sultan's army during the second siege of Vienna allowed the Habsburgs to take control of the whole of Hungary, Transylvania and Croatia.

Panel inscribed "AEIOU", Frederick III's motto

Following the abdication of King Charles in 1556, the imperial crown passed to his brother Ferdinand (1556–64); he represented the

---

# The First Habsburg Monarchy

The Habsburgs rose to the ranks of the most influential German feudal families during the first half of the 1300s, and in the following centuries they became the rulers of one of Europe's most powerful countries. This advancement was due mainly to their far-sighted dynastic policy and expedient marriages. Strategic matches brought under their control territories far beyond the seat of their power in Austria and Styria, to include Tyrol, Flanders, the Netherlands, Bohemia, Hungary and the possessions of the Spanish crown in both Europe and South America. The Habsburgs' marriage policy was later summed up in the motto "Let others fight wars, you, lucky Austria, get married".

**Austria of Rudolf I**
▦ Austria in 1278

**Sauce Boat of Rudolf II**
This sauce boat from the famous collection of objets d'art from the Mannerist period, collected by Rudolf II, can be seen in Vienna's Kunsthistorisches Museum *(see pp88–91)*.

**Regalia of Rudolf II**
The intricate sceptre, orb and crown became the insignia of the Austrian Empire.

Maximilian I —

**Ferdinand I**, grandson of Maximilian I, ruled Bohemia, Austria and Hungary.

**Relief of the Siege of Vienna in 1683**
The 70,000-strong Christian army, led by the Polish King Jan III Sobieski, broke through the ring around Vienna and forced the 110–115,000 Turkish troops of the Grand Vizier Kara Mustapha to flee.

**Rudolf II**
During his reign, Rudolf II attracted scholars such as Kepler, as well as famous sorcerers, alchemists and seers to the imperial court.

**Philip I**, son of Maximilian I, gained control of Spain as the result of his marriage to Joanna the Mad.

**Mary of Burgundy,** wife of Maximilian I

**Family of Maximilian I**
*This painting by Bernhard Strigel (c.1520) depicts Maximilian I with his family, a dynasty that turned Austria into a powerful empire.*

**Rudolf I**
The first Habsburg king of Germany, having defeated Bohemian King Ottokar II in 1276, seized Austria, Carinthia and Styria.

**Karl V**, grandson of Maximilian I, inherited Spain from his mother.

**Rudolf IV the Founder**
Rudolf IV died very young (only 26 years old) and was buried in St Stephen's Cathedral – the church he had founded in Vienna.

## Where to See Gothic Austria

The most interesting early-Gothic remains to be found in Austria, dating back to the 13th–14th centuries, are the cloisters of the Cistercian abbeys in Heiligenkreuz *(see p140)* in the Wienerwald, as well as Lilienfeld and Zwettl, both in Lower Austria. Among the best examples of Gothic architecture are the impressive Stephansdom (St Stephen's Cathedral) in Vienna, the Franciscan church in Salzburg *(see p223)*, and the four-nave parish church in Schwaz *(see pp248–9)*, in Tyrol. The most famous late-Gothic (1481) winged altar, an outstanding work by the Tyrolean artist Michael Pacher, is found in St Wolfgang *(see p209)*, in the Salzkammergut. Many churches feature original Gothic sculptures.

**Stephansdom** (St Stephen's Cathedral) in Vienna *(see pp62–3)* is Austria's best-known Gothic building.

**Goldenes Dachl** The "Golden Roof" in Innsbruck *(see p242)* is an attractive example of secular Gothic architecture.

## The Struggle for Spanish and Austrian Succession

The expiration of the Spanish line of Habsburgs led to the Spanish War of Succession (1701–14), which brought further territorial gains for Austria, including Belgium, Milan, Naples and Sardinia. Soon the problem of succession also arose in Austria, where Emperor Charles VI (1711–40) had died without a male heir. The so-called Pragmatic Sanction, established by Charles in 1713, stipulated that the Habsburg Austrian territories remain an integral, indivisible whole, with female members of the house also eligible for succession. The emperor's only daughter, Maria Theresa (1740– 80), however, was forced to defend her rights by fighting Prussia, France, Spain and a number of German states in the War of Austrian Succession (1740–48), during which she lost Silesia to Prussia. In 1772 and 1775, Austria participated in the first and third Partitions of Poland, annexing that country's southern territories.

## Enlightened Absolutism

Maria Theresa and her son Joseph II (1780–90) embarked on an extensive course of reforms, in the spirit of enlightened absolutism. They curtailed the rights of the Church, abolished serfdom, created a new administrative structure of the state and declared German the official language for all institutions. Their aim was to obliterate the differences between the individual

Apotheosis of Eugene of Saxony

countries of the empire, to unify the multi-ethnic state and to centralize power.

## Revolution and Restoration

During the revolutionary changes that took place in Europe at the turn of the 18th century, the Habsburgs joined the anti-French coalition forces. Initially they suffered major territorial losses (Belgium, Lombardy, southern Poland). Franz II, Maria Theresa's grandson, relinquished his title of Holy Roman Emperor and in 1806 declared himself Emperor Franz I of Austria. Following the defeat of Napoleon and the Congress of Vienna, where proceedings were dominated by the Austrian Foreign Minister, Klemens Metternich, the Habsburg Empire became once again a European superpower. Metternich, who from 1821 held the office of chancellor,

Emperor Franz I of Austria and Maria Theresa surrounded by their children

**1701–14** War of Spanish Succession. Austria acquires Belgium, Milan, Naples, Parma and Sardinia

**1740–48** War of Austrian Succession. Prussian-French-Spanish coalition opposes Maria Theresa's right to the imperial throne

| 1700 | 1720 | 1740 | 1760 | 1780 |

*Maria Theresa*

**1756** Birth of Wolfgang Amadeus Mozart

*Wolfgang Amadeus Mozart*

**1795** Austria participates Third Partition of Pola

**1772** Austria participates in First Partition of Poland

The Congress of Vienna in 1815

and in fact ruled Austria, became the main exponent of absolutism and the policy of ethnic oppression; hence his nickname, "Europe's coachman".

## The 1848 Revolution

In 1848–9, a wave of revolutions swept across Europe and the Austrian Empire. Uprisings against absolute government broke out in Vienna, Milan, Venice, Budapest, Cracow and Prague; the Hungarian revolution was suppressed only with the help of the Russian army. Emperor Ferdinand I saw himself forced to grant several concessions, including giving Austria a constitution (1848). Badly affected by the revolutionary events, the emperor abdicated in 1848 and the Austrian throne passed to his 18-year-old nephew, Franz Joseph I (1848–1916), who quickly reintroduced absolute rule, thus inviting increased resistance, particularly in the Hungarian part of the empire.

## The Austro-Hungarian Empire

Defeat suffered in the with Sardinia and France (1859), and with Prussia and Italy (1866), testified to the weakening position of Austria, particularly when confronted with the growing power of the unifying Germany. Defeat in the international arena also brought about changes in internal policy. In 1867, the emperor signed a treaty with Hungary and transformed the Austro-Hungarian Empire into a state consisting of two parts, united under one common ruler as well as a common army, finances and foreign policy. The adopted model of government eased the tensions in Austro-Hungarian relations, but did not contribute to the solution of other conflicts, including those with the Czechs, who revolted afresh, led by nationalist feelings.

Internationally, the empire's attention was focused on the Balkans where, with Russian approval, it occupied Bosnia and Herzegovina (1878). Key to Vienna's political strategy was the political-military treaty signed in 1882 with Germany and Italy, the Triple Alliance.

In the late 1800s, Vienna developed as a centre of fashion and became the birthplace of the avant-garde Viennese Secession style.

Buildings on fire in Vienna during the Austrian Revolution of 1848

**1806** Franz II relinquishes title of Holy Roman Emperor

*Johann Strauss (the Younger)*

**1867** Austria becomes Austro-Hungarian state

**1815** Congress of Vienna

**1848** Revolution in Vienna

**1898** Assassination of Empress Elisabeth by an Italian anarchist

| 1820 | 1840 | 1860 | 1880 | 1900 |

**1825** Birth of Johann Strauss (the Younger)

**1848** Ferdinand I abdicates and Franz Joseph I ascends the throne

**1889** Death of the Crown Prince, Archduke Rudolf

**1805** Napoleon defeats the Austrian and Russian armies in the Battle of Austerlitz

**1866** Defeated by Prussia, Austria loses its status as the main German power

# The Monarchy of Franz I

At the turn of the 19th century, Austria had to face
social and political changes brought about by the French
Revolution. Franz II ascended the Austrian throne as Holy
Roman Emperor in 1792, and Austria entered a 22-year-
period of war with France. Franz II declared his opposition
to all reformist ideas and, in response to Napoleon's self-
coronation, he established the Austrian Empire in 1804.
As Emperor Franz I, and with his all-powerful chancellor
Klemens Metternich, his main concern in the field of
domestic policy was the preservation of the monarch's
absolute power.

**After the Vienna Congress**
◻ Austria in 1815

**The coffin contains the body of
Franz I**, which was later laid in a
sarcophagus in the crypt of the
Capuchin church in Vienna *(see p75)*.

**Franz I Crosses the Vosges Mountains**
Following Napoleon's defeat at Waterloo in 1815,
Franz I marched into France at the head of troops
belonging to the coalition's occupying forces.

An officer in
Austrian uniform

**The imperial crown of Austria** –
once the crown of Emperor Rudolf II.
Alongside lie other regalia.

**Radetzky Statue**
Johann Radetzky was one of the most
outstanding commanders in Austrian
history. After the victory over Italy in the
Battle of Custozza (1848), the 82-year
old became famous as the mainstay
of the Habsburg monarchy.

**Emblem of
the Empire**
In 1836, Austria's
national emblem
combined Lorraine's
two-headed eagle,
with imperial crown,
sword, sceptre and
a shield with
the Habsburg
family crest.

**Technological Progress**
The first railway line on the European continent was built in Austria, in 1832. It linked Linz with České Budejovice.

An officer in
Hungarian uniform

## Where to See Biedermeier Style in Austria

The Biedermeier style of furniture, interior design and painting, popular during the early 19th century, reflected the virtues and aspirations of the middle classes. Draped curtains, patterned carpets, bureaus and glazed cabinets became standard features. Domestic architecture flourished. Typical interiors can be seen in Vienna, in the Geymüllerschlössel, which is part of the Museum of Applied Arts (MAK – *see p64*), and the Dreimäderlhaus. Works of prominent artists such as Ferdinand Waldmüller, Josef Danhauser and Moritz Daffinger can be found in the Belvedere (*see pp102–3*), the Wien Museum Karlsplatz (*see p101*), and in the Schlossmuseum in Linz (*see p194*), among other places.

## Funeral Ceremony of Franz I

*When Napoleon declared himself Emperor of France in 1804, Franz II countered by proclaiming himself Franz I, Emperor of Austria. He was the last ruler of the Holy Roman Empire of the German Nation. He died in 1835.*

**Biedermeier-style furniture** was highly valued by the prosperous middle classes, particularly in the first half of the 19th century.

**Franz I in his Coronation Robes**
In 1804, Franz I took on the newly created role of Emperor of Austria and King of Hungary. Two months later, he added the title King of Bohemia.

**The Dreimäderlhaus**, at No. 10 Schreyvogelgasse, is one of the most beautiful examples of Viennese Biedermeier.

Depiction of the sensational murder of Archduke Franz Ferdinand and his wife, Sophie

## World War I

In 1908, Austria-Hungary decided on a formal annexation of Bosnia-Herzegovina, leading to increased tensions with Russia, which had begun to strengthen its position in the Balkans, and with Serbia, which pursued its own expansionist aims. On 28 June 1914, in Sarajevo, the Serbian student Gavrilo Princip shot dead the heir to the Austrian throne, Franz Ferdinand. His assassination resulted in the outbreak of World War I. Germany, Austria's old ally from the Triple Alliance, declared itself on the side of Austria (Italy remained neutral for a while), while the Triple Entente countries – Russia, France and England – sided with Serbia. The war exposed the weakness of the Habsburg monarchy and brought about its collapse. Charles I, Austria's last emperor, was exiled to Madeira in 1921.

## The First Republic

On 12 November 1918, the Provisional National Assembly proclaimed the birth of the Austro-German Republic. Its first elected chancellor was the socialist Karl Renner. The peace treaty, signed in St-Germain-en-Laye (1919), imposed war compensations on Austria and forbade unification with Germany. During the 1920s, Austria's economic situation steadily worsened, giving rise to radical sentiments. The worsening internal problems were exploited by nationalist circles calling for Austria to join with Germany. Chancellor Engelbert Dollfuss, elected to office in 1932, tried to counteract such dangers by introducing "strong-arm government", repressing the Social-Democratic opposition and dissolving Communist and Nazi parties. These steps led to bloody riots in Vienna and Linz in February 1934. In July of that year, the Nazis unsuccessfully attempted a coup, and murdered Dollfuss in the process. The new chancellor, Kurt Schuschnigg, under pressure from Adolf Hitler, agreed in February 1937 to admit Nazi politicians into his government, but resigned in the face of demands for Austria to be incorporated into Germany. His successor, the Nazi activist Arthur

Townspeople give the Nazi salute as German troops march into Austria during the annexation

---

| | | | | |
|---|---|---|---|---|
| **1908** Annexation of Bosnia and Herzegovina | **1914** Assassination of Archduke Franz Ferdinand, in Sarajevo. Outbreak of WWI | | **1938** Anschluss – Austria's integration into the Third Reich | |
| | **1934** Workers riot in Vienna and Linz; bloody suppression by the police | | **1943** Moscow Conference | |

| **1900** | **1910** | **1920** | **1930** | **1940** | **1950** |
|---|---|---|---|---|---|

| | | | | |
|---|---|---|---|---|
| **1916** Death of Franz Joseph I. Emperor Charles I ascends the throne | **1918** End of WWI. Collapse of Austria-Hungary. Creation of the Republic of Austria | **1934** Nazi coup failed. Engelbert Dollfuss killed | **1955** Treaty of State restoring full sovereignty to Austria. Parliament declares Austria to be neutral for all time | |
| *Archduke Franz Ferdinand's jacket* | | *Engelbert Dollfuss* | | |

Soldiers of the occupying forces salute each other in Vienna, 1951

Seyss-Inquart, proclaimed Austria's integration into the Third Reich (Anschluss) on 13 March 1938, which met with the approval of the majority of the Austrian population. German troops marched into the country. In 1938, some 200,000 Jews lived in Vienna, yet after the Holocaust only 7,000 remained.

## World War II and the Second Republic

Following the Anschluss, Austria became a part of Greater Germany until the end of World War II. Opposition against the Nazi administration was negligible. Before the end of the war, at the Moscow Conference in 1943, the Allied forces decided to restore an independent Austrian state. In April 1945, Karl Renner formed the first provisional government of the restored Second Republic, and in December he was elected president. In July 1945, Austria

was divided into four occupation zones by the Allied powers.

The first parliamentary elections, in November 1945, were won by the Christian-Democratic Party (ÖVP), with the Socialist Party (SPÖ) coming second. Both parties were to control the political life of the country for the next 50 years. De-Nazification continued until 1948. In 1955 the Austrian State Treaty was signed, restoring Austria to full sovereignty. Foreign troops were withdrawn from its territory and parliament proclaimed permanent neutrality. In December 1955, Austria became a member of the United Nations, and in 1995 joined the European Union (EU).

From the 1990s onwards, attention has been focused on the rise of the right and reaction to the global refugee crisis. In 2000, Austria was sanctioned by the EU for seven months, after the right-wing Freedom Party became part of the coalition government. Austria has also adopted several contentious measures regarding refugees and in 2017 banned the wearing of the Islamic veil in schools and courts.

Simon Wiesenthal and Ariel Musicant, Austrian investigators into Nazi crimes, at the Jewish memorial

**1973** Konrad Lorenz receives Nobel Prize in Physiology and Medicine

**1995** Austria joins the EU

**2004** Elfriede Jelinek receives Nobel Prize for Literature

**2006** Austria heads EU Presidency

**2008** Far-right leader Jörg Haider dies in car crash

**2012** New right-wing political party, Team Stronach, is launched

| 1970 | 1980 | 1990 | 2000 | 2010 | 2020 |

Vienna ...t of John F. ...dy and ...Khrushchev

**1972–81** Austrian diplomat Kurt Waldheim holds office of UN Secretary General

*Austrian anti-globalization protest*

**2000** Nationalist Austrian Freedom Party enters government coalition

**2010** Heinz Fischer of the Social Democractic Party wins the presidential elections with just under 80 per cent of the vote

# VIENNA
# AREA BY AREA

# Introducing Vienna

Central Vienna includes the Inner City, demarcated by the Ringstrasse (often shortened to Ring) and Franz-Josefs-Kai, plus the area between Ring and Gürtel. Gürtel is Vienna's second ring road, running almost parallel with the Ring. In this guide, central Vienna is divided into three districts, in line with its administrative sectors. The most interesting sights outside the centre are also featured.

**Majolikahaus**
The façade of Majolikahaus, at No. 40 Linke Wienzeile, was designed in 1899 by Otto Wagner, one of the foremost representatives of Viennese Secession style.

**Freyung**
Freyung Square is dominated by the Austria Fountain; in the background is the Schottenkirche, the church of Vienna's Benedictine monks.

◀ Aerial view of the city of Vienna from the bell tower of Stephansdom

**Pallas Athene Fountain**
The statue of the goddess Pallas Athene, by Carl Kundmann, was placed on the fountain in front of the Parliament building in 1902.

**Staatsoper**
The Vienna State Opera House was the first building Franz Joseph I had erected on the prestigious Ringstrasse, built along the route of the old city walls.

**Stephansdom**
The interior of the Gothic St Stephen's Cathedral has been modified many times through the centuries.

**Key**

⬜ Major sight

⬜ Pedestrian street

**For keys to symbols** *see back flap*

# INNER CITY

The first steps of any visitor to Vienna should be taken in the old quarter. Vienna's Innere Stadt, or "inner city", is easy to negotiate on foot and is well defined: the Danube canal forms a natural barrier on the east, and the Ringstrasse provides a binding circle around the other sides. At the very centre, Stephensdom stands proud in the city's main square, Stephensplatz. A clutch of must-see attractions are located here, including the Spanish Riding School, Alte Burg and several important churches.

It is also one of Vienna's liveliest areas, with lavish traditional cafés and restaurants, including the famous Café Central, as well as elegant shops awaiting visitors.

## Sights at a Glance

### Streets and Squares
2 Graben
8 Dr-Ignaz-Seipel-Platz
12 Schwedenplatz
14 Jewish Quarter
17 Hoher Markt
19 Schulhof
20 Am Hof
21 Freyung
22 Herrengasse
23 Minoritenplatz
24 Michaelerplatz
26 Heldenplatz
29 Josefsplatz
34 Kärntner Strasse

### Historic Buildings
5 Mozarthaus Vienna
11 Urania

16 Altes Rathaus
18 Böhmische Hofkanzlei
27 *Alte Burg pp72–3*
28 *Spanish Riding School p71*
33 Winterpalais des Prinzen Eugen

### Churches
1 Peterskirche
3 *Stephansdom pp62–3*
6 Deutschordenskirche St Elisabeth
7 Franziskanerkirche
9 Dominikanerkirche

13 Ruprechtskirche
15 Maria am Gestade
30 Augustinerkirche
32 Kapuzinerkirche, Kaisergruft

### Museums
4 Dom- und Diözesanmuseum
10 Österreichisches Museum für Angewandte Kunst
31 Albertina

### Parks and Gardens
25 Volksgarten

*See Street Finder, maps 2 & 3*

| 0 metres | 250 |
| 0 yards | 250 |

◀ Spectacular frescoes adorning the dome and altar of Peterskirche

# Street-by-Street: Around Stephansdom

The origins of this district date back to the 13th century, but much of it was changed in the 17th and 18th centuries, when many churches and public buildings were refashioned in the spirit of the increasingly powerful Habsburg monarchy. Narrow, medieval alleys adjoin monumental Baroque structures and bourgeois town houses, whose ground floors are often occupied by shops, cafés and restaurants. In the evenings, when the churches and museums close for the night, the area is still lively with people.

**❹ ★ Dom- und Diözesanmuseum**
This crucifix, containing the relics of St Andrew, is one of the many treasures of medieval sacred art kept in the Cathedral Museum.

**Haas & Haas** provides a change from the ubiquitous coffee house, serving a wide selection of teas as well as light meals. The tea house has an attractive courtyard filled with lush greenery.

**❸ ★ Stephansdom**
St Stephen's Cathedral has a Baroque main altar, the work of Tobias Pock, showing the martyrdom of its patron saint.

STEPHANS PLATZ

BLUTGASSE

**❻ Deutschordenskirche St Elisabeth**
This church belonged to the Teutonic Order which, after having been banned from Eastern Prussia by Napoleon, moved its headquarters to Vienna.

**Along Blutgasse** and neighbouring streets the tenement houses feature lovely green courtyards.

**❺ Mozarthaus Vienna**
Wolfgang Amadeus Mozart lived in this house from 1784 to 1787 and composed *The Marriage of Figaro* here.

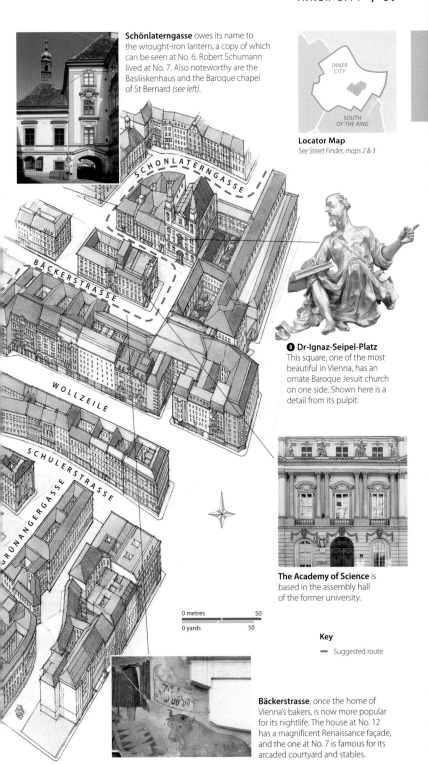

**Schönlaterngasse** owes its name to the wrought-iron lantern, a copy of which can be seen at No. 6. Robert Schumann lived at No. 7. Also noteworthy are the Basiliskenhaus and the Baroque chapel of St Bernard *(see left)*.

**Locator Map**
*See Street Finder, maps 2 & 3*

**➑ Dr-Ignaz-Seipel-Platz**
This square, one of the most beautiful in Vienna, has an ornate Baroque Jesuit church on one side. Shown here is a detail from its pulpit.

**The Academy of Science** is based in the assembly hall of the former university.

0 metres    50
0 yards     50

**Key**
— Suggested route

**Bäckerstrasse**, once the home of Vienna's bakers, is now more popular for its nightlife. The house at No. 12 has a magnificent Renaissance façade, and the one at No. 7 is famous for its arcaded courtyard and stables.

# ❶ Peterskirche

Petersplatz 6. **Map** 2 B4. **Tel** 53 36 443. Ⓤ Stephansplatz. 🚌 1A, 2A, 3A. **Open** 7am–8pm Mon–Fri, 9am–9pm Sat, Sun. 

St Peter's church, one of Vienna's oldest, was, according to legend, founded in 792 by Charlemagne, as commemorated in a marble relief on the church's façade, *The Placing of the Cross by Charlemagne*, by Rudolf Weyr (1906).

The site was occupied by a Romanesque basilica in the Early Middle Ages. The present Baroque church was built in the 18th century to designs by Gabriele Montani. It received its final form from Johann Lukas von Hildebrandt, who also gave the church its magnificent green patina-covered dome, which towers over the whole district. The frescoes inside the dome, depicting the Assumption of the Virgin Mary, were created by Johann Michael Rottmayr.

The Chapel of St Michael, the first on the right, holds a glass coffin containing the relics of St Benedict.

The striking patina-covered copper dome of Peterskirche

# ❷ Graben

**Map** 2 B4, C4. Ⓤ Stephansplatz. 🚌 1A, 2A, 3A. Jewish Museum: **Tel** 53 50 431. **Open** 10am–6pm Sun–Fri. 🖼 ⬛ 🆆 jmw.at

This fully pedestrianized street, running through a bustling part of the city centre, is one of the most fashionable shopping areas

The Baroque plague column on Graben

in Vienna, full to bursting with lively restaurants and cafés. There are two identical fountains in the square, St Joseph Fountain on the northwestern side and St Leopold Fountain on the southeastern side.

In the centre of the square stands the Baroque Pestsäule (Plague Column), also known as the Dreifaltigkeitssäule (Trinity Column), which the Emperor Leopold I had erected after the end of the 1679 plague that decimated the town. It depicts the Holy Trinity, with a statue of the praying emperor at the top. A carved group, entitled *Faith Conquers the Plague*, adorns the southern side of the column. A short distance from here, towards Stephansplatz, stands a modest statue of St John of Nepomuk, which is a favourite spot with buskers.

The modern Haas-Haus on Graben, at Stephansplatz, was built in 1985–90 on the site of older buildings destroyed during a bombing raid. Made from glass and aluminium, it is the most controversial building in the heart of the city. Its windows beautifully reflect the cathedral towers. The top floor houses a café-restaurant, offering great views.

One of the original Baroque structures is the Bartolotti Palace, at the corner of Dorotheergasse. Further along Dorotheergasse, at No. 11, is the **Jewish Museum** (Jüdisches Museum Wien), which moved to the former Eskeles Palace from the old synagogue. The oldest Jewish museum in the world, founded in 1895, the structure preserves remnants of a medieval synagogue.

Otto Wagner, an outstanding architect of the Viennese Secession, had his studio at Graben No. 10; in the 1980s, the house belonged to the eccentric Austrian artist Friedensreich Hundertwasser.

# ❸ Stephansdom

*See pp62–3.*

# ❹ Dom- und Diözesanmuseum

Stephansplatz 6. **Map** 2 C4. **Tel** 51 552-35 60. Ⓤ Stephansplatz. 🚌 1A, 2A, 3A. **Open** 10am–6pm Tue–Sat. 🖼 🆆 dommuseum.at

Reopened in 2017 after three years of extensive renovations, with a new design by architect Boris Podrecca, this museum features striking juxtapositions of medieval and avant-garde art. Many pieces were donated to the cathedral by Duke Rudolf IV. Highlights include a famous portrait of the duke (c.1360), and the *Erlacher Madonna*, a life-size statue of the Madonna and Child, a Gothic masterpiece (c.1330) from Lower Austria. The cathedral museum also holds sacral vessels and reliquaries from St Stephen's Cathedral, valuable masterpieces of the Gothic, Baroque and Romantic eras, and the Otto Mauer collection of 20th-century Austrian art.

Gothic Madonna and Child, Cathedral Museum

## ❺ Mozarthaus Vienna

Domgasse 5. **Map** 2 C4.
**Tel** 51 21 791. ⓤ Stephansplatz.
🚌 3A. **Open** 10am–7pm daily. 🏛
📷 🅦 **mozarthausvienna.at**

Domgasse 5 is the most famous of Mozart's various homes in Vienna. He lived here with his family in 1784–7, and composed many of his masterpieces here, including *The Marriage of Figaro*. Restored for the anniversary year of 2006, the Mozarthaus Vienna has exhibitions on two upper floors as well as the Mozarts' first-floor flat.

## ❻ Deutschordens-kirche St Elisabeth

Singerstrasse 7. **Map** 2 C4.
**Tel** 51 21 065. ⓤ Stephansplatz.
🚌 1A, 2A, 3A. Church: **Open** 7am–7pm daily. Treasury: **Open** 10am–noon Tue, Thu & Sat, 3–5pm Wed, Fri. 🏛

The knights of the Teutonic Order arrived in Vienna in the 13th century. They established their quarters near the Stephansdom, but only the tower still stands today. In the 15th century, they built the present Gothic **church** of St Elizabeth. Its Baroque façade, added between 1725 and 1735, hides the original Gothic features.

In 1807, when Napoleon abolished the Order of Teutonic Knights in Eastern Prussia, the knights moved their headquarters to Vienna and brought the Order Treasury here. The four rooms of the **Treasury** hold collections of historical objects: insignia of the Grand Masters, coins, medals, seals, sacral vessels and tableware, and masterpieces of European art collected by the knights.

The walls of the church are hung with the coats of arms of the Teutonic knights. The beautiful winged altar (1520) is made from elaborate carved and painted panels depicting scenes from the Passion, surrounded by intricate tracery.

Within the complex of build-ings belonging to the Order is the apartment where Mozart first lived in Vienna, later occupied by Johannes Brahms (1863–5).

## ❼ Franziskaner-kirche

Franziskanerplatz 4. **Map** 2 C4.
**Tel** 51 24 578. ⓤ Stephansplatz.
**Open** 6:30am–noon, 2–5:30pm Mon–Sat, 7am–5:30pm Sun.

In the 14th century, the Franciscans took over this church, originally built by wealthy citizens as a "house of the soul" for prostitutes wishing to reform. The present church, designed in the South German Renaissance style by Bonaventura Daum, was built in 1601–11. Its façade is topped by a scrolled gable with obelisks and carvings. The interior was decorated by Austrian and Italian masters of the Baroque, including Andrea Pozzo and Johann Georg Schmidt. An axe has been stuck in the wooden statue of the Madonna and Child above the tabernacle, known as Madonna and Axe, ever since an attack during the religious wars of the 17th century. The Moses Fountain in front of the church dates from 1798.

A charming 18th-century wall fountain, Academy of Sciences

## ❽ Dr-Ignaz-Seipel-Platz

**Map** 3 D4. ⓤ Stephansplatz, Schwedenplatz. 🚌 3A.

Dr Ignaz Seipel, a conservative politician, was twice Chancellor of Austria in the 1920s. The square bearing his name is one of the most attractive in Vienna. At its centre (at No. 2) stands a Rococo structure designed by Jean Nicolas Jadot de Ville-Issey, originally intended as an auditor-ium for the Old University. Since 1857 it has served as the head-quarters of the Österreichische Akademie der Wissenschaften (Austrian Academy of Sciences). The frescoes on the ceiling of the Rococo assembly hall, painted by Gregorio Guglielmi, show an allegory of the four academic faculties. Damaged by fire in 1961, they have been meticulously restored.

Opposite the Academy of Sciences stands the impressive High Baroque Jesuitenkirche. The Jesuits took over the university in the 1620s and from 1703 to 1705, rebuilt the church next to it with a new façade and interior, the works of the Italian painter Andrea Pozzo.

The impressive winged altarpiece in Deutschordenskirche

# ❸ Stephansdom

Marking the centre of Vienna, the cathedral, dedicated to the first Christian martyr, St Stephen, is the very soul of the city. Although built on this site some 800 years ago, the present building is mainly late-Gothic – the only fragments remaining of the original 13th-century Romanesque church are the Giants' Doorway and the Towers of the Heathens. Largely destroyed during World War II, the cathedral was restored to its former glory by the efforts of the entire nation. In a vault beneath its main altar are urns containing the internal organs of some of the Habsburgs – other body parts were interred elsewhere in Vienna.

★ Giants' Doorway

This masterpiece of late-Romanesque art, with its richly carved portal and the twin Towers of the Heathens, stands on the site of an earlier heathen shrine.

Entrance to the catacombs

★ Cathedral's Pulpit

The pulpit in the main nave is decorated with portraits of the Four Fathers of the Church. The sculptor himself looks on from a "window" below, under the stairs.

**KEY**

① **The North Tower** houses the Pummerin Bell.

② **The Bronze Sphere** is crowned with a twin-headed eagle – the Habsburg emblem.

③ **Viewing platform**, at 72 m (236 ft)

④ **The mosaic roof** is covered with almost 250,000 glazed tiles.

⑤ **Lifts** to the bell

⑥ **Singer Gate** was at one time the entrance for male visitors. The superb sculptures depict scenes from the life of St Paul and Duke Rudolf IV the Founder.

Main entrance

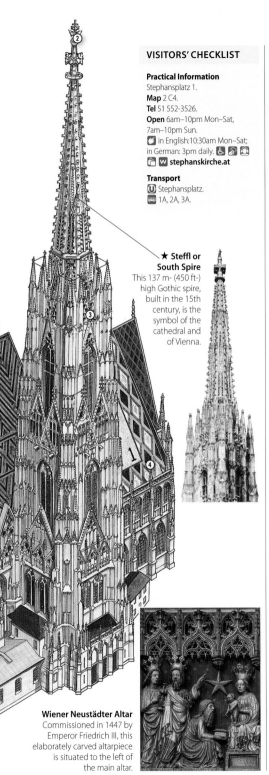

## VISITORS' CHECKLIST

**Practical Information**
Stephansplatz 1.
**Map** 2 C4.
**Tel** 51 552-3526.
**Open** 6am–10pm Mon–Sat,
7am–10pm Sun.
🕭 in English:10:30am Mon–Sat;
in German: 3pm daily. ♿ 🈂 📷
📷 🖥 stephanskirche.at

**Transport**
Ⓤ Stephansplatz.
🚌 1A, 2A, 3A.

★ **Steffl or
South Spire**
This 137 m- (450 ft-)
high Gothic spire,
built in the 15th
century, is the
symbol of the
cathedral and
of Vienna.

**Wiener Neustädter Altar**
Commissioned in 1447 by
Emperor Friedrich III, this
elaborately carved altarpiece
is situated to the left of
the main altar.

The majestic Baroque façade
of Dominikanerkirche

## ❾ Dominikaner-kirche

Postgasse 4. **Map** 3 D4. **Tel** 51 29 174.
Ⓤ Stubentor, Schwedenplatz,
Stephansplatz. 🚋 2. 🚌 3A, 74A.
**Open** 7am–7pm Mon–Sat, 7:30am–
9pm Sun. 🖥 mariarotunda.at

Dominican monks came
to Vienna in 1226, at the
invitation of Duke Leopold VI.
They built and consecrated their
first church and convent here
in the second half of the 13th
century. The church that stands
now, built between 1631 and
1674, was designed by Cypriano
Biasino and Antonio Canevale.

The church has a richly
ornamented interior, with a
ring of chapels surrounding
the nave, early-Baroque frescoes
on the ceiling and a painting by
Franz Geyling inside the dome.
The second chapel on the right,
St Vincent Chapel, has swirling
Rococo grilles and candelabra,
and there is a very beautiful gilt
organ above the west door, set
within a mid-18th-century
decorative enclosure.

Niches in the majestic façade
contain statues of Dominican
saints. The two statues in the
corner recesses commemorate
two great scientists and medieval
religious figures, St Albert the
Great and St Thomas Aquinas.

Worth seeing are the frescoes
by Tencalla and Rauchmüller,
and the high altar (1839–40) by
Karl Rösner, with a painting by
Leopold Kupelwieser.

## ⓿ Österreichisches Museum für Angewandte Kunst

Stubenring 5. **Map** 3 D4. **Tel** 712 80 00. Ⓤ Stubentor, Landstrasse 🚋 2. 🚌 1A, 74A.. Ⓢ Landstrasse. **Open** 10am–10pm Tue, 10am–6pm Wed–Sun. 🅿 Admission free Tue. ♿ Ⓦ **mak.at**

The Austrian Museum of Applied Arts (MAK), founded in 1864 and the first of its kind in Europe, exercised a strong influence on the development of the applied arts for some time. It houses the archives and collections of the Wiener Werkstätte – workshops famous for their promotion of good design.

The building was designed by one of the Ring architects, Heinrich von Ferstel, in Florentine Renaissance style. A new wing was added in 1909, and in 1994 the flak tower in Arenbergpark became an annexe of the museum. Each room is unique, designed by a different artist, thus creating a fine setting for the items on display.

The eclectic permanent collection includes glass, pottery, porcelain, jewellery, metalwork, furniture, textiles, Eastern carpets and decorative items from the Far East. Separate rooms are devoted to the Secession period.

Biedermeier-style sofa, MAK

## ⓫ Urania

Uraniastrasse 1. **Map** 3 E3. Ⓤ Schwedenplatz. 🚋 1, 2, N. Planetarium: **Tel** 89 174 150 000. **Open** Term time: 9am–8pm Mon–Fri, 2–8pm Sat, Sun; school hols: 9am–4pm Mon–Fri, 2–8pm Sat, Sun. Ⓦ **planetarium-wien.at**

On the east side of Julius-Raab-Platz, on the banks of the Danube Canal, stands a round

building with a distinctive dome that is visible from afar. Urania, named after the Greek muse, was built in 1910 to designs by Max Fabian. It is home to Vienna's oldest educational establishment that is not a school. Inside the building are lecture halls and a theatre for visiting theatre performances, as well as a resident puppet theatre; it is also home to a cinema and a **planetarium**. Every year, Urania holds a symposium devoted to the outstanding Austrian writer and Nobel prize winner Elias Canetti.

## ⓬ Schwedenplatz

**Map** 3 D3. Ⓤ Schwedenplatz.

Schwedenplatz, the Swedish Square, is one of Vienna's busiest spots. Here, on the banks of the Danube Canal, under Schwedenbrücke, is a landing stage with riverboats inviting visitors on to a variety of pleasure cruises. It is a lively area, with several snack and ice cream stands, and buskers playing violins providing entertainment.

In Laurenzberg, on the south side of Schwedenplatz, remains of the old town wall can be seen, with a metal ring that was used to tie up horses and an old sign with traffic regulations. At Fleischmarkt 11, steep, narrow steps lead down to the wine bar Griechenbeisl, which claims to be the oldest restaurant in the city. Visitors are welcomed by a board showing the *Lieber Augustin*; from the entrance hall you can see down to a small, illuminated cellar where his statue is on display. The story of Augustin, a piper, goes back to the times of the Great Plague in Vienna. In a drunken stupor, he slumped into the gutter. When undertakers mistook him for dead and threw him into a plague pit, he woke up and terrified them by singing: *O du lieber Augustin…* (Oh, dear Augustin). Miraculously, he survived, and today, tourists wishing to return to Vienna throw a coin into the cellar.

Striking ivy-clad façade of Ruprechtskirche, Vienna's oldest church

## ⓭ Ruprechtskirche

Ruprechtsplatz. **Map** 2 C3. **Tel** 53 56 003. Ⓤ Schwedenplatz. 🚋 1, 2, N. 🚌 1A, 2A, 3A. Mass: 9pm–midnight Fri (German), 5pm Sat (German). Ⓦ **ruprechtskirche.at**

The church of St Ruprecht, rising on an escarpment overlooking Ruprechtsplatz, is Vienna's oldest church. At one time, an arm of the Danube flowed nearby with a landing stage for salt transported from Salzburg. According to legend, the church was founded in 740 by disciples of the Salzburg bishop St Ruprecht, patron saint of salt merchants. The Romanesque nave and three lower floors of the tower date from the 11th century. In the choir is a 12th-century stained-glass window, Vienna's oldest, depicting the Crucifixion and the Virgin Mary on the throne.

## ⓮ Jewish Quarter

**Map** 2 C2, 3. Ⓤ Schwedenplatz, Herrengasse. 🚌 1A, 2A, 3A. Jewish Museum: Palais Eskeles, Dorotheergasse 11. **Tel** 535 04 31. Ⓤ Stephansplatz. **Open** 10am–6pm Sun–Fri. 🅿 Museum Judenplatz: Misrachi-Haus, Judenplatz 8. Ⓤ Schwedenplatz, Herrengasse. **Open** 10am–6pm Sun–Thu, 10am–2pm Fri. 🅿

A tangle of narrow streets west of Rotenturmstrasse makes up the earliest Jewish quarter in Vienna. Today, the Jewish quarter is a busy area of clubs, bars and kosher restaurants, but during the Middle Ages, Judenplatz was the site of the Jewish ghetto, with a synagogue, the remains of which can be seen under the square. There was also a Jewish hospital, rabbi's house, bathhouse and school.

In 2000, the **Museum Judenplatz**, devoted to medieval Jewish life, opened in Misrachi House. A modern monument by Rachel Whiteread at the centre of the square commemorates the victims of the Holocaust.

Stadttempel, Vienna's only synagogue to have survived World War II, is hidden behind a façade on Seitenstettengasse. It is now guarded by armed police, a precaution taken following a terrorist attack in 1983.

In 1895, the world's first **Jewish Museum** was founded here. It was closed down by the Nazis, but a new museum opened in 1993 in Palais Eskeles in Dorotheergasse *(see p60)*.

The Gothic interior of the church Maria am Gestade

## ⓮ Maria am Gestade

Salvatorgasse 12. **Map** 2 C3.
**Tel** 533 959 40. Ⓤ Schwedenplatz, Stephansplatz. 🚋 1A, 3A. **Open** 7am–6pm daily. 🖥 **maria-am-gestade.redemptoristen.at**

The church of St Mary's on the riverbank was once flooded by the waters of an old Danube canal. Today it rises on a steep escarpment, its 56-m- (180-ft-)

high Gothic steeple dominating the city. The stone helmet atop the steeple is a masterpiece of Viennese Gothic art.

First mentioned in the 12th century, the present building dates from the late 1300s, and is one of Vienna's oldest churches. It was used as an arsenal during Napoleon's occupation of the city in 1809, but later restored.

Inside, the stained-glass panes behind the main altar are mostly original medieval features. The pillars are adorned with six Gothic statues, plus some from the 17th and 19th centuries. To the left of the main altar is a chapel with a Renaissance stone altar, with colourful painted carvings. The church also holds the tomb of Clemens Maria Hofbauer, the city's patron saint.

## ⓰ Altes Rathaus

Wipplingerstrasse 8. **Map** 2 B3.
Ⓤ Schwedenplatz, Stephansplatz. 🚋 1, 2. 🚌 1A, 3A. Archives and Museum of the Austrian Resistance: **Tel** 228 9469 319. **Open** 9am–5pm Mon–Wed, 9am–7pm Thu. 🗓 by appointment.

Vienna's Old Town Hall probably first stood at neighbouring Tuchlaubenstrasse. The building at Wipplingerstrasse was once owned by the rich and influential brothers Otto and Haimo von Neuhaus, who headed a burghers' rebellion against the Habsburgs. In 1309, Prince Friedrich the Fair confiscated the building and

Ironwork at the entrance to the Altes Rathaus, Wipplingerstrasse

gave it to Vienna. It served as the city's main administrative centre until 1883.

The entrance of the Altes Rathaus is festooned with lovely Baroque ironwork. In the courtyard stands the Andromeda Fountain (1741), the last work of the sculptor Georg Raphael Donner. A door leads from the courtyard to Salvatorkapelle (St Saviour's chapel), the former Neuhaus family chapel, which has a Renaissance portal (1520–30) facing Salvatorgasse, a rare example in Vienna of the Italian Renaissance style.

Today, the Altes Rathaus houses the **Archives and Museum of the Austrian Resistance**, devoted to the memory of those who risked their lives by opposing National Socialism in Austria, in the years 1934–45.

## Vienna's Jews – Past and Present

A Jewish merchant community thrived in Vienna from the 12th century, with the original Jewish quarter centred around Judenplatz. During the 1421 persecutions many Jews were murdered, while others were forced to convert to the Christian faith or to leave the town. The 1781 Edict of Tolerance, issued by Joseph II, lifted legal constraints on Jews, and the centre of Jewish life gradually moved to the opposite bank of the Danube Canal, around the Prater. In 1938, some 200,000 Jews lived in Vienna, contributing to its cultural and intellectual life. After the Nazi genocide, only 7,000 remained. Now Eastern European immigrants are again adding to their total number.

The lavish interior of the Stadttempel

Anker Clock in Hoher Markt, with cut-out historical figures

## ⑰ Hoher Markt

**Map** 2 C3. Ⓤ Stephansplatz, Schwedenplatz. 🚌 1A, 3A.

Hoher Markt is the oldest square in Vienna. After World War II, the foundations of the Roman military camp of Vindobona, where Emperor Marcus Aurelius died in AD 180, were discovered under the square. They now form part of a popular museum.

In medieval times, fish and cloth markets, as well as executions, were held in the square. Since the early 18th century, it has been a venue for town court trials.

The Ankeruhr (Anker Clock), above the entrance to Bauernmarkt, is a copper and bronze sculptural clock designed in 1911 by Franz von Matsch. It features 12 historical figures who contributed to Vienna's development and reputation. Every hour one of these emerges, and at noon the entire set parades past. The procession is headed by Marcus Aurelius, followed by Rudolf IV, and closes with the composer Joseph Haydn.

In the centre of the square stands the remarkable Baroque Josephsbrunnen (Joseph's fountain) or Vermählungsbrunnen (nuptial fountain), commissioned by Leopold I and designed by Johann Bernhard Fischer von Erlach, depicting Joseph and Mary's betrothal by the high priest.

## ⑱ Böhmische Hofkanzlei

Judenplatz 11. **Map** 2 B3. **Tel** 53 122. Ⓤ Stephansplatz. 🚌 1A, 3A. **Open** 8am–3:30pm Mon–Fri. Ⓦ vfgh.gv.at

The Habsburg rulers were also kings of Bohemia, which was initially governed from Prague. In 1627, however, Emperor Ferdinand II transferred the administration to Vienna. In 1714, the Bohemian Court Chancery moved into this grand palace, designed by Johann Bernhard Fischer von Erlach, and henceforth the Austrian emperors ruled Bohemia from here.

The vast original Baroque portals, with sculptures added later by Lorenzo Mattielli, create a harmonious exterior, which is subtle yet powerful. Also noteworthy are the beautifully carved and elegantly curved window frames.

## ⑲ Schulhof

**Map** 2 B3. Ⓤ Stephansplatz, Herrengasse. 🚌 1A, 2A, 3A. Clock Museum: **Tel** 53 32 265. **Open** 10am–6pm Tue–Sun. **Closed** 1 Jan, 1 May, 25 Dec. 🅿

Schulhof is a small alley connecting the imperial Am Hof square with the elegant, Baroque residential area of Kurrentgasse. The building at No. 2, the former Obizzi Palace (1690), now houses

Entrance to the unique Clock Museum in Schulhof

a fascinating **Clock Museum**, which has more than 3,000 exhibits. The museum provides its visitors with a comprehensive account of the history of chronometry through the ages and of clock technology from the 15th century to the present day. The Biedermeier and Belle Epoque periods are particularly well presented. A major highlight is the interesting 18th-century astronomical clock by the Augustinian friar David a Sancto Cajetano.

At every full hour the three floors of the museum resound to the striking, chiming and playing of numerous clocks. All are carefully maintained to keep the correct time. This is something of a startling experience, although quite enchanting.

A short distance from here, at No. 10 Kurrentgasse, is the bakery Grimm, one of the most famous in Vienna.

## ⑳ Am Hof

**Map** 2 B3. Ⓤ Stephansplatz, Herrengasse. 🚌 1A, 2A, 3A.

The name of this square (meaning "by the Court") refers to the medieval princes' residence nearby. This later housed the mint, and then the royal military chancery. Today it is a bank.

The main architectural gem of present-day Am Hof is the church of the Nine Angel Choirs, which was built in the late 14th century by Carmelite Friars and rebuilt after the fire of 1607. It is adorned with a Baroque façade crowned with a triangular pediment featuring Our Lady, the queen of the nine angel choirs. The dissolution of the Holy Roman Empire was proclaimed from the church's terrace on 6 August 1806.

There are a number of other interesting houses in the square. The building at No. 10, with a magnificent façade incorporating sculptures by Lorenzo Mattielli, is the former citizens' armoury, today housing the headquarters of the city's fire services. No. 14 is the

Statue on top of No. 10 Am Hof, the former citizens' armoury

Collalto Palace, where, in 1762, the six-year-old Mozart gave his first performance.

In front of the church stands the Mariensäule (Column of Our Lady), a monument commissioned by Ferdinand III to commemorate the end of the threat of the Swedish invasion, at the conclusion of the Thirty Years' War.

## ㉑ Freyung

**Map** 2 B3. **Ⓤ** Herrengasse, Schottentor. ▤ 1, 71, D. ▥ 1A, 2A.

This square derives its name from the right of sanctuary (*frey* is an old word for "free") granted to any fugitive seeking refuge in the Schottenkirche (Scottish church), now at No. 6. The priory church was founded by Irish Benedictine friars, who came to Vienna in 1177. Although much altered, the church has

Fountain in Fersel Passage, linking Freyung with Herrengasse

a Neo-Classical façade and a magnificent Baroque interior, which still bears features of its former Romanesque decor. Above the tabernacle stands the 13th-century statue of Our Lady, the oldest Romanesque sculpture in Vienna.

The adjacent abbey buildings house a picture gallery with an interesting collection of medieval art.

Other interesting buildings in Freyung include the Baroque Harrach Palace at No. 3, designed by Domenico Martinelli (1690) and, at No. 4, the Kinsky Palace, designed by Johann Lukas von Hildebrandt, who became the court architect in 1700.

Nearby is one of the few remaining, largely unaltered Renaissance buildings, the Porcia Palace of 1546, one of the oldest in Vienna.

At the centre of the square, in a glass-roofed, hexagonal atrium, stands the Austria Fountain. Erected in 1846, it shows an allegorical figure of Austria surrounded by four mermaids representing the major rivers (Danube, Elbe, Po, Vistula) in the Habsburg Empire at the time.

## ㉒ Herrengasse

**Map** 2 A3, B4. **Ⓤ** Herrengasse. ▥ 1A, 2A.

Herrengasse was once one of the smartest addresses in Vienna, where the nobility had their palaces. Nowadays, most buildings are occupied by government offices.

Herrengasse's name, meaning gentlemen's alleyway, dates from the 16th century, when the Landhaus at No. 13 was the seat of the provincial government of Lower Austria, the province surrounding Vienna. It fulfilled this function until 1986, when the small town of St Pölten became the new capital of the province. Some very old parts of the Landhaus still remain; the chapel is believed to have been built by Anton Pilgram, one of the architects of Stephansdom. The present building was

rebuilt in 1837–48, under the supervision of Ludwig Pichl. In the courtyard, a tablet from 1571 warns visitors not to carry weapons or fight here. The injunction was famously ignored when the 1848 Revolution was ignited on this very spot. In 1918 the Republic was proclaimed from the Landhaus.

Liechtenstein Palace, seen from Minoritenplatz

## ㉓ Minoritenplatz

**Map** 2 A4, B3. **Ⓤ** Herrengasse. ▤ 1, 71, D. ▥ 1A, 2A.

The dominant feature of this square is the Minoritenkirche. Built originally by Minor Friars in 1224, the present structure is a Franciscan church from the 14th century. It was rebuilt during the Baroque period, and restored to its original Gothic form in the 19th century. The church retains a fine west portal (1340). The tower acquired its unusual pyramid shape during the Turkish siege of Vienna in 1529, when a shell sliced the top off the steeple. Inside the church is a mosaic copy of Leonardo da Vinci's *Last Supper*.

Between Minoritenplatz and Bankgasse is the town palace of the Liechtenstein family.

On the south side of the square, at No. 3, is the former palace of the Dietrichstein family. This palace, an early work of 1755 by Franz Hillebrand, houses the Austrian Chancellor's Office and the Foreign Office. Its rooms have witnessed many historic events.

# Street-by-Street: The Hofburg Complex

The Hofburg Complex, the former
emperor's residence, is a permanent
reminder of the glory of the Habsburg
Empire, with its majestic palace –
particularly impressive when seen from
Heldenplatz – and the harmony of the
squares and palaces in Augustinerstrasse.
This part of Vienna is one of the capital's
most fashionable and lively areas, both
during the daytime and at night, when
the former palace rooms serve as theatre
and concert halls.

**㉔ Michaelerplatz**
The Michaelertrakt, on the site of the former
court theatre on the south side of this square, was
commissioned by Franz Joseph as a passageway and
built to designs by Ferdinand Kirschner.

MICHAELE
PLATZ

**㉖ Heldenplatz**
The square between
the Ring and Hofburg
is used for
large public
gatherings.

**㉗ ★ Alte Burg**
The Old Palace was the official
Habsburg residence from the
13th century.

**Neue Burg**, the last wing
of the Hofburg, was built
just before the outbreak of
World War I, during the
final days of the monarchy.

**Kohlmarkt** has some of the smartest shops in town, including some designed by the renowned architect Hans Hollein.

**Locator Map**
*See Street Finder, map 2*

**Inside Michaelerkirche** the Rococo main altar and the 14th-century Renaissance frescoes are spectacular.

**28 Spanish Riding School**
The Riding School, where shows with the graceful, white Lipizzaner stallions take place, is one of Vienna's star attractions.

0 metres 30
0 yards 30

**Key**
— Suggested route

**30 Augustinerkirche**
The church's Loreto chapel contains silver urns preserving the hearts of the Habsburg family.

**31 ★ Albertina**
This palace, built in 1781, now houses one of the finest collections of graphic art in Europe.

**29 ★ Josefsplatz**
This beautiful square was named after Emperor Joseph II, whose statue stands at its centre.

Stucco angels in Michaelerkirche, Michaelerplatz

## ❷❹ Michaelerplatz

**Map** 2 B4. 🚇 Herrengasse. 🚌 2A, 3A.

Michaelerplatz faces the grand main entrance into the imperial residence, the Michaelertor (St Michael's Doorway), which leads to the Hofburg's inner courtyard. On both sides of the doorway are 19th-century wall fountains designed by Rudolf Weyr which represent the empire's land and sea power.

Michaelerkirche (St Michael's church) was once the parish church of the court. Its oldest parts date from the 13th century. According to legend, the church was built in 1221 by Leopold VI of Babenberg. Its present form dates from 1792, when it was given a Neo-Classical façade, while still preserving its Baroque portal. The interior features one of the most beautiful Rococo altars in Vienna. Above the altar is a stucco relief depicting the expulsion of the rebel angels from heaven and the Archangel Gabriel at the head of the heavenly host.

In the 17th and 18th centuries, affluent parishioners were buried under the church. Their well-preserved corpses, clothed in their burial finery, are displayed in the crypt, in open coffins.

The remains of a Roman encampment, as well as some medieval foundations, were discovered underneath the square in 1990.

## ❷❺ Volksgarten

Dr-Karl-Renner-Ring. **Map** 2 A4. 🚇 Herrengasse. 🚋 1, 2, 71, D. 🚌 2A. **Open** Apr–Oct: 6am–10pm daily; Nov–Mar: 7:30am–5:30pm daily.

Volksgarten (the People's Garden) was created in 1820, when Napoleon had the city walls destroyed. The sophisticated, formal plantations created in the French style, particularly the splendid rose gardens, became a place of relaxation for fashionable society.

In the middle of the park is the Theseustempel (the Temple of Theseus), a classical-stye structure by Peter von Nobile. Von Nobile was also responsible for the Cortisches Kaffeehaus, remains of which are visible in today's Garden Café. In front of the temple is a statue of an athlete (1921) by Josef Müllner. A monument devoted to the writer Franz Grillparzer and a fountain memorial dedicated to Empress Elisabeth can also be found in the garden. A modern pavilion provides refreshments and evening entertainment.

## ❷❻ Heldenplatz

**Map** 2 A4, A5. 🚇 Volkstheater, Herrengasse. 🚋 1, 2, 71, D. 🚌 1A, 2A, 46, 49, 57A. Neue Burg museums: **Tel** 52 524-5202. **Open** 10am–6pm Wed–Sun. 🚫 📷

During Vienna's grand 19th-century reconstruction, Heldenplatz was planned as the centre of a majestic imperial forum that was to adjoin the old Hofburg complex, surrounded by new buildings housing the emperor's art collection. Neue Burg (New Castle) was completed in 1913, but by then the monarchy was dying out.

The vast, undeveloped Heroes' Square, the largest public space in Vienna, remained. It was here, in March 1938, that Adolf Hitler announced Austria's incorporation into the German Reich.

The entrance to the square is via Ballhausplatz or Burgtor (Palace Gate), built in 1824 to commemorate the victory of the coalition against Napoleon in the Battle of Nations, at Leipzig (1813). Later, it served as the Monument to the Unknown Soldier. The two equestrian statues in the square, by Anton Dominik von Fernkorn, are of Archduke Charles and Prince Eugene of Saxony.

The latter stands in front of the Neue Burg, which now houses a number of museums including the Ephesos Museum, named after the archaeological site in Turkey which yielded the finds on display here; a collection of early musical instruments, some owned by famous musicians; and one of the most impressive arms collections in Europe.

The equestrian statue of Prince Eugene of Saxony, Heldenplatz

## ❷❼ Alte Burg

See pp72–3.

# ㉘ Spanish Riding School

The Spanish Riding School was founded in 1572. Initially, its training of horses served a practical purpose, but today performances are staged purely for entertainment, and have become one of the city's top attractions. Shows are held in the building known as the Winterreitschule (Winter Riding School), constructed between 1729 and 1735 by Joseph E. Fischer von Erlach. The Hofburg fire in 1992 destroyed some of the stables and almost put an end to the school's activities.

## VISITORS' CHECKLIST

**Practical Information**
Michaelerplatz 1. **Map** 2 B4.
**Tel** 53 39 031. **Open** 9am–4pm
daily. Shows: Jan–Jun, Aug–Dec:
10am– noon Tue–Sat. 🅿 🎫 2pm,
3pm & 4pm daily. 🔲 srs.at

**Transport**
Ⓤ Herrengasse, Stephansplatz.
🚌 1A, 2A.

Black bicorn hat with gold braid stripe

Coffee-coloured jacket with rows of brass buttons

Long boots covering the knees

Pale leather gloves

**Interior of the Winter Riding School**
The opulent interior is lined with 46 columns and adorned with stucco ornaments, chandeliers and a coffered ceiling.

Buckskin jodhpurs

### Rider in Typical Uniform
*The riders of the Winter Riding School wear historical uniforms, which are complemented by elegant saddles with embroidered cloth.*

## The Horses' Steps

*The riders perform on the specially trained white Lipizzaner stallions, a breed originally produced by crossing Spanish, Arab and Berber horses. The steps made by the horses are part of a carefully orchestrated ballet.*

**The Levade**
The horse stands on its hind legs, hocks almost touching the ground.

**The Capriole**
The horse leaps into the air with a simultaneous kick of the hind legs.

**The Piaffe**
The horse trots on the spot, often between two pillars.

**The Croupade**
The horse leaps into the air with hind legs and forelegs bent under its belly.

# ㉗ Alte Burg

The Imperial Palace, or Old Palace, is a vast complex. Its construction was started by the Babenbergs, but the Neue Burg (New Castle wing) was not completed until 1913. As well as housing several museums, including in the royal apartments a museum dedicated to Empress Elisabeth, the Alte Burg is today also a conference centre. Different architectural styles are represented in various parts of the complex: the Gothic Schweizerhof, the Renaissance Stallburg courtyard and the Baroque Josefsplatz.

**In der Burg**
This large inner courtyard, called "inside the fortress", has a large statue of Franz I, built by Pompeo Marchesi, in 1842–46.

**The Silberkammer**
The Silver Chamber displays stunning silver, gold and porcelain tableware, and vessels used at official receptions, such as this 1821 goblet.

**Amalienburg**
In the 19th century, this Renaissance palace, built for Rudolf II in 1575, was the home of Empress Elisabeth. Shown here is her dressing room with gymnastic equipment.

## KEY

① **The Leopoldinischer Trakt**, dating from 1660–70 and built by Leopold I, today houses the offices of the President of Austria.

② **Michaelertor**, leading to Hofburg

③ **The Spanish Riding School** stages its world-famous horse-riding performances at the Winterreitschule (Winter Riding School).

④ **Stallburg**, a Renaissance palace, houses the riding school stables.

⑤ **Redoutensäle**, the former ballrooms

★ **Schweizertor**
The 16th-century Baroque Swiss Gate leads to the oldest parts of the castle, originally a four-tower stronghold.

**★ Reichskanzleitrakt**
Franz Joseph's apartments in the Imperial Chancery Wing, built in 1726–30, are open to visitors. This portrait of Empress Elisabeth (1865) hangs in the Sisi Museum.

## VISITORS' CHECKLIST

**Practical Information**
Michaelerplatz 1. **Map** 2 B4.
**Tel** 533 75 70.
Imperial Apartments: **Tel** 533 75 70.
**Open** 9am–5:30pm daily (until 6pm Jul & Aug). ♿ 🎧 ⬇
🌐 **hofburg-wien.at**
Schatzkammer: **Tel** 525 240.
**Open** 9am–5:30pm Wed–Mon.
🎧 🌐 **kaiserliche-schatzkammer.at**

**Transport**
Ⓤ Stephansplatz, Herrengasse.
🚋 1, 2, 71, D. 🚌 1A, 2A, 49, 57A.

**★ Schatzkammer**
The collection of sacred and secular treasures, including this 10th-century crown, is regarded as the most magnificent of its kind in the world.

**The Burgkapelle**
The Gothic Royal Chapel was completed in 1449. The Wiener Sängerknaben (the Vienna Boys' Choir) sings here on Sundays.

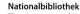

**Nationalbibliothek**
The showpiece of the Austrian National Library (1722–35) is the opulent Prunksaal, or Hall of Honour, panelled in wood.

The magnificent Prunksaal in the National Library, Josefsplatz

## ❷ Josefsplatz

**Map** 2 B4. Ⓤ Stephansplatz, Herrengasse. 🚌 1A, 2A.

In the centre of Josefsplatz stands an equestrian statue (1807) of Joseph II portrayed as a Roman emperor, by Franz Anton Zauner.

Behind the statue, to the right, is the entrance to the National Library building designed by Johann Bernhard Fischer von Erlach. Its Prunksaal (Hall of Honour) is regarded as the most beautiful library in Europe. Frescoes by the Baroque painter Daniel Gran adorn its vault. The walls of the historic reading room are graced by Johann Bergl's frescoes.

Perhaps the grandest items in the library's rich collection are the cartographic treasures exhibited just behind the Prunksaal.

The Redoutensäle, in the wing adjacent to the library and once the court ballrooms, now serve as the head office of the Vienna Congress Centre.

On the opposite side of Josefsplatz are two interesting palaces: at No. 5 is the 18th-century Pallavicini Palace by Johann Ferdinand Hetzendorf von Hohenberg, and at No. 6 the 16th-century Palffy Palace

by Nikolaus Pacassi. They now serve as cultural venues for the city.

## ❸ Augustinerkirche

Augustinerstrasse 3. **Map** 2 B5. **Tel** 53 37 099. Ⓤ Stephansplatz, Karlsplatz, Oper. 🚌 2A. **Open** 7am–6pm daily. Mass: 11am Sun & church hols.

The 14th-century Gothic Augustinian church was refurbished in the Baroque style, but some 100 years later was restored to its original character. Inside is one of the most powerful works by Antonio Canova (1805), the tomb of Maria Christina, Maria Theresa's favourite daughter. It is shaped like a pyramid, approached by a funeral procession. St George's Chapel, on the right, contains a marble cenotaph dedicated to Emperor Leopold II, while further along, in the Loreto chapel, are silver urns containing the hearts of members of the Habsburg family, including Leopold II's, as well as the heart of Napoleon's son, the King of Rome, who died when young.

The church was once the Court Chapel and, as such, the scene of many historic

Tomb of Maria Christina in Augustinerkirche

events, including the royal wedding of Marie Louise (1812) to Napoleon, and that of Elisabeth of Bavaria (known by her popular nickname, Sisi) to Franz Joseph (1854).

## ❹ Albertina

Albertinaplatz 1. **Map** 2 B5. **Tel** 534 830. Ⓤ Stephansplatz, Karlsplatz. 🚋 1, 2, 62, 71, D. 🚌 2A. **Open** 10am–6pm daily, 10am–9pm Wed. 🅿 ♿ 🆆 albertina.at

The Albertina was once the Habsburg palace of Duke Albert of Sachsen-Teschen and his wife Archduchess Maria Christina, the favourite daughter of Maria Theresa.

The Albertina houses one of the world's finest collection of prints and drawings, including works by famous artists such as Leonardo da Vinci, Michelangelo, Dürer, Rubens, Manet and Cezanne, as well as by Schiele, Klimt and Picasso. It has a million prints, over 65,000 watercolours and drawings, and some 100,000 photographs. It is also home to the Sammlung Batliner, a collection of paintings under the title "Monet to Picasso".

The beautiful Neo-Classical Historic State Rooms in the palace are among the most valuable examples of this style of architecture.

## ❷ Kapuzinerkirche and Kaisergruft

Neuer Markt. **Map** 2 B5. **Tel** 51 26 853.
Ⓤ Stephansplatz, Karlsplatz. 🚌 2A.
**Open** 10am–6pm daily. 📷

The Capuchin church stands at the southwestern corner of Neuer Markt, formerly a cereal and flour market. In 1617, Anna of Tyrol, wife of Emperor Matthias, founded a crypt in its vaults in which the Habsburg family members were laid to rest. Today, the Kaisergruft (imperial crypt) contains the earthly remains of 138 family members. On their death, the Habsburgs were dismembered; their hearts are kept in silver urns in August-inerkirche, their entrails in the catacombs of Stephansdom (*see pp62–3*). The only Habsburg monarchs not present are Ferdinand II, whose vast tomb-mausoleum is in Graz, and Charles I. The last Austrian emperor, he died in exile and is buried on Madeira. The only non-Habsburg buried here is Maria Theresa's governess, Countess Caroline Fuchs.

The most poignant tomb is the crypt of Franz Joseph I. The monarch is flanked by separate tombs containing the remains of his wife Elisabeth, assassi-nated by an Italian anarchist, and their only son Crown Prince Rudolf, who committed suicide in 1889. Also of note is the double sarcophagus of Maria Theresa and her husband Franz Stephan I. It bears the statues of the imperial couple and four figures with the crowns of Austria, Hungary, Bohemia and Jerusalem (the Habsburgs were also the titular Kings of Jerusalem).

## ❸ Winterpalais des Prinzen Eugen

Himmelpfortgasse 8. **Map** 2 C5.
**Tel** 51 433. Ⓤ Stephansplatz. 🚋 2.
🚌 2A. **Open** 10am–6pm daily.
Ⓦ **belvedere.at**

The Winter Palace was commiss-ioned in 1694, by Prince Eugene of Savoy, one of the most

Grand stairway in the Winterpalais des Prinzen Eugen

brilliant military commanders of his day. The task was entrusted to Johann Bernhard Fischer von Erlach, and the palace was subsequently extended by Johann Lukas von Hildebrandt. Its central part includes the original magnificent staircase, adorned with sculptures by Giovanni Giuliani. The central portal reliefs depict the figure of Aeneas carrying his father out of the burning city of Troy, and the hero Hercules, who is slaying a monster.

From 1848 until 2006, the palace was home to the Ministry of Finance. After extensive renovation, the palace today houses the Baroque collection of the Belvedere (*see pp102–3*).

Nearby, at Seilerstätte No. 30, is the Haus der Musik (House of Music). A museum dedicated to the Wiener Philharmoniker (Vienna Philharmonic), it also houses a high-tech exhibition on the nature of sound, which allows visitors to see and feel as well as hear music.

## ❹ Kärntner Strasse

**Map** 2 B5, C4, C5. Ⓤ Stephansplatz, Karlsplatz. 🚋 1, 2, 62, 71, D.
🚌 1A, 2A, 3A.

Kärntner Strasse was once the main road running south across town to Kärnten (Carinthia), hence its name.

Today, the view down the street is blocked at its Ring end by the silhouette of the opera house, and at the Stock-im-Eisen-Platz end by the modern Haas-Haus, which reflects the spires of the Stephansdom. At Stock-im-Eisen-Platz there is a wooden block into which every passing apprentice ironworker used to drive a nail, in the hope that this would ensure his safe return.

In the mid-section, at No. 37, stands the Malteserkirche (church of the Knights of Malta). The Maltese Knights came to Vienna in the early 13th century, and the church remains under their jurisdiction to this day. The church walls display the coats of arms of the Grand Masters of the Maltese Order.

Malteserkirche is one of the few older buildings in the street. When Kärntner Strasse was widened during the 19th century, to transform it into the old town's main artery, most of the buildings were demolished.

Today, the pedestrianized street is one of Vienna's most fashionable and expensive shopping streets. Here, you can shop at one of many exclusive boutiques, eat and drink in busy restaurants, bars and outdoor cafés, and listen to street musicians or just watch others stroll by.

Kärntner Strasse, one of Vienna's most fashionable shopping streets

# NORTH OF MARIAHILFER STRASSE

This district, to the north of Mariahilfer Strasse and along the Ring, includes some of the most magnificent and monumental buildings in Vienna. The semicircular Ring or Ringstrasse, developed during the 1870s and 1880s, is a grand boulevard divided into nine sections, each named after architectural landmarks or prominent politicians from the Habsburg era. Today, this is still one of Vienna's most prestigious

areas and is home to several important sights. Here visitors will find many of the city's cultural institutions, including the biggest concentration of museums in Austria. Mariahilfer Strasse itself is a very busy shopping street, with large department stores and many quaint cafés and bars around it, concentrated especially in the cobbled, pedestrianized streets of the bustling Spittelberg area.

## Sights at a Glance

**Streets**
- ⑱ Mariahilfer Strasse
- ⑲ Spittelberg

**Historic Buildings**
- ① Neues Rathaus
- ② Parlament
- ③ Burgtheater pp82–3
- ④ Universität
- ⑦ Josephinum
- ⑧ Old AKH – University Campus
- ⑫ Theater in der Josefstadt
- ⑬ Palais Trautson
- ⑭ Volkstheater

**Churches**
- ⑤ Votivkirche
- ⑨ Dreifaltigkeitskirche
- ⑪ Maria-Treu-Kirche

**Museums and Galleries**
- ⑥ Freud-Museum
- ⑩ Museum für Volkskunde
- ⑮ Naturhistorisches Museum
- ⑯ Kunsthistorisches Museum pp88–91
- ⑰ MuseumsQuartier

0 metres / 0 yards 300

*See also Street Finder, maps 1, 2 & 4*

◄ Impressive Gothic spires of the Votivkirche

# Street-by-Street: Around the Town Hall

The most prestigious buildings in Vienna were erected in the second half of the 19th century, on Ringstrasse, at the command of Emperor Franz Joseph I. These include the Neues Rathaus (new town hall, seat of the town administration), the immense Parlament (the seat of Austria's upper and lower houses), the magnificent buildings of the University, and the Burgtheater.

The square in front of the town hall, with its adjacent park, is Vienna's largest open-air arena, serving as a stage for theatre and concert performances, and in the summer for vast film screenings.

**The Town Hall forecourt** turns into a vast Christmas market in December, selling gifts and Christmas decorations.

❶ ★ **Neues Rathaus**
This Neo-Gothic building, modelled on Brussels' town hall, is the seat of the Vienna City and Provincial Assembly.

**Arkadenhof**, the courtyard of the town hall, serves as a concert venue in summer.

0 metres         100
0 yards          100

❷ ★ **Parlament**
The main decorative feature inside the Neo-Classical parliament building is the stylized Austrian eagle.

*For hotels and restaurants in this area see p293 and pp312–13*

**4 ★ Universität**
The University courtyard is surrounded by arcades lined with busts of its professors.

REICHSRATSSTRASSE

GRILLPARZERSTRASSE

UNIVERSITÄTSRING

**Locator Map**
See Street Finder maps 1 & 2

INNER CITY

NORTH OF MARIAHILFER STRASSE

SOUTH OF THE RING

**Plaque from the Pasqualati house** at Mölker-Bastei No. 8, which, in 1804–8 and again in 1810–15, was the home of Ludwig van Beethoven. It was here that he composed his opera *Fidelio*, as well as Symphonies 4, 5, 7 and 8. Today, the house is a small museum.

**Statue of Liebenberg**, the gallant mayor of Vienna during the Turkish siege of the town in 1683.

**Café Landtmann**, opened in 1873, is the coffee house of the affluent middle classes, and was once Sigmund Freud's favourite haunt.

**Key**

— Suggested route

**3 ★ Burgtheater**
The high panel above the centre of the building is decorated with a frieze depicting a Bacchanalian procession.

Pallas Athena monument in front of the parliament building

the representatives of the 17 peoples of the empire. The magnificently decorated state apartments and conference rooms can be visited in a guided tour. The lower vestibule contains busts of prominent members of the Austrian National Assembly.

The side wings have four bronze chariot groups, each driven by Nike, the Greek goddess of victory. Another, smaller statue of Nike is held aloft by her fellow goddess, of wisdom, Pallas Athena, whose 5-m (16-ft) statue is the main feature of the monumental fountain in front of the central portico, designed by Carl Kundmann and placed here in 1902. It is flanked by allegorical figures representing Law Enforcement (left) and Legislation (right), as well as figures symbolizing the major rivers of the empire.

# ❶ Neues Rathaus

Friedrich-Schmidt-Platz 1. **Map** 1 C3. **Tel** 52 550. Ⓤ Rathaus. 🚋 1, 71, D. **Open** 8am–6pm Mon–Fri. ♿ 1pm Mon, Wed & Fri. **Closed** during meetings and public holidays. ♿

The New Town Hall, built in 1872–83 by Friedrich Schmidt, lies in an attractive park. The symmetrical, triple façade of the Neo-Gothic building faces Ringstrasse. Its central tower, 98 m (321 ft) high, is topped by the statue of a knight in armour, one of Vienna's symbols. The main tower is flanked by two smaller towers, 60 m (197 ft) high. The town hall cellar is a restaurant. The whole length of the first floor is taken up by a reception hall. The forecourt is used for many events, including a Christmas fair.

# ❷ Parlament

Dr-Karl-Renner-Ring 3. **Map** 1 C4. **Tel** 40 11 00-25 70. Ⓤ Volkstheater. 🚋 1, 2, 71, D. ✂ Sep–mid-Jul: 11am, 2pm, 3pm, 4pm Mon–Sat (also 1pm Fri, noon & 1pm Sat); mid-Jul–Aug: 11am, noon, 1pm, 2pm, 3pm, 4pm Mon–Sat. Ⓦ parlament.gv.at

Today's assembly hall of Austria's two-chamber parliament originally served as the location of the highest legislative body of the Austrian part of the Austro-Hungarian Empire. An imposing Neo-Classical building, the Parlament was completed in 1883 to designs by the Dutch architect Theophil Hansen.

The entrance is raised above street level. A gently sloping ramp leads to the main portico, which is modelled on a Greek temple. Both the ramp and the pediment are adorned with carved marble figures of Greek and Roman historians, scholars and statesmen. The relief depicts the Emperor Franz Joseph I handing the constitution to

# ❸ Burgtheater

See pp82–3.

# ❹ Universität

Universitätsring. **Map** 2 A3. **Tel** 42 77 0. Ⓤ Schottentor. 🚋 1, 37, 38, 40, 41, 42, 43, 44, 71, D. 🚌 1A.

Vienna University is the oldest university in the German-speaking world and the third oldest in Central Europe, after Prague and Cracow. It was founded in 1365 by Rudolf IV, and flourished and grew in the late 15th century. Its present

The main building of Vienna University

home, designed by Heinrich von Ferstel in Italian Renaissance style, was completed in 1883.

The university complex has its buildings arranged around one large and eight smaller courtyards. The courtyard arcades, modelled on the Palazzo Farnese in Rome, are adorned with statues of famous scholars associated with Vienna University, including one of Freud.

Neo-Gothic stone figures from the façade of the Votivkirche

## ❺ Votivkirche

Roosevelkplatz. **Map** 2 A2. **Tel** 40 61 192. Ⓤ Schottentor. 🚊 1, 37, 38, 40, 41, 42, 43, 44, 71, D. **Open** 7am–6pm daily. Ⓦ votivkirche.at

Opposite the spot where a deranged man tried to assassinate Franz Joseph I in 1853, stands this Neo-Gothic church with its two 99-m-(325-ft-) high, lacy steeples completed 26 years later as a grateful offering for sparing the emperor's life. The architect was Heinrich von Ferstel.

The most beautiful historic relic in the Votivkirche is its late-15th-century Antwerpian altar, a masterpiece of Flemish woodcarving, representing scenes from Christ's Passion. The main portal sculptures depict the four Evangelists and figures from the Old Testament, along with four patrons of the empire's regions.

Many of the chapels inside the church are dedicated to the Austrian regiments and to military heroes.

Sigmund Freud's waiting room in the Freud-Museum

## ❻ Freud-Museum

Berggasse 19. **Map** 2 A1. **Tel** 31 91 596. Ⓤ Schottentor. 🚊 37, 38, 40, 41, 42, D. 🚌 40A. **Open** 10am–6pm daily. 🎧 Ⓦ freud-museum.at

Berggasse No. 19, a typical 19th-century Viennese town house, was the home of Sigmund Freud, the famous doctor and father of psychoanalysis, from 1891 to 1938. Here he wrote his most acclaimed works and treated patients before he was forced to flee Austria on the arrival of the Nazis.

The room in which Freud received patients is on the mezzanine floor. In the small, dark lobby hangs Freud's frayed hat; in a corner stands his travel trunk. His walking stick can also be seen here. A cabinet contains some archaeological objects collected by Freud. The world-famous couch, however, is now on display in the Freud Museum in London. There is a research library and archive on site.

Visitors can book an evening meal, for up to 12 guests, in the former consulting room.

### Freud's Theories

With his theory of psychoanalysis, Sigmund Freud (1856–1939) has exerted a lasting influence not only on medicine but also on our culture generally. In 1896 he coined the term "psychoanalysis". According to Freud, the unconscious psyche, driven by certain instincts and impulses, in particular the sexual instinct (libido), is the main engine behind all our conscious and unconscious actions. An imbalance in the psychological system, so Freud suggested, could lead to very serious emotional disorders and might result in severe mental disturbance.

## ❼ Josephinum

Währingerstrasse 25. **Map** 1 C2. **Tel** 40 160-26 001. Ⓤ Schottentor. 🚊 37, 38, 40, 41, 42. **Open** 10am–6pm Mon–Sat. **Closed** public holidays. 🎧

Designed by Isidor Canevale and built in 1783–5, this building once housed the Military Surgical Institute. Life-sized anatomical wax models, commissioned by Joseph II to teach human anatomy to his army surgeons, are now the main attraction of the medical museum based here today.

## ❽ Old AKH – University Campus

Alser Strasse 4/Spitalgasse 2. **Map** 1 A1, B1. Ⓤ Schottentor. Federal Museum of Pathological Anatomy: Spitalgasse 2. **Tel** 521 77 606. **Open** 10am–6pm Wed, 10am–1pm Sat. **Closed** public holidays. Ⓦ univie.ac.at

Vienna's Old General Hospital (AKH), built in 1784, was donated to the University of Vienna in 1988 and adapted to house the 15 academic faculties of the university.

It was inaugurated in 1998 as the university campus. The huge complex consists of several buildings around one vast and 12 smaller courtyards. The Narrenturm (Madman's Tower) of the former lunatic asylum, designed by architect Isidor Canevale, now houses the **Federal Museum for Pathological Anatomy**.

Various objects used by Sigmund Freud

# ❺ Burgtheater

The Burgtheater is one of the most prestigious stages in the German-speaking world. The original theatre, built in Maria Theresa's reign, was replaced in 1888 by today's Italian Renaissance-style building by Karl von Hasenauer and Gottfried Semper. In 1897, after the discovery that the auditorium had several seats with no view of the stage, it closed for refurbishment. A bomb devastated the building in 1945, leaving only the side wings and Grand Staircases intact, but subsequent restoration was so successful that today the damage is hard to see.

**Busts of Playwrights**
Lining the walls of the Grand Staircases are busts of playwrights whose works are still performed here, including this one of Johann Nepomuk Nestroy *(left)* by Hans Knesl.

**★ Grand Staircases**
The two majestic gala staircases in the side wings are the only original parts of the building that escaped destruction in World War II.

Main entrance on Universitätsring

## KEY

① **Ceiling frescoes** by the Klimt brothers, Gustav and Ernst, and Franz Matsch cover the north and south wings.

② **Statue of the muse Melpomene**

③ **Statue of the muse Thalia**

**Foyer**
The walls of the curving first-floor foyer are lined with the portraits of famous actors and actresses.

**Auditorium**
During rebuilding after the war, the original layout was kept in the auditorium with the imperial colours of red, gold and cream. It seats over 1,000 spectators.

★ **Der Thespiskarren**
The ceiling frescoes in the side wings are by the Klimt brothers and Franz Matsch. This fresco detail by Gustav Klimt depicts the cart of Thespis, first performer of a Greek tragedy.

★ **Front Façade**
The façade is crowned by a frieze of Bacchus and Ariadne, by Rudolf Weyr. Above the frieze towers the statue of Apollo.

**1741** Maria Theresa founds the Burgheater in an empty ballroom at the Hofburg, to stage mainly Italian operas

*The old Burgtheater on the Michaelaplatz in Hofburg, in the mid-18th century*

**1955** After its destruction in World War II, the theatre reopens with Grillparzer's *King Ottokar*

1750  1850  1950  2050

**1776** Joseph II reorganizes the theatre and promotes it to the status of a national theatre

**1874** Work on the present building begins

**14 Oct 1888** The Burgtheater opens in the presence of the Emperor Franz Joseph I and family

## 9 Dreifaltigkeits-kirche der Minoriten

Alser Strasse 17. **Map** 1 B2. **Tel** 40 57 225. **U** Rathaus. 5, 33, 43, 44. **Open** 7:30am–noon Mon–Fri, Sun, 7:30–8:30am Sat.

Built between 1685 and 1727, the church of the Holy Trinity is a typical Baroque structure, with a twin-tower façade. It contains an altarpiece (1708) in the north aisle by the painter Martino Altomonte, and a beautiful crucifix in the south aisle from the workshop of Veit Stoss.

In 1827, the body of the composer Ludwig van Beethoven was brought to this church from Schwarzspanierhaus in neighbouring Garnisonsgasse, where he had died. Following the funeral service, attended by his contemporaries (including Schubert and the playwright Franz Grillparzer), the cortège conveyed his coffin to its final resting place, the cemetery in Währing, on the city outskirts.

Striking crucifix in the Dreifaltigkeitskirche der Minoriten

## 10 Museum für Volkskunde

Laudongasse 15–19. **Map** 1 B3. **Tel** 406 890 50. **U** Rathaus. 5, 33, 43, 44. 13A. **Open** 10am–5pm Tue–Sun. **W** volkskundemuseum.at

Near a quiet park stands the charming Austrian Folklore Museum. Founded in 1895, it moved in 1917 to its present

Entrance to the Museum für Volkskunde, Schönborn Palace

premises, the former Schönborn Palace, built in 1706–11 to designs by Johann Lukas von Hildebrandt as a homely two-storey mansion, and altered in 1760 by court architect Isidor Canevale. The building has a rather imposing façade with statues running along its top.

In the museum you will find artifacts reflecting popular culture in Austria and neighbouring countries that were once part of the Habsburg Empire. The collection includes furniture, textiles and ceramics, household and work tools, religious objects, and two complete living rooms that illustrate lifestyle, customs and rituals in the various regions. The core of the collection consists of objects from the 17th to 19th centuries.

On Lange Gasse, a couple of blocks along towards Josefstädter Strasse, you will pass the **Alte Backstube**, at No. 34. This old bakery is one of the loveliest town houses in Vienna. It was built in 1697 by the jeweller Hans Bernhard Leopold and was in continuous use until 1963. The rooms have been lovingly restored, retaining the old baking ovens, and house a traditional restaurant and café, and a small baking museum where baking equipment from the early 18th century can be seen.

## 11 Maria-Treu-Kirche

Jodok-Fink-Platz. **Map** 1 B3. **Tel** 40 50 425. **U** Rathaus. 2. 13A. **Open** 9am–11am Mon, Wed & Fri, 4–6pm Wed. **W** mariatreu.at

Originally designed by Johann Lukas von Hildebrandt in 1716, Maria Treu Kirche (church of Mary the Faithful) acquired its present form in the mid-19th century, when the twin towers were added.

The church, as well as the adjacent monastic buildings, was founded by fathers of the Piarist order, one of whose main aims is education; they also founded a primary and a secondary school next door. The homely cellar of the former monastery is today a pleasant restaurant.

The interior of the church is one of the best preserved in Vienna. Its Baroque ceiling frescoes, the work of the great Austrian painter Franz Anton Maulbertsch, are very lovely. They depict scenes from the life of the Virgin Mary and events from the Old and New Testaments. In one of the chapels, to the left of the presbytery, you can see an altarpiece of the Crucifixion, also painted by Franz Anton Maulbertsch.

The Chapel of Our Lady of Sorrows contains a *pietà* known as Our Lady from Malta, which was brought here by the Knights of Malta.

In front of the church is a striking Baroque pillar, topped with a statue of the Madonna (1713), one of many such plague columns erected in Vienna as thanksgiving at the end of the plague era. In this case the column commemorates the epidemic of 1713.

Baroque frescoes in Maria-Treu-Kirche

The opulent auditorium of Theater in der Josefstadt

## ⓬ Theater in der Josefstadt

Josefstädter Strasse 26. **Map** 1 B4.
**Tel** 427 003 00. Ⓤ Rathaus. 🚊 2.
🚌 13A. 🌐 josefstadt.org

This intimate theatre, one of the oldest still standing in Vienna, has enjoyed a glorious history. First established in 1788, the theatre was later much altered. After renovation by Joseph Kornhäusel, for its reopening in 1822 Ludwig van Beethoven composed his overture *The Consecration of the House*, conducting it himself at the reopening gala.

In 1924, the directorship of the theatre was given to Max Reinhardt, one of the most outstanding theatre directors and reformers, who supervised its further restoration and introduced an ambitious modern repertoire as well as magnificent productions of classic drama. He transformed what was once a middle-of-the-road provincial theatre into the most exciting stage in the German-speaking world.

The theatre is worth a visit to view its interior alone. As the lights slowly dim, the crystal chandeliers float gently to the ceiling. It offers excellent productions of Austrian plays, with an emphasis on comedy, classics and the occasional musical.

## ⓭ Palais Trautson

Museumstrasse 7. **Map** 1 C5.
Ⓤ Volkstheater. 🚊 49. 🚌 48A.
**Closed** to the public.

The Baroque Trautson Palace, built between 1710 and 1712 for Prince Johann Leopold Donat Trautson, to a design by Johann Bernhard Fischer von Erlach, was acquired by Maria Theresa in 1760. She then donated it to the Royal Hungarian Bodyguard, which she had founded.

The Neo-Classical façade, with rows of Doric columns, is heavily ornamented. Its finest sculptures, including that of Apollo playing the lyre, tower above the first-floor windows. The palace has a beautiful staircase, decorated with carvings of the Sphinx and columns of male figures who support the ceiling, by the sculptor Giovanni Giuliani. Since 1961 the palace has housed the Ministry of Justice, so there is no public access.

## ⓮ Volkstheater

Neustiftgasse 1. **Map** 1 C5.
**Tel** 52 111-0; tickets 52 111-400.
Ⓤ Volkstheater. 🚊 1, 2, 46, 49, 71, D.
🚌 48A. 🌐 **volkstheater.at**

Famed as a venue able to combine classic and modern drama with popular Viennese plays, the Volkstheater (People's Theatre) was, for many years, a staging post for directors and actors on their way from the provincial theatres to the renowned Burgtheater. Today, classic and modern, or even experimental, drama dominate the repertoire. The Volkstheater presents many plays for the first time, or for the first time in the German language.

The Volkstheater was built in 1889 by the Austrian architects Ferdinand Fellner and Hermann Helmer. They employed the latest in theatre technology, including electric lighting throughout, and many theatre designers later copied their work. The auditorium, with more than 1,000 seats, is one of the largest in a theatre devoted to German-language drama, and is a great example of Viennese *fin-de-siècle* architecture. In front of the theatre stands a statue (1898) of the dramatist Ferdinand Raimund.

The majestic entrance to the 19th-century Volkstheater

The dinosaur room in the
Naturhistorisches Museum

## ⓯ Naturhistorisches Museum

Burgring 7. **Map** 2 A5. **Tel** 52 177-0.
Ⓤ Volkstheater. 🚋 1, 2, 46, 49, 71, D.
🚌 48A. **Open** 9am–6:30pm Thu–
Mon, 9am–9pm Wed. **Closed** Tue,
1 Jan, 1 May, 1 Nov, 25 Dec. 🅿 ♿
🆆 nhm-wien.ac.at

On two sides of Maria-Theresien-
Platz are two identical buildings,
designed by Gottfried Semper
and Karl von Hasenauer. They
were both built as museums
at the time of Franz Joseph I, as
part of the Ringstrasse development. Today, one is an art
museum (Kunsthistorisches
Museum, *see pp88–91*), the
other the Natural History
Museum, home to one of the
richest and most wide-ranging
collections in the world.

Many exhibits originally
belonged to Maria Theresa's
husband, Francis Stephen of
Lorraine. The present permanent
exhibition occupies two floors
and consists of archaeological
and anthropological displays,
reconstructed specimens of
extinct animals and one of
the best gem collections in
the world.

Among the key exhibits
are the Hallstatt archaeological finds, dating from the
early Iron Age, and the famous
Venus of Willendorf – a
25,000-year-old stone statuette
of a woman. The life-sized
replicas of dinosaur skeletons
in the Dinosaur Hall are also a
major attraction.

The Natural History Museum
plays a very important role
within the education system
and its temporary exhibitions are
organized mainly with
schools in mind. Its exhibition
showing the imaginary life
of dinosaurs toured much of

the world in the wake of Steven
Spielberg's hugely popular film
*Jurassic Park*.

In the square between the
buildings stands an imposing
monument of Maria Theresa
(1888) by Kaspar von Zumbusch.
It shows the empress clasping
the Pragmatic Section of 1713,
enabling women to ascend to
the throne. Below her are her
generals and her principal
nobles and advisors.

## ⓰ Kunsthistorisches Museum

*See pp88–91.*

## ⓱ MuseumsQuartier

Museumsplatz 1. **Map** 1 C5. **Tel** 52 35
881. Ⓤ MuseumsQuartier, Volkstheater. 🚋 1, 2, 46, 49, 71, D. 🚌 48A.
Information: **Open** 10am–7pm daily.
🆆 mqpoint.at. Museum of Modern
Art: **Tel** 525 000. **Open** 2–7pm Mon,
10am–7pm Tue–Sun (to 9pm Thu).
🅿 🆆 mumok.at Leopold Museum:
**Tel** 525 70. **Open** 10am–6pm daily (to
9pm Thu). **Closed** Tue, public holidays.
🅿 🆆 leopoldmuseum.org
Kunsthalle Wien: **Tel** 5521 890. **Open**
10am–7pm Mon–Sat (to 9pm Thu).
🅿 ♿ 🆆 kunsthallewien.at

Johann Bernhard Fischer
von Erlach was
commissioned
by Emperor Karl VI
to build the
imperial stables

*Rossbändiger* (1892), the tamer of horses,
near the MuseumsQuartier

on the escarpment behind the
old town fortifications. In 1921,
these Baroque buildings became
a venue for fairs, and in the
1980s they were converted into
a museum complex to designs
by Laurids and Manfred Ortner.
They changed the fittings of
the existing structures and
added new ones, resulting in
one of the world's largest
cultural centres.

The MuseumsQuartier
(Museum District) includes the
**Kunsthalle Wien** (Vienna Art
Hall) opposite the main entrance,
behind the former premises
of the Spanish Riding School.
Vienna's main showcase for
international contemporary art,
the Kunsthalle is one of the city's
most important art spaces,
focusing on transdisciplinary
work including photography,
video, film and new media, as
well as modern-art retrospectives.

To the left of the Kunsthalle
is the white limestone façade
of the **Leopold Museum**, which
houses the art collection of
Rudolph Leopold. This encompasses over 5,000 works of art,
including major pieces by
Gustav Klimt, together with
the world's largest Egon
Schiele collection.

The **Museum of Modern Art
Ludwig Foundation Vienna**,
or **MUMOK**, to the right of the
Kunsthalle, is clad in contrasting dark basalt. It contains
one of the largest European
collections of modern art,
from American Pop to Cubism,
Expressionism and Viennese
Actionism, as well as contemporary art from Central and
Eastern Europe.

The **Architektur Zentrum
Wien** is a venue for interesting
temporary exhibitions of modern
architecture and architectural
history. Its permanent exhibition
features 20th-century Austrian
architecture.

The **Tanzquartier Wien** is
dedicated to dance, providing
facilities and training to performers and choreographers, and
presenting various types of dance
and other performances to the
public. The MuseumsQuartier
also has archives and facilities
for lectures, workshops and

Schiele's *Kneeling Female Nude* (1910), Museum of Modern Art, MuseumsQuartier

seminars, as well as Austria's first centre for museum and exhibition studies. Children can play, explore and learn about a variety of subjects in the **ZOOM Kindermuseum**, an unconventional centre.

Amid this extraordinary cultural setting are numerous cafés, bars, green spaces, shops and bookstores.

## 18 Mariahilfer Strasse

**Map** 4 A1, B1. U Westbahnhof, Zieglergasse, Neubaugasse, MuseumsQuartier. 2A, 13A.

Mariahilfer Strasse is one of the longest streets in Vienna, a main artery running west from the town centre to the area around Schönbrunn.

The part between Getreidemarkt (Grain Market) and Westbahnhof (the Western Railway Station) is also the busiest shopping street in this part of the city. Here you will find Vienna's largest department stores and its best window displays. Shopping tends to be better value here than on Kärntner Strasse (*see p75*), but is still more costly than at the mall complex at the Meidling train station, or further out in the Favoriten district.

Mariahilfer Strasse took its name from the church of St

Mary, Our Lady of Perpetual Succour, built in the late 17th century on the site of an older church, but not consecrated until 1730. Its façade is an austere pyramidal structure, rising to a bulbous steeple, and there are lively Rococo reliefs set in its walls. In front of the church stands a monument to the composer Joseph Haydn (*see p28*), who lived at this address for 12 years. Mariahilfer Strasse No. 45 is the longest and most famous double-exit house in Vienna, and the birthplace in 1790 of the popular Austrian playwright Ferdinand Raimund.

## 19 Spittelberg

**Map** 1 C5. U Volkstheater. 49. 48A. Amerlinghaus: Stiftgasse 8. **Tel** 52 36 475. **Open** during events. W amerlinghaus.at

Spittelberg is the oldest and most colourful part of the elegant 7th District. In the 17th century, the cluster of streets between Siebensterngasse and Burggasse, around Spittelberggasse, was Vienna's first immigrant worker district. Its inhabitants were mainly craftsmen, merchants and servants from Croatia and Hungary, brought here to work at the court. Today, the district's crafts heritage lives on in the

street market, held on the first weekend of each month and prior to Christmas. Among the stalls with wood carvings, tie-dyed fabrics and silver jewellery, waiters from the local bars negotiate the busy crowds; there are some 58 bars in this small area, which contains just 138 houses. The number of bars may change from one week to the next, but the bustling, festive party atmosphere can be experienced almost every evening. The Spittelberg area also comprises small art galleries, and artists display their work in the restaurants.

At one time, attractive barmaids offered "additional services", and legend has it that Emperor Joseph II once decided to explore the Spittelberg district for himself. However, when in disguise he entered the Witwe Bolte (Widow Bolte) restaurant, still open today, he was unceremoniously thrown out.

Nos. 18 and 20 Spittelberggasse are fine Baroque houses.

The beautifully restored **Amerlinghaus**, in which the painter Friedrich Amerling (1803–87) was born, is now a cultural and community centre, and a restaurant.

A little further along, between Siebensterngasse and Mariahilfer Strasse, is an enclosed area around former barracks now housing the Military Academy, and the Stiftkirche, topped with an onion-shaped cupola, which serves as a garrison church. Its walls are lined with very expressive late-Baroque reliefs.

Amerlinghaus communitiy centre, Spittelberg

# ⑯ Kunsthistorisches Museum

The world's fourth largest gallery, the Museum of Art History houses a collection based on works amassed over the centuries by generations of Habsburg monarchs. The public was given access to these art treasures when two museums were built on Ringstrasse to designs by Karl von Hasenauer and Gottfried Semper. One was to house the art collection, a second, identical building the Natural History Museum *(see p86)*. Both opened in 1891. The art museum's lavish interior complements its exhibits, today seen by more than one and a half million people each year.

Second floor

First floor

Ground floor

**★ Hunters in the Snow (1565)**
The last in a cycle of seasonal paintings by Pieter Bruegel the Elder, this winter scene graces a gallery room containing the world's largest collection of this artist's work.

**★ The Artist's Studio (1665)**
This painting, one of the most famous by Vermeer, is believed by some to be a self-portrait of the artist at work.

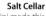

**Salt Cellar**
Benvenuto Cellini made this sumptuous *Saliera* of the sea god Neptune and an earth goddess for the French King François I.

**Key**

- ☐ Egyptian and Near Eastern collection
- ☐ Collection of Greek and Roman antiquities
- ☐ Kunstkammer Wien
- ☐ Picture gallery
- ☐ Coin cabinets
- ☐ Non-exhibition space

## Museum Guide

*The ground floor area to the right of the main entrance displays artifacts from the ancient civilizations of Egypt, Greece, Rome and the Near East. The area to the left houses the Kunstkammer, with a collection of sculpture and decorative arts. The picture gallery takes up the entire first floor, while the second floor houses the impressive coin collection as well as temporary exhibitions.*

★ **Velázquez's Infanta**
The Spanish artist Diego Velázquez immortalized the eight-year-old Margarita Teresa (1659), the future wife of Emperor Leopold I.

★ **Gemma Augustea**
The famous Roman cameo, carved with great precision from onyx, shows the goddess Roma and Emperor Augustus welcoming his son Tiberius after his heroic victory over the barbarians in Pannonia.

Rooms 1–7

**King Thutmosis III**
This king from the 18th Dynasty (c.1500 BC) was one of the foremost warriors of ancient Egypt. He is depicted in the style typical of the Late Kingdom period.

**Hippopotamus**
This blue ceramic figure from Middle-Kingdom Egypt (around 2000 BC) was placed in the tombs of important persons, to mark their status in society.

## Decoration of the Museum

The museums built on Ringstrasse in the 1890s were among the first to be designed with particular collections in mind. Many prominent artists were employed to decorate the interiors. Their great masterpiece is the main staircase in the Kunsthistorisches Museum. Hans Makart created the symbolic scenes above the windows, while Gustav and Ernst Klimt painted frescoes depicting stages in the development of art. The *Apotheosis of the Renaissance* (1890) is a fabulous *trompe l'oeil* ceiling fresco by Michael Munkácsy.

**Apotheosis of the Renaissance**

# Exploring the Kunsthistorisches Museum

The Museum of Art History has a fine collection of Egyptian, Greek and Roman objects, which provide an intriguing record of the world's earliest civilizations. The European sculpture and decorative art in the Kunstkammer Wien dates from the 15th to the 18th centuries. This period is also the focus of the picture gallery, which largely reflects the personal tastes of its Habsburg founders. Venetian and 17th-century Flemish paintings are well represented, and there is an excellent display of works by earlier Dutch and German artists. There is also a vast coin collection.

## Oriental and Egyptian Antiquities

At the core of this collection are the objects unearthed by Austrian archaeologists in Giza. Particularly fascinating are the well-preserved relics from the tomb of Ka-Ni-Nisut, dating from the Early Kingdom era, including a meticulously reconstructed burial chamber. The blue ceramic figure of a hippopotamus dates from the Middle Kingdom era. Such animal figures were placed in the tombs to mark the social status of the deceased – the hippopotamus was regarded as a royal beast and could be hunted only with the pharaoh's permission. The exhibits from the Late Kingdom, mainly associated with the mortuary cult, include a papyrus book of the dead, the mummified corpses of people and animals, sarcophagi and Canopic jars used to preserve the entrails of mummified corpses.

Near Eastern antiquities are represented in the museum collections by Babylonian reliefs, including a glazed-brick frieze depicting a striding lion from the Ishtar Gate in Babylon and various exhibits from Arabia.

## Greek and Roman Antiquities

Only part of the museum's Greek and Roman collection is housed in the main building; the finds from Ephesous and on Samothrace are on display in the Ephesous Museum in Neue Burg (see p70). The main building on Maria-Theresien-Platz has a beautiful collection of early Greek urns, in a variety of shapes, including vessels presented to winners at the Panathenaic Games. The sculpture rooms house many examples of early Greek and Roman art. Some are of outstanding quality: for example, the Youth from Magdalensburg, a cast of a lost Roman statue found buried in an Austrian field; the huge Head of Athena, probably from the school of Phidias; and fragments of a frieze with a dying Amazon. The Hellenic era is represented by the magnificent Head of a Philosopher, likely to have been that of Aristotle. One of the most precious items in the entire collection of antiquities is Gemma

Augustea, a Roman cameo depicting Emperor Augustus welcoming his son Tiberius on his return from war, together with Roma, the goddess of Rome.

The antiquities section also contains some Etruscan ceramics and statuettes from Tanagra. Early Coptic, Byzantine and German items are shown in the other rooms, but the true jewel among the later antiquities is the Treasure of Nagyszentmiklós, a collection of 9th-century golden vessels with stunning reliefs, showing Far Eastern influences, found in Romania in 1799.

## Kunstkammer Wien

This museum within a museum is spread over twenty galleries filled with magnificent works of art bought or commissioned by successive Habsburg rulers, scientific instruments and clocks regarded as masterpieces of applied art, and curiosities and artifacts from the rulers' Kunstkammern (chambers of art). Some of the royals worked in the studio; exhibits include, for example, glass blown by Archduke Ferdinand II and embroidery by Maria Theresa.

Some of the most intriguing items, however, are splendid examples of craftsmanship, including pieces of jewellery and items made from gold. The showpiece of the collection is the golden Saliera or Salt Cellar (see p88), made by the Italian goldsmith and sculptor Benvenuto Cellini for the French King François I.

Other gems in these rooms include the magnificent chalice from the collegiate church in Wilten and the precious Burgundy cup of Friedrich III.

A separate section is devoted to wood and stone sculptures from the Middle Ages, mainly of religious subjects, among them the amazing Madonna from Krumlowa (c.1400), the poignant Virgin with Child

Room I of the Egyptian galleries

*Virgin with Child (c.1495) by Tilman Riemenschneider*

*Susanna and the Elders* (1555) by Tintoretto

by Tilman Riemenschneider (c.1495) and stone statues from the cathedral churches of Bamberg and Naumburg.

Highlights of the Italian Renaissance and Baroque rooms are the marble bust of a laughing boy by Desiderio da Settignano, a marble relief of Bacchus and Ariadne, and a fine bronze and gilt figurine known as *Venus Felix*, after an antique marble statue.

The collection of decorative arts also includes fine pieces of furniture and tapestries, gilded table ornaments and vases, a number of statuettes and figurines, miniature clocks and jewellery.

## Picture Collection

Exhibits in the painting galleries are mostly hung according to regional schools or styles of

*Summer* (1563) by Italian painter Giuseppe Arcimboldo

painting, and arranged chronologically. Paintings go back as far as the 16th century, and include several works by early Flemish masters, such as Rogier van der Weyden, Hans Memling and Jan van Eyck. The highlight is the collection of Pieter Bruegel the Elder's surviving works, the largest collection of his work and the museum's greatest treasure.

Two rooms are devoted to Rubens, with large-scale religious works and an intimate portrait of his wife. Antony van Dyck is represented by some outstanding works, and there are paintings by Dutch genre painters. All the Rembrandts on show are portraits. The only painting by Johannes Vermeer is *The Artist's Studio*, an enigmatic work.

The Italian collection of 16th-century paintings from Venice and the Veneto include works by Titian, from his early *Gypsy Madonna* (1510) to the late *Nymph and Shepherd* (1570–75). Other highlights are Giovanni Bellini's graceful *Young Woman at her Toilette* (1515) and Tintoretto's *Susanna and the Elders*, one of the major works of Venetian Mannerism. There is a series of allegorical portrait heads representing the elements and the seasons by Giuseppe Arcimboldo. Italian Baroque painting includes works

by Annibale Carracci and Michelangelo Merisi da Caravaggio, including the huge *Madonna of the Rosary* (1606–7).

French treasures include the formal court portrait of the youthful Charles IX of France (1569) by François Clouet, and *The Destruction of the Temple in Jerusalem* (1638) by Nicolas Poussin.

Among the few British works are Thomas Gainsborough's *Landscape of Suffolk* (c. 1750) and paintings by Reynolds. The German collection contains several works by Albrecht Dürer, including his *Madonna with the Pear* (1512), and by Lucas Cranach the Elder and Hans Holbein the Younger.

There are several fine portraits of the Spanish royal family by Diego Velázquez, including his *Portrait of the Infanta* (1659).

## Coin Cabinets

The coin and medal collection of the Museum of Art History comprises 500,000 individual items, making it one of the most extensive numismatic collections in the world. Its first inventory was compiled in 1547. The nucleus of the collection derives from the former possessions of the Habsburgs, but has been added to by modern curators. The exhibits illustrate the history of money, with coins from ancient Egypt, Greece and Rome, and examples of Celtic, Byzantine, medieval and Renaissance money, right up to present-day Austrian currency.

**Medal of Ulrich II Molitor** (1581)

Also on display is a collection of medals, with portraits that are often outstanding miniature works of art. Particularly noteworthy are the 16th-century silver and gilt medals of Ulrich II Molitor, the Abbot of Heiligenkreuz, and the 19th-century silver medallion engraved by Bertrand Andrieu and minted to commemorate the baptism of Napoleon's son, showing the emperor as proud father.

# SOUTH OF THE RING

This part of town is an area of great diversity, ranging from the stateliness of the Opera House to the raucous modernity of bustling Karlsplatz, from the magnificence of Karlskirche – one of Johann Bernhard Fischer von Erlach's greatest churches – to the secular attractions of the Belvedere. Once Prince

Eugene of Savoy's palace, the Belvedere is now the home of the Gallery of Austrian Art, which includes works by Gustav Klimt. The district also has beautiful buildings with façades decorated in the Vienna Secession style. The stalls of the bustling Naschmarkt are also a popular attraction.

## Sights at a Glance

### Streets and Squares
⑬ Schwarzenbergplatz

### Historic Buildings
① Hotel Sacher
② Staatsoper
⑤ Theater an der Wien
⑦ Technische Universität
⑨ Karlsplatz Pavilions
⑪ Musikverein

### Museums and Galleries
③ Academy of Fine Arts
④ Secession Building
⑩ Künstlerhaus
⑫ Wien Museum Karlsplatz
⑮ 21er Haus
⑯ Belvedere see pp102–3

### Market
⑥ Naschmarkt

### Church
⑧ Karlskirche see pp98–9

### Parks
⑭ Stadtpark

See also Street Finder,
maps 2, 3, 4 & 5

0 metres        500
0 yards         500

◄ The opulent interior of the State Opera House

For keys to symbols see back flap

# Street-by-Street: Around the Opera

Between two of Vienna's key landmarks, the
Opera House and Karlskirche, lies an area
that typifies the varied cultural vitality of the
city as a whole. Here, you will find cultural
monuments such as an 18th-century theatre,
a 19th-century art academy and the superb
Secession Building, mixed in with emblems
of the Viennese devotion to good living: the
Hotel Sacher and the Café Museum, both
as popular today as ever, and the colourful
Naschmarkt, Vienna's best market for
vegetables and exotic fruits.

❸ **Academy
of Fine Arts**
This Italianate
building is home
to one of the best
collections of old
masters in Vienna.

Goethe Statue

The **Schiller
Statue** dominates
the park in front
of the Academy
of Fine Arts.

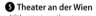

❹ ★ **Secession Building**
This delightful structure, built in 1898 as a showroom
for the Secession artists, houses Gustav Klimt's
*Beethoven Frieze*, created for an exhibition in honour
of the great composer.

❺ **Theater an der Wien**
The 18th-century theatre on
the banks of the Wien river is a
prime operatic venue in a
historic setting. The
programme also includes
ballet and concerts.

SCHILLERPLATZ

ELI

NIBELUNG

MAKARTGASSE

GETREIDEMARKT

LINKE WIENZELLE

❻ ★ **Naschmarkt**
Fresh produce is sold here Monday to
Saturday, and a flea market operates
on Saturday mornings.

**1 Hotel Sacher**
Home of the famous *Sachertorte*, which you can eat in its café.

**Locator Map**
*See Street Finder, maps 2 & 4*

**2 ★ Staatsoper**
The majestic state opera, erected on this site in 1869, is still the hub of Vienna's glorious cultural life.

**The Café Museum's** interior was originally designed by early minimalist Adolf Loos in 1899. It was remodelled in the 1930s by Josef Zotti, who installed curved booths.

0 metres       50
0 yards        50

**Key**

— Suggested route

**The Mark Anthony Statue
(1899)**, alongside the Secession Building, is a gloriously decadent bronze statue by Arthur Strasser. It depicts the Roman leader sitting in a chariot drawn by lions.

The imposing structure of the Vienna State Opera House

## ❶ Hotel Sacher

Philharmonikerstrasse 4. **Map** 2 B5.
**Tel** 51 45 60. Ⓤ Karlsplatz. 🚊 1, 2, 71,
D. 🚌 2A. 🗺 **sacher.com**

Hotel Sacher is one of the "must-see" sights in Vienna. It was founded by the son of Franz Sacher, who created the famous *Sachertorte* in 1832. Although this cake is now sold in almost every café around the city, this is its true home and visitors can treat themselves to a slice in the hotel's Café Sacher Wien.

The hotel came into its own under Anna Sacher, the founder's cigar-smoking daughter-in-law, who ran the hotel from 1892 until her death in 1930. She collected autographs and, to this day, a vast white tablecloth signed by Emperor Franz Joseph I is on display. During her time, the Sacher became a venue for the extra-marital affairs of the rich and noble. It is now a discreetly sumptuous hotel with red velvet sofas, draped curtains and stylish furniture.

## ❷ Staatsoper

Opernring 2. **Map** 2 B5. **Tel** 51 444-2250. Ⓤ Karlsplatz. 🚊 1, 2, 71, D. 🚌 2A. 🗺 **wiener-staatsoper.at**

In May 1869, Vienna's State Opera House opened to the strains of Mozart's *Don Giovanni*. Built in Neo-Renaissance style, the opera house initially failed to impress the Viennese. The distressed interior designer, Eduard van der Nüll, committed suicide and, two months later, the architect, August Sicard von Sicardsburg, also died. Yet, when the opera was hit by an allied bomb in 1945, the event was seen as a symbolic blow to the city. With a new state-of-the-art auditorium and stage, the opera house eventually reopened on 5 November 1955 with a performance of Beethoven's *Fidelio*. Its illustrious directors have included Gustav Mahler, Richard Strauss and Herbert von Karajan.

The hall is renowned for its exceptional acoustics and some

300 performances are held every year, including premieres of new operas. The programme changes daily. For those that can't make a performance, some events are streamed live on the internet.

Each year, on the last Thursday of Carnival, the stage is extended to create a vast dance floor for the Vienna Opera Ball (*see p39*).

## ❸ Academy of Fine Arts

Schillerplatz 3. **Map** 4 C1. **Tel** 588 16 22 22. Ⓤ Karlsplatz. 🚊 1, 2, 71, D. 🚌 57A, 59A. **Open** 10am–6pm Tue–Sun and public holidays. **Closed** 1 Jan, 1 May, 24, 25, 31 Dec. ♿ 🗺 **akademiegalerie.at**

The Gemäldegalerie der Akademie der Bildenden Künste, as signposted in German, was built in 1872–6 by Theophil Hansen as a school and museum. In 1907, Adolf Hitler applied to be admitted but was refused a place on the grounds that he lacked talent.

Today, the academy is both a research centre and a picture gallery, hosting changing exhibitions. Its pride is late-Gothic and early-Renaissance works, including some pieces by Rubens, a winged altarpiece by Hieronymus Bosch depicting the Last Judgement and works by Titian, Cranach and Botticelli. It also has some 17th-century Dutch and Flemish landscapes and an Austrian collection.

## ❹ Secession Building

Friedrichstrasse 12. **Map** 4 C1.
**Tel** 58 75 307. Ⓤ Karlsplatz. 🚊 1, 2, 62, 71, D. 🚌 57A, 59A. **Open** 10am–6pm Tue–Sun & hols. **Closed** 25 Dec. 🚫 📷 🗺 **secession.at**

The unusual Secession Building was designed in *Jugendstil* style by Joseph Maria Olbrich, as a showcase for the Secessionist artists, including Gustav Klimt, Koloman Moser and Otto Wagner, who broke away from Vienna's traditional art scene. The almost windowless building, with its

### Otto Wagner (1841–1918)

The most prominent architect at the turn of the 20th century, Wagner studied in Vienna and Berlin. Initially, he was associated with the historicist style, but in time he became the foremost representative of the Austrian Secession. He prepared plans for the re-routing of the Wien river and the modernization of the town's transport system. His most outstanding works include the **Majolikahaus** (*see Naschmarkt, opposite*), train stations (*see p100*), the Post Office Savings Bank building, a hospital and the Kirche am Steinhof (*see p112*).

Detail of Otto Wagner design

Façade of the Secession Building, with its golden filigree dome

# ⑥ Naschmarkt

**Map** 4 C1. **Tel** 400 005 430. Ⓤ
Kettenbrückengasse, Pilgramgasse.
🚌 59A. **Open** 6am–7pm Mon–Fri,
6am–5pm Sat. **W** **naschmarkt-**
**vienna.com**. Schubert Memorial
Apartment: **Tel** 58 16 730. **Open**
10am–1pm, 2pm–6pm Wed & Thu.
**Closed** 1 Jan, 1 May & 25 Dec. 🎟

The Naschmarkt is Vienna's
liveliest market, selling all types
of market goods as well as
delicatessen food. The weekly
Saturday flea market is popular.
Nearby, at Kettenbrückengasse
No. 6, is the **Schubert Memorial**
**Apartment**, where the composer Franz Schubert died in
1828. It displays facsimiles, prints
and a piano.
Overlooking Naschmarkt, at
Linke Wienzeile Nos. 38 and 40,
are two remarkable apartment
blocks. Designed by Otto
Wagner in 1899, and known as
the Wagner Apartments, they
represent the peak of *Jugendstil*
style. No. 38 has gilt ornament,
mostly by Koloman Moser.
No. 40 is known as Majolikahaus,
after the glazed pottery used
to weather-proof the walls. Its
façade has subtle flower patterns
in pink, blue and green; even
the sills are decorated.

filigree globe of entwined laurel
leaves on the roof, is a squat
cube with four towers. Gustav
Klimt's *Beethoven Frieze* (1902) is
its best known exhibit. Designed
as a decorative painting running
along three walls, it shows
interrelated groups of figures
thought to be a commentary
on Beethoven's *Ninth Symphony*.
The Secession Building is
Vienna's oldest independent
exhibition space. Owned by
the Austrian Association of
Visual Artists, it favours shows
of experimental works.

# ⑤ Theater an
der Wien

Linke Wienzeile 6. **Map** 4 C1.
**Tel** 58 83 06 65/58 885 (tickets).
Ⓤ Kettenbrückengasse. 🚌 59A.
**W** theater-wien.at

The "Theatre on the Wien
River", one of the oldest theatres
in Vienna, was founded by
Emanuel Schikaneder. A statue
above the entrance shows
him playing Papageno in the
premiere of Mozart's *The Magic*
*Flute*. Schikaneder, who had
written the libretto for this

opera, was the theatre's first
director. The premiere of
Beethoven's *Fidelio* was staged
here in 1805, and for a while
the composer lived in the
theatre. Many plays by prominent playwrights such as Kleist,
Grillparzer and Nestroy, and
many Viennese operettas were
premiered here, too, including
works by Johann Strauss (son),
Zeller, Lehár and Kalman. After
many years as a venue for
musicals, the Theater an der
Wien now stages only opera.

The Neo-Classical entrance to the
Theater an der Wien

# ⑦ Technische
Universität

Karlsplatz 13. **Map** 5 D1.
**Tel** 588 01–0. Ⓤ Karlsplatz.
🚋 1, 2, 62, 71, D. 🚌 2A, 4A, 59A.

Vienna's Technical University
has a Neo-Classical façade,
beautiful colonnades and rooftop statues by Joseph Klieber. It
was built in 1816 by Joseph
Schemerl von Leytenbach, to
the designs of the Imperial
Office of Public Works. Klieber
also created the eight stone
heads flanking the main
entrance, featuring some of the
university's famous professors.
Inside, the most beautiful
room is the Assembly Hall,
with carved wall panelling.
The University fronts on
to Resselpark, which contains
many busts and statues of
Austria's most important
scientists and engineers.

# ❽ Karlskirche

During Vienna's plague epidemic of 1713, Emperor Karl VI vowed that should the city be delivered from its plight he would build a church dedicated to St Charles Borromeo (1538–84), the patron saint of the plague. Johann Bernhard Fischer von Erlach created a richly eclectic building, later completed by his son. At 72 m (236 ft), it is the tallest Baroque church in Vienna. The Neo-Classical giant dome and portico are flanked by two minaret-like towers and Oriental-style gatehouses. The most striking features inside are the beautiful cupola frescoes, high altar and side altarpieces painted by the foremost artists of the day – Martino Altomonte, Daniel Gran and Sebastiano Ricci.

**The Pulpit**
Two putti crown the canopy of the richly gilded pulpit, adorned with rocailles and flower garlands.

**★ High Altar**
A stucco relief by Albert Camesina shows St Charles Borromeo being assumed into heaven on a cloud laden with angels and putti.

## KEY

① **Pediment reliefs** by Giovanni Stanetti show the suffering of the Viennese population during the 1713 plague.

② **The two gatehouses** leading into the side entrances of the church seem to combine the architecture of Roman triumphal arches with that of Chinese pavilions.

③ **Stairway** (closed to the public)

Main entrance

★ **Cupola Frescoes**
Johann Michael Rottmayr's frescoes, painted in 1725–30, depict the Apotheosis of St Charles Borromeo. This was the painter's last commission.

## Johann Bernhard Fischer von Erlach

An outstanding architect of the Austrian Baroque, Fischer von Erlach (1656–1723) designed many of Vienna's finest buildings, including the palaces of Schönbrunn, Prince Eugene of Savoy and the Trautson family. He died before he finished the Karlskirche; his son, Joseph Emanuel, completed it in 1737, and also took over as court architect.

★ **The Two Columns**
Inspired by Trajan's Column in Rome, these two columns feature scenes from the life of St Charles Borromeo, illustrating the qualities of Steadfastness and Courage.

**St Charles Borromeo**
Lorenzo Mattielli's statue of the patron saint and protector from the plague crowns the pediment.

Sunflower motif on the façade of the Karlsplatz Pavilions

## ❾ Karlsplatz Pavilions

Karlsplatz. **Map** 5 D1. Ⓤ Karlsplatz. 🚋 Kärntner Ring. 🚌 1, 2, 62, 71, D. 2A, 4A, 59A. **Tel** 50 58 747-85 177. **Open** Apr–Oct: 10am–6pm Tue–Sun & public hols.

Otto Wagner *(see p96)* was responsible for designing and engineering many elements of Vienna's light urban railway, the Stadtbahn, in the late 19th century. A few of Wagner's stations remain to this day – it is worth looking at the stations in Stadtpark, Kettenbrückengasse and Schönbrunn, for example – but none can match his stylish pair of railway exit pavilions (1898–9) alongside Karlsplatz. The patina-green copper roofs and the ornamentation complement the Karlskirche beyond. Gilt patterns are stamped onto the white marble cladding and eaves, with repetitions of Wagner's beloved sunflower motif. The greatest impact is made by the buildings' elegantly curving rooflines.

Today the western pavilion holds an exhibition devoted to the architect and urban planner. It covers his most important designs including the Kirche am Steinhof *(see p112)* and the revolutionary Stadtbahn, as well as his theories of design, which were radical for the time. The eastern pavilion houses a café.

## ❿ Künstlerhaus

Karlsplatz 5. **Map** 5 D1. **Tel** 58 79 663. Ⓤ Karlsplatz. 🚌 1, 2, 62, 71, D. 2A, 4A, 59A. **Open** check website for opening hours. 🎨 🆆 k-haus.at

Commissioned by the Vienna Artists' Society as an exhibition hall for its members, the Künstlerhaus (Artists' House) was completed in 1868. The society favoured grandiose, academic styles of painting in tune with the historicist Ringstrasse architecture which was also being developed around that time. The Artists' House itself is typical of this style. Designed by August Weber (1836–1903) to look like a Renaissance *palazzo*, it is decorated with marble statues of the masters of art, including Albrecht Dürer, Michelangelo, Raphael, Peter Paul Rubens, Leonardo da Vinci, Diego Velázquez and Titian, symbolizing the timeless value of art.

The Künstlerhaus has been undergoing renovation work for several years, during which exhibitions are housed at Künstlerhaus 1050 on Siebenbrunnengasse. It is expected to reopen in September 2018.

## ⓫ Musikverein

Bösendorferstrasse 12. **Map** 5 D1. **Tel** 50 58 190. Ⓤ Karlsplatz. 🚋 1, 2, 62, 71, D. 🚌 2A, 4A, 59A. **Open** guided tours: phone for details; box office: 9am–8pm Mon–Fri, 9am–1pm Sat and 1hr before concerts. 🆆 musikverein.at

Next to the Künstlerhaus is the Musikverein, headquarters of the Society of the Friends of Music. It was designed by Theophil Hansen between 1867 and 1869 and the exterior of the building features terracotta statues and balustrades.

The Musikverein is the home of the famous Vienna Philharmonic Orchestra. The concert hall, seating almost 2,000, has excellent acoustics, and the decor is superb. The balcony is supported by vast columns; the gilded ceiling shows nine muses and Apollo; and lining the walls are the statues of various famous musicians.

The most well-known annual event here is the New Year's Day concert, which is broadcast live around the world.

The monumental, historicist façade of the Musikverein

# ⑫ Wien Museum Karlsplatz

Karlsplatz 8. **Map** 5 D1. **Tel** 50 58 747.
Ⓤ Karlsplatz. 🚋 1, 2, 62, 71, D. 🚌 2A, 4A, 59A. **Open** 10am–6pm Tue–Sun & hols. **Closed** 1 Jan, 1 May, 25 Dec. 🎫 (free first Sun of every month and for under 19s). ♿ 🅦 **wienmuseum.at**

Visitors to the Historical Museum of the City of Vienna are greeted by a vast model of the city from the era when the Ringstrasse was developed. The exhibition covers nearly 3,000 years of urban history, illustrating the lives of its first settlers; life in the Roman camp of Vindobona; the threat from Turkish invaders; and the subsequent rise of Vienna to the magnificent capital of a great empire.

The museum has collections of memorabilia of many of Vienna's famous citizens. Perhaps the most interesting of these are the reconstructed apartments of the writer Franz Grillparzer (1791–1872) and the architect Adolf Loos (1870–1933).

# ⑬ Schwarzenbergplatz

**Map** 5 E1. Ⓤ Karlsplatz. 🚋 71. 🚌 4A.

The elongated Schwarzenberg Square, one of the city's grandest spaces, is best seen from the Ringstrasse, from where several important structures come into view together. In the foreground is an equestrian statue of Prince Karl Philipp Fürst zu Schwarzenberg, who commanded the Austrian and allied armies in the Battle of Leipzig in 1813 against the French army under Napoleon.

The Hochstrahlbrunnen (high jet fountain) was built in 1873 to mark the connection of Vienna's first Alpine water supply. The fountain is floodlit in summer. Once the focal point of the square, it now partly obscures the heroic-style Soviet monument to the Red Army that commemorates the Russian liberation of Vienna. Beyond the Russian monument, the beautiful Schwarzenberg

Fountain and Soviet Monument at Schwarzenbergplatz

Palace can be seen. It was built in 1697 by Johann Lukas von Hildebrandt and altered by the Fischer von Erlachs, Johann Bernhard and Joseph Emanuel. One wing houses the Swiss Embassy but most of the building remains closed awaiting further development.

# ⑭ Stadtpark

**Map** 3 D5. Ⓤ Stadtpark, Stubentor, Landstrasse–Wien Mitte. Ⓢ Wien Mitte. 🚋 2. 🚌 3A, 74A.

On the Weihburggasse side of the municipal park stands one of the most photographed sights in Vienna, the gilded statue of the King of Waltz, Johann Strauss the Younger. It was designed by Edmund Hellmer in the Neo-Romantic

Gilded statue of composer Johann Strauss the Younger in Stadtpark

style of the 1920s. The park, opened in 1862, also contains statues of the composers Franz Schubert and Franz Lehár, the painter Hans Makart and portraitist Friedrich von Amerling. Parallel to the Ringstrasse, along the Wien river, runs an attractive promenade designed in Secession style by Friedrich Ohmann. It includes several magnificent portals, part of a project to regulate the flow of the Wien river, as well as several pavilions, bridges and stone playgrounds.

# ⑮ 21er Haus

Arsenalstrasse 1. **Map** 5 F5. **Tel** 795 57 770. 🚋 18, O. 🚌 69A. **Open** 11am–6pm Thu–Sun (until 9pm Wed). 🎫 🅵 🖥 ♿ 🅦 **21erhaus.at**

At the south end of the Belvedere (see pp102–3), not far from the Military Museum, is Vienna's temple to contemporary art: the 21er Haus.

Built of steel and glass, the museum is an example of modernist architecture and was originally designed for the World Exhibition in 1958. Reopened in 2011 as a modern and contemporary art gallery, the 21er Haus celebrates Austrian art from 1945 to the present day, with changing exhibitions, performance art, lectures and a sculpture garden in the courtyard.

# 🔟 Belvedere

The Belvedere was built as the summer
residence of Prince Eugene of Savoy by Johann
Lukas von Hildebrandt. A brilliant military commander
whose strategies helped vanquish the Turks
in 1683, the prince became a favourite
at the Austrian court and with the
people. Situated on a gently sloping
hill, the Belvedere consists of two palaces
linked by a formal garden designed in the
French style by Dominique Girard. The garden
is laid out on three levels, each conveying a
complicated series of classical allusions:
the lower part represents the domain of the
Four Elements, the centre is Parnassus and
the upper section Mount Olympus.

**Chapel**
Prince Eugene's
former chapel is
now part of a gallery
with works by
Caspar David
Friedrich, F. G.
Waldmüller,
Edvard Munch,
Renoir and Monet.

**★ Gustav Klimt
Collection**
Klimt's portrait of
the Old Testament
figure of *Judith I*
(1901, *left*) and
his famous *The Kiss*
(1907–8) hang
in this superb
collection.

Main entrance leading
to Lower Belvedere

**Figures from the
Providentia Fountain
(1739)**
The original lead
figures that Georg
Raphael Donner made
for the Providentia
Fountain in Neuer
Markt are displayed
in the Marble Hall; this
central statue shows
Providence. The figures
that now stand in the
market are copies.

*For hotels and restaurants in this area see pp293–4 and pp313–14*

Entrance to the Upper
Belvedere from
Prinz-Eugen-Strasse

★ **Sala Terrena**
One of the finest rooms of
the Upper Belvedere, this hall
has beautiful stucco work by
Santino Bussi and statues
by Lorenzo Mattielli.

**Statues of Sphinxes**
With their lion bodies
and human heads, the
imposing Sphinx statues
adorning the Belvedere
gardens represent strength
and intelligence.

★ **Hall of Mirrors**
A statue of Prince Eugene by
Balthasar Permoser stands in
this richly ornamented
Baroque room, whose
walls are covered
with huge gilt-
framed mirrors.

**KEY**

① **Upper cascade**

② **Main gate** leading to the
Upper Belvedere

③ **Upper Belvedere**

④ **The Orangerie** houses
temporary exhibitions.

⑤ **The Palace Stables** house
the collection of medieval art
(Study Collection).

# FURTHER AFIELD

For a city of over 1.7 million inhabitants, Vienna is surprisingly compact. However, some of its most interesting sights are a fair distance from the historic city centre. Beyond the Ring sprawls Schönbrunn, a vast Neo-Classical palace and former summer home of the Habsburgs, with Rococo state rooms and superb gardens. The expressionist, brightly coloured apartment blocks of the Hundertwasser district are equally fascinating. Outside of the city you will also find Europe's largest cemetery; its biggest open-air festival; the Prater, the city's famed funfair; period swimming baths; and even a wild animal park. A visit to the headquarters of the United Nations takes you out of Austria altogether and onto international soil.

## Sights at a Glance

### Historic Buildings
3 Karl-Marx-Hof
4 Liechtenstein Garden Palace
5 Augarten
9 Hundertwasser-Haus
11 Amalienbad
15 Schönbrunn Palace see pp114–15
17 Wagner Villas

### Museums and Galleries
10 Heeresgeschichtliches Museum
13 Haydnhaus
14 Museum of Technology

### Parks and Gardens
6 Donauinsel
8 Prater
18 Lainzer Tiergarten

### Interesting Districts
1 Kahlenberg
2 Grinzing
7 UNO-City

### Churches
16 Kirche am Steinhof
19 Wotrubakirche

### Cemeteries
12 Zentralfriedhof see pp110–11

### Key
Central Vienna
Greater Vienna
Motorway
Motorway tunnel
Major road
Other road

◀ A section of the façade of the eccentric Hundertwasser Haus, created in 1985

**For keys to symbols** see back flap

Cobenzlgasse, one of the charming streets in Grinzing

# ❶ Kahlenberg

🚌 38A.

North of the city, on the edge of the Vienna Woods, rise two almost identical peaks. The lower of the two, with ruins visible on top, is Leopoldsberg, the former seat of Margrave Leopold who ruled Austria in the 12th century. The second, with a television mast and the outline of a white church at the top, is Kahlenberg, the highest peak in Vienna.

It was from here, on 12 September 1683, that the Polish King Jan III Sobieski led his troops to relieve the besieged city. Pope Innocent III's papal legate celebrated a thanksgiving mass in the ruins of the church, which had been destroyed by the Turks.

The restored St Josefkirche on Kahlenberg is now maintained by Polish monks. Two tablets beside the church door commemorate the battle and the visit by Pope John Paul II, in 1983. Inside the church is a chapel with frescoes by the Polish artist Jen Henryk de Rosen, and a display of the coats of arms of families whose members took part in the battle.

A short distance behind the church is an observation terrace and a restaurant. The views over the vineyards below and the city beyond are fabulous, with the Danube bridges to the left and the Vienna Woods to the right. Kahlenberg is a popular weekend excursion for the Viennese.

# ❷ Grinzing

🚋 38. 🚌 38A.

The quiet villages scattered among the vineyards on the slopes of the Vienna Woods come to life during the wine-making season, when large groups of tourists arrive to sample the new-vintage *Heuriger*. Originally, the vintners were licensed to sell their own wine, while snacks were offered for free. This tradition developed into today's *Heurigen* – new-vintage wine taverns, typical of Vienna.

Today, of course, such hospitality is no longer offered for free. At *Heurigen* inns, wine and other drinks are served at the table and food is available from self-service buffets. Guests sit on benches around wide wooden tables, where they can drink and enjoy themselves until the early hours. There are many such

A plaque on No. 31 Himmelstrasse in Grinzing

villages in the area around Vienna, but undoubtedly the most famous of all is Grinzing. Although it may have lost some of its original charm, this is still a nice place to spend an evening.

On the way to Grinzing, it is worth taking the time to visit the Heiligenstädter Testament-Haus at No. 6 on the narrow Probusgasse – Ludwig van Beethoven's most famous home in Vienna. It was here that the great composer tried to find a cure for his worsening deafness; when he failed, he wrote a dramatic letter to his brothers, known as *The Testament*.

# ❸ Karl-Marx-Hof

Heiligenstädterstrasse 82–92. Ⓤ Heiligenstadt. 🚋 D. 🚌 5A, 10A, 11A, 38A, 39A.

In the 1920s, Vienna was governed by a Social-Democratic town council, elected mainly thanks to the votes of first-time women voters, a period known as Red Vienna. The council formed the ambitious plan to build houses for its entire working population. As a result, between 1923 and 1933 more than 60,000 new apartments, well-appointed for the time, were built. The programme was financed by a luxury tax imposed on wealthy citizens. Its execution was so strict that the municipal finance director, Hugo Breitner, earned himself the nickname the "financial vampire". Karl-Marx-Hof is an

The peach- and salmon-coloured façade of the Karl-Marx-Hof

*For hotels and restaurants in this area see p294 and pp314–16*

The Baroque building of the Augarten Porcelain Manufactory

immense complex of 1,382 assisted housing apartments and recreational facilities, and is the most celebrated of the housing developments of that period. The project's architect, Karl Ehn, was a pupil of Austrian architect, Otto Wagner.

The delightful ceiling frescoes in the Liechtenstein Garden Palace

## ❹ Liechtenstein Garden Palace

Fürstengasse 1. **Map** 2 A1. **Tel** 319 57 67-167. 🚇 Friedensbrücke. 🚌 40A.
🚊 D. **Open** for guided tours by reservation only.

Completed in 1692 to designs by Domenico Martinelli in the Rococo style, this was the Liechtenstein family's summer palace. It has a monumental façade, with tall pilasters and typically Baroque windows.

Inside, the colourful ceiling paintings in the vast ground-floor room are the work of Johann Michael Rottmayr. Vault paintings by Antonio Belucci can be seen on both sides of the stairway. The grand hall is decorated with frescoes by Andrea Pozzo, a masterpiece of Baroque interior design.

The palace houses the art collection of Prince Hans-Adam II von und zu Liechtenstein – one of the richest private collections in the world. The collection is centred on the Baroque with special focus on Rubens, and ranges from the Renaissance (for example, Raphael and the Bruegels) through to the early 19th century (Waldmüller and Füger). The Liechtenstein family also acquired many masterpieces of modern art, dating from the early 20th century. The palace stands in an extensive garden, which was remodelled in the 19th century in the English style.

## ❺ Augarten

Obere Augartenstrasse 1. **Map** 3 D1.
**Tel** 21 12 418. 🚇 U-Taborstrasse.
🚊 2, 5, 31. 🚌 5A, 5B. Augarten.
Palace: **Open** guided tours 10:15am
& 11:30am Mon–Fri (manufactory),
10am–6pm Mon–Sat (museum).
**Closed** Sun & public hols.
🌐 **augarten.at**

There has been a palace on this site since the days of Leopold I, but it was destroyed by the Turks in 1683 and then rebuilt around 1700 to designs attributed to Johann Bernhard Fischer von Erlach. Since 1948 it has been the home of the world-famous Vienna Boys' Choir and is consequently closed to the public.

The surrounding park is one of the oldest in Vienna; it was first planted in 1650 by Emperor Ferdinand III, later renewed and opened to the public in 1775. Topiary lines long paths and the handsome gates were designed by Isidor Canevale. Mozart, Beethoven and Johann Strauss (the Elder) all gave concerts in the park pavilion, which was once the imperial porcelain factory. Renovated in 2011, the pavilion now houses the Porcelain Museum. This museum illustrates the history of Vienna porcelain. Several exhibits on display highlight the craftsmanship and techniques. The manufactory is open to the public for guided tours.

## ❻ Donauinsel

🚇 Donauinsel, Handelskai.
🎪 Donauinselfest:
🌐 **danauinselfest.at**

The numerous side-arms and rivulets of the Danube river regularly flooded the town until it was first canalized between 1870 and 1875. The second period of canalization in the Vienna region began in 1972 and was completed in 1987. The New Danube, a 5-km (3-mile) canal that acts as an "overflow", dates from this period.

The wooded island created between the Danube and its canals by the first stage of canalization is known as Donauinsel, or Danube Island. It is Vienna's largest recreation area and a favourite with the local population, who come here to swim and sunbathe in the summer. The vast park is criss-crossed by dozens of avenues, walking and cycling paths, and picnic areas with built-in barbecues, as well as nudist areas. Even water-skiing and surfing are possible.

The Danube Island Festival, held each June, is the biggest free open-air festival of music and food in Europe, claiming as many as three million visitors.

The vast, modern complex of UNO-City on the Danube

## ❼ UNO-City

Wagramerstrasse 5. **Tel** 26060-5596.
Ⓤ Kaisermühlen, Vienna International
Center. 🚌 20A, 92A, 92B. 🕐 11am,
2pm, 3:30pm Mon–Fri (plus 12:30pm
Jul & Aug); ID required. Donauturm:
**Tel** 263 35 72. 🆆 unvienna.org

On the left bank of the Danube
is UNO-City, one of only three
United Nations headquarters.
The complex stands on international, non-Austrian territory;
its post office uses its own special
postage stamps and UN post-
marks. UNO-City consists of four
vast semicircular buildings and
a large congress hall, one of the
most strikingly modern pieces of
architecture in Europe, designed
by the architect Johann Staber
and opened in 1979. Today,
visitors can join one of the regular
guided tours of the complex.

UNO-City is surrounded by a
green park, covering an area of
over 600,000 sq m (700,000 sq yds),
with excellent recreational
facilities. One of the main attractions is the **Donauturm**, a TV
tower rising to 252 m (827 ft),
with two revolving restaurants
and an observation platform.

## ❽ Prater

Praterverband: **Tel** 728 05 16; Ferris
wheel: **Tel** 72 95 430. Ⓤ Praterstern.
Ⓢ Wien Nord. 🚋 5, O. 🚌 5B, 80A.
**Open** Funfair mid-Mar–Oct: 10am–
midnight daily. 🆆 prater.at

Originally an imperial
hunting ground, the
woods and meadows
between the Danube and
its canal were opened
to the public by Joseph II
in 1766. The amusement
park at Prater, called
Wurstelprater, is the oldest
in the world. It is still one
of the most entertaining,
with a roller coaster,
miniature steam train and the
world's tallest flying swing
attraction. Unlike similar parks
in most countries, admission to
the grounds is free, and charges
for the rides are very modest; a
ride on the roller coaster costs
€3.50. Overlooking all is Vienna's
iconic Riesenrad (Ferris wheel),
built in 1896 by the English
engineer Walter Basset. The
setting for a tense scene in
Carol Reed's film *The Third Man*
(1949), it is now one of the
city's symbols.

The Prater is also a vast sports
park, home to a soccer and a
trotting stadium, the Freudenau
racetrack, swimming pools,
tennis courts, a golf course
and cycling trails, as well as
a planetarium and open-air
restaurants and bars.

Nearby are the pavilions
and vast grounds of the annual
Vienna Fair.

The Wurstelprater funfair at night

## ❾ Hundertwasser-Haus

Löwengasse/Kegelgasse.
Ⓤ Landstrasse. 🚋 1.
**Closed** no admission to the public.
Kunsthaus Wien: **Tel** 712 0491.
**Open** 10am–7pm daily.
🆆 hundertwasser-haus.info

Hundertwasser-Haus is a
municipal apartment block
created in 1985 by the artist
Friedensreich Hundertwasser. An
eclectic-style building, combining
the elements of a Moorish
mosque with features of Spanish
villages and Venetian palaces, it
has become one of Vienna's main
attractions. The shopping centre
opposite was also designed by
the artist, whose work is on show
at the **Kunsthaus Wien**, Untere
Weissgerberstrasse 13.

Apartments
delineated by
colour

Typically irregular
window

Main entrance
on Löwengasse

# ⑩ Heeresgeschichtliches Museum

Ghegastrasse Arsenal, Objekt 18.
**Tel** 79 56 10. Ⓤ Südtiroler Platz,
Schlachthausgasse. Ⓢ Quartier
Belvedere. 🚋 18, O & D. 🚌 13A, 69A.
**Open** 9am–5pm daily. Guided tours
(in English), call 0664 622 2248.
**Closed** 1 Jan, Easter Sunday, 1 May, All
Saints, 25 & 31 Dec. 🅿 Ⓦ **hgm.or.at**

The impressive Museum of
Army History is housed in the
military complex known as the
Arsenal, built as a fortress in
1856. The museum's collection is
based around the theme: "wars
belong in museums". Many of the
exhibitons have been designed
for children.

Exhibits relate to the Turkish
Siege of Vienna in 1683, the
French Revolution and the
Napoleonic wars. There are
documents relating to the battles
fought by the Habsburgs, a
collection of arms, banners,
uniforms and military vehicles.
Among the most fascinating
exhibits are memorabilia relating
to Prince Eugene of Savoy,
as well as a collection of model
ships that illustrates the past
glories of imperial power at sea –
since it is landlocked, it is easy
to forget that Austria was once
a formidable naval power.
A separate section is devoted to
the events in Sarajevo on 28 June

Decorative tiling from the 1920s in Amalienbad

1914, when Archduke Franz
Ferdinand and his wife Sophie
von Hohenberg were assassin-
ated by a Serbian nationalist,
provoking a crisis that led to the
outbreak of World War I.

# ⑪ Amalienbad

Reumannplatz 23. **Tel** 60 74 747.
Ⓤ Reumannplatz. 🚋 6, 67. 🚌 7A,
65A, 66A, 67A, 68A, 68B, 70A.
**Open** 9am–6pm Tue, 9am–9:30pm
Wed, Fri, 7am–9:30pm Thu, 7am–8pm
Sat, 7am–6pm Sun.

Public baths may not seem like
an obvious tourist attraction,
but the *Jugendstil* Amalienbad
(1923–6) is a fine example of a
far-sighted municipal authority

providing essential public
facilities for the local working
population, and doing so with
style and panache. Named after
one of the councillors, Amalie
Pölzer, the baths were designed
by Otto Nadel and Karl
Schmalhofer, employees of the
city's architectural department.

The magnificent main pool,
overlooked by galleries, is covered
by a glass roof that can be
opened in minutes. There are
saunas, baths and therapeutic
pools. When first opened, the
baths were one of the largest of
their kind in Europe. The interior is
enlivened by fabulous Secession
tile decorations. The baths were
damaged in World War II but have
been impeccably restored.

Corner of block
with first-floor
café and staircase
topped by an
onion dome

Uneven
ceramic line

Roof gardens planted with
hundreds of trees and shrubs

# ⑫ Zentralfriedhof

Austria's largest burial ground, containing 300,000 graves – the largest number of any cemetery in Europe – and covering over 2.5 sq km (1 sq mile), was opened in 1874. The central section includes the graves of artists, composers, architects, writers and local politicians. Funerals in Vienna are often quite lavish affairs, and the cemetery contains a vast array of funerary monuments, from the humble to the ostentatious.

★ **Friedhofskirche zum Heiligen Karl Borromäus**
This Art Nouveau church is decorated with Egyptian elements.

## KEY

① **The Presidential Vault** contains the remains of Dr Karl Renner, the first President of the Austrian Republic after World War II.

② **Arcades** around the cemetery's Secession church.

③ **Monument (1894) to Dr Johann Nepomuk Prix**, mayor of Vienna, by Viktor Tilgner

④ **The main entrance** to the cemetery is from Simmeringer Hauptstrasse, with the Secession-style Gate II designed by Max Hegele in 1905.

## Cemetery Layout

The cemetery is divided into numbered sections: apart from the central garden of honour (reached via gate II), where VIPs are buried, there are old (gate I) and new (gate IV) Jewish cemeteries, a Protestant cemetery (gate III), a Russian Orthodox section, and various war graves and memorials. It is easiest to explore the cemetery on board the circulating minibus.

**The Monument to the Dead of World War I** is a powerful representation of a grieving mother by Anton Hanak.

Old Jewish cemetery

Main entrance

Islamic area

New Jewish cemetery

Protestant cemetery

**Arnold Schönberg's Cube**
The grave of the modernist composer Arnold Schönberg, creator of dodecaphonic music, is marked with this bold cube by Fritz Wotruba.

**Theophil Hansen's Grave**
Danish architect Theophil Hansen made Vienna his home and designed the city's Parliament building. He died in 1891.

**VISITORS' CHECKLIST**

**Practical Information**
Simmeringer Hauptstrasse 234.
**Tel** 534 69-28405. **Open** Nov–Feb: 8am–5pm daily; Mar & Oct: 7am–6pm daily; Apr–Sep: 7am–7pm daily (until 8pm Thu May–Aug). **W** friedhoefewien.at

**Transport**
Ⓢ Zentralfriedhof. 🚃 6, 71.

**The Arcades**
Some spectacular monuments can be seen carved in the semi-circular arcades facing the main entrance, including this memorial (1848) to the miner August Zang. It shows the entrance to a mine.

★ **Graves of the Musicians**
The musicians buried here include Johann Strauss the Elder and the Younger *(shown left)*, Brahms, Beethoven and Schubert. There is also a monument to Mozart.

**Russian Orthodox Chapel**
This small chapel, built in traditional Russian Orthodox style in 1894, is used by Vienna's Russian community.

Brahms' Room in the Haydnhaus

## ⓭ Haydnhaus

Haydngasse 19. **Tel** 59 61 307.
Ⓤ Zieglergasse. 🚍 57A. **Open** 10am–
1pm, 2–6pm Tue–Sun. **Closed** 1 Jan,
1 May, 25 Dec. 🅿️

Haydn built this house in what
was then a new suburb with
money that he had earned on
his successful trips to London
between 1791 and 1795.
He lived in the house from
1797 until his death in 1809,
and composed many major
works here, including *The
Seasons* and *The Creation*.

The museum was extensively
renovated and reopened in 2009
to commemorate the 200-year
anniversary of Haydn's death.
The exhibits include portraits,
documents and original scores
as well as Haydn's clavichord,
which was bought by Johannes
Brahms. The museum's garden,
in the middle of Mariahilfer
Strasse, is open to the public.

## ⓮ Museum of Technology

Mariahilfer Strasse 212. **Tel** 89 998-0.
Ⓤ Schönbrunn, Johnstrasse. 🚊 10,
52, 58. 🚍 10A, 57A. **Open** 9am–
6pm Mon–Fri, 10am–6pm Sat, Sun
and hols. **Closed** 1 Jan, 1 May, 1 Nov,
25 & 31 Dec. 🅦 tmw.at

Originally founded by Franz
Joseph I in 1908, Vienna's
Museum of Technology
covers a massive area since
its renovation in the 1990s.

The museum documents
technical progress over the
past centuries, from domestic
appliances to heavy industry,
with a particular emphasis on
Austrian engineers and scientists.
Exhibits include the world's first
sewing machine (Madersperger,

1830), the oldest
typewriter (Mitterhofer,
1860), the ship's
propeller, designed by
Ressel in 1875, and the
first petrol-driven car
built in the same year
by Siegfried Marcus. A
major section features
displays on computer
technology and oil-
and gas-refining, as
well as a reconstruc-
ted coal mine.

The Railway Museum, which is
an integral part of the museum,
houses a large collection of
imperial railway carriages and
engines. Its prize exhibit is the
carriage used by Franz Joseph I's
wife, the Empress Elisabeth.
The Post Office Museum displays
the world's first postcard – an
Austrian invention.

A huge lighthouse at the
entrance recalls the Habsburg
Empire's once formidable
extent, from the Tatra Mountains
to the Atlantic Ocean.

## ⓯ Schönbrunn Palace

*See pp114–15.*

## ⓰ Kirche am Steinhof

Baumgartner Höhe 1. **Tel** 91 060-11007.
**Open** 4–5pm Sat, noon–4pm Sun.
🚍 47A, 48A. 🅿️ (free on Sat). 🕐 3pm
Sat, 4pm Sun & by appointment.

At the edge of the Vienna Woods
rises the conspicuous copper
dome of the astonishing Church
at Steinhof. Built in 1902–7 by
Otto Wagner, the church is
considered to be one of the most
important works of the Secession.
It is an integral part of the large
mental hospital complex, also
designed by Wagner, who laid
out the church to facilitate access
for disabled churchgoers.

The church, dedicated to
St Leonard, is clad in marble
with copper nailhead ornament,
and has spindly screw-shaped
pillars topped by wreaths
supporting the porch, and four
stone columns. The light and airy
interior is a single space with
shallow side chapels. Its main
decoration consists of gold and
white friezes as well as gilt
nailhead and beautiful blue
stained-glass windows by
Koloman Moser. The altar
mosaics are by Rudolf Jettmar.

The Secession-style interior of the Kirche am Steinhof

Hermesvilla in Lainzer Tiergarten, retreat of the imperial family

fully equipped with electricity, and bathtubs and toilets were added in the 1890s. Attractive murals show scenes from Shakespeare's *A Midsummer Night's Dream*, designed by Hans Makart and painted by the young Gustav Klimt.

Today, Hermesvilla holds exhibitions, while the stables act as summer quarters for the Lipizzaner horses from the Spanish Riding School.

**Hermesvilla**
**Tel** 80 41 324. **Open** Apr–Oct: 10am–6pm Tue–Sun & public hols.
**w** wienmuseum.at

## ⑰ Wagner Villas

Hüttelbergstrasse 26 & 28. **Tel** 914 85 75. **U** Hütteldorf. 43B, 52A, 52B. Ernst Fuchs-Museum: **Open** 10am–4pm Tue–Sat, by appointment Mon & Sun.

Hidden behind dense, leafy greenery, at the start of a road to Kahlenberg, stand two villas built by the architect Otto Wagner. The oldest, built for himself, still has some classical elements such as Ionic columns, once favoured by Wagner. It was meticulously restored by the present owner, the painter Ernst Fuchs, who added his own colours and established a museum. The villa is now a famous meeting place for Vienna's artistic community as well as a venue for fund-raising auctions. The second villa, built some 20 years later, was completed in pure Secession style. Privately owned, it can be viewed only from outside.

## ⑱ Lainzer Tiergarten

Hermesstrasse. 60 to Hermesstrasse, then 55A. **Tel** 400 049 200. **Open** daily. **w** lainzer-tiergarten.at

The Lainzer Tiergarten in the Vienna Woods, once an imperial hunting ground, was enclosed within a 25-km- (16-mile-) long wall on the orders of Maria Theresa. The wall still stands today and successfully stops herds of deer and wild boar escaping. It also prevents modern building developments

from encroaching on this beautiful space.

The Tiergarten was opened to the public in 1923, and in 1941 the entire area was declared a nature reserve. Walks in the woods and meadows of this large park will transport the visitor into another world. It is forbidden to disturb the animals; bikes and dogs are banned, turning the reserve into a true haven for wildlife. From the observation platform on top of Kaltbründlberg, there are great views over Vienna and the Vienna Woods.

A 15-minute walk along paths brings you to the **Hermesvilla**. In 1885, Emperor Franz Joseph I ordered a hunting lodge to be built here and presented it to his wife Elisabeth, in the hope that this would stop her from perpetually seeking to escape the clamour of the city. He did not succeed, but the beautiful Hermesvilla was built by Karl von Hasenauer as a retreat for the imperial family. The couple's rooms were on the first floor; Elisabeth's quarters were designed with flourish and elegance; Franz Joseph's were much more spartan. The villa, named after a marble statue of Hermes, was

Detail on the stables in Hermesvilla

## ⑲ Wotrubakirche

Georgsgasse/Rysergasse. **Tel** 888 61 47. 60A. **Open** 2–8pm Sat, 9am–4:30pm Sun and public holidays. by appointment.

Standing on a hillside close to the Vienna Woods, this church was designed in uncompromisingly modern style in 1965 by the Austrian sculptor Fritz Wotruba (1907–75), after whom it is named. It was built in 1974–6 by Fritz Gerhard Mayr. The church is made up of a pile of uneven concrete slabs and glass panels that provide its principal lighting and views for the congregation out onto the hills.

The building is raw in style, but powerful and compact. The church looks different from every angle and has a strong sculptural quality. The central section, consisting of 152 concrete blocks, can accommodate a congregation of up to 250.

The sculptural Wotrubakirche

# ⓯ Schönbrunn Palace

In 1695, Emperor Leopold I asked Johann Bernhard Fischer von Erlach to rebuild the former summer residence of the imperial family. However, it was not until the reign of Maria Theresa that the project was completed by Nikolaus Pacassi (1744–9). It is to him that the palace owes the magnificent Rococo decorations of its state rooms. Schönbrunn has been the scene of many important historic events.

**Round Chinese Cabinet**
Maria Theresa used this room for private discussions with her State Chancellor, Prince Kaunitz. The walls of the white-and-gold room are adorned with lacquered panels.

**★ Great Gallery**
Used for imperial banquets, this room has a lovely ceiling fresco by Gregorio Guglielmi.

**A hidden staircase**
leads to the apartment of the State Chancellor, above which he had secret conferences with the Empress.

**Blue Chinese Salon**
The last Austrian emperor, Karl I, signed his abdication in 1918 in this Rococo room with Chinese scenes.

Napoleon Room

**Millionen-Zimmer**
(Millions Room) was Maria Theresa's conference room.

**★ Vieux-Lacque Room**
During her widowhood, Maria Theresa lived in this room, which is decorated with exquisite oriental lacquered panels.

Main entrance

**Miniatures Cabinet**
The paintings on the wall of Maria Theresa's breakfast room are copies of Dutch and German paintings by Franz Stephan and his daughters Maria Anna, Maria Christine and Maria Antonia.

## VISITORS' CHECKLIST

**Practical Information**
Schönbrunner Schlossstrasse 47.
**Tel** 81 11 32 39.
Palace: **Open** Apr–Jun, Sep–Oct: 8:30am–5:30pm daily; Jul–Aug: 8:30am–6:30pm daily; Nov–Mar: 8:30am–5pm daily. Gardens: **Open** morning till dusk.
**W** schoenbrunn.at

**Transport**
Schönbrunn, Hietzing. 10, 58, 60. 10A, 56A, 56B, 58A.

**Large Rosa Room**
This is one of three rooms decorated with monumental Swiss and Italian landscape paintings by Josef Rosa, after whom the room is named.

**Palace Guide**
*On the first floor, the suite of rooms to the right of the Blue Staircase was occupied by Emperor Franz Joseph I and his wife Elisabeth. The rooms in the east wing include Maria Theresa's bedroom and rooms used by Archduke Franz Karl.*

**The Blue Staircase** leads to the entrance for all tours of the state rooms.

### The Coach Museum

One wing of Schönbrunn Palace, formerly housing the Winter Riding School, now contains a marvellous collection of coaches – one of the most interesting in the world. It includes over 60 carriages dating back to the 17th century, as well as riding uniforms, horse tackle, saddles, coachman liveries, and paintings and drawings of horses and carriages. The pride of the collection is the coronation coach of Emperor Karl VI. Other exhibits include sleighs and sedan chairs belonging to Maria Theresa, among others.

**Coronation coach of Karl VI**

#### Key
- Franz Joseph I's apartments
- Empress Elisabeth's apartments
- Ceremonial and reception rooms
- Maria Theresa's rooms
- Archduke Franz Karl's rooms
- Closed to visitors

# SHOPPING IN VIENNA

With a compact, eminently walkable city centre, and a variety of shops to suit any budget and taste, Vienna is a great place to shop. The pedestrian shopping areas of Kärntner Strasse, Graben and Kohlmarkt in the Old Town have a plethora of upmarket stores, as does Vienna's longest shopping street, Mariahilfer Strasse. Bargains are to be had in street flea and antiques markets, while the side streets south of the MuseumsQuartier cry to be explored. There are several shopping centres in the suburbs, including Wien Mitte Landstrasse, Stadion Center and BahnhofCity West. These can all be reached on the U-Bahn. Look out for glassware, traditional crafts and, of course, sweet treats.

## Where to Shop

The most elegant shops – and the most attractive window displays – are found within the Ring. Kärntner Strasse, Graben, Kohlmarkt and the central shopping passage connecting Kärntner Strasse with Weihburggasse, as well as the Goldenes Quartier on Kohlmarkt, are full of designer brands and upmarket stores. As everywhere, these kinds of shops tend to be expensive. Tastefully decorated smaller shops scattered around the Old Town offer goods of guaranteed quality that are often truly unique. Shoppers will find an array of clothes, glass and porcelain, confectionery, books and decorative items to choose from.

The shops along Mariahilfer Strasse offer more variety; this is where you will find many of the multi-national chains, as well as large shoe shops, book- and stationery shops, and a variety of food shops. There are a number of chain stores on Graben and Kärntner Strasse, too, such as H&M and Mango. A similar range of goods, but at lower prices, can be found on Meidlinger Hauptstrasse and Favoritenstrasse.

## Opening Hours

Shops generally open at 8:30 or 9am and close at 6 or 7pm. Almost all stay open till 5pm on Saturday and close on Sundays and public holidays.

The supermarket chain Billa is open on Sundays at the main railway stations and Vienna airport. Most bakeries also open on Sundays. It is possible to buy some items at petrol stations.

## How to Pay

All major credit and debit cards, including Visa and MasterCard, are widely accepted, though a minimum purchase amount may be required. Visitors normally resident outside the EU are entitled to claim back the VAT (*Mehrwertsteuer* – MwSt) if the total value of goods

A chest of drawers with chocolates from Altman & Kühne

purchased in any one shop exceeds €75. Take your passport when shopping and ask the shopkeeper to complete the appropriate form; keep the receipts. The VAT rate is 20 per cent and the goods listed on the form must be unused and available for inspection by customs officers.

## Rights and Services

If you have purchased goods that turn out to be defective, you are usually entitled to a refund, provided you have kept the receipt. Some exceptions include goods bought in the sales or at street markets. Many shops offer a free gift-wrapping service; many will also ship items anywhere in the world – for a fee.

## Antiques and Art

A pawnshop established by Emperor Joseph I in 1703 has been transformed into Austria's largest auction house. Called **Dorotheum,** it mainly sells antique furniture and objects of decorative value. Its vast store at Dorotheergasse No. 17 is one of several branches throughout

The elegant interior of J. & L. Lobmeyr

the country. Lovely second-hand and antique items can also be bought at the flea markets that take place regularly in various parts of town; the largest of them, but also the most expensive, is held on Saturday at the **Naschmarkt** *(see p97)*. The **Kunst- und Antikmarkt am Hof** offers high-quality antique paintings, porcelain, furniture and books.

## Food and Drink

Vienna is justly famous for its cakes, pastries and *Torten*, and any good *Café-Konditorei* will post cakes back home for you. In the pre-Christmas period, try the buttery Advent *Stollen* from **Meinl am Graben**, or the original *Sachertorte*, directly from the **Hotel Sacher**, at any time of year. **Lebzelterei Pirker** sells traditional *Lebkuchen*. Specialist chocolate shops, such as **Altmann & Kühne**, are worth a visit if you have a sweet tooth. And look out for *Eiswein*, a delicious dessert wine made from grapes left on the vine after the first frosts, available at **Vinothek St. Stephan**.

## Souvenirs

There are many things you can buy to remind you of Austria. A

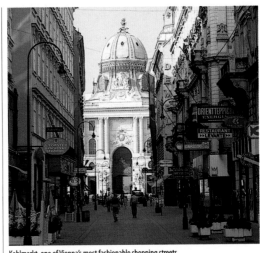
Kohlmarkt, one of Vienna's most fashionable shopping streets

large selection of souvenirs can be found at the bazaar-like **Hundertwasser Village**. Biedermeier-style flower posies and pretty handbags embroidered with folkloric designs are available at **Maria Stransky** and **Petit Point**, beautiful glassware and handpainted porcelain can be found at **J. & L. Lobymeyer**, and there are exquisite figurines and tableware at the famous **Augarten** porcelain factory. Other souvenirs include cups with the profile of Romy

Schneider in her role as Sissi, or pictures of the young Franz Joseph I. Traditional Austrian clothes, or *Trachten*, are sold by **Witzky Landhausmode**. Products here include *Loden*, a felt-like fabric used to make warm coats, jackets and capes, and *Dirndls* (dresses). **Zauberklingl** is the place for practical jokers, with great party jokes. A wide range of traditional handicrafts, designer jewellery, glass, porcelain and fashion accessories are stocked at **Österreichische Werkstätten**.

## DIRECTORY

### Antiques and Art

**Dorotheum**
Dorotheergasse 17.
**Map** 2 B4.
**Tel** 515 600.
w dorotheum.com

**Kunst- und Antikmarkt am Hof**
Am Hof.
**Map** 2 B3.
**Open** Mar–Nov: 10am–6pm Fri, Sat.
w antikmarkt-hof.at

**Naschmarkt**
**Map** 4 C1.
**Open** 6am–7pm Mon–Fri, 6am–6pm Sat.
Flea market: 6am–2pm Sat.
w naschmarkt-vienna.com

### Food and Drink

**Altmann & Kühne**
Graben 30.
**Map** 2 B4.
**Tel** 533 09 27.

**Hotel Sacher**
Philharmonikerstrasse 4.
**Map** 2 B5.
**Tel** 514 560.

**Lebzelterei Pirker**
Stephansplatz 7.
**Map** 2 C4.
**Tel** 512 03 69.

**Meinl am Graben**
Graben 19. **Map** 2 B4.
**Tel** 532 33 34.

**Vinothek St. Stephan**
Stephansplatz 6.
**Map** 2 C4.
**Tel** 512 68 58.

### Souvenirs

**Augarten**
Spiegelgasse 3.
**Map** 2 C4. **Tel** 512 14 94.

**Hundertwasser Village**
Kegelgasse 37–39.
**Map** 3 F4. **Tel** 710 46 16.

**J. & L. Lobmeyr**
Kärntner Strasse 26.
**Map** 2 C5.
**Tel** 512 05 08-88.

**Maria Stransky**
Hofburg Passage 2.
**Map** 2 B4. **Tel** 533 60 98.

**Österreichische Werkstätten**
Kärntner Strasse 6.
**Map** 2 C4.
**Tel** 512 24 18.

**Petit Point**
Kärntner Strasse 16.
**Map** 2 C4.
**Tel** 512 48 86.

**Witzky Landhausmode**
Stephansplatz 7.
**Map** 2 C4.
**Tel** 512 48 43.

**Zauberklingl**
Linke Wienzeile 16.
**Map** 2 C4.
**Tel** 586 43 05.

# ENTERTAINMENT IN VIENNA

Vienna offers a wide range of entertainment, from street theatre in the famous Wurstelprater funfair to classical drama in one of the opulent theatres. But most of all, Vienna is a musical town, with grand opera at the Staatsoper; the latest musicals at the Theater an der Wien; dignified orchestral music and elegant waltzes; relaxed dances in the Stadtpark and free open-air concerts. Even the famous Lipizzaner horses perform to Viennese music. The city also takes pride in its Burgtheater, one of the foremost stages in

the German-speaking world, as well as its many smaller dramatic theatres. There are two excellent theatres that have performances in English and several cinemas that specialize in classic films. Restaurants tend to close early but you can still be entertained around the clock at one of the many nightspots: jazz clubs, nightclubs, casinos and bars with live music all beckon within the Ringstrasse. Or you can end your day sipping coffee and indulging in gorgeous pastries at one of the late-night cafés.

The giant Ferris wheel in the Wurstelprater funfair

## Practical Information

Listings of current events and theatre, concert and cinema programmes can be found in most daily newspapers; check *Neue Kronen Zeitung, Die Presse, Standard* or *Kurier*. The weekly guide *Der Falter* (www.falter.at) is entirely devoted to the arts. The Vienna Tourist Office (Wiener Tourismusverband) publishes a monthly guide with listings of art and sports events taking place that month, and every hotel has a range of free leaflets with details of concerts, theatre performances and other artistic events. You can also check the fat round billboard columns all over the city, which have posters advertising the latest events. By law, theatres, concert halls and public buildings are adapted with ramps, lifts and special seating

areas to accommodate disabled spectators. All have at least one disabled toilet.

## Booking Tickets

Given the huge demand for classical music in Vienna, it is highly recommended to book performances months in advance. The online services listed in the directory *(opposite)* are a good place to start, or try the websites for specific theatres and venues. You can buy tickets in person at the state-run **Bundestheaterkassen**.

Theatres offer various concessions and the opera house sells cheap tickets for standing-only places. Tickets bought in advance tend to be up to 10 per cent cheaper than those bought just before the start of a performance.

## Music

The principal venues for classical concerts, including the ever-popular waltzes, are the **Staatsoper** (State Opera), the concert halls of the **Musikverein**, home to the Wiener Philharmoniker, and the **Konzerthaus**. Here you can hear the world's greatest performers. Classical music concerts are also held in many churches. Open-air concerts are very popular during the summer season. Another Viennese favourite is the **Kursalon Hübner**, where you can enjoy old and new tunes while overlooking the Stadtpark.

The **Donauinselfest**, staged in June on the Danube Island, is a great way to hear free concerts by some of the world's most popular performers. During local festivals, in wine bars and cafés you can often hear Viennese folk music called *Schrammelmusik*. Kärntner Strasse is another kind of music venue – many street

A young street musician entertaining with his cello

performers and buskers here hope for hand-outs from the generally well-to-do passers-by.

## Theatre

Vienna's Staatsoper enjoys an excellent international reputation. Opera is also shown at the **Wiener Volksoper** (Vienna People's Opera) and the **Wiener Kammeroper** (Vienna Chamber Opera). The **Raimund Theater** is one of the best places for musicals. The **Theater an der Wien** specializes in opera productions. The **Burgtheater** is one of the most important German-language theatres in the world. The **Akademietheater** is more intimate. The **Volkstheater** stages modern plays and the occasional classic drama, while the **Theater in der Josefstadt** produces mostly comedies. **Vienna's English Theatre** is the oldest English-language theatre in Europe.

## Cinema

Most films are dubbed and shown in German; those that can be watched in their original language are always advertised as such in the programme.

The famous Vienna State Opera Ball

Some cinemas specialize in foreign films. The **Österreichisches Filmmuseum** in the Albertina building offers visitors inexpensive membership, and screens both classic and cult films, while the **Votivkino** and the **Filmhaus Stöbergasse** cinemas often put on a season of films devoted to one artist or subject.

## Casinos

**Casino Wien** is set in the fabulous Baroque Esterházy Palace, where a full range of games, including blackjack, roulette and poker,

Billboard column

is on offer. For slot machines there is **Casino Admiral Prater**. Austria's biggest tables can be found in the smoke-filled rooms of the **Concord Grand Casino**, in the Simmering suburb.

## After a Night Out

At night, public transport is provided by a network of half-hourly buses, departing from the central points at Schwedenplatz, Franz-Josef-Kai and the opera. Tickets are availble from the kiosk or on the bus. The U-Bahn runs all night on weekends and the night before a public holiday. Taxis can be found outside all major venues and at taxi ranks.

## DIRECTORY

### Bookings

**Bundestheaterkassen**
Operngasse 2. **Map** 2 B5.
**Tel** 51 444-7810. **Open** 8am–6pm Mon–Fri, 9am–noon Sat, Sun.
Ⓦ bundestheater kassen.at

**Online booking sites**
Ⓦ koeticket.com
Ⓦ viennaticketoffice. com
Ⓦ viennaclassic.com

### Music

**Donauinselfest**
Ⓦ donauinselfest.at

**Konzerthaus**
Lothringerstrasse 20.
**Map** 5 D1. **Tel** 24 20 02.
Ⓦ konzerthaus.at.

**Kursalon Hübner**
Johannesgasse 33.
**Map** 3 D5. **Tel** 51 257 90.

**Musikverein**
Bösendorferstrasse 12.
**Map** 5 D1. **Tel** 50 58 190.
Ⓦ musikverein.at.

**Staatsoper**
Opernring 2. **Map** 2 B5.
**Tel** 51 444-2250.
Ⓦ wiener-staatsoper.at.

### Theatre

**Akademietheater**
Lisztstrasse 1. **Map** 5 E1.
Tickets: Opernring 2.
**Tel** 51 444-4140.

**Burgtheater**
Universitätsring 2.
**Map** 2 A3.
**Tel** 51 444-4400.

**Raimund Theater**
Wallgasse 18–20.
**Tel** 588 85.

**Theater an der Wien**
Linke Wienzeile 6.
**Map** 4 C1. **Tel** 588 301 010.

**Theater in der Josefstadt**
Josefstädter Strasse 26.
**Map** 1 B4. **Tel** 42 700.

**Vienna's English Theatre**
Josefsgasse 12. **Map** 1 C4.
**Tel** 402 12 60-0.

**Volkstheater**
Neustiftgasse 1.
**Map** 1 C5.
**Tel** 52 111-400.

**Wiener Kammeroper**
Fleischmarkt 24. **Map** 3 D3.
**Tel** 58 885.

**Wiener Volksoper**
Währingerstrasse 78.
**Map** 1 C1. **Tel** 51 444–3670.

### Cinema

**Filmhaus Stöbergasse**
Stöbergasse 11–15.
**Map** 4 A 4/5. **Tel** 54 666-30.

**Österreichisches Filmmuseum**
Augustinerstrasse 1.
**Map** 2 B5. **Tel** 53 370 54.

**Votivkino**
Währingerstrasse 12.
**Map** 2 A2. **Tel** 31 735 71.

### Casinos

**Casino Wien**
Kärntner Strasse 41.
**Map** 2 B5. **Tel** 51 248 36.

# VIENNA STREET FINDER

The map references given for all the sights, hotels, restaurants, bars, shops and entertainment venues described in this book refer to the maps in this section. Most of the city's famous sights, historic buildings, tram, bus, U-Bahn and railway stations, and river landing-stages have been marked on the map. Others are indicated by symbols, which are explained in the key below. The names of the streets and squares on the map are given in German. The word *Strasse* (Str.) translates as street, while *Gasse* is a smaller street, *Platz* means square, *Hof* means a courtyard, *Brücke* translates as bridge and a *Bahnhof* is a railway station.

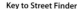

0 kilometres 1
0 miles 1

**Key to Street Finder**

- Major sight
- Place of interest
- Other building
- U U-Bahn station
- Bundesbahn station
- S Schnellbahn station
- Badner Bahn stop
- i Tourist information office

- Hospital with casualty unit
- Police station
- Church
- Synagogue
- Railway line
- Pedestrianized street

**Scale of Maps 1–5**

0 metres 200
0 yards 200

1:11,500

# Street Finder Index

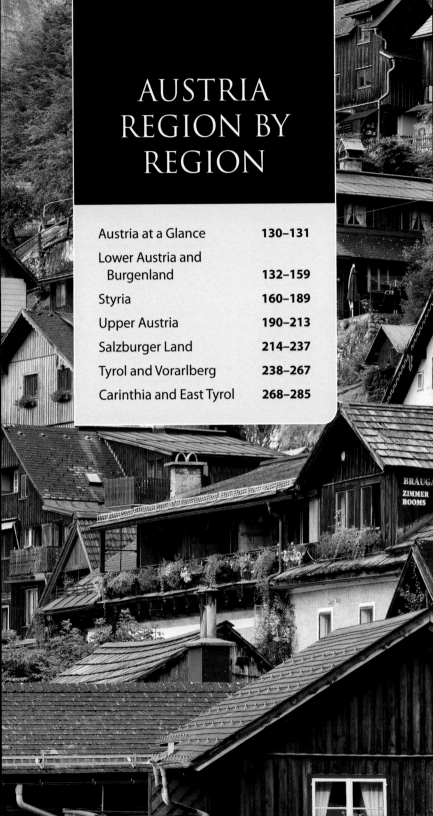

# AUSTRIA REGION BY REGION

BRÄUGA
ZIMMER
ROOMS

# Austria at a Glance

Situated at the heart of Europe, Austria is at once an efficient, industrialized country and a dreamlike wonderland effusing cultural and natural charm. Beautiful countryside abounds – from Neusiedler Lake in the east, surrounded by vast, flat steppes, to the three majestic Alpine ranges that cut across the country. These glorious settings provide stunning backdrops for the fairytale castles, Benedictine abbeys and Baroque palaces that form just a handful of Austria's cultural highlights. And Austria isn't just a feast for the eyes; *The Sound of Music* and the sounds of Mozart, Strauss and Haydn fill every corner of the country. Add world-renowned museums and cafés that hark to a time gone by, and you have a country that offers an experience like no other.

**The Mirabell Palace in Salzburg** was built in the 17th century for Salome Alt, the mistress of Archbishop Wolf Dietrich von Raitenau. The magnificent stairway is adorned with sculptures by Raphael Donner.

**Innsbruck**, with its picturesque Old Town and church spires rising against the majestic backdrop of the snow-covered Alps, is the capital of Tyrol, the picture-postcard province most popular with visitors.

UPPER
AUSTRIA
*(see pp190–213)*

Salzburg

Lofer

Bregenz

Reutte

Wörgl

Radsta

TYROL AND
VORARLBERG
*(see pp238–67)*

Schwaz

Zell am See

Bludenz

Innsbruck

SALZBURGER LAND
*(see pp214–37)*

CARINTHIA
AND EAST TYRO
*(see pp268–85)*

Lienz

Villa

**Houses in Bregenz**, capital of Vorarlberg province, are decorated with early heraldic paintings and the figures of saints.

**Schloss Bruck in Lienz**, in East Tyrol, was built in 1252–77 for the Görz family. Today, it is home to a museum with a fine collection of 19th- and 20th-century Austrian art and folklore items.

◄ Charming view of Hallstatt, one of Austria's most picturesque villages

**Hauptplatz in Linz**, capital of Upper Austria, is one of the most beautiful architectural sights in Central Europe. In the centre of the square stands the marble column of the Holy Trinity (1723).

**A Monument to Strauss and Lanner** was erected in the spa park of Baden, a sleepy town close to Vienna, famous for its sulphuric baths and casino, one of the oldest in Austria.

Gmünd

Hollabrunn

LOWER AUSTRIA
AND BURGENLAND
*(see pp132–59)*

Stockerau

VIENNA
*(see pp54–127)*

Linz

Melk

St Pölten

Steyr

Baden bei
Wien

Mitterbach

Wiener Neustadt

Eisenstadt

Oberpullendorf

Leoben

STYRIA
*(Ssee pp160–89)*

Murau

Graz

Wolfsberg

Leibnitz

Klagenfurt

**The Zeughaus in Graz**, capital of Styria province, is an impressive display of the city's armoury and former power.

**The Landhaus in Klagenfurt**, seat of the Carinthian provincial government, was built in the 16th century in an Italianate style, and is one of Klagenfurt's most attractive buildings. Its glorious galleried inner courtyard remains intact to this day.

| 0 kilometres | 50 | |
|---|---|---|
| 0 miles | | 50 |

# LOWER AUSTRIA & BURGENLAND

Lower Austria is the largest province in Austria, both in terms of area and population. It surrounds the Austrian capital, Vienna, which for many years doubled as capital of the province. Following a plebiscite in 1986, the provincial capital was moved to St Pölten. At the edge of Lower Austria, bordering Hungary along one side, is the low-lying province of Burgenland, with its capital Eisenstadt.

Lower Austria, together with Upper Austria, covers the area that was once the cradle of the country. The low-lying and gently undulating terrain make this region easily accessible. During Roman times, its southern reaches belonged to the provinces of Noricum and Pannonia, while the areas north of the Danube frequently changed hands as Slav and German tribes fought over them. From AD 791, Lower Austria belonged to the Franks and, in AD 970, it was given the name Ostmark (Eastern Margravate). Today, it occupies an area of 19,163 sq km (6,930 sq miles) and stretches along the Danube valley, from the German border in the west, to Hungary in the east. In the south it reaches the slopes of the limestone Rax Mountains, with their highest peak, Schneeberg, and the popular winter resort of Semmering.

Lower Austria's main towns, beside Vienna and St Pölten, are Krems, Mödling, Wiener Neustadt, Klosterneuburg and Baden bei Wien. In the north of the province, adjoining the Czech Republic and Slovakia, lies the vine-growing region of Weinviertel. Further west is the wooded Waldviertel.

To the southeast of Lower Austria, from Neusiedler See down, is the narrow province of Burgenland, covering an area of 3,965 sq km (1,530 sq miles), with a population of 278,000. Historically, it was a part of Hungary, but after the Turkish wars (1529–1791) it was settled by Germans and Croats, and finally incorporated into Austria in 1921.

The main town in Burgenland is Eisenstadt, where the mighty Esterházy family established their seat; to this day they continue to play an important role in the region's development.

The ornate 19th-century casino in the spa town of Baden bei Wien

◀ Beautiful spiral staircase with *trompe l'oeil* moulding, Melk Abbey

# Exploring Lower Austria and Burgenland

The Wachau, a narrow stretch of the Danube valley, forms the heart of Lower Austria, famous for its fertile plains, its vineyards and picturesque villages. Formidable fortresses, castles and fortified abbeys rise along the high banks of the river, including the imposing Benedictine Abbey in Melk. Further east, the Wienerwald (Vienna Woods) is perfect for walking and cycling. Burgenland Province has its own unique flora and fauna around Neusiedler See. It produces the finest red wines in Austria and celebrates the memory of Joseph Haydn, former court musician to the Esterházy family in Eisenstadt.

## Sights at a Glance

1. *St Pölten pp136–7*
2. Tulln
3. Klosterneuburg
4. Korneuburg
5. Laxenburg
6. Wiener Neustadt
7. Baden bei Wien
9. Stift Göttweig
10. Krems
12. Dürnstein
13. Weissenkirchen
14. Spitz
15. Burg Aggstein
16. *Melk Abbey pp146–7*
17. Schloss Schallaburg
18. Amstetten
19. Waidhofen an der Ybbs
20. Neuhofen an der Ybbs
22. Burg Forchtenstein
23. *Neusiedler See pp156–7*
24. *Eisenstadt pp158–9*
25. Bruck an der Leitha
26. Rohrau
27. Hainburg
28. Schloss Hof

## Tours

8. Wienerwald Tour
11. *Waldviertel Tour pp144–5*
21. Schneeberg Tour

*Gossiping Women* on Herrenplatz in St Pölten

The Gothic parish church in Spitz, overlooking the picturesque Wachau valley

*For hotels and restaurants in this region see p295 and pp316–18*

0 kilometres 20

0 miles 20

16th-century Teisenhoferhof, with its attractive galleried courtyard, now home of the Wachaumuseum, Weissenkirchen

The mock-Gothic Franzensburg Castle, Laxenburg

Jihlawa

Brno

ellerndorf

Laa an der Thaya

Poysdorf

Hohenau

Hollabrunn

Mistelbach

ÖSTERREICH

Dürnkrut

Stockerau

Wolkersdorf

ULLN

4 KORNEUBURG

Gänserndorf

2

3 KLOSTERNEUBURG

SCHLOSS HOF

arkersdorf

VIENNA

28

27

Donau (Danube)

HAINBURG

Schwechat

Petronell

Mödling

5 LAXENBURG

26 ROHRAU

WIENER WALD

8

7 BADEN BEI WIEN

25 BRUCK AN DER LEITHA

Ebreichsdorf

Neusiedl am See

Györ

ndorf

Podersdorf

EISENSTADT

Frauenkirchen

WIENER NEUSTADT

6

24

Rust

23 NEUSIEDLER SEE

chberg

BURGENLAND

22

Ilmitz

Neunkirchen

BURG FORCHTENSTEIN

sloggnitz

Aspang Markt

Deutschkreutz

Oberpullendorf

Mannersdorf an der Rabnitz

Pinkafeld

Oberwart

Szombathely

Grosspetersdorf

Graz

Güssing

Jennersdorf

## Key

━━━ Motorway

━━━ Major road

┄┄┄ Minor road

━━━ Scenic route

╼╾ Main railway

─── Minor railway

▬▬▬ International border

▬▬▬ Province border

## Getting Around

The main airport for these provinces is Vienna-Schwechat International Airport, which is served by every major airline. St Pölten is a major railway and road hub, situated on the route of the Westbahn line, with branch lines to Mariazell, Krems, Tulln and Gaming. St Pölten is also served by the Westautobahn (motorway) and the road connecting Vienna and Salzburg. The entire region is covered by a dense road network.

**For keys to symbols** *see back flap*

# ❶ St Pölten

The capital of Lower Austria since 1986, St Pölten was the first Austrian city to be granted municipal rights, in 1159. Its history dates back to Roman times, and it achieved considerable status under the Augustinian orders in the 8th century. St Pölten's fastest period of growth, however, was during the Baroque period, when outstanding masters of that era, such as the architect Jakob Prandtauer and the painters Daniel Gran, Paul Troger and Bartolomeo Altomonte, made their home here. Economically, St Pölten became the most important city in Lower Austria when trade switched from the Danube waterways to overland roads.

Rathausplatz in St Pölten, with the Holy Trinity column

### Exploring St Pölten

The beautiful Baroque centre, with several older buildings, lies to the south of the railway station between Domplatz, Riemerplatz and Rathausplatz. The town centre is compact and easy to explore on foot, being largely pedestrian-ized. Apart from fascinating Baroque buildings and those associated with the town's administrative role, St Pölten also has more recent architecture of interest.

**A detail on the cathedral door**

### 🏛 Domkirche Mariä Himmelfahrt

Domplatz 1. **Tel** (02742) 353 402. Diocesan Museum: **Tel** (02742) 324 331. **Open** May–Oct: 10am–noon, 2–5pm Tue–Fri, 10am–1pm Sat. 

In the 12th century, a church dedicated to St Hippolytus stood on this site. Destroyed by fire in 1278, and again in 1621, the church was rebuilt in Baroque style to designs by Jakob Prandtauer. Deceptively plain on the outside, the cathedral's interior is a typical example of exuberant Baroque ornamen-tation. Daniel Gran and Bartolomeo Altomonte created the large wall and ceiling paintings, depicting scenes from the life of Jesus. Adjoining the cathedral is the Bishops' Palace, once an abbey, with a lovely staircase, also by Prandtauer, and a magnificent library decorated by Paul Troger.

The **Diocesan Museum** houses a collection of sculptures, paintings and decorative art objects dating from the Gothic and Baroque periods. Behind the palace, at No. 1 Klostergasse, is the apartment of Jakob Prandtauer.

### 🏛 Franziskanerkirche

Rathausplatz.
The Franciscan church of the Holy Trinity, together with its friary, occupies the narrow, northern end of the Rathausplatz. A Rococo church with a delightful pink façade, it is unusual because it has no tower. The church interior, also decorated in Rococo style, features an altarpiece by Andreas Gruber. There are four wing paintings by another well-known Austrian Baroque artist, Martin Johann Schmidt, known as Kremser Schmidt.

### 🏛 Rathaus

Rathausplatz 1.
**Tel** (02742) 333 3000.
The present town hall was built in the 16th century by combining two Gothic buildings in a mishmash of incongruous styles. The niches of the Gothic entrance gate abut a Renaissance portal, the Gothic tower has a Baroque onion dome on top, and the entire structure has been concealed behind a Baroque façade. Inside, however, it is worth seeing the ceiling stuccowork in the Mayor's Chamber and sculptures by Christoph Kirschner.

The town hall occupies the southern side of Rathausplatz, once considered the most beautiful square in Austria. Today, it is lined with modern buildings, and has lost some of its Baroque charm. Next to the town hall you can see the house where Austrian composer Franz Schubert once lived, and at No. 5 is the Montecuccoli Palace. The façades of both buildings were created by Prandtauer's nephew, Joseph Munggenast.

At the centre of the square stands the marble column of the Holy Trinity, with a fountain and statues of saints.

Portraits line the walls in the Mayor's Chamber, Rathaus

### 🏛 Institut der Englischen Fräulein

Linzer Strasse 9–11.
**Tel** (02742) 3521 88–0.
Church: **Open** 10am–5pm daily.

The Institute of the English Ladies, founded by the English Catholic nun Mary Ward, established several schools in St Pölten to educate the girls of aristocratic families. The institute, one of the most beautiful Baroque buildings in Lower Austria, was begun in 1715 and enlarged some 50 years later. Prandtauer created the beautiful white and pink façade, punctuated by black wrought-iron grills on the windows, with three groups of sculptures on two floors.

A statue outside the Institut der Englischen Fräulein

St Mary Column, in the centre of the Baroque Herrenplatz

### 🏛 Riemerplatz

Riemerplatz is another beautiful Baroque square, lined with exquisite buildings such as the striking Herberstein Palace, at the wider end of Wiener Strasse. At no. 41 Kremser Gasse, which runs north from the square, stands the delightful Stöhr-Haus with its breathtakingly beautiful Art Nouveau façade. It is the work of the architect Joseph Maria Olbrich, who also designed the superb Secession Building in Vienna (see pp96–7).

### 🏛 Herrenplatz

This is yet another attractive Baroque square in the city; its most outstanding features are the Baroque façades of the buildings around the square. Mostly attributed to Jakob Prandtauer, these façades often hide much earlier medieval niches and arcaded courtyards. On top of the house at No. 2 is a lovely sculpture by Georg Raphael Donner, called Dispersing of Darkness by Light. At the centre of the square stands St Mary's Column (1718).

### 🏛 Wiener Strasse

Wiener Strasse, adjacent to Herrenplatz, has been a main thoroughfare since Roman times, as is still obvious today from its many inns. There are a number of interesting historical buildings in this road, including St Pölten's oldest pharmacy, at No. 1, dating back to 1595. Its façade, built in 1727 by Joseph Munggenast, still displays the pharmacist's original coat of arms from 1607 and the 19th-century sign "Zum Goldenen Löwen" (To the Golden Lion).

## VISITORS' CHECKLIST

**Practical Information**
Road map F3.
🚗 50,000.
ℹ️ Rathausplatz 1.
**Tel** (02742) 333 3000.
🌐 stpoeltentourismus.at

**Transport**
🚌 🚆

## St Pölten City Centre

① Domkirche Mariä Himmelfahrt
② Franziskanerkirche
③ Rathaus
④ Institut der Englischen Fräulein
⑤ Riemerplatz
⑥ Herrenplatz
⑦ Wiener Strasse

0 metres        250
0 yards          250

Thirteenth-century funerary chapel of the Three Wise Men in Tulln

## ❷ Tulln

**Road map** F3. 🗺 16,000. 🚊 🚌 🚆
ℹ Minoritenplatz 2, (02272) 69 00.
🌐 **tulln.at**

Tulln, on the right bank of the Danube river, was the site of the Roman camp of Comagena and is one of the oldest towns in Austria. Two structures remain from that period: the 3rd-century Roman Tower, probably the oldest structure in Austria, and a milestone.

Tulln is famous as the birthplace of Egon Schiele, one of the foremost painters of the early 20th century, best known for his provocative nudes. The **Egon-Schiele-Museum**, housed in an old prison on the banks of the Danube, shows 90 original works by the artists and the permanent exhibition *Egon Schiele and his Times*.

The former monastery, Minoritenkloster, houses Tulln's town hall, as well as the **Zuckermuseum**, on the top floor, which is devoted to the history of sugar.

The Romanesque **Pfarrkirche St Stephan**, the parish church of St Stephen, was built in the 12th century, but subsequently altered, first in Gothic, then in Baroque style. It has an interesting Romanesque portal with 12 reliefs, probably representing the apostles. Next to the church is the 13th-century mortuary, one of the more interesting historic sites in town. It holds the impressive cemetery chapel of the Three

Wise Men, combining elements of late-Romanesque style with early Gothic, and featuring a beautifully decorated portal and well-preserved murals.

The remains of the old city walls are also still preserved.

🏛 **Egon-Schiele-Museum**
Donaulände 28. **Tel** (02272) 645 70.
**Open** Apr–Oct: 10am–5pm
Tue–Sun & hols. 📷 on request.
🌐 **egon-schiele.eu**

🏛 **Zuckermuseum**
Minoritenplatz 1. **Tel** (02272) 602 11 237. **Open** 8am–3:30pm Mon, Tue & Wed, 8am–7pm Thu, 8am–noon Fri. 📷

## ❸ Klosterneuburg

**Road map** G3. 🗺 26,000. 🚊 🚌
🚆 ℹ Niedermarkt 4 (02243) 320 38 600. 🌐 **klosterneuburg.at.**

This small town, just outside Vienna, was once the main seat of the Babenberg rulers. In the early 12th century, Margrave Leopold III built his castle here, and later the collegiate church, the magnificent **Stift Klosterneuburg**, supposedly in atonement for an act of treason he committed against Heinrich V.

The Romanesque church of the Augustinian Abbey was altered many times until the 17th and 18th centuries, when it acquired its present Baroque interior, designed by Joseph Fischer von Erlach and Donato Felice d'Allio, among others. Original features include the early-Gothic cloister and burial chapel of Leopold III; the latter contains the town's greatest treasure, an altarpiece by Nicolas of Verdun, a goldsmith and master of enamel from Lorraine. The altar, completed in 1181 after 10 years' work, has 51 enamelled panels arranged in three horizontal layers, depicting Bible scenes. The chapel has fine stained-glass windows.

A wine barrel in Klosterneuburg

The museum in the former imperial residence holds a valuable collection of paintings and Gothic and Baroque sculptures.

Near Klosterneuburg, a small museum in **Kierling** is devoted to the writer Franz Kafka, based in the former Hoffmann Sanatorium where he died.

🏰 **Stift Klosterneuburg**
**Tel** (02243) 411-212. **Open** May–mid-Nov: 9am–6pm daily; mid-Nov–Apr: 10am–5pm. **Closed** 25, 26, 31 Dec. 📷
📷 ♿ 🅿 🌐 **stift-klosterneuburg.at**

🏰 **Essl Collection of Contemporary Art**
An der Donau-Au 1. **Tel** (02243) 370 50 150. **Open** 10am–6pm Tue–Sun, 10am–9pm Wed. 📷 ♿
🌐 **essl.museum**

## ❹ Korneuburg

**Road map** G3. 🗺 12,000.
🌐 **korneuburg.gv.at**

Korneuburg once formed a single town with Klosterneuburg. In 1298 it became independent, and grew into an important trading and administrative centre.

Hauptplatz, the main square, is surrounded by houses with late-Gothic, Renaissance and Baroque façades. Other interesting sights include the late-Gothic St-Ägidius-Kirche (church of St Giles) and the Rococo Augustinerkirche (church of St Augustine), whose

The main altarpiece in Korneuburg

Franzensburg Castle, a mock-Gothic folly in Laxenburg

main altarpiece shows the sky resting on four columns, with God the Father sitting on his throne, holding the Earth in his hand. The altar painting of the *Last Supper* is the work of Franz Anton Maulbertsch.

**Burg Kreuzenstein**, on the road to Stockerau, is a fascinating folly of a Gothic castle. Built in the 19th century by Count Johann Nepomuk Graf Wilczek, on the site of a former fortress (1140) that was almost entirely destroyed by Swedish forces during the Thirty Years' War, it holds the count's extensive collection of late-Gothic art and handicrafts.

## ❺ Laxenburg

**Road map** G3. 🚌 ℹ️ Schlossplatz 7–8, (02236) 711 010. 🅦 laxenburg.at

This small town, situated 15 km (9 miles) outside Vienna, is a favourite place for daytrips from the capital. It began as a hunting lodge, Lachsenburg, around which a settlement grew. Destroyed during the last Turkish wars, but restored and enlarged in the 17th century, it became a favourite retreat for Maria Theresa and other members of the imperial family. Laxenburg was chosen as a venue for the signing of many important state treaties, including the Pragmatic Sanction which made it possible for a woman, Maria Theresa, to accede to the throne. Today, the former imperial palace is the seat of the

International Institute for Applied Systems Analysis (IIASA), and it also houses the Austrian Film Archives. The palace is surrounded by a landscaped, English-style **Schlosspark**, one of the grandest such palace parks in Europe at the time of Emperor Joseph II.

The park is dotted with many follies, and one particularly worth visiting is the early-19th-century **Franzensburg**, a mock-Gothic castle, built on an island in an artificial lake within the palace grounds at the height of the fashion for all things historic. It was furnished with original objects collected and pillaged from all over the empire, such as the 12th-century columns with capitals in the chapel, from Klosterneuburg, and the ceiling in the Hungarian Coronation Room from the Hungarian town of Eger. In the summer, open-air theatre performances take place on the castle island.

## ❻ Wiener Neustadt

**Road map** G3. 🚹 42,000. 🚆 🚌 ℹ️ Neunkirchner Strasse 17, (02622) 373-311. 🅦 wiener-neustadt.at

This large town, some 40 km (25 miles) south of Vienna, is an industrial city and an important road and rail transport hub, and also the largest shopping city of Lower Austria.

In the centre of the town is the attractive Hauptplatz, with a part-Gothic **Rathaus** (town hall) rebuilt in Baroque style. Gothic houses line the northern side of the square, and the St Mary's Column (1678) stands in the centre. The **Dom** (cathedral church of the Ascension of Our Lady) was built in the 13th century. Its outstanding features include 12 wooden statues of the apostles by the columns of the central nave, and the Baroque main altar. The Brautportal (Portal of the Betrothed) dates from 1230.

In **Stift Neukloster** (Holy Trinity church) you can see a beautifully carved stone on the tomb of Eleanor of Portugal, wife of Emperor Friedrich III, by Niklas Gerhaert of Leyden, dating from 1467.

The former castle now houses the prestigious Military Academy, once commanded by General Rommel. In its west wing is the 15th-century **St-Georgs-Kathedrale** (St George's Cathedral), with the tomb of Maximilian I under the main altar. A corner tower, a remnant of the old fortified city walls, now houses a criminology museum and a gruesome exhibition of instruments of torture.

The town hall on Hauptplatz, Wiener Neustadt

One of the many attractive villas in Baden bei Wien

## ❼ Baden bei Wien

**Road map** G3. 🚗 25,000. 🚊 🚉 🚌
ℹ️ Brusattiplatz 3 (02252) 22 600–600.
🎉 Festival of Roses (Jun).
🌐 baden.at

The spa town of Baden, on the eastern slopes of the Vienna Woods, was already known in Roman times, when it was called *Aquae Pannoniae* and Emperor Marcus Aurelius praised its sulphuric springs. Today, its 15 hot springs make Baden a popular destination with older patients, but taking a hot sulphur bath is a relaxing experience for younger visitors too. In summer, you can swim in the open-air Art Deco baths.

The small town was completely rebuilt after a fire in 1812, and many of its attractive Neo-Classical town houses and Biedermeier-style villas hail from this period. The main architect at the time, Joseph Kornhäusel (1786–1860), largely shaped the look of the town.

At one time, the list of Baden visitors read like a *Who's Who* of the rich and famous, and included such luminaries as Wolfgang Amadeus Mozart, who composed his *Ave Verum* here; Franz Schubert; and, most importantly, Ludwig van Beethoven. It was here that he composed his *Ninth Symphony*. Baden was frequented by the maestros of Viennese operetta as well: Strauss (the Elder and the Younger), Lanner and Zeller. Napoleon also holidayed here with his wife Marie Louise.

## ❽ Wienerwald Tour

The Vienna Woods (Wienerwald), to the west of the capital, are a favourite weekend destination for the Viennese. Crossed by numerous walking and cycling tracks, the wooded hills covering an area of 1,250 sq km (480 sq miles) are a perfect place for recreation. The main town in the area is Baden bei Wien, one of Europe's most famous spa towns, and to the north lie Klosterneuburg, former capital of the Babenbergs, and Tulln *(see p138)*. There are also some interesting works of art and unique scenery.

**② Heiligenkreuz**
The Cistercian Abbey (1133) at Heiligenkreuz, founded by Leopold III of Babenberg, has retained its fine Romanesque-Gothic character and some Baroque furnishings to this day.

**• Alland**

**Key**

— Suggested route
— Scenic road
═ Other road
═ River, lake

**③ Mayerling**
After the suspected double suicide of Rudolf and Mary von Vetsera, Franz Joseph I had the famous hunting lodge converted into a Carmelite chapel of atonement.

### The Mayerling Mystery

Rudolf, the only son of Franz Joseph I and Elisabeth, was a restless man, unable to adjust to the rigours of court. After a fierce quarrel with his father, he went to Mayerling with his mistress, Mary von Vetsera. On 30 January 1889, the two lovers' bodies were found in the lodge. Both had been shot. Had they been murdered, was it joint suicide, or did Rudolf kill Mary and then turn the gun on himself? The reason behind the tragedy also remains a mystery to this day.

The tombstone of Mary von Vetsera

### ① Burg Liechtenstein
The castle in Maria Enzersdorf, originally built in 1166, has been altered many times and now resembles a Gothic castle, with imposing towers and battlements.

### ⑦ Mödling
This small, picturesque town, once a retreat for artists, is situated in beautiful natural scenery of limestone rocks.

0 kilometres          3

0 miles                    3

### ⑥ Gumpoldskirchen
This small wine-making town has become famous for its countless *Heurigen* wine bars and cheerful restaurants.

### ⑤ Bad Vöslau
Poised on the southern slopes of the Vienna Woods, this village has two claims to fame: its wines and its baths (1837), built by Count Moritz von Fries, with crystal-clear natural mineral water.

### ④ Baden bei Wien
Frauenbad, one of the original 19th-century baths, is today no longer in use but makes an interesting historic sight.

### Tips for Drivers

**Length of route:** 60 km (37 miles).

**Stopping places:** most of the best restaurants can be found in Gumpoldskirchen and Baden.

**Suggestions:** visit the abbey in Heiligenkreuz. **Tel** (02258) 8703-0; take a boat excursion on the underground lake in Seegrotte, Hinterbrühl. **Tel** (02236) 26364.

The magnificent organ in Stift Göttweig

## 🄰 Stift Göttweig

**Road map** F3. 🚌 🚐 **Tel** (02732) 85 581-0. **Open** mid-Mar–Oct: 8am–6pm daily. Museum: **Open** mid-Mar–Oct: 10am–6pm daily (from 9am Jun–Sep). 📷 🄲 (02732) 855 810 to book. 🖥 Ⓦ stiftgoettweig.or.at

Stift Göttweig, a Benedictine abbey, crowns a hilltop on the south bank of the Danube, near Krems. Founded in 1083, it was inhabited by Benedictine monks from St Blasien in the Black Forest from 1094. Stift Göttweig is sometimes referred to as the Austrian Monte Cassino because, superficially, it resembles the Benedictine mother abbey. The abbey was rebuilt after a fire in 1718, according to plans by Johann Lukas von Hildebrandt. The project was never completed, however, and the present abbey has an interesting but somewhat asymmetrical outline, with a Neo-Classical façade. In 1739, a magnificent flight of stairs, known as Kaiserstiege (imperial staircase), was added to the western section of the abbey. The stairs are lined with statues representing the four seasons and the twelve months of the year. Inside, the abbey is adorned with a fresco by Paul Troger, depicting the

Exhibit in the Museum Krems

apotheosis of Karl VI. The abbey has an interesting collection of sculptures, paintings and graphic art. The abbey restaurant affords great views of the surroundings.

## 🄼 Krems

**Road map** F3. 🏔 24,000. 🚌 🚐 🛈 Utzstrasse 1 (02732) 82676. 🎭 Donaufestival (late Apr/early May), Folklore Festival (Jul). Ⓦ krems.gv.at

During the 11th and 12th centuries, Krems, then known as *Chremis*, was a serious rival to Vienna. Today, this attractive town, together with neighbouring Stein, is a popular destination. Visitors are enchanted by the beautiful architecture of its town houses and courtyards, which give Krems a southern, Italian feel. There are remains of the old town walls, but the greatest attraction is the late-Gothic **Piaristenkirche**, an imposing Piarist church built on the foundations of an older church. It boasts a beautiful Baroque altarpiece by the local artist Johann Martin Schmidt, known as Kremser Schmidt. The **Veitskirche**, the parish church of St Veit, is the earliest Baroque church in Austria, the work of Cypriano Biasino. The former Dominican

abbey has a lovely early-Gothic cloister and now houses the **Museum Krems**, with exhibits on the town's history. Krems also has a Renaissance town hall and the vast, 13th-century **Gozzoburg**, a palace built by Judge Gozzo.

The Minoritenkirche, the Church of the Minorite Monks in Stein dates from the same period. It is adorned with 14th-century paintings of the Virgin Mary on a throne. The parish church of St Nicholas has a beautiful altarpiece and ceiling frescoes.

## 🄻 Waldviertel Tour

*See pp144–5.*

## 🄼 Dürnstein

**Road map** F3. 🏔 900. 🚌 🚐 🛈 Dürnstein 25, (2711) 219. Ⓦ duernstein.at

Much of the popularity of the idyllically situated town of Dürnstein is due to the adventures of the English king, Richard the Lionheart. On the Third Crusade, undertaken with the French king Philip August and the Austrian margrave Leopold V, Richard fell out with his fellow crusaders. On his journey home through Babenberg territories, in 1192, he was imprisoned in Kuenringer castle above Dürnstein, whose ruins can still be seen today. As legend has it, the King's faithful French minstrel, Jean Blondel, discovered him with a song known only to the two of them. A ransom of 35,000 kg (77,100 lbs) of silver was paid and Richard released. The Babenbergs used the money to fortify Enns, Hainburg, Wiener Neustadt and Vienna, while the name of the faithful servant lives on in many of Dürnstein's establishments.

The Baroque silhouette of the **Stiftskirche** (collegiate Church of the Assumption of the Virgin Mary) towering above the town was created by the masters of the day. The courtyard is probably the work of Jakob Prandtauer; the entrance is embellished with lovely, decorated portals. The former convent of St Claire is now an inn; the Renaissance castle a hotel.

The Baroque tower of the Stiftskirche in Dürnstein

## ⑬ Weissenkirchen

**Road map** F3. ⛰ 1,500. 🚌 ⛴ ℹ️ (02715) 2600. 🅆 **weissenkirchen.at**

The small village in the heart of the Wachau Valley has attracted artists since 1900, who come to paint the magnificent scenery of the Danube gorge and to enjoy the cosy inns. Today, their works can be seen in the **Wachaumuseum**, in the Teisenhoferhof, a Renaissance mansion. Another attraction is the Wehrkirche Mariä Himmelfahrt (Church of the Assumption of the Virgin Mary), on a hilltop, fortified against Turkish raiders. The well-preserved defence towers are remains of those fortifications. The main entrance to the church is through the western portal, which has fine mouldings. Inside, on the rainbow arch, is a beautiful painting (1520) of the Madonna, from the Danube School.

🏛 **Wachaumuseum**
**Tel** (02715) 2268. **Open** Apr–Oct: 10am–5pm Tue–Sun. 📷

**Environs:** Situated between Weissenkirchen and Spitz is the small village of **St Michael**, with another example of a fortified church. A few miles beyond

Spitz is **Willendorf**, where the famous statuette of the *Venus of Willendorf* was found. This representation of female fertility is believed to be over 25,000 years old. The figure itself is now kept in Vienna's Natural History Museum *(see p86)*, while an over-life-sized copy stands in a field near Willendorf.

## ⑭ Spitz

**Road map** F3. ⛰ 1,600. 🚌 ⛴ ℹ️ Mittergasse 3a, (02713) 23 63.

On the banks of the Danube at the foot of the Tausendeimerberg (thousand bucket hill, so called because of the amount of wine it was said to produce), nestles the enchanting town of Spitz an der Donau. The river was once important to the town's economic life, and the **Schifffahrtsmuseum** explores this history.

Another famous sight is the **Pfarrkirche**, the early-Gothic parish church of St Maurice, furnished in late-Gothic style. The church has a presbytery (1508), crisscross vaulting and elaborate window lacework. The altar painting is by Kremser Schmidt. Lovely wooden statues from around 1380, showing Christ and the apostles, are set in niches along the Gothic gallery.

High above the town looms the ruin of Hinterhaus Castle, with its Gothic bulwark and Renaissance fortifications.

🏛 **Schifffahrtsmuseum**
Auf der Wehr 21. **Tel** (02713) 2246. **Open** Apr–Oct: 10am–noon, 2–4pm Mon–Sat, 10am–4pm Sun & hols.
🅆 **schifffahrtsmuseum-spitz.at**

Remains of the formidable 12th-century Burg Aggstein

## ⑮ Burg Aggstein

**Road map** F3. ⛴

The impressive ruins of Burg Aggstein, built into the rock, are poised high above the banks of the river. Today the castle lies in ruin, but once it measured some 100 m (330 ft) in length, with tall stairs leading to the Upper Castle. Built by the notorious Kuenringers, a band of robber barons, it served to repel attacks by Turks and Swedes during the 16th and 17th centuries, thus cementing its rank as one of the most important fortresses in the region.

Many gruesome stories are told about the castle's early days. Its owner, a notorious thief, was said to have laid in wait for passing barges and demanded a hefty toll to allow them passage. Those who refused to pay were imprisoned in the Rosengärtlein, a rose garden set on a rocky shelf, where they would either die of hunger or jump to their death.

Today, the picturesque Burg Aggstein and its café are popular destinations for a day trip from Vienna.

The romantic ruins of Hinterhaus Castle in Spitz

# ⓫ Waldviertel Tour

Bitterly fought over by Germans and Slavs, who both wanted to settle here and exploit the area's natural resources, Austria's Waldviertel boasts numerous historic sights, from abbeys built as defensive structures to the magnificent residences of the nobility built during times of peace. The wooded region became known as an idyllic spot for hunting trips and excursions, and today it is still its natural beauty and recreational facilities that draw most visitors. The traditional crafts practised in the area's numerous villages are another attraction.

### ① Gmünd
This town, on the Czech border, has a fascinating glass and stone museum. To the north is the Naturpark Blockheide-Eibenstein, with its vast granite rock formations and an unusual open-air exhibition of minerals.

### ② Rosenau
First built in 1590 as a Renaissance palace, Rosenau was remodelled some 150 years later in Baroque style. Its owner, Leopold Schallenberg, set aside some rooms for use as a Masonic lodge; today, it is a Masonic museum.

**Key**

━━━ Suggested route

═══ Other road

――― River, lake

0 kilometres 5

0 miles 5

### ③ Zwettl
This lovely old town boasts several original Baroque houses with interesting pediments. Nearby is one of the region's gems, the magnificent Cistercian monastery (1137–8), with a Gothic church and Baroque interior.

## Tips for Drivers

**Length of the route:** 152 km (94 miles).
**Stopping places:** the tourist office at Zwettl is a useful stop. Sparkenplatz 1. **Tel** (02822 541 09).
**Suggestions:** visits to Altenburg Abbey and Schloss Greillenstein; falconry shows at Schloss Rosenburg.

**⑦ Greillenstein**
Set in woodland in the Kamp river valley, this Renaissance castle features a beautiful arcaded courtyard and has several tall chimneys.

**⑥ Eggenburg**
A small, medieval town, Eggenburg has two attractions: 1,900 m (6,200 ft) of original town walls and towers, and the Rollipop museum, which is dedicated to scooters, motorbikes and tiny cars.

**⑤ Rosenburg**
One of Austria's most famous castles, Schloss Rosenburg was rebuilt in Neo-Classical style after a fire. The former state rooms house a splendid museum of old furniture, paintings and arms.

**④ Altenburg**
This gorgeous Benedictine abbey (1144) has a large library, a treasury and, above all, a crypt entirely covered in stunning ceiling paintings depicting the dance of death.

## Freemasonry in Austria

Francis Stephen, future husband of Maria Theresa, introduced Freemasonry to Austria from Holland. In the late 18th and early 19th centuries, it played a very important role in the Austro-Hungarian Empire, with many prominent politicians and artists being counted among its members. An increasing desire for national self-determination and liberal thought slowly removed the Masons from power. In 1945, the Grand Masonic Lodge of Austria renewed its activities. Today, it has some 2,400 members in 52 lodges, including many public figures, financiers and artists.

Masonic Lodge in Rosenau

# ⑯ Melk Abbey

The town and abbey of Melk, the original seat of the Babenbergs, tower above the left bank of the Danube, some 60 km (37 miles) west of Vienna. In the 11th century, Leopold II invited the Benedictines from Lambach to Melk and granted them land and the castle, which the monks turned into a fortified abbey. Almost completely destroyed by fire in 1297, the abbey was rebuilt many times. In the 16th century, it withstood a Turkish invasion. In 1702, Abbot Berthold Dietmayr began a thorough remodelling of the complex. Jakob Prandtauer, Johann Michael Rottmayr, Joseph Munggenast and other renowned artists of the day helped to give the present abbey its magnificent Baroque form.

**Stairwell**
A spiral staircase with ornamental balustrade connects the library with the Stiftskirche, the monastery church of St Peter and St Paul.

**★ Library**
The impressive library holds some 100,000 volumes, including 2,000 manuscripts and 1,600 incunabula. It is decorated with a beautiful ceiling fresco by Paul Troger.

**Crowning with the Crown of Thorns**
This powerful painting by Jörg Breu (1502) is exhibited in the Abbey Museum.

**KEY**

① The **Marble Hall**, a magnificent room decorated with a painting by Paul Troger, was once used for receptions and ceremonies.

② **Convent courtyard**

③ **17th-century two-tiered fountain**

④ **The grand staircase** leading to the imperial apartments is adorned with putti and sculptures.

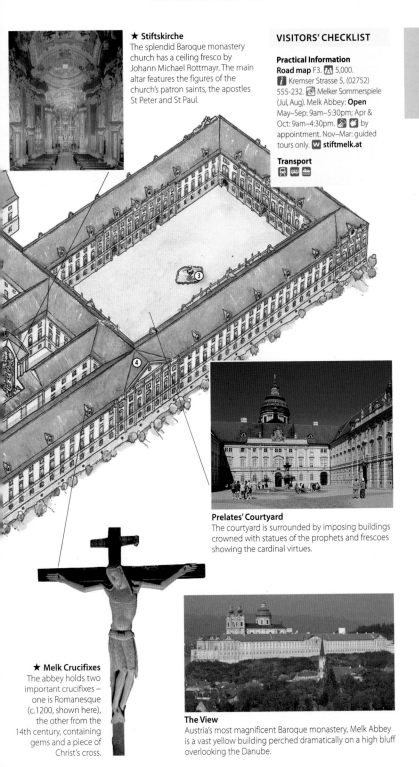

### ★ Stiftskirche
The splendid Baroque monastery church has a ceiling fresco by Johann Michael Rottmayr. The main altar features the figures of the church's patron saints, the apostles St Peter and St Paul.

### VISITORS' CHECKLIST

**Practical Information**
**Road map** F3. 🅼 5,000.
ℹ️ Kremser Strasse 5, (02752) 555-232. 🎭 Melker Sommerspiele (Jul, Aug). Melk Abbey: **Open** May–Sep: 9am–5:30pm; Apr & Oct: 9am–4:30pm. 🅿️ 📷 by appointment. Nov–Mar: guided tours only. 🆆 stiftmelk.at

**Transport**
🚌 🚠 🚤

**Prelates' Courtyard**
The courtyard is surrounded by imposing buildings crowned with statues of the prophets and frescoes showing the cardinal virtues.

### ★ Melk Crucifixes
The abbey holds two important crucifixes – one is Romanesque (c.1200, shown here), the other from the 14th century, containing gems and a piece of Christ's cross.

**The View**
Austria's most magnificent Baroque monastery, Melk Abbey is a vast yellow building perched dramatically on a high bluff overlooking the Danube.

Figure decorating an elevation of Schallaburg Castle

## ⓱ Schloss Schallaburg

**Road map** F3. 🚌 **Tel** (02754) 6317-0. **Open** 9am–5pm Mon–Fri, 9am–6pm Sat, Sun, public holidays. 🅿 🚻 ♿
🌐 **schallaburg.at**

Schallaburg Castle counts as one of the most beautiful Renaissance castles in Lower Austria. It has some early remains of medieval Romanesque and Gothic architecture, but these are overshadowed by later additions. Particularly impressive are the Renaissance courtyard and the two-storey red-and-white terracotta arcades by Jakob Bernecker. Carved terracotta atlantes support the second-storey arcades; sculptures and terracotta masks decorate the lower niches and walls of the castle. One of the best of these is the mask of a court jester holding a wand. Wilhelm von Losenstein, who owned the castle when the arcades were created, was a Protestant and a Humanist, a fact that is reflected in the works commissioned by him.

At the end of World War II, the castle was totally destroyed by the Russians, and it was not until 1970, when it came into state administration, that work began to return it to its former glory.

Today, Schallaburg houses Lower Austria's Cultural and Educational Centre, and serves as a venue for excellent exhibitions and lectures.

## ⓲ Amstetten

**Road map** E3. 🚹 23,000. 🚊 🚌
ℹ **Tel** (07472) 601 454.

A major transport hub, the town of Amstetten is situated on the Ybbs River near the border with Upper Austria. Originally known as Amistein, the town witnessed the arrival of Illyrian, Celts and Roman settlers over time. It is the largest town in the Mostviertel region and boasts an attractive town hall, the 15th-century parish church of St Stephen with frescoes depicting the Last Judgement, and the Gothic church of St Agatha. The **Mostviertler Bauernmuseum**, set in a former farmhouse, covers traditional country life.

🏛 **Mostviertler Bauernmuseum**
Gigerreith 39. **Tel** (07479) 73 34-1.
**Open** call ahead. 🅿 📷

**Environs:** Some 6 km (4 miles) southwest of the town is the medieval **Burg Ulmerfeld**, first recorded in the 10th century. From the 14th century until 1803, the castle belonged to the bishops of Freising. Later transformed into a papermill, it is now an important cultural centre and has a collection of arms.

## ⓳ Waidhofen an der Ybbs

**Road map** E3. 🚹 11,000. 🚊 🚌
**Tel** (07442) 511255. 🌐 **waidhofen.at**

In the 16th century, this little town in the Ybbs valley was an important centre of iron processing and arms production. Its medieval old town is dominated by church spires and two towers, remains of the medieval fortifications. The 13th-century Ybbsturm and the Stadtturm were raised by 50 m (164 ft) in 1534 to celebrate the town's victory over the Turks. Since then, the clock on its north side on Stadtturm has shown 11:45am, the hour of victory. The city's **5e Museum** in Rothschild Castle focuses on the elements that have

Attractive houses and onion-domed spires in Waidhofen an der Ybbs

shaped Waidhofen's history and offers state-of-the-art interactive exhibits.

🏛 **5e Museum**
Oberer Stadtplatz 32. **Tel** (07442) 511 255. **Open** 10am–5pm daily. 📷
🌐 **5e-waidhofen.at**

**Environs:** The Carthusian Marienthron Monastery in **Gaming**, the most important structure of its kind in Central Europe, was founded in 1332 by Prince Albrecht II. The monks' cells and the fortified walls with round turrets remain to this day. Its Baroque library has frescoes by the Prague painter Wenzel Lorenz Reiner, his only work on display outside his Czech homeland. Today, the monastery is used as a venue for cultural events. Containing one of the best Austrian concert halls, it is much-liked by pianists, and the annual Chopin Festival is held at Marienthron in late summer.

The town also has an interesting Baroque church, several early buildings, a St Mary's Column and a pillory.

The Marienthron Monastery in Gaming, seen from the Prelates' Courtyard

# Benedictine Abbeys

Benedictine monasticism was established in the 6th century, in Italy, by St Benedict of Nursia, and its mother abbey was Monte Cassino. The first Benedictine abbey in Austria was founded in the 8th century, in Salzburg, but it was not until the 11th century that the order became a major force. Its growth was linked to the increased importance given to the Austrian state under the rule of the Babenbergs, whose history was chronicled by the Benedictines. Fortified abbeys were built on unassailable hilltops, and rural settlements grew up in the shadow, and under the protection of, the abbeys. The beautiful silhouettes of the abbey buildings tower over their surroundings. Stunningly decorated inside, they boast marvellous libraries that house outstanding records of the past.

**Altenburg Abbey** *(see p145),* from the 12th century, was altered in Baroque style in the 18th century. Its façade is adorned with statues and paintings.

**Kremsmünster Abbey** *(see p204)* contains a tombstone with the figure of Knight Gunther. The inscription tells the legend of how his father founded the abbey in 777, following his son's death.

**St Paul im Lavanttal Abbey** *(see p272)* houses one of the most extensive Benedictine libraries, with over 40,000 volumes and manuscripts.

**The grand imperial staircase in Stift Göttweig** *(see p142),* lined with statues, was designed by F. A. Pilgram in 1739.

**The family tree** of the Babenberg dynasty, who brought the Benedictine monks to their seat in the stunning monastery of Melk, can be studied in Klosterneuburg Abbey *(see p138),* just outside Vienna.

**In front of the Stiftskirche in Melk** *(see pp146–7),* one of the most magnificent abbeys in Austria, a terrace extends affording fabulous views far across the Danube and the surrounding countryside.

## ⑳ Neuhofen an der Ybbs

**Road map** E3. 🚶 2,900. 🚌
ℹ️ (07475) 52700-40.
🌐 neuhofen-ybbs.at

Neuhofen is a small town on the Ybbs river, in the foothills of the Alps. Its centre is occupied by a Gothic church with a tall spire. The town was once a stopping place for pilgrims travelling to nearby Sonntagberg, whose Baroque basilica is an important place of worship for Austrian Catholics.

Today, the **Ostarrichi Kulturhof**, a museum of Austrian history on the outskirts of the village, is the town's top attraction. The modern building was erected in 1980 to designs by Ernst Beneder, who also landscaped the surroundings in an attempt to make new and old blend in a single composition. The museum was built in record time, at a cost of 28.8 million shillings, and in 1996 it was the focus of Austria's 1,000th anniversary celebrations.

The most important exhibit, from which the centre has taken its name, is the facsimile of a document which first mentions the term *Ostarrichi* (the original document is kept in archives in Munich). In this document, dated 1 November 996, Emperor Otto III, ruler of

Facsimile of the AD 996 document, Ostarrichi Kulturhof, Neuhofen an der Ybbs

the German Roman Empire, presented the land around Niuvanhof (present-day Neuhofen), known as *Ostarrichi* in the local language, to Gottschalk, bishop of Freising in Bavaria. It was the first time that this name was used to describe the land that was controlled by the Babenbergs and which eventually, in the 11th–12th centuries, would become Austria. The bishops of Freising had owned estates in this district from as early as the 9th century, and they regularly toured their territories. The names "Osterriche" and "Osterland", which appeared later, referred to the land east of the Enns river. It is fairly likely that originally the name referred to the entire country of Eastern Franconia. With time, Niuvanhof became Neuhofen and, if etymologists are to be believed, the present name of Austria (Österreich) derives from

*Ostarrichi*. According to the most widely believed interpretation, it meant "eastern territories", but an alternative view also exists: at the time when the name *Ostarrichi* first appeared, the area in this part of the Danube valley was still populated by Slav tribes, and the names of many surrounding towns and villages reveal a Slav origin. It is possible that *Ostarrichi*, as it was then, comes from the Slav word "ostrik", meaning a hill.

Whichever interpretation is accurate, the year 996 is recognized here as the beginning of Austrian history, and the Neuhofen Museum informatively presents the story of the remarkable rise of a small German duchy to the heights of European power as the multi-ethnic Habsburg Empire, and the tangled web of history that eventually, in 1918, led to the creation of the Austrian Republic.

The permanent exhibition in the Kulturhof consists of three parts. The first shows a facsimile of the *Ostarrichi* document in the original Latin version and in its German translation, together with photographs. The second exhibition is devoted to the etymological changes that the term has gone through, including its geographical, linguistic and political transformations. The third part of the exhibition is devoted to present-day Austria and its provinces. It illustrates how the distinct areas grew together into the Austrian Republic of today, and how each province has managed to preserve its own regional identity, customs, traditions, arts and culture.

🏛️ **Ostarrichi Kulturhof**
Millenniumsplatz 1. **Tel** (07475) 52700-40. **Open** mid-Apr–Oct: 9am–noon Mon, Tue, Thu & Fri; 10am–noon, 1–5pm Sat, Sun & hols.
🌐 ostarrichi-kulturhof.at

Gothic church in the centre of Neuhofen an der Ybbs

# ㉑ Schneeberg Tour

Both the Schneeberg and Raxalpen mountain ranges are popular with the Viennese for short winter breaks. Situated some 100 km (60 miles) from the capital, they offer excellent and well-developed skiing areas as well as many attractive walking trails for summer outings. The world's first high-mountain railway line was laid here, through the town of Semmering. To this day a ride on the railway is a thrilling experience.

## Tips for Drivers

**Length of route:** 130 km (80 miles). **Stopping places:** hotels and restaurants can be found in Puchberg, Semmering, and at the upper station on Schneeberg. **Suggestions:** ride on the railway from Puchberg to Schneeberg (mid-Apr–Oct).
ℹ️ (02742) 360 99 099.
🌐 **schneebergbahn.at**

④ **Schneeberg**
The highest peak in the range and in Lower Austria, whose distinctive silhouette is clearly visible from the motorway between Vienna and Graz, rises to 2,076 m (6,811 ft). The summit affords magnificent views of the Raxalpe range.

⑤ **Höllental – Hell Valley**
The ravine along the Schwarza river starts from the slopes of Hirschwang, where the world's first cable car was built in 1926.

① **Puchberg am Schneeberg**
A rack-railway links Schneeberg with Puchberg, a popular resort which also boasts an old castle.

⑥ **Semmering**
A popular health resort since the early 19th century, this town is known for its long sunshine hours, great views and interesting architecture.

### Key

━━ Suggested route
━━ Scenic road
══ Other road
┈┈ River, lake

0 kilometres    5
0 miles         5

② **Neunkirchen**
One of the oldest towns in Lower Austria, Neunkirchen has original Renaissance buildings and a church with late-Romanesque details.

③ **Ternitz**
This small town, in the Sierningbach valley, is a resort as well as a nature reserve. It has a modern church with a large mosaic.

**For keys to symbols** *see back flap*

## ㉒ Burg Forchtenstein

**Road map** G3. 🚌 Mattersburg. 🚌
ℹ️ Hauptstrasse 31, (02626) 631 23.
Castle: **Tel** (02626) 81212. **Open** Apr–
Oct: 10am–6pm daily; Nov–Mar:
groups by appointment. 🎫
🌐 **esterhazy.at**

Perched unassailably on the
rocky slopes of Rosaliengebirge
stands Forchtenstein Castle,
built in the 14th century by
the Mattersdorfer family.
Bought and extended by the
Esterházys, it now houses a
magnificent and extensive
private collection of arms. The
castle armoury exhibits arms
and war trophies dating from
the 16th to the 19th centuries
as well as memorabilia and
pictures from the wars with
Turkey, France and Prussia.
Forchtenstein Castle was one of
the fortresses that defended
the Habsburg state during the
Turkish raids of 1529 and 1683.
Other trophies from that period
include a captured Turkish tent,
one of the most interesting
exhibits, and a tank, dug 142 m
(466 ft) deep into the castle
courtyard by the captive Turks.
There are also vast paintings
of battle scenes. Having played
its part in repelling the Turkish
threat, the heavily fortified
castle became a museum
in 1815.

The equestrian statue in the
courtyard is of Paul, the first
prince of the Esterházy family,
which still owns the castle

The birthplace of Franz Liszt in Raiding, near Forchtenstein

today. In summer the castle
hosts a popular festival.

**Environs:** In the village of
Raiding, 24 km (15 miles) to
the south of Forchtenstein, is a
lovely cottage, the birthplace
of the composer Franz Liszt.
The house is now a museum,
the **Liszt-Haus**. Every March,
Raiding hosts the Liszt Festival,
a celebration of Liszt's music.

### 🏛 Liszt-Haus

Lisztstrasse 46. **Tel** (02619) 510 47-16.
**Open** mid-Mar–May: 9am–5pm Tue–
Sat; Jun–mid-Nov: 9am–5pm Mon–
Sat, 10am–5pm Sun & hols.

## ㉓ Neusiedler See

*See pp156–7.*

## ㉔ Eisenstadt

*See pp158–9.*

## ㉕ Bruck an der Leitha

**Road map** G3. 🚗 7,500. 🚉 🚌
ℹ️ Hauptplatz 16, (02162) 622 21.

This small town, situated 30 km
(19 miles) east of Vienna, was
established as a Babenberg
fortress in 1230, and formed
the main border point between
Austria and Hungary. Its present
form dates mainly from the turn
of the 17th century, but the
remains of the medieval
fortifications from the 13th
century, as well as several old
houses, remain in the main
square today.

In this square, the Hauptplatz,
there is an attractive town hall
with a Rococo balcony and an
arcaded courtyard. Also here is
the Baroque Pfarrkirche, built by
Heinrich Hoffmann. In Friedrich-
Schiller-Gasse stands the

The imposing 14th-century Burg Forchtenstein on the slopes of Rosaliengebirge

◀ The tranquil waters of Neusiedler See, in Burgenland

Kapuzinerkloster, the Capuchin Friary, with its church dating from 1629.

The town's greatest architectural attraction, however, is the Prugg, a 13th-century castle with an original early-Gothic turret. In 1707, Johan Lukas von Hildebrandt altered the castle in the Baroque style. The chapel also dates from this period.

The Stadtmuseum Ungarturm, located in a 13th-century tower on Burgenlandstrasse, exhibits prehistoric and Roman finds, along with armaments and handicrafts. It also provides background on the town's past.

## ㉖ Rohrau

**Road map** G3. ㊂ 1,600.
㊂ Bad Deutsch Altenburg, Petronell.

East of Vienna lies the small town of Rohrau, with two attractions: Haydn's birthplace and the Harrach family castle, **Schloss Rohrau**. The pretty house in which the composer and his brother Michael were born, is now a small museum, the **Haydn-Geburtshaus**, devoted to both composers.

The nearby Schloss Rohrau contains beautiful private art galleries with a splendid collection of 17th- and 18th-century paintings, mainly from Spain and Naples, but also some work from the Netherlands. The castle dates from the 16th century but was rebuilt in the 18th century.

▥ **Haydn-Geburtshaus**
**Tel** (02164) 2268. **Open** 10am–4pm Tue–Sun & hols. **Closed** 1 Jan, 24 Dec.
㊂ ⓦ haydngeburtshaus.at

⌂ **Schloss Rohrau**
**Tel** (02164) 2253 16. **Open** Easter–Oct: 10am–5pm Fri–Sun. ㊂
ⓦ schloss-rohrau.at

## ㉗ Hainburg

**Road map** G3. ㊂ 6,000. ㊂
ⓘ Ungarstrasse 3, (02165) 62 111 23.

Hainburg on the Danube was once a fortified border town of the Eastern Margravate, and it is still a gateway into Austria from the east. The ruins of an

Heathen's Gate in the Carnuntum Archaeological Park near Hainburg

11th- century castle and three substantial town gates remain from this period. The small town has many historic sights, such as the Romanesque cemetery chapel and the Rococo Mary Column in Hauptplatz. The best way to travel to Hainburg is along the Danube. The marshy area around the town is a nature reserve, and home to rare bird species no longer seen elsewhere. The area west of Hainburg is preserved as a nature reserve.

**Environs:** 38 km (24 miles) east of Vienna is the village of Petronell-Carnuntum, where archaeologists unearthed a Roman town, Carnuntum, and the remains of a military camp.

The sights open to visitors in the **Carnuntum Archaeological Park** include a Roman triumphal arch known as Heidentor (Heathens' gate), public baths, a reconstructed town villa and two huge amphitheatres. The ruins of ancient Carnuntum, the former

capital of the Roman province of Pannonia, extend to nearby Bad Deutsch-Altenburg, where many of the unearthed objects are on display in the **Museum Carnuntinum**.

🏛 **Carnuntum Archaeological Park**
ⓘ Petronell Carnuntum, Hauptstrasse 296, (02163) 33 77-0. **Open** mid-Mar–mid-Nov: 9am–5pm daily. ㊂
ⓦ carnuntum.co.at

▥ **Museum Carnuntinum**
Bad Deutsch-Altenburg, Badgasse 40–46. **Tel** (02163) 33 77-0. **Open** mid-Mar–mid-Nov: 9am–6pm daily. ㊂
ⓦ carnuntum.co.at

## ㉘ Schloss Hof

**Road map** G3. **Tel** (02285) 20 000. ㊂ from Marchegg. **Open** mid-Mar–Oct: 10am–6pm daily. ㊂ (for families).
ⓦ schlosshof.at

Schloss Hof has long been an appealing excursion from Vienna. From 1725 Prince Eugene of Savoy made the palace into his principal country seat and laid out a formal country garden that survives to this day.

Extended a generation later under Empress Maria Theresa, the palace contains state and private rooms from both these periods. The Schloss Hof complex also includes an idyllic estate farm with herb gardens, craft workshops and numerous attractions for the young, such as animal enclosures, and pony and carriage rides.

The Danube snaking through Hainburg

# ⓑ Neusiedler See

The jewel of Burgenland, Neusiedler See is the largest steppe lake in Central Europe. On the border between Austria and Hungary (a small section – around one-fifth of its total area – at the southern end belongs to Hungary), it covers an area of 320 sq km (124 sq miles) and has no natural in- or outlets apart from the Wulka river. The water is slightly saline and never more than 2 m (6½ ft) deep, so it warms up quickly in summer. The banks are densely overgrown with reeds, which make ideal nesting grounds for birds, while the lakeside beaches are popular with visitors. In 2001, the lake and the surrounding countryside were declared a World Heritage Site by UNESCO.

**Neusiedler See**
Neusiedler See, Vienna's "seaside", attracts visitors with its wide range of water sports facilities and enchanting, melancholy landscapes.

**★ Rust**
This attractive town on the western lake-shore has a perfectly preserved old town with many Renaissance and Baroque buildings. Star sights include the town hall and Fischerkirche.

*Eisenstadt* ←

*Wien (Vienna)* ↖

• Purbach

Rust

Neusiedler See

**Mörbisch am See**

• Klingenbach

• Sopron

Keszthely ↘

**Mörbisch am See**
Situated on the border with Hungary, this village produces an excellent white wine. Its charming, whitewashed houses, laden with flowers, create a truly unique atmosphere.

### Neusiedl am See
A well-known resort and agricultural centre, Neusiedl is situated at the northern end of Neusiedler See. It has a museum devoted to local fauna and flora, and a small ruin.

## VISITORS' CHECKLIST

**Practical Information**
**Road map** G3.
Rust (02685) 502; Neusiedl am See (02167) 2229; Illmitz, National Park Information Centre (02175) 3442; Neusiedlersee Tourismus (02167) 8600.
w neusiedlersee.com

**Transport**

### ★ Podersdorf
With its access to the water unencumbered by the wide band of reeds that separates other villages from the lake, and with swimming, boating and windsurfing facilities, Podersdorf is the most popular resort on the lake's eastern shores.

### Illmitz
Situated amid the marshes of the Seewinkel national park, this is a good base for exploring the surrounding grass- and wetlands.

### Seewinkel
This national park, a naturalist's paradise of reedbeds, small lakes and marshes, is home to over 250 different bird species.

**Key**
- ▬▬ Motorway
- ─── Major road
- ─── Minor road
- ▪ ▬ Walking route
- ▬▪▬ National border
- ─── River

0 kilometres    5

0 miles    5

# ㉔ Eisenstadt

This small town lies on the southern slopes of the Leitha hills, 50 km (31 miles) south of Vienna. It became the capital of Burgenland province in 1925, when international border adjustments put the larger and more notable Ödenburg – today the town of Sopron – in Hungary. From this date Eisenstadt underwent a remarkable growth, and today it is an important transport hub and wine-making centre. The town is mainly associated with the Hungarian Esterházy family and their famous choirmaster, Joseph Haydn. Another great musician, Franz Liszt, was born on the Esterházys' estate, in the village of Raiding *(see p154)*.

Ornamental grille on Joseph Haydn's tomb in the Bergkirche

## Exploring Eisenstadt

Above all, Eisenstadt is the town of Haydn, and the main tourist trails retrace his footsteps. Most of the town's historic sights are clustered around the inner town centre, south of Schlosspark. Only the Bergkirche, with its calvary, and the Jewish quarter of Unterberg are situated further to the west.

### 🏛 Bergkirche

Joseph-Haydn-Platz 1. Haydnmausoleum: **Open** Apr–Oct: 9am–5pm daily. 🖼

In 1715, Prince Paul Esterházy ordered a hill to be created to the west of the castle and of Eisenstadt's centre. He then had a church built on top of that hill, dedicated to the Visitation of the Virgin Mary, with a Way of the Cross made up of 24 stations. The Passion figures are life-size and each tableau stands in a specially laid out room. The rather theatrical, Baroque-style figures are carved from wood or stone. The north tower of the church contains the most-visited attraction of the church: the tomb of Joseph Haydn. In 1932, on the 200th anniversary of the composer's death, a small mausoleum was built here by the Esterházys for the marble sarcophagus containing Haydn's remains.

### 🕎 Jüdischer Friedhof

Unterbergstrasse. Jewish Museum: Unterbergstrasse 6. **Tel** (02682) 65145. **Open** May–Oct: 10am–5pm Tue–Sun; Nov–May: 9am–4pm Mon–Thu, 9am–1pm Fri; groups only. **Closed** 24 Dec–6 Jan.

From medieval times until 1938, a Jewish settlement existed in Eisenstadt. Confined to the district of Unterberg, it played an important role in the city's development. Inhabitants of the district included the Chief Rabbi of the Hungarian Jewry, banker Samson Wertheimer, and Sandor Wolf, a famous art collector. Eisenstadt was one of a handful of towns where old traditions were still observed, such as the closing of the district for Sabbath, and the chains that were once used for that purpose are preserved to this day. The two Jewish cemeteries in Eisenstadt are among the best-preserved in Austria. The adjacent house, which once belonged to Samson Wertheimer, now houses the Jewish Museum.

### 🏛 Landesmuseum Burgenland

Museumgasse 1–5. **Tel** (02682) 719-4000. **Open** Timings vary, check website for opening times. 🌐 landesmuseum-burgenland.at

This museum houses a large collection of objects associated with the history and art of the Burgenland province. Its geological collection comprises minerals and exhibits on the local Ice Age fauna. Archaeological findings include the Drassburg Venus, items from burial mounds in Siegendorf and objects which represent the Hallstatt and Roman cultures.

### 🏰 Schloss Esterházy

Esterházyplatz. **Tel** (02682) 63 004-7600. **Open** May–Sep: 10am–6pm daily; Apr & Oct: 10am–5pm daily; Nov–Mar: 10am–5pm Fri–Sun & hols. 🖼 🖼 🌐 esterhazy.at

The Esterházy Castle was built around 1390, on the site of earlier fortifications, remains of which were discovered in the course of excavations. In 1663–72, Carlo Martino Carlone transformed the castle into a magnificent Baroque palace. The main attraction inside is the Haydnsaal, a concert hall beautifully decorated with frescoes and boasting truly

Tombstones in one of the Jewish cemeteries in Unterberg

Prince's apartments in Esterházy Castle

amazing acoustics. Joseph Haydn once used to conduct the castle orchestra here.

Today, the larger part of the castle is leased to the Burgenland provincial authorities. The castle is surrounded by a beautiful English-style park.

### 🏛 Domkirche
Domplatz 1a.

This late-Gothic church was built in the 15th century on the site of an earlier medieval structure. As with many other churches in this part of Austria, its builders were conscious of the permanent threat of Turkish invasion, and its lofty steeple contains lookout holes on all sides.

The eclectically decorated interior features some medieval tombstones and a relief in the church's vestibule depicting the Mount of Olives. The pulpit and the beautiful organ are Baroque, as are the two altar paintings by German-born artist, Stephan Dorfmeister. The large bronze sculpture of the Pietà is the work of Anton Hanak. The Domkirche was given cathedral status in 1960.

### 🏛 Franziskanerkirche
Joseph-Haydn-Gasse.

The Franciscan church of St Michael was built between 1625 and 1630. Most of its interior hails from a later period, but the magnificent reliefs in the altarpiece date from 1630. Beneath the church you will find the crypt of the powerful local dynasty, the Esterházy family.

### 🏛 Haydn-Haus
Joseph-Haydn-Gasse 21. **Tel** (02682) 719 6000. **Open** Apr & May: Tue–Sat; Jun–mid-Nov: daily. 🅿
### 🌐 haydn-haus.at

The house where Joseph Haydn lived between 1766 and 1778 is now a small museum displaying a number of the composer's possessions. From 1761, Haydn was employed by the Esterházy family as their *Kapellmeister*

(music director), and in the evenings he conducted the court orchestra for performances of his own music. Many of his beautiful compositions were first heard in Eisenstadt.

Haydn's home for 12 years, now a museum devoted to the composer

---

## Eisenstadt City Centre

① Bergkirche
② Jüdischer Friedhof
③ Landesmuseum Burgenland
④ Schloss Esterházy
⑤ Domkirche
⑥ Franziskanerkirche
⑦ Haydn-Haus

0 metres       250
0 yards        250

# STYRIA

Austria's second-largest province, in the country's southeast, Styria has a population of 1.2 million. It is dominated by forests, meadows and vineyards covering some three-quarters of its total area of 16,387 sq km (6,327 sq miles). It is also an area of iron ore extraction and processing, and Erzberg (Iron Ore Mountain), glittering in every hue of red and brown, is a major tourist attraction.

Iron ore was first extracted by the Romans, who named this part of Austria the Roman province of Noricum. The mineral shaped the history of the province through the centuries, and its traces survive to this day. Following the highs and lows of the early Middle Ages, Styria fell into the hands of the Habsburg dynasty in the 13th century and shared in its fate and fortunes. The province was repeatedly ravaged by Hungarians and Turks, and, after having staved off the Turkish threat in the 17th century, also became susceptible to attacks by the French.

A legacy of these times are its numerous hilltop castle strongholds and imposing fortified abbeys. Some have survived intact, others have been meticulously restored to their former splendour to capture the imagination of visitors to the region.

Styria's great attractions include the south-facing slopes of Raxalpen, its gentle climate and its rural idylls – it is known as "the green heart" of Austria. In the west, along its border with the Salzburger Land, the area is dominated by the lofty peaks of the Salzburg Alps and Lower Tauern. Here you will find excellent winter sport centres around Schladming, and at the foot of Dachstein, the highest peak in the region, with the best cross-country-skiing trails.

The Salzkammergut in the north is a stunningly beautiful lake district. The province's main rivers are the Mur, which flows through Graz, its tributary the Mürz, and the Salza.

Bad Blumau, an architectural complex based on Friedensreich Hundertwasser's designs

◀ Steep, terraced vineyards near Gamlitz

# Exploring Styria

Styria, or Steiermark, is rich in attractions and its capital, Graz, is Austria's second-largest city. The west of the province offers excellent winter sports facilities; in the north lie the beautiful Mur and Mürz valleys, and many lakes. The quiet, agricultural southeast is covered with vineyards. Special sights are the National Austrian Open-Air Museum in Stübing, the Lipizzaner stud in Piber, and the Mariazell Basilica, the country's largest Marian sanctuary.

Tobacco, one of the products grown in eastern Styria

One of the grand villas in the spa town of Bad Gleichenberg

*For hotels and restaurants in this region see pp295–6 and pp318–20*

## Getting There

Graz has an international airport, Flughafen Graz-Thalerhof. The Province of Styria extends either side of the main road and rail connections crossing Austria from north to south. Local rail and road networks are also well developed.

Watermill in Mureck, on the Mur river

Statue of St Roch in the Wine Museum in Kitzeck, near Graz

### Key

━━━ Motorway
━━━ Major road
┈┈┈ Minor road
━━━ Scenic route
▬▬▬ Main railway
┈┈┈ Minor railway
▬▬▬ International border
━━━ Province border
△ Summit

## Sights at a Glance

1 Graz pp164–9
2 Stübing pp170–71
3 Lurgrotte
4 Frohnleiten
5 Bruck an der Mur
6 Mürzzuschlag
7 Vorau
8 Pöllau
9 Schloss Herberstein
10 Bad Blumau
11 Schloss Riegersburg

12 Bad Gleichenberg
13 Bad Radkersburg
15 Piber
16 Judenburg
17 St Lambrecht
18 Turracher Höhe
19 Murau
20 Oberwölz
21 Schladminger Tauern pp182–3
22 Ramsau
23 Bad Aussee

24 Admont
25 Hohentauern
26 Eisenerzer Alpen
27 Seckau
28 Leoben
30 Mariazell Basilica pp188–9

### Tours

14 Steirische Weinstrasse Tour pp176–7
29 Salzatal Tour pp186–7

For keys to symbols see back flap

# ❶ Graz: Street-by-Street

Graz, the capital of Styria, is the second largest city in Austria. During the Middle Ages it was the seat of a junior branch of the Habsburg family, and later of Emperor Friedrich III. The legacy of the Habsburgs is Graz's lovely Altstadt (Old Town), one of the best preserved in Central Europe and a UNESCO World Heritage Site. Graz was also a stronghold against Turkish incursions.

The modern city extends from the foot of Schlossberg (Castle Mountain), on both sides of the Mur river. Graz is famed for its universities, architecture, cultural attractions and culinary traditions. It hosts two classical music festivals each year, one in the summer at the Music College and the "Styriarte", as well as the avant-garde "Styrian Autumn".

**Haus am Luegg**
This town house at Nos 11 & 12 Hauptplatz (c.1690) has a striking façade, with Renaissance frescoes and early Baroque stucco work.

**Rathaus**
The new town hall, built in the late 19th century on the southern side of Rathausplatz, replaced the smaller Renaissance palace that had previously occupied the same site.

**Hauptplatz**
The Old Town's triangular main square is surrounded by 17th-century town houses.

FÄRBERGASSE

HERRENGASSE

ALBRECHTGASSE

LANDHAUSGASSE

SCHMIEDGASSE

**★ Landhaus**
The inner courtyard of this government building has three magnificent storeys of arcaded Renaissance galleries.

**★ Landeszeughaus**
The jewel of this old armoury, the largest in the world that has been preserved intact, is the collection of weapons from Austria's 16th- and 17th-century Turkish wars (see pp168–9).

**Key**

— Suggested route

**Burg**

The impressive double spiral staircase was built in 1499 on the orders of Maximilian I. He extended this vast Gothic castle built by his father, Friedrich III, who had made Graz one of his three capitals.

**VISITORS' CHECKLIST**

**Practical Information**
Road map F4.
275,000.
Graz Tourismus, Herrengasse 16, Graz, (0316) 8075-0.
Styriarte (mid Jun–mid Jul); Springfestivale (mid Jun).
graztourism.at

**Transport**

**Dom**

The beautifully carved reliquary chests in the choir of the cathedral were originally made to hold the dowry of Paola di Gonzaga, duchess of Mantua.

★ **Mausoleum**

The tomb of Emperor Ferdinand II, built next to the cathedral in 1614–38, is considered a perfect example of the Mannerist style in Austrian architecture.

0 metres 100
0 yards 100

View of the city of Graz and the Mur river from the Clock Tower

### Exploring Graz

The city is built on both banks of the Mur river; the Altstadt, with most of the tourist sights, is on the left bank. It can be reached by tram from the railway and bus stations. The Island in the Mur is Graz's newest attraction.

### 🏰 Schlossberg

Hofgasse.

At the north of the Altstadt rises the 473-m- (1,552-ft-) high Schlossberg. The top is reached by a funicular or by a 20-minute walk. The 28-m- (92-ft-) high Clock Tower (1561), a symbol of Graz, offers splendid views over the city. It houses a museum.

### 🏛 Dom

Hofgasse.

The cathedral is a former castle church, built between 1439 and 1464 for Emperor Friedrich III. Its west portal bears the emperor's coat of arms and his famous motto, AEIOU (see pp42–3). Originally, the cathedral was built as a defensive church on the outskirts of town. It has survived almost intact to this day and the interior still features some original elements, including Gothic frescoes showing life during the plague, although most of the decorations stem from the Baroque period.

### 🏛 Franziskanerkirche

Franziskanerplatz.

This church once belonged to the Minorite friars, but in 1515 it was handed over to the Franciscans. Inside, the St James's chapel dates from 1320–30, and there are also Gothic cloisters with beautiful tombstones. The interior was redesigned after World War II, and the combination of the restored vault and modern stained-glass windows with earlier details creates a very striking effect. Next to the church is a monastery with a distinctive tower. Both the church and the monastery are in an unusually shaped square, surrounded by many interesting buildings with Baroque façades.

### 🏛 Hauptplatz

The triangular square at the heart of the Old Town is an excellent starting point for exploring the city of Graz. It is surrounded by many original town houses from different periods, including the famous Haus am Luegg, with its Renaissance and Baroque façade decorations. To the north of the

Hauptplatz, the distinctive triangular main square in Graz's centre

square, at No. 4, stands Graz's oldest pharmacy, in a house dating from 1534 with some earlier features. The south side of the square is occupied by the neo-Renaissance town hall, built in the 1880s. In the middle of the square stands the fountain of Archduke Johann, who contributed much to the city's development. The four female figures around it symbolize Styria's four main rivers: the Mur, the Enns, the Drau and the Sann.

### 🏛 Universalmuseum Joanneum

Old Gallery Schloss Eggenberg: *see below*. **Tel** (0316) 8017 9560. New Gallery: Joanneumviertel entrance Kalchberggasse. **Tel** (0316) 8017 9100. **Open** 10am–5pm Tue–Sun. Schloss Eggenberg: Eggenberger Allee 90. **Open** Apr–Oct: 10am–5pm Wed–Sun; Nov–Mar: Sun & hols as part of a tour.
**w** museum-joanneum.at

The memory of Archduke Johann remains alive in Graz to this day. The grandson of Maria Theresa, he played an important role in the political life of the country and participated in military campaigns, until he finally settled in Graz to devote time to his favourite pursuit of scientific research. He founded the Technical University as well as the Joanneum, Austria's first public museum, which is named after him. Today the Joanneum has 17 departments and holds several exhibitions, some bequeathed by the archduke.

The Old Gallery, the most interesting display, is located in the lovely Baroque Eggenberg Palace, 3 km (2 miles) west of Graz, and contains some magnificent medieval paintings by Cranach, Pieter Bruegel the Younger, and Styrian 17th- and 18th-century artists. A collection of coins and medals is also to be found there. The most valuable exhibit in the museum is the Strettweg chariot, which dates from the 7th century BC. The Natural History Museum provides an insight into the geological and mineralogical history of Styria.

The New Gallery, a collection of 19th- and 20th-century paintings, drawings and sculptures,

The Italianate galleried courtyard of the Landhaus

previously housed in the Rococo Herberstein Palace, is now part of the Joanneum Quarter.

### Landhaus
Herrengasse 16.
The Landhaus, one of the most beautiful Renaissance buildings in Styria, was once the seat of the Styrian diet, which under Habsburg rule also covered areas that are now part of Slovenia and Italy. Today it houses the provincial parliament.

The building was altered in the 16th century by the Italian military architect Domenico dell'Allio. The stairs on the north-western side of the courtyard are the work of another Italian, Bartolomeo di Bosio. The front, with its loggia and vast arched windows, is in the Venetian style. Well worth seeing is the beautiful courtyard, with its three storeys of balustraded galleries linked by a raised walkway, and a fountain topped with a forged bronze cupola. In summer months it serves as a venue for festival events. Inside the Landhaus is the Baroque Landtag conference room, which has beautifully carved doors crowned by allegorical scenes, and ceiling stucco work by Johann Fromentini, depicting scenes from Styrian history. Also worth seeing is the Knight's Hall, which was decorated by the same artist.

### Mausoleum
Hofgasse.
This small building, commissioned by Emperor Ferdinand II (1578–1637) as a tomb for himself and his family, is one of the most unusual and

magnificent in Graz. A devout Catholic, the emperor became especially notorious for the extremely harsh measures he took to introduce the Counter-Reformation in his territories, as well as for provoking the outbreak of the Thirty Years' War.

The mausoleum is one of the foremost examples of Austrian Mannerism, successfully blending various different styles. It was designed by an Italian architect, Pietro de Pomis, and completed by another Italian, Pietro Valnegro, who also built the belfry by the eastern apse. Its narrow façade, exuberantly decorated with sculptures, consists of several architectural planes that create an exceptionally harmonious composition. The interior design is the work of Johann Bernhard Fischer von Erlach, who was born in Graz and began his life and career here.

### Palais Attems
Sackstrasse 17.
Palais Attems is the city's most attractive Baroque palace. Built in 1702–16, it was designed by

Johann Joachim Carlone. The palace's main features are its monumental staircase with frescoes and stucco ornaments, and its richly ornamented façades (inside and out, beyond the drive). The uniform furnishing of the rooms, with ceiling stuccos and lovely fireplaces and tiled stoves, is testimony to the Austrian aristocracy's standard of living during the Baroque period.

### Grazer Congress
Albrechtgasse 1. **Tel** (0316) 8088-400.
Next to the town hall stands an old palace which, in 1980, was transformed into a modern congress centre with multiple facilities for arts performances. The building has two magnificent conference suites as well as contemporary entertainment venues furnished with state-of-the art technology. It also houses the city's largest concert hall, the Stefaniensaal.

### Kunsthaus Graz
Lendkail 1. **Tel** (316) 801 792 00
**Open** Tue–Sun 10am–5pm
**W** kunsthausgraz.at
This gallery opened in 2003 in conjunction with Graz's year as European Capital of Culture. Owing to its "biomorphous" construction, using organic cellulose materials, and striking modern blue structure, it has been nicknamed the "friendly alien", and has become an attraction in itself, thanks in part to its riverside setting. Exhibitions are wildly eclectic – from Japanese woodcuts to street theatre – but the main focus is on contemporary art post-1960.

Kunsthaus Graz, known as the "friendly alien"

# Landeszeughaus

The Landeszeughaus, or armoury, was built between 1642 and 1645 as a stock of arms to be handed to the local population in the fight against the Turks. Graz was in the vanguard of defending and guarding access to the threatened Austrian provinces of Styria, Carinthia and Carniola, which gave its armoury great importance. With a collection of over 32,000 objects, the Graz armoury today ranks as the world's best-preserved early arsenal. The museum's beautiful Renaissance façade was designed by the Italian Antonio Solar.

**Minerva Statue**
The Minerva statue in a niche to the right of the entrance, like the Mars statue on the left, is the work of Giovanni Mamolo.

**17th-century Muskets**
These front-loading firearms, with smooth barrels, were widely used in Europe throughout the 16th and 17th centuries.

## Museum Guide

*The first floor is devoted to heavy guns, flintlock pistols and rifles. The second floor holds the store of armour used by infantry and cavalry units, and pistols. The third floor displays the armour used by nobles and in tournaments. The fourth floor is devoted to staffs and edged weapons. The cloakroom, toilets and museum shop are located on the ground floor.*

**Cannons**
The first-floor exhibition includes field guns and old naval deck guns.

**Wheel-lock Pistol**
This type of pistol, with a spherical barrel-end, was introduced to the German and Austrian cavalries in the 17th century.

★ **Helmets**
Most of the 16th-century helmets adorning the third floor ceiling were made in the Nuremberg and Augsburg workshops.

**VISITORS' CHECKLIST**

**Practical Information**
Herrengasse 16.
**Tel** (0316) 80179810.
**Open** Apr–Oct: 10am–5pm
Tue–Mon; Nov–Mar: admission
only during a guided tour at 1pm
Tue–Mon. **Closed** 24 & 25 Dec.
w landeszeughaus.at

★ **Hungarian Sabres**
The 16th-century sabres are the pride of the side-arms collection exhibited on the fourth floor.

**Fluted Armour**
Made in a Nuremberg workshop during the 16th century, this suit of armour is one of the earliest in the collection.

**Key**
First floor
Second floor
Third floor
Fourth floor

★ **Horse Armour**
Dating from 1505, this armour hails from the workshop of Konrad Seusenhofer, master armourer of Innsbruck.

# ❷ Stübing

In the Styrian village of Stübing, just outside Graz, is the Österreichische Freilichtmuseum (Austrian Open-Air Museum). Covering 66 ha (24 acres) of picturesque woodland, this collection of buildings, representing Austria's regional architecture through the ages, was transported here from almost every part of the country. Each building, reconstructed and preserved with original furnishings, tools and decor, presents a unique insight into the everyday life of its former inhabitants, as well as contributing to a fascinating overview of how working life has changed throughout the years.

**Farmstead from Alpbach**
This Tyrolean farm is called Hanslerhof and dates from 1660. It unites all the essential areas of a farmstead under one single roof.

| 0 metres | | 50 |
|---|---|---|
| 0 yards | | 50 |

*Pigsty from Gstadtterboden in the Enns valley*

*Granary (1620) from Hintertux in Tyrol*

*Chapel from Haag in Upper Austria*

*8th-century farm buildings from Waldviertel in Lower Austria*

**Residential House**
St Walburg in southern Tyrol was the original location of this house, which was reconstructed in its present form following a fire in 1811.

**House from Schwarzenberg**
This 17th-century building is typical of the rural architecture in Bregenzer Wald (the Bregenz Forest) in Vorarlberg.

**Brenner Kreuz**
A brick shrine from Ebene Reichenau in Carinthia, this little chapel houses a statue of St Florian, the patron saint of fire fighters, who is invoked against fire.

## Museum Activities

Every day, the Open-Air Museum offers activities associated with traditional customs and crafts, in which visitors are invited to participate. You can try your hand at lace-making, or on special days sing folk songs or listen with children to classic fairy tales. *Erlebnistag*, or adventure day, held every year on the last Sunday in September, combines a picnic with instruction into the secrets of traditional craft skills, customs and entertainments.

Traditional needlework display in Stübing

### VISITORS' CHECKLIST

**Practical Information**
**Road map** F4.
**Tel** (03124) 53700.
**Open** Apr–Oct: 9am–5pm daily.
**w** freilichtmuseum.at

**Transport**

**Crucifix**
This cross was taken from a granary in Oberzeiring, which was used as the main food store.

Main entrance

*Single-class village school from Styria*

*buildings eastern*

*Apiary from the Enns valley*

*Belfry from Schallendurf in Burgenland*

*Sawmill from Festritz, near Birkfeld*

*Barn from St Nikolaus in Burgenland*

★ **Farmstead from Western Styria**
The main room in the 16th-century part of this house is the large "black room", where the entire family used to gather around the hearth and stove to cook, eat and socialize.

★ **Kitchen**
This typical kitchen from a house in Burgenland province, is whitewashed and chimneyless, with an open hearth and traditional bread oven.

The astonishing Lurgrotte caves close to Peggau

## ❸ Lurgrotte

**Road map** F4. 🚗 ℹ️ (03127) 2580.
**Open** Peggau: Apr–Oct: 9am–4pm daily (last guided tour 3pm); Semirach: mid-Apr–Oct: 10am–4pm; Nov–mid-Apr: guided tours 11am & 2pm. 🎫
🆆 **lurgrotte.com**

The Lurgrotte is the largest and most interesting cave in Austria, with superb stalactites and stalagmites. Starting at the entrance at either Peggau or Semirach, guides lead visitors through this world of icy wonders, along an underground stream. The largest dripstone, 13 m (43 ft) tall, is nicknamed the "Giant" (der Riese). A railway takes you to the caves from Semirach.

## ❹ Frohnleiten

**Road map** F4. 🚗 6,500. 🚗 🚌
ℹ️ (03126) 2374. 🆆 **frohnleiten.or.at**

Set among gentle hills on the Mur river, the town of Frohnleiten is surrounded by a network of clearly marked rambling trails which invite visitors to take long walks.

At one time Frohnleiten was an important transhipment post on the Mur. In 1763, the town almost burned to the ground in a fire. Sights worth visiting include the Servite monastery and the parish church, with Rococo figures in the altarpiece by Veit Königer and ceiling frescoes by Josef Adam von Mölk. Frohnleiten has won several awards for its impressive flower

displays, and has a splendid Alpine garden on 90,000 sq m (107,000 sq ft) of land, stocked with some 10,000 species from around the world.

**Environs:** A short way to the west, in Adriach, is the **St Georgskirche**, church of St George, with an altarpiece of the martyrdom of St George and four frescoes in the main nave by Josef Adam von Mölk.

## ❺ Bruck an der Mur

**Road map** F4. 🚗 16,000. 🚗 🚌
ℹ️ Koloman-Wallisch-Platz 1 (03862) 890-121. 🎭 Murenschalk (2nd Thu and Fri in Aug).

This major industrial centre lies at the mouth of the Mürz river, where it flows into the Mur. Bruck flourished during the 14th and 15th centuries, thanks to its trade with Venice, when it had the right to store grain and salt. The small but attractive old town in the fork of the Mürz and Mur rivers dates from this period. Bruck was once a town of blacksmiths and their works are now its chief historical attractions. On the main square stands an iron well (1626) by the local master, Hans Prasser, sporting an intricate wrought-iron canopy. The **parish church of Mariä Geburt** features an interesting door (1500) to the vestry, a beautiful example of Styrian metalwork. This Gothic church was later altered in the Baroque style. The former Minorite church has several important 14th-century frescoes. In the main square, Koloman-Wallisch-Platz, stands the town hall, with an attractive arcaded courtyard, in a former

ducal residence. The town's loveliest building is the late-Gothic **Kornmesserhaus**, built for the ironmonger Kornmess. It has open arcades on the ground floor and a first-floor loggia.

A small distance away, on the other side of the Mur, stands St Rupert's church, with a superb *Last Judgement* fresco (1420), uncovered in the 1930s. Above the town rise the ruins of **Landskron** fortress, whose only remaining feature is the bell tower.

Poster from the Winter Sports Museum in Mürzzuschlag

## ❻ Mürzzuschlag

**Road map** F4. 🚗 9,000. 🚗
ℹ️ Wiener Strasse 9, (03852) 3399.

This town on the Mürz at the foot of Semmering mountain is Austria's oldest winter sports resort. Skiing here dates back to 1893, and in 1934 the town was the venue for the Nordic Games, which inspired the Winter Olympics. The town's first historic records date from 1469, when Emperor Friedrich III ordered it

Ruins of Landskron Castle rising above Bruck an der Mur

The richly ornamented library in the 12th-century Augustinian Vorau Abbey

to be burned to the ground following a rebellion led by Count Andreas Baumkircher. Today its main sights of interest are the parish church, with a lovely Renaissance altarpiece, and its picturesque old houses, including **the house of Johannes Brahms** at No. 4 Wiener Strasse. Also worth visiting is the **Winter Sports Museum** which has a large collection of objects and memorabilia relating to all aspects of winter sports.

**🏛 Winter Sports Museum**

Wiener Strasse 13. **Open** 9am–12:30pm & 2–5pm Tue–Sun. **Closed** 1 Jan, Shrove Tuesday, 1 Nov, 24–25 Dec, 31 Dec. 📷

## ❼ Vorau

**Road map** F4. 🏯 4,800. 🚌 🛈 Stift Vorau, (03337) 2351.

On a remote hill stands the 12th-century Augustinian **Vorau Abbey**. In the 15th century, the abbey was turned into a fortress; its present form is the result of alterations made throughout the 17th and 18th centuries. The main entrance has symmetrical wings on both sides, adjoining two identical towers. One wing contains the cloister; in the other wing are the prelacy and the magnificent fresco- and stucco-adorned library with its low barrel-vaulted ceiling. On the floor above is the cabinet of manuscripts, decorated with ceiling paintings of the Gods, the Virtues and The Immaculate. It contains some 415 valuable manuscripts, including the oldest annals of poetry in the German language – the *Vorauer Handschrift* and the famous *Kaiserchronik*.

Bust of Johannes Brahms, who lived in Mürzzuschlag

The abbey church, dedicated to St Thomas, acquired its sumptuous decor in 1700–5. It has a main altarpiece by Matthias Steinl, who also created the beautifully ornamented pulpit.

The small nearby town of Vorau has an **Open-air Museum** (Freilichtmuseum) with a fascinating collection of typical homes and public buildings (school, pharmacy, smithy) from neighbouring villages, complete with their distinctive furnishings.

**🏛 Open-air Museum**

Tel (03337) 3466. **Open** Apr–Oct: 10am–5pm daily (Jul & Aug: 9am–5pm daily). 📷

## ❽ Pöllau

**Road map** F4. 🏯 6,000. 🛈 (03335) 4210. 🌐 naturpark-poellauertal.at

Pöllau lies at the centre of a national park, surrounded by woodland, vineyards and walking trails. The town's main attractions are the former **Augustinian Abbey** and, above all, the lovely **St Veit's church**. Built between 1701 and 1712 by Joachim Carlone of the famous family of architects from Graz, this is a splendid example of Styrian Baroque. The building is vast: the main nave and presbytery measure 62 m (203 ft), the transept 37 m (121 ft) and the dome is 42 m (138 ft) high. The vaults and the inside of the dome are decorated with *trompe l'oeil* frescoes by Mathias von Görz, depicting the four fathers of the church, two Augustinian saints and the 12 apostles. The main altarpiece has a monumental painting by Josef Adam von Mölk showing the martyrdom of the patron saint, St Veit.

**Environs:** About 6 km (4 miles) northeast of Pöllau, high up on Pöllauberg, stands the 14th-century Gothic pilgrimage church of **Maria-Lebing**, with vault frescoes by Mölk and two statues of the Virgin Mary from the 15th and 17th centuries.

# ❾ Schloss Herberstein

**Road map** F4. 🚗 300. 🚌 **Tel** (03176) 88250. **Open** Mar–Apr: 10am–4pm daily; May–Sep: 9am–5pm daily; Oct–Mar: 10am–4pm daily. 🅿
**w** herberstein.co.at

Schloss Herberstein, perched on a steep rock amid wild countryside, has remained in the hands of the same family since 1290. Since the Herbersteins still live in the castle, a visit feels a bit like peeping through a keyhole at history.

The medieval fortress, rebuilt numerous times, achieved its present form in the late 16th century. Its most magnificent part is the Florence Courtyard, a lovely arcaded enclosure more reminiscent of Renaissance Italian palaces than of northern European fortresses. At one time the castle was a venue for knightly tournaments.

The rooms that are open to visitors today display many items relating to the Herberstein family, and an exhibition that gives a unique insight into aristocratic life in the 18th and 19th centuries. There is even an original kitchen from the 16th century. there are temporary exhibitions in summer.

One of the most interesting places within the castle grounds is the nature reserve, **Tierwelt Herberstein**, which is home to wild plants and animals. Its origins can be traced back to the 16th century, when the castle was inhabited by Count Sigmund von Herberstein, the author of pioneering works on the agriculture and geography of Eastern Europe.

Bad Blumau resort, designed by Friedensreich Hundertwasser

🏰 **Tierwelt Herberstein**
**Open** mid-Mar–Apr & Oct: 10am–4pm daily; May–Sep: 9am–5pm daily; Nov–mid-Mar: 10am–3:30pm Thu–Sun & hols. 🅿 **w** tierwelt-herberstein.at

# ❿ Bad Blumau

**Road map** F4. 🚗 1,600. 🚊 🚌
ℹ️ Rogner–Bad Blumau, (03383) 51000.📧 **w** blumau.com

In eastern Styria, in an area that has long been famed for its crystal-clear mineral waters, is a spa resort that is certainly worth a detour. The entire resort of Bad Blumau was designed by the painter and architect Friedensreich Hundertwasser, in a style similar to his building in Vienna (*see pp108–9*). The rounded façades, rippling roofs, colourful walls and irregularly shaped terraces and balconies transport you into a strange and surreal fairyland. As you stroll along an

avenue lined with trees and shrubs that represent the Chinese horoscope, you suddenly realize that the grass you are walking on grows on the roof of a building below.

The outside of the complex can be seen with a guided tour but the main reason for a visit to the spa is, of course, taking the waters. Admission to the complex is available for half and full days, and will prove both an artistic experience and a pleasant way to while away some time.

# ⓫ Schloss Riegersburg

**Road map** F5. 🚗 5,000. 🚌
**Tel** (03153) 8670. **Open** Apr & Oct: 10am–6pm daily; May–Sep: 9am–6pm daily. **w** riegersburg.com

On a steep basaltic rock high above the Grazbach stream stands Riegersburg Castle, a mighty medieval fortress that was once Styria's most easterly outpost against raiders from Hungary, then Turkey, and, more recently,

The medieval fortress of Riegersburg, rebuilt in the 17th century

*For hotels and restaurants in this region see pp295–6 and pp318–20*

a German stronghold during World War II. The present castle dates from the 17th century. The fortress is surrounded and defended by a 3-km- (2-mile-) long wall with eleven bastions, seven gates and two moats, and can only be approached by a long steep climb.

A good handful of the castle's rooms serve as a museum. One section is dedicated to an extensive collection of armour and armoury. Dating from the Middle Ages to the 17th century, the weapons include swords, pistols and rifles, and range from those used during warfare to those kept for hunting. Several rooms explore the lives of the Liechtenstein family, now owners of the castle, who played an important role in the turbulent history of Austria and Europe. The Witches' Museum looks at the Styrian witch trials of the 17th century; it features gruesome instruments of torture and grim tales of persecution.

In the castle's first courtyard stands a monument to soldiers killed during World War II. Beyond the second moat, in the inner courtyard, you will find a well surrounded by an intricate wrought-iron enclosure featuring a horseshoe. Is it said that those who succeed in tracing the horseshoe among the intricate decorations may count on good luck.

## ⓬ Bad Gleichenberg

**Road map** F5. 🏔 5,500. 🚌
ℹ️ (03159) 2203.
🌐 bad-gleichenberg.at

Once the most popular health resort in Styria, Bad Gleichenberg was developed in 1834 by Matthias Constantin Capello Graf von Wickenburg. When the therapeutic properties of the local spring waters – already known to the Romans – were

brought to his attention, he set about developing them. A shrewd businessman, he soon turned this quiet corner of southeastern Styria into a modern resort that attracted visitors with its promise of painless treatments for heart disease, circulatory and respiratory ailments, problems of the digestive tract and rheumatic conditions. Consequently, Bad Gleichenberg became one of the most popular destinations for the health-conscious Austrian aristocracy, who also congregated on the local promenade, and in the magnificent park, which now displays statues of its former visitors hidden among the shrubbery. The town has many surviving villas and Secession-style palaces; one of the most beautiful is the old theatre, now housing a cinema.

Statue of Graf von Wickenburg, Bad Gleichenberg

**Environs:** A short way north of the spa town, in Gleichenberg village, stands the medieval **Schloss Kornberg**. Built as a fortress in the 13th century, it was transformed into a residential palace in the 17th century. Today it is a two-storey castle complex with four towers, and a magnificent Renaissance courtyard.

## ⓭ Bad Radkersburg

**Road map** F5. 🏔 3,100. 🚌 🚌
ℹ️ (03476) 25450.

Bad Radkersburg, on the Slovenian border, was founded as a town in 1265 by the Bohemian King Ottokar. Once a fortified border post as well as an important trade centre and transhipment harbour on the Mur river, today it is a peaceful small town, which still bears many signs of its former glory. In the main square stands the

Octagonal tower of the late-Gothic town hall, Bad Radkersburg

late-Gothic town hall, with its octagonal clock tower topped by a belfry. The Marian or Plague Column in the square dates from 1681, and the surrounding houses with their patios and shaded galleries are the former homes of noblemen and rich citizens. The house at No. 9 once belonged to the Von Eggenbergs, one of Styria's most powerful families.

Like many of its neighbours, Bad Radkersburg is also a spa town and health resort whose health-giving mineral waters attract numerous visitors.

Plague Column on Hauptplatz in Bad Radkersburg

# ⑭ Steirische Weinstrasse

Much of southern Styria is given over to vineyards, with vines planted on steep, south-facing slopes. The roads along the foot of the hills run through fields of maize, the region's second crop. The third crop is pumpkins, and pumpkin seeds are used to make *Kürbiskernöl*, a popular salad oil. Visitors following the Styrian wine routes will find many pleasant places to stop for a meal, but more importantly, a chance to sample the local wine and learn about the grape varieties that cloak the gardens of the restaurants.

### ① Gundersdorf
At the entrance to the village stands a high pole with four vanes clattering in the wind. This is the *Klapotetz*, a scarecrow that guards the vineyards against birds. There are many such devices throughout the region, but the one in Gundersdorf is the largest.

### ② Stainz
This town owes its former wealth to the wine trade. The Augustinian Abbey, converted into a palace by Archduke Johann, now houses part of the Graz Joanneum Museum *(see p166)*, dedicated to the history of farming and hunting in the region.

### ③ Bad Gams
A health resort with iron-rich mineral waters, Bad Gams owes its fame mainly to its superb pottery products.

### ④ Deutschlandsberg
This village is the centre of production for Schilcher rosé wine. It is dominated by the ruins of a former castle, whose remaining 12th-century turret affords spectacular views over the valley.

```
0 kilometres          5
0 miles               5
```

**Key**

— Suggested route

═ Other road

⋯ River, lake

## Austrian Wines

Austria can boast some truly excellent wines, in particular its white wines, and production meets almost the entire domestic demand. The largest wine-producing area is Lower Austria, particularly the Weinviertel and the Wachau valley. Burgenland, southern Styria and the environs of Vienna are also key regions. The most popular white wines are Grüner Veltliner, Welschriesling and Weissburgunder. The land around Neusiedler See produces white wines, but is particularly famous for its reds: Zweigelt and the full-bodied Blaufränkisch. The light Schilcher rosé comes from Deutschlandsberg in Styria. The sweet dessert wine Eiswein, made from grapes picked after the first frosts, is also produced in Austria.

Label for Austrian red wine from Gumpoldskirchen

### ⑤ Kitzeck

In the centre of town, in an old inn between the church and the pub, is a fascinating wine museum. Kitzeck also boasts the highest vineyards in Europe, growing on steep slopes at an altitude of 564 m (1,850 ft).

### ⑥ Leibnitz

Several traces reveal earlier Roman settlements in the town of Leibnitz. The archaeological finds are now on display in nearby Seggau Castle.

*Graz*

*Feldbach*

67

⑥

⑤

*Mur*

74

*Weisse Sulm*

*Maribor*

⑦

*Eibiswald*

### ⑦ Ehrenhausen

Vineyards form the pristine landscape surrounding Ehrenhausen. The greatest attraction of this historic town is the mausoleum of Rupert von Eggenberg (died 1611), a hero of the Turkish wars, with an interior designed by Johann Bernhard Fischer von Erlach.

### Tips for Drivers

**Length of route:** 66 km (41 miles).
**Stopping places:** inns and rooms to rent are dotted along the route.
**Suggestions:** a visit to the Steirisches Weinmuseum (wine museum) in Kitzeck: Steinriegel 15. **Tel** (03456) 3000. **Open** Apr–Oct: 10am–noon, 2–5pm daily; Nov–Mar: 9am–noon Mon–Fri.

## ⑮ Piber

**Road map** F4. 🚗 Köflach. 🚌
🏔 500. 🅸 (03144) 72 777-0.
Stud: **Tel** (03144) 3323-100. **Open**
Apr–Oct: 9:30am–5pm daily; Nov–
Mar: guided tours only. 🅿 📷

Piber is the location of the Piber
Federal Stud, the breeding farm
for Vienna's Spanish Riding
School (see p71). When the town
of Lipizza was incorporated into
Slovenia after World War I, it
was in a former castle in Piber,
a small Styrian village, that the
famous Lipizzaner horses found
a new home.

The horses are a complex
mixture of six different breeds.
Born dark-chestnut or black,
they acquire their famous white
colour between the ages of four
and ten. In Piber, the initial
selection of 5 out of 40 stallions
takes place: they are assessed
for their suitability and stage
talents before five years of
training at the Spanish Riding
School. Those with a keen
passion for horses can purchase
one of the stallions here.

## ⑯ Judenburg

**Road map** E4. 🏔 10,000. 🚍 🚌
🅸 Hauptplatz 20, (03572) 85000.
🆆 judenburg.com

This town at the fork of a road is
an old mercantile centre that took
its name from the Juden, or Jews,
who once lived and traded here.
When Emperor Maximilian
expelled the Jews in 1496, the
town went into decline. Not much
remains of the medieval Jewish
quarter, but it is worth visiting
**Nikolauskirche**, the church of

St Nicholas. The only original
feature is the presbytery. Rebuilt
in 1673 in the Baroque style, the
church was subsequently given
a Neo-Renaissance facelift
during the Neo-Classical period.
Inside are statues of the
12 apostles by the local artist
Balthasar Brandstätter. A side
altar contains a small wooden
statue of the Madonna and Child,
dating from 1500. The Magda-
lenenkirche, church of St Mary
Magdalene, features lovingly
restored Gothic stained-glass
windows. The town also has a
museum devoted
mainly to the region's
history and art.

**Environs:** East of
the town, on the
ledge of a rock,
stand the ruins of an
old Liechtenstein
**castle**, once only
accessible by step
ladder. Beyond
Judenburg are
some interesting
archaeological
sites, which date
from prehistoric times. The
famous chariot, now displayed
in the Joanneum Museum in
Eggenberg Castle in Graz, was
unearthed in nearby **Strettweg**.

## ⑰ St Lambrecht

**Road map** E4. 🏔 1,900. 🚍 🚌
🅸 Hauptstrasse 12 (03585) 2305.
🆆 stlambrecht.at

St Lambrecht, a Benedictine
abbey, was founded in the
12th century by Henry III, duke
of Carinthia. The monastery

complex was built in 1640 to
designs by Domenico Sciassia.
The church dates from the
14th century, but it was rebuilt
in the Baroque style and today
it is a triple-nave basilica with
medieval frescoes on the walls
and presbytery ceiling, and
statues of the church's fathers
in the organ enclosure. The
main altar (1632) by Valentin
Khautt is 16 m (52 ft) high.

North of the church, by the
cemetery, stands a 12th-century
Romanesque chapel. The abbey
also has a magnificent library
and an interesting
museum with a collec-
tion of the old
furnishings of
church and abbey,
including Roman-
esque sculptures, a
15th-century votive
painting, *The Mount
of Olives*, by Hans
von Tübingen, and
15th-and 16th-
century stained-
glass panels. The
gem of the
museum, however,
is its collection of birds. Some
1,500 species were assembled in
the 19th century by the amateur
collector Blasius Hanf.

Image of the patron saint of
St Lambrecht Abbey

🏛 **St Lambrecht Abbey Museum**
Hauptstrasse 1–2. **Tel** (03585) 2305-29.
**Open** for guided tours only mid-May–
mid-Oct: 10:45am, 2:30pm Mon–Sat,
2:30pm Sun & hols.

## ⑱ Turracher Höhe

**Road map** E5. 🏔 100. 🚌 🅸 (04275)
8392. 🆆 turracherhoehe.com

This small ski resort nestles at
an altitude of 1,700 m (5,575 ft)
high in the Nockbergen (Nock
mountains), one of Austria's
most scenic Alpine ranges, on
the border between Styria and
Carinthia. The town makes a
great base for year-round walks
in the woods and mountain
meadows. Nearby are the
remains of an old iron-smelting
plant. The blast furnace ended
its operation in the early 20th
century, but the remains of
heavy industry create a very
striking feature set against the

The world-famous Lipizzaner horses in a paddock near Piber

*For hotels and restaurants in this region see pp295–6 and pp318–20*

Splendid autumn colours in the woods around Turracher Höhe

backdrop of the pistes and the beautiful snow-covered hills of the ski resort.

## ⑲ Murau

**Road map** E4. 🚇 3,700. 🚌 🚉
ℹ️ (03532) 2720. 🆆 **murau.at**

Murau sprang up in the 13th century at a crossroads of trading routes on the scenic Mur river and became a local centre for commerce and industry. The historic town centre of Murau lies on the left bank of the Mur river. Its Renaissance houses are dominated by the Gothic **Matthäuskirche**, the church of St Matthew, consecrated in the 13th century and later altered in the Baroque style. The church contains some interesting tombs of the Liechtenstein

family but its star attraction is the main altar (1655), a magnificent work by local Baroque masters, incorporating a Gothic painting of the Crucifixion (c.1500). Also worth seeing are the medieval frescoes of St Anthony in the transept, and the Entombment of Christ and Annunciation in the main nave.

The castle behind the church, **Schloss Murau**, was founded by the Liechtenstein family and later passed into the hands of the Schwarzenbergs. It has an interesting museum of metallurgy. In the vaults of **Elisabethkirche**, at No. 4 Marktgasse, is a Diocesan Protestant Museum that holds documents relating to the events around the Reformation and the Counter-Reformation in this part of Austria.

## ⑳ Oberwölz

**Road map** E4. 🚇 1,000.
ℹ️ Hauptplatz 15, (03581) 8420.
🆆 **oberwoelz-lachtal.at**

This small town, which grew rich through its trade in salt and the smelting of silver excavated in the surrounding hills, has preserved some of its former glory. In its environs many archaeological finds from the Hallstatt period have been unearthed, revealing a long history. Oberwölz once belonged to the bishopric of Freising and up to the time of the Napoleonic wars its envoy resided in the neighbouring **Schloss Rothenfels**.

The town has some well-preserved remains of medieval fortifications, including three turrets and two town gates. Its pride is the Gothic **Stadtpfarrkirche St Martin**, the parish church of St Martin, a triple-nave basilica with an early-Gothic chapel and a 15th-century Gothic vestibule. In 1777, J. A. von Mölk painted the ceiling frescoes in the chapel vault. On the external south wall is a relief from 1500, showing the Last Judgement. Next to the church stands the 14th-century chapel of St Sigismund, with the Way of the Cross by Johann Lederwasch from the turn of the 18th century. In the Cultural Centre is a regional museum with a collection of archaeological finds from the area, and a museum of wind instruments.

Historic buildings in the old town of Murau on the Mur river

Traditional huts in an Alpine village, Goeriachtal valley ▶

# ㉑ Schladminger Tauern

The small town of Schladming lies at the foot of the Niedere (Lower) Tauern that extend along the Enns valley. Rising to 2,800 m (9,200 ft), their gentle slopes provide excellent conditions for downhill skiers, from the beginner to the professional. The scenery is superb, excellent for walking in summer, with an efficient bus network, cable cars and ski lifts in winter. If you are looking for more of a challenge, you can find this in the Dachstein massif close by. But for a relaxing break it is still worth going down to Schladming, with its tempting restaurants and cosy cafés lining the broad promenade.

★ **Schladming**
The little town of Schladming has a rich history. Once a centre of peasant revolts, it remains to this day the centre of Austrian Protestantism.

★ **Ennstal – the Enns Valley**
One of Austria's major rivers, the Enns, separates the Schladminger Tauern (part of the Niedere Tauern) from the Dachstein massif.

```
0 kilometres          5
0 miles               5
```

*Hunerkogel*

**Filzmoos**

**Ramsau
am Dachstein**

①

*ENNSTAL*

**Schladr**

**320**

**E651**

**Rohrmoos**

*Hochwurzen*

**Radstadt**

*Forstaubach*

**99**

↓ *Klagenfurt*

## KEY

① **The ascent** by cable car from the small village of Ramsau am Dachstein *(see p184)* takes visitors to the tops of Dachstein and Hunerkogel. Climbing instructors also give advice to rock climbers.

② **Gröbming** has an attractive late-medieval church of the Assumption of the Virgin Mary, with a winged altar (1520).

③ **Hochgolling**, rising to 2,863 m (9,393 ft), is the highest peak in the Schladminger Tauern. The long, arduous climb rewards with stunning views of the mountains from the top.

**Rohrmoos**
This resort, just outside Schladming, is a good base for climbing the neighbouring Hochwurzen and Planai summits.

**★ Dachstein Massif**
The highest, most impressive peak is Dachstein itself, which rises to 2,995 m (9,826 ft). A glacier, it is perfect for year-round skiing.

**VISITORS' CHECKLIST**

**Practical Information**
Road map D4, E4.
🛈 Schladming, Ramsauerstrasse 756, (03687) 23 310.
🅦 schladming-dachstein.at

**Transport**
🚉 🚌

**Haus**
A resort and winter sports centre, Haus has a beautiful Baroque church. It is a good starting point for mountain walks to the nearby scenic lakes, including Bodensee, Hüttensee and Obersee.

**Riesachsee**
One of many mountain lakes set amid beautiful scenery, the Riesachsee lies at an altitude of 1,333 m (4,373 ft). It is a perfect spot for trout fishing.

**Key**

— Major road
— Minor road
···· Mountain railway
═ River

**For keys to symbols** *see back flap*

The resort of Ramsau, famed for cross-country skiing

## ㉒ Ramsau

**Road map** D4. 2,800.
Ramsauerstrasse 756, (03687)
81 833. **ramsau.com**

At an altitude of 1,000 m
(3,280 ft) lies the small town of
Ramsau am Dachstein, renowned
for its superb cross-country ski
runs, extending over some
230 km (143 miles). Snow is
almost guaranteed from
November until March and the
efficient interconnecting system
of lifts, cable cars, trains and
buses also puts more difficult
runs within easy reach. The peaks
opposite the Dachstein massif
have slopes that are perfectly
suited to moderately skilled
downhill skiers. In the summer
the *Loipen,* or cross-country ski
runs, turn into excellent long-
distance walking routes.

From the Ramsau side, visitors
can ascend the famous Dachstein
south face by cable car. Cable
cars also travel up Hunerkogel
(2,694 m/8,836 ft), from where a
lovely panoramic view of the
area unfolds. The descent takes
you to nearby Filzmoos, a resort
with views of the spectacular
Bischofsmütze (Bishop's Mitre).

There are many attractions on
offer in Ramsau, such as feeding
alpine animals and night toboggan runs. The **Alpinmuseum**
illustrates the history of
mountaineering in the region.
The **Wassermühle Rössing** is one
of several waterwheels that has
been built in the area since the
17th century. It lies at the foot
of Sattelberg, near the start of

the children's *via ferrata* (climbing
path), the Kali-Kinderklettersteig.
The old waterwheel creaks into
motion on Friday afternoons.

**Alpinmuseum**
**Tel** (03687) 70 63 836. **Open** May–Oct:
10am–4pm daily. on request.

**Wassermühle Rössing**
**Tel** (03687) 81 874. **Open** mid-Jun–Sep.

## ㉓ Bad Aussee

**Road map** D4. 4,800.
Hauptstrasse 48, (03622) 54040-0.
**badaussee.at**

Bad Aussee, the main town
in the Styrian part of the
Salzkammergut, lies at the fork
of the Traun river, which cuts
a scenic gorge between the
Dachstein massif and the Totes
Gebirge (Dead Mountains). The
region's wealth was founded on
its salt deposits. Later, Bad Aussee
achieved renewed fame when,
in 1827, Archduke Johann

married Anna Plochl, daughter
of the local postmaster. The
archduke, who made many
important contributions to the
life of Styria, was a grandson of
Maria Theresa and the 13th child
of future Emperor Leopold II.

The former seat of the Salt
Office, in Chlumeckyplatz, is a
lovely 14th-century building
which now houses the city's
regional museum with an
exhibition on salt mining.
The 13th-century Romanesque
St Paul's church has a notable
stone statue of the Madonna.

**Environs:** A scenic road
northwest of Bad Aussee will
take you to **Altausseer See** and
the Loser peak. On the road is
an old salt mine, open to the
public. During World War II it
was reputedly used to hide
works of art.

## ㉔ Admont

**Road map** E4. 5,000.
(03613) 21160-10. **admont.at**

At the centre of the village of
Admont stands a **Benedictine
abbey** whose importance once
reached far beyond the region.
Built in the 11th century and
often rebuilt, it burned down
in 1865, but the fire spared its
priceless collection: with nearly
160,000 volumes, it is said to
hold the world's largest
monastic library. The library's
magnificent Rococo interior,
dating from 1773, was designed
by the Viennese architect Josef
Hueber. The large hall holding
two-storey cabinets is 72 m

A picturesque street in Bad Aussee

Richly ornamented interior of Admont's library

(236 ft) long. The ceiling frescoes by Bartolomeo Altomonte show vast allegorical scenes of the arts, the natural sciences and religion. The abbey's south wing has been converted into a museum showcasing both historic treasures and modern art.

**🏛 Benedictine Abbey**
**Tel** (03613) 2312-604. Library & Museum: **Open** mid-Mar–Oct: 10am–5pm daily; Nov–Feb: on request. **W stiftadmont.at**

**Environs:** 5 km (3 miles) beyond Admont, high above the Enns river, stands the 15th-century pilgrimage church of **Frauenberg**, rebuilt in the Baroque style. It has a beautiful altarpiece by Josef Stammel.

## ㉕ Hohentauern

**Road map** E4. 🚗 430. 🚌
**ℹ** (03618) 335. **W hohentauern.at**

Hohentauern (1,274 m/4,180 ft) is the highest village in the Rottenmanner Tauern, surrounded by more than 20 peaks higher than 2,000 m (6,560 ft). This mountain range is part of the Niedere (Lower) Tauern, which extend to Salzburger Land. Other ranges in the Niedere Tauern include Radstädter *(see p232)*, Schladminger *(see pp182–3)* and Wölzer Tauern.

Hohentauern was founded by the Celts. From the 12th century it became important as a commercial centre along Hohentauernpass, the mountain pass connecting the Enns and Mur valleys. St Bartolomäus church has magnificent carvings by Josef Stammel.

The Hohentauernpass crosses the range at a height of 1,260 m (4,134 ft). A drive along Hohentauernpassstrasse is one of the best ways to enjoy the superb mountain scenery.

From the north, you pass through **Rottenmann** with its old city walls; **Möderbrugg**, a former centre of the metal industry; **Oberzeiring** and its disused salt mine; and **Hanfelden**, with its large ruined castle. Nearby is the ruined **Schloss Reifenstein**.

## ㉖ Eisenerzer Alpen

**Road map** E4. Eisenerz: 🚌 🚗 4,300.
**ℹ** Dr-Theodor-Körner-Platz 1, (03848) 2511-81.

You can reach the Eisenerzer Alpen (Iron Ore Alps) by following the steep, narrow valley of the Enns river. This gorge, called Gesäuse, begins a short distance from Admont, near Hieflau. The entrance to the gorge presents great views of the river and the Hochtor massif, rising 2,369 m (7,772 ft) above. The surrounding area is used as a training ground for advanced mountaineering and as a base for expeditions to the neighbouring peaks. Easily the most famous mountain in the Eisenerzer Alpen is **Erzberg**, which has has been exploited for its large iron ore deposits since ancient times. It looks like a stepped pyramid, the red pigment contrasting with the green forests and meadows.

The area around Erzberg is the largest iron ore basin in this part of Europe. In **Eisenerz**, an old mining town at the foot of Erzberg, visitors can join an underground tour with **Abenteuer Erzberg**, which includes a ride on a large dump truck. The village also has a lovely old town and the fine 16th-century church of St Oswald.

**🏛 Abenteuer Erzberg**
Erzberg 1. **Tel** (03848) 3200.
**Open** May–Oct daily.
🕐 10am–3pm; obligatory.
 **W abenteuer-erzberg.at**

The shimmering Erzberg – the red iron-ore mountain in the Eisenerzer Alpen

# ㉙ Salzatal Tour

The small Salza river, a tributary of the upper Enns, cuts its way across the eastern end of the High Limestone Alps. A journey along the Salza valley is an expedition through a thinly populated area of entrancing beauty. The trail leads along the foothills of the Hochschwab massif, beside wild mountain streams, small barrier lakes and through dense woodlands. The river flows through virgin mountain terrains and its waters are so crystal clear that you can see every detail reflected in it.

**Brunnsee ②**
Beyond the village of Wildalpen, a magnificent view opens onto the valley and the lake at the very heart of the Hochschwab massif. The northern slopes of the mountains can been seen in their full glory.

**Prescenyklause ③**
Beyond a rock gate is an old dam that once held back the waters of the Salza river so rafts could carry timber to the valleys.

**Hieflau ①**
This former centre of the metal industry is hidden amid dense forests. The local village museum displays objects associated with the region's history.

0 kilometres 5

0 miles 5

**Key**

— Suggested route

— Scenic road

═ Other road

⋯ River, lake

**Hochschwab ⑤**
The highest summit in this vast mountain range is the 2,277-m- (7,470-ft-) high Hochschwab, the destination of both summer and winter excursions.

_Mariazell_

The main nave of the abbey church in Seckau Abbey

## ㉗ Seckau

**Road map** E4. 🔼 1,300. 🚗 🚌
ℹ (03514) 5205-3. 🅦 seckau.at

The small town of Seckau, established in the 13th century, has some interesting houses and the late-Gothic chapel of St Lucia in the town square. But its main claim to fame is **Seckau Abbey**, originally Augustinian and taken over by the Benedictines in the 19th century. Its present shape, dating from the 17th century, is the work of Pietro Francesco Carlone, but the abbey's basilica of the Assumption of the Virgin Mary has maintained its original late-Gothic character.

Among its treasures is the Crucifixion group in the presbytery, highly expressive figures from the 12th and 13th centuries. The lion figures in the portal and the Madonna and Child in the church vestibule are Romanesque or early Gothic, and on the south wall, 13th-century frescoes were discovered.

## ㉘ Leoben

**Road map** F4. 🔼 25,000. 🚗 🚌
ℹ Hauptplatz 3, (03842) 48148-0.

Leoben, Styria's second largest town, is an industrial and academic centre. Beautiful mansion houses line the Hauptplatz (the main square), and the adjacent streets bear witness to the town's early wealth derived from the local iron deposits. There is a lovely old town hall with coats of arms, and the Hacklhaus has a glittering red façade.

Also worth seeing in the old town is the **Pfarrkirche St Xaver**, the church of St Xavier, built in the 17th century by the Jesuits, with its beautiful Baroque main altar and a Romanesque crucifix on the south wall. On the other side of the bridge across the Mur river stands the Gothic church of **Maria am Waasen**, with original stained-glass windows in the presbytery. On the southern outskirts, in the district of Göss, stands Styria's first Benedictine **abbey**, built around 1000 by Archbishop Aribo. It is now mainly 16th-century with some earlier elements. The church's main nave is a monument to Styria's late-Gothic architecture. Other original features include 14th-century frescoes in the presbytery and an 11th-century, early-Romanesque crypt.

Austria's most famous brewery, **Gösser**, a short way from the abbey, is also open to the public. In the city centre, at No. 6 Kirchgasse, is the **Kunsthalle Leoben**, a museum of fine arts.

**Weichselboden** ④
It is worth stopping off in this small village, one of very few along this route, to visit its lime-tree-shaded church. A very small old hotel invites visitors to stay.

The elegant Baroque façade of the Hacklhaus in Leoben

_For hotels and restaurants in this region see pp295–6 and pp318–20_

# ③ Mariazell Basilica

The earliest records of a church devoted to the Birth of the Virgin Mary date from 1243, but it is believed to have been established in 1157 and its 850th anniversary was celebrated in 2007. Mariazell is the main pilgrimage centre for the Roman Catholic population in this part of Europe. Pilgrims arrive all year, but high points are Assumption (15 Aug) and the Birth of the Virgin (8 Sep). Mariazell became famous in the 14th century, when King Louis of Hungary founded the Gnadenkapelle (Chapel of Mercy) to give thanks for his victory over the Turks.

**View of the Church**
In the 17th century, the church was extended to accommodate the growing number of pilgrims, and the central tower was supplemented by two Baroque side towers.

**Church Interior**
The basilica was originally a Gothic hall church, which is still apparent despite the Baroque-style alterations carried out in the late 17th century by Domenico Sciassia.

## KEY

① **14th-century Gothic tower**

② **Vault frescoes** by Giovanni Rocco Bertoletti

**★ Treasury**
The treasury is home to various precious objects, including a wooden statuette of the Madonna and Child and an ivory relief, both from the 14th century.

Main entrance

**Madonna and Child**
*Magna Mater Austriae* – the
Great Mother of Austria, a late-
Romanesque statue of the
Madonna and Child – is the
main object of veneration by
pilgrims to Mariazell.

## VISITORS' CHECKLIST

**Practical Information**
**Road map** F4.
Kardinal-Tisserant-Platz 1, Mariazell.
**Tel** (03882) 2595. **Open** May–Oct:
7:45am–8pm daily (until 9pm Sat);
Nov–Apr: 7:45am– 7:15pm daily.
Treasury: **Open** May–Oct: 10am–
3pm Tue–Sat, 11am–4pm Sun &
hols; Advent: 1–5pm Fri–Sun.
🌐 basilika-mariazell.at

**★ Main Altar**
The monumental altar
showing the Crucifixion is
the work of Johann
Bernhard Fischer von Erlach.
The silver figures on the
altar were created by
Lorenzo Mattielli.

## Cardinal Joseph Mindszenty (1892–1975)

The Hungarian primate,
imprisoned for his opposition
to the communist regime, was
released in the 1956 uprising.
When this was crushed, he took
refuge in the US Embassy in
Budapest for 15 years. He later
lived in Austria and was buried
in Mariazell. His body was later
moved to Hungary.

**★ Gnadenkapelle**
This chapel, with a statue
of the Virgin Mary is said
to have been founded
by King Louis of Hungary
and was decorated in
Baroque style by Fischer
von Erlach the Younger
and Lorenzo Mattielli.

# UPPER AUSTRIA

Upper Austria, so called because of its location in the upper reaches of the Austrian Danube, occupies an area of about 12,000 sq km (4,600 sq miles) and has 1.4 million inhabitants. Its borders are marked by the rivers Enns to the east and Inn to the west. To the north, the Czech Republic is its neighbour, to the south are Styria and the Salzburger Land, to the west is Germany.

Upper Austria is, after Vienna, the most industrialized Austrian province and has remained the richest area of the country since the time when Austria was part of the Roman province of Noricum. In later years, Upper Austria joined Bavaria. Then, under Babenberg rule in the 13th century, it became the cradle of the great future empire, together with neighbouring Lower Austria.

Historically, the province of Upper Austria is divided into five districts: Mühlviertel, which stretches south to the Danube and occupies the Czech massif, with Freistadt its largest town; the westernmost district of Innviertel, which lies in the foothills of the Alps and includes the towns of Ried and Braunau; Hausruckviertel, named after the Hausruck massif and with Vöcklabruck as its largest town; and Traunviertel, which includes the Salzkammergut, one of the most picturesque and popular natural areas in Austria. The Danube valley is generally considered to be a separate region, with scores of small towns, lofty fortresses and magnificent abbeys, including the most glorious of them all – St Florian, a jewel of Austrian Baroque architecture.

The province's capital, Linz, is Austria's third-largest city. It is an important industrial centre, contains the largest Austrian Danube port, and is a major transport hub. It is beautifully situated in an extensive valley, surrounded by gently rolling hills, and has a charming old town district.

View from the Krippenstein peak across to the imposing Dachstein massif

◀ Houses situated on the banks of the glorious Hallstätter See, Hallstatt

# Exploring Upper Austria

Upper Austria is an exceptionally diverse province, with something to interest everyone. Linz, the capital city, has both the oldest church in Austria and a state-of-the-art virtual technology museum. On the banks of the rivers Danube and Enns rise the magnificent abbeys in Kremsmünster, Steyr and St Florian. The caves in the Dachstein range are fascinating natural monuments. However, Upper Austria's greatest attraction are its glorious lakes, set amid limestone peaks in the beautiful Salzkammergut. The mild climate and therapeutic facilities attract visitors to the area's small resorts, and Bad Ischl was once the summer home of the emperor.

Aigen im Mühlkreis

Regensburg

Rohrb

Lembach im Mühlkreis

**7 SCHÄRDING**

Natternbach

Andorf

Peuerbach

**8 OBERNBERG AM INN**

Neumarkt im Hausruckkreis

Bad Schallerbach

**9 BRAUNAU AM INN**

Altheim

Ried im Innkreis

**SCHMIDING**

München (Munich)

Mauerkirchen

Haag am Hausruck

**OBER-ÖSTERREICH**

Eggelsberg

Mattighofen

Frankenberg

**LAMBACH 11**

**16**

**SCHWANENSTADT 17**

**STADL-PAURA**

Salzburg

Lengau

**VÖCKLABRUCK 18**

Gampern

Laakirch

St. Georgen

Schörfling

**19 GMUND**

**SALZKAMMERGUT LAKES 21**

Traunsee

Salzburg

**TRAUNKIRCHEN 20**

Mondsee

Attersee

Ebensee

Mondsee

**22 SCHAFBERG**

**ST WOLFGANG 23**

**24 BAD ISCHL**

Gosau

**DACHSTEIN-HÖHLEN**

**HALLSTATT 25**

**27**

**26 GOSAUSEEN**

Steyr's trademark – the Gothic Bummerlhaus with its steeply pitched roof

## Sights at a Glance

*For hotels and restaurants in this region see pp296–7 and pp320–21*

Zwettl
Sandl
310
38
38
Bad Leonfelden
**FREISTADT 6**
Zwettl an
der Rodl
126
310
Pregarten
124
St. Georgen
am Walde
Königswiesen
**5 KEFERMARKT**
ensheim
A7
Gallneukirchen
lhering
**1 LINZ**
Leonding
**4 PERG** Grein
Traun
DANUBE
Wien
(Vienna)
Haid
A1
Enns
VALLEY
**3** 
**ST FLORIAN**
2
(Danube)
WELS
139
Neuhofen
**13 KREMSMÜNSTER**
**15 BAD HALL**
**14 STEYR**
122
A9
115
138
Ternberg
Kirchdorf an
der Krems
Großraming
121
Klaus
Weyer Markt
115
A9
Windischgarten
138
Trieben

Houses with flower-decked balconies
in St Wolfgang

The attractive riverfront esplanade in Gmunden

0 kilometres     15
0 miles     15

## Getting There

Although Linz-Hörsching Airport is served by some international flights, most visitors fly to Vienna. Linz lies on the Vienna–Salzburg railway line and the A1 motorway, which traverses the province east to west and also connects with the southern A9 motorway. There is a dense network of roads and bus routes throughout. From spring until autumn, boats on the Danube river connect Passau with Linz and Linz with the Wachau valley.

Statue in front of the Kaiservilla,
in Bad Ischl

**Key**

Motorway
Major road
Minor road
Scenic route
Main railway
Minor railway
International border
Province border

**For keys to symbols** *see back flap*

# ❶ Linz

Straddling the Danube and surrounded by picturesque hills, Linz owes its former importance and wealth to its location at an intersection of waterways. This strategic position led the Romans to found a substantial settlement called Lentia on the site, and since the 15th century, Linz has been the capital of Upper Austria. The European Capital of Culture in 2009 and a UNESCO City of Media Arts, Linz is a vibrant city with numerous galleries and museums, as well as the futurist Ars Electronica Center. It also claims the largest urban square in Europe and is home to Austria's biggest church, the Mariendom, or New Cathedral.

Looking over the rooftops of Linz

## Exploring Linz

The town of Linz sprawls across both banks of the Danube, with the historic old town on the right (south) bank, in the bend of the river. The majority of the town's main sights are located near the Hauptplatz. Europe's largest city square, it is some 13,200 sq m (142,000 sq ft), and is enclosed by magnificent Baroque buildings. The Ars Electronica Center is situated on the left (north) bank of the Danube.

## 🏠 Martinskirche

Römerstrasse/Martinsgasse.
**Tel** (0732) 777454. 📷

A modest façade hides what is considered to be Austria's oldest surviving church. Dedicated to St Martin, it was first mentioned in the 8th century, during the time of Charlemagne, as part of the Carolingians' former royal residence. The Gothic and Romanesque windows

and portals are particularly noteworthy. There was an older Roman wall on the same site, and ten Roman tombstones, together with other ancient stones, were used as building material to erect the church. The interior dates from the Carolingian period, the only later addition being the Neo-Gothic presbytery. The rainbow arch that separates the nave from the presbytery and the north wall of the church are adorned with 14th–15th-century frescoes of the Virgin Mary on a throne. Much of the interior can only be seen with a guide.

The tiny Martinskirche, Austria's oldest church

## 🏛 Linzer Schloss

Schlossberg 1. **Tel** (0732) 7720 523 00.
**Open** 9am–6pm Tue–Wed & Fri, 9am–9pm Thu, 10am–5pm Sat, Sun, public holidays. 📷
🔲 landesmuseum.at

In the 15th century, Emperor Friedrich III built his residence on the Römerberg (Roman Mountain), on the foundations of an earlier structure. The castle acquired its present shape between 1600 and 1607, and its distinctive silhouette has become one of the most famous sights in Linz. Since 1966, this former imperial residence has housed a branch of the Oberöster-reichisches Landesmuseum. Exhibits include paintings and sculptures from early medieval times to the 19th century and the Secession, 12th–18th-century arms, 16th–19th-century musical instruments, furniture and handicrafts, golden, ceramic and glass objects, and a permanent archaeological exhibition. Part of the museum is devoted to folk traditions; there's a recon-structed physics laboratory from the Jesuit school in Linz and the Schloss Weinberg pharmacy (c.1700). From the castle, there are superb views over Linz.

## 🎭 Landhaus

Theatergasse 1. **Tel** (0732) 77200.
The regional government is based in a Renaissance palace built on the site of a former Minorite monastery. Its north portal, on Klosterstrasse, is a beautiful marble work by Renaissance artists. The inner courtyard is surrounded by a colonnade. Here you will find the Planetenbrunnen (Fountain of the Planets), built to com-memorate the outstanding astronomer and mathematician Johannes Kepler, who lectured at the college, then based in the Landhaus, for 14 years (1612–26). The seven figures on the fountain's bronze plinth show the planets known at the time. Close by is the Minoritenkirche, a former Minorite church, the earliest documented record of which is in the town chronicles of 1288. Altered in the

The Planet Fountain in the inner courtyard of the Landhaus

Baroque style in 1751–8, the church has an unusual façade with oval telescopes between the storeys. The lovely Rococo interior is decorated with charming stuccowork and paintings by Martin Johann Schmidt and Bartolomeo Altomonte.

## Hauptplatz

The Hauptplatz, in Linz's Old Town, is Europe's grandest in scale, and one of the finest to visit. It is 220 m (720 ft) long and 60 m (200 ft) wide, and overall it creates a much stronger impression than its component

parts would suggest. Many of its buildings are worth a closer look, though. The Gothic Altes Rathaus (Old Town Hall) at No. 1 was built around 1513, and still has its original octagonal tower with an astronomical clock. In the 17th century, the town hall was given a new façade supported by columns. Other interesting buildings are the Gothic and Baroque houses, including Feichtingerhaus, a former mail inn (No. 21), a Gothic building with an early-Baroque façade. The Plague Column (1723) in the centre of the square was funded jointly

### VISITORS' CHECKLIST

**Practical Information**
**Road map** E3.
270,000. Hauptplatz 1, (0732) 7070-2009.
Pflasterspektakel (end Jul); Brucknerfest (Sep); Ars electronica (Sep). linztourismus.at

**Transport**

by the local council and all citizens, in thanksgiving for sparing Linz and the Linzers from three deadly disasters: war, fire and the Black Death plague.

Hauptplatz, with its Baroque Plague Column

## Linz City Centre

1. Martinskirche
2. Schloss
3. Landhaus
4. Hauptplatz
5. Alter Dom
6. Stadtpfarrkirche
7. Landesgalerie
8. Stadtmuseum Nordico
9. Seminarkirche
10. Mariendom
11. Ars Electronica Center
12. Lentos Kunstmuseum

The towers of Alter Dom

### ⌂ Alter Dom

Domgasse 3. **Tel** (0732) 770866-0.
**Open** 7:30am–6:30pm daily.

The capital of the archbishopric of Upper Austria was established in Linz in 1783, and in 1785 the former Jesuit church was chosen as the cathedral. Ignatiuskirche, the church of St Ignatius, was built in the second half of the 17th century to designs by Pietro Francesco Carlone, and today its green façade and onion-dome-topped twin towers are distinctive features in the town panorama. The modest exterior of the church conceals a beguiling Baroque interior. The wide main nave has three side chapels on each side. Particularly fascinating are the beautifully engraved stalls in the presbytery, where local artists carved the figures of dwarfs and monsters peeping out from behind the backrests and armrests.

From 1856 until 1868 the composer Anton Bruckner was the cathedral's organist. The present organ, by the famous master Krismann, was altered according to Bruckner's own instructions.

### ⌂ Stadtpfarrkirche

Pfarrplatz 4. **Tel** (0732) 776120.

The parish church of the Assumption of the Virgin Mary (Mariä Himmelfahrt) was built in the 13th century as a triple-nave basilica with a Gothic presbytery, and altered in the 17th century, when it received a new interior and further chapels. The

presbytery contains the tombstone of Emperor Friedrich III, who resided in Linz for a while. The urn containing his heart is concealed behind a marble slab in the church wall to the right of the altar. In the eastern end of the south nave is the chapel of St John of Nepomuk. Its lovely Baroque interior is decorated with frescoes and an altar by Bartolomeo Altomonte. St John of Nepomuk was one of the most revered saints in the Austrian empire. Many towns erected statues to him, and the Stadtpfarrkirche in Linz houses two of these. One stands in the external chapel by the presbytery, probably created by Georg Raphael Donner. The chapel's architecture and dome shape are the work of another Austrian master of the Baroque, Johann Lukas von Hildebrandt.

### 🏛 Landesgalerie

Museumstrasse 14. **Tel** (0732) 7720-52200. **Open** 9am–6pm Tue, Wed & Fri, 9am–9pm Thu, 10am–5pm Sat, Sun & hols. ♿ 🖥 **landesmuseum.at**

Reminiscent of a grand manor house, this magnificent building is the headquarters of the Oberösterreichisches (Upper Austria) Landesmuseum group, which includes the museum at Linzer Schloss (see p194) and the Biologiezentrum. The Landesgalerie features a superb collection of 20th-century and contemporary art, and an extensive archive of photographs, with an emphasis placed on artists and works from Upper Austria.

### 🏛 Stadtmuseum Nordico

Dametzstrasse 23. **Tel** (0732) 7070-1912. **Open** 10am–6pm Tue–Sun (to 9pm Thu). ♿ 🖥 **nordico.at**

In 1675, this Baroque complex was the home of the college known as "Nordisches Stift", which had as its aim the education of young boys from Nordic countries – hence the name – and their transformation into good Catholics. Today, this imposing building, now owned by the council, houses the Nordico Town Museum, with its collection of objects relating to the history of Linz from ancient times onwards, including a model of the town from 1740. The top floor is given over to temporary exhibitions, mainly of Modern art.

### ⌂ Seminarkirche

Harrachstrasse 7. **Tel** (0732) 771205. **Open** 7am–5pm daily.

The former Deutschordenkirche (church of the Teutonic Order) is now a seminary church. Artistically, this is the most valuable historic church building in Linz. It was built in the early 18th century, to a design by Johann Lukas Hildebrandt. Its beautiful Baroque façade is topped with the decorative coats of arms of the Harrach family. The tower, crowned with a distinctive flattened dome, is surrounded by sandstone statues depicting the virtues expected of a Knight of the Order. The interior is in the shape of an ellipse and is covered with an oval dome.

The Neo-Classical façade of the Landesgalerie

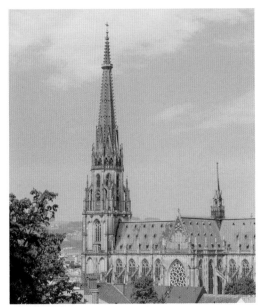

The impressive Mariendom, Austria's largest cathedral

The Crucifixion in the main altar is the work of Martino Altomonte. To the right of the entrance stands a statue of St John of Nepomuk, facing which is a painting of the death of St Joseph. The beautiful ceiling relief shows God the Father reigning among a host of angels on a sky adorned with filigree leaf ornaments.

### ☗ Mariendom
Herrenstrasse 26. **Tel** (0732) 946100. **Open** 7:30am–7pm Mon–Sat, 8am–7pm Sun.

Construction of the New Cathedral, known as the Mariendom, started in 1862, but it was not completed until 1924. Its architect was Vincenz Statz, the builder of Cologne cathedral. The Neo-Gothic cathedral is Austria's largest sacred structure, with a capacity of 20,000. It is said that only one condition was stipulated by the local council: the steeple must not be taller than that of the Stephansdom in Vienna (see p62). Statz complied with the request and the tower in Linz is 134 m (440 ft) high – 3 m (10 ft) lower than its counterpart. There is a platform at 65 m (213 ft) which offers great views of the city. The most interesting features of the cathedral are its modern, colourful stained-glass windows, which depict often complex scenes, such as the history of the city.

### ⛭ Ars Electronica Center
Ars-Electronica-Strasse 1. **Tel** (0732) 7272-0. **Open** 9am–5pm Tue, Wed, Fri, 9am–7pm Thu, 10am–6pm Sat, Sun. **aec.at**

At the entrance to the Nibelungenbrücke (Nibelungs Bridge), on the north bank of the Danube, stands one of Austria's most unusual museums, or rather exhibition centres. The Ars Electronica Center is a highly original museum of virtual worlds, created with the help of modern computer technology. It demonstrates the latest computer wizardry and virtual-reality simulations of space and time travel. Visitors can, for example, journey inside various parts of the universe, visit imaginary Renaissance towns or see a flying saucer disappear into space. There is also a 3D virtual space in the basement where you can explore other worlds with special headsets.

### ⛭ Lentos Kunstmuseum
Ernst-Koref-Promenade 1. **Tel** (0732) 7070 3614. **Open** 10am–6pm Tue–Sun (to 9pm Thu). **lentos.at**

The striking glass façade of this modern museum reflects the Danube. Its collection focuses on contemporary pieces, and features Expressionism (Kokoschka, Klimt), Op and Pop Art (Warhol), Pluralism and Austrian photography.

### ⛭ Biologiezentrum Linz
Johann-Wilhelm-Klein-Str. 73. **Tel** (0732) 7720 521 00. **Open** 9am–5pm Mon–Fri, 10am–5pm Sun. **landesmuseum.at**

This is Upper Austria's largest plant and animal research and exhibition centre. There are special interactive exhibits for children, plus plenty of creepy crawlies and tanks of exotic fish. Outside gardens are devoted to rare and threatened flora.

### Pöstlingberg
A short distance from the centre of Linz rises the 537-m (1,762-ft) Pöstlingberg. The electric mountain train, built in 1898, that climbs almost to the top is the steepest of its kind in Austria. The route is 2.9 km (2 miles) long, and the incline reaches a staggering 10.6 per cent.

At the top is a funfair and a viewing platform, as well as a zoo and the Wallfahrtskirche zu den Sieben Schmerzen Mariens, the pilgrimage church of Our Lady of Seven Sorrows.

Pilgrimage church built in 1738–47 on Pöstlingberg

# ❷ The Danube Valley

Europe's second-longest river, the Danube is unrivalled for its romantic charms, which have inspired so many poets and musicians. Passing through ten countries, the Danube enters Austria as a mountain river just outside of Passau, traverses Upper and Lower Austria for some 360 km (240 miles), and exits after the Hainburg marshes en route to Bratislava in Slovakia. The majestic river is perhaps best experienced by bicycle or foot, if not by boat. By any means, a tour of the river provides stunning views of dense woodland and sprawling vineyards, interspersed with looming fortresses and monasteries nestled along the banks.

**Burg Clam**
The romantic silhouette of Clam Castle, rising above a deep ravine has remained virtually unchanged since the 12th century.

**★ Wilhering**
The collegiate church of the 12th-century Cistercian abbey in Wilhering has a beautiful Rococo interior with frescoes by Bartolomeo Altomonte.

**★ Enns**
The Renaissance municipal tower of Enns was built in 1565–8. It stands on the Hauptplatz, on the left bank of the Enns river, just before it joins the Danube.

*For hotels and restaurants in this region see pp296–7 and pp320–21*

### Grein
Grein's most popular sight is its late-Gothic castle, extended in the 17th century.

## VISITORS' CHECKLIST

**Practical Information**
Road map E3.
*i* Lindengasse 9, 4040 Linz,
(0732) 7277 800 for full details
of hotels, restaurants and
cycling tours.
w donauregion.at

### St Nikola an der Donau
The Danube ends its journey through Upper Austria near St Nikola, an area of outstanding natural beauty.

## Concentration Camps

During the Third Reich, more than 50 concentration camps were built on Austrian territory. Most were destroyed immediately after the war, but some commemorative plaques and symbolic sites have been preserved: there is a memorial crematorium at Gusen, and in Ebensee the cemetery and underground mine tunnels where prisoners once worked can be seen. The most important memorial, however, is the former camp at Mauthausen, where the quarry, original buildings and the "ash dump" have been preserved. Just outside the camp is a visitors' centre and musuem operated by the Austrian government. Each year the liberation is celebrated on the Sunday nearest 8 May.

Mauthausen Todesstiege (Stairway of Death) between the quarry and the camp

### Key

▬▬ Motorway

═══ Major road

═══ Minor road

┄┄ River

▪ ▪ Bundesland (province) border

0 kilometres    5
0 miles          5

One of the magnificent rooms in the emperor's apartments in St Florian Abbey

## ❸ St Florian

**Road map** E3. 6,000.
(07224) 5690. **Open** Abbey:
Guided tours: 11am, 1pm, 3pm.
Bruckner organ: mid-May–mid-Oct:
2:30pm Wed–Fri, Sun, Mon.

Florian, the prefect of the Roman
Noricum Province, converted
to Christianity and was tortured
and thrown into the Enns river in
304 as a result.
His body was
retrieved and, in
the 11th century,
a magnificent
abbey and a
church were built
on the site of his
burial place by
Augustinian monks;
they remain the
keepers of St Florian to this day.
The present appearance of the
abbey and church is the work
of two outstanding Baroque
architects: Carlo Carlone and
Jakob Prandtauer.

St Florian is an impressive
complex of buildings, with
monks' quarters, reception
rooms and a church with an
adjoining chapel of the Virgin
Mary. The main feature in
the large courtyard is the
Adlerbrunnen (Eagle Well), built
in 1603. The east wing houses
the library, with its vast collection
of over 140,000 volumes,

*Alter Codex* from
the library of St Florian

incunabula and manuscripts.
The ceiling painting by
Bartolomeo Altomonte shows
the marriage of Virtue with
Knowledge. Next to the library is
the Marble Hall with huge
columns, designed by Jakob
Prandtauer. The grand staircase
in the west wing, also by
Prandtauer, leads to the emperor's
apartments, where important
guests stayed.
Adjacent is the
room of Anton
Bruckner, who
was associated
with St Florian for
many years.
Carlo Carlone
remodelled the
abbey church – his
great masterpiece.
Worth seeing inside are the
stained-glass windows, the lovely
pulpit and the main altar with a
painting of the Assumption of
the Virgin Mary flanked by
columns of pink Salzburg marble.
The abbey also has an art gallery.

## ❹ Perg

**Road map** E3. 8,000.
(07262) 53150.

Perg, a small town with a long
history situated 30 km (19 miles)
east of Linz, was once owned
by the mighty Von Perg family,

whose last member died in the
12th century, during the Third
Crusade. Until the 19th century
Perg was the largest centre of
millstone production; it is also
the home of Manner, the largest
manufacturer of sweet wafers in
the world. Worth seeing today
are some attractive houses on
Herrengasse, a 1683 Baroque
pillory in the main square and
St Jacob's church (1416), which
has retained its Gothic interior.

In Perg's environs, graves
and numerous remains of the
Hallstatt civilization have been
unearthed (*see p212*). The
Heimathaus, at No. 1
Stifterstrasse, exhibits finds
from that period. It also
documents the production of
millstones and has an interesting
collection of 16th–17th-century
ceramics, decorated using a
special local technique.

## ❺ Kefermarkt

**Road map** E3. 2,000.
Oberer Markt 15, (07947) 591 00.
kefermarkt.at

The main attraction in this
little town is its 15th-century
Wallfahrtskirche (pilgrimage
church), built by Christoph
von Zelking, the master of
Kefermarkt's castle, Schloss
Weinberg. He also commis-
sioned its altar, dedicated to
his favourite saint, St Wolfgang
(died 994), bishop of Regensburg
and Henry II's tutor. The creator
of the altar is unknown, but
the result is a masterpiece of
medieval art. Carved entirely
from limewood, it was probably
once painted, but now the
original texture and colour of
the wood are revealed. Its
centre is made up of the figures
of saints Peter, Wolfgang and
Christopher. On the wings of
the altar, the artist has placed
scenes of the Annunciation, the
Birth of Christ, the Adoration of
the Magi and the Death of Mary.
The altar was once riddled
with woodworm and only
narrowly escaped total destruction. It was carefully restored in
1852–5, under the supervision
of Adalbert Stifter, a writer and
school inspector for Upper

Austria. There is also an interesting permanent exhibition in the church called "Jesus on the Road".

Statue on the splendid wooden altar in Kefermarkt church

## ❻ Freistadt

**Road map** E3. 🏛 7,500. 🚌 🚉
ℹ Hauptplatz 1, (07942) 75700-30.
W freistadt.at

Freistadt, the largest town in the Mühlviertel region, was once the last border fortress on the route leading from the Alpine countries to Bohemia. Much of the medieval **town wall** has survived to this day, including several bastions and two impressive gateways; one of these, the late-Gothic Linzer Tor, is the symbol of the town. The focal point of the old town centre, the rectangular Hauptplatz, is lined

### Jakob Prandtauer (1660–1726)

Austria's outstanding architect of the Baroque, Prandtauer specialized in sacred buildings and shaped the present look of several medieval abbeys. His greatest masterpiece is generally agreed to be the Benedictine abbey in Melk (*see pp146–7*). He also created the church of the Carmelite nuns in St Pölten, and gave a Baroque face to the Augustinian abbey in St Florian and the Benedictine abbey in Kremsmünster. Distinctive features of his work are the variety of forms he used, and the way in which he blended architecture with the surrounding countryside.

Jakob Prandtauer

with historic houses. On its east side stands the town hall, with a carved fountain.

The 15th-century **Katharinenmünster**, the church of St Catherine, on the southwest side of the square, was altered in the Baroque style by Johann Michael Prunner. The altar paintings are the work of Carlo Carlone. The castle, not far from the main square, was built in 1397 for the widow of Prince Albert III. It was devastated by a fire in 1888 and subsequently turned into a military barracks. The building now houses the **Schlossmuseum**, a regional museum holding a large collection of glass paintings, along with 11th-century pottery and handicrafts.

🏛 **Schlossmuseum**
Schlosshof 2.
**Tel** (07942) 72 274.
**Open** 9am–noon, 2–5pm Mon–Fri.

## ❼ Schärding

**Road map** D3. 🏛 4,900. 🚌
ℹ (07712) 4300. W schaerding.at

This town on the banks of the Inn river was, until 1779, owned by the Bavarian family of Wittelsbach, whose influence can be seen in the local architecture. Schärding's most beautiful feature is **Stadtplatz**, the central square cut in half by buildings. At the north end of the upper square, **Silberzeile** is a row of beautiful houses with gabled roofs. It is overslooked by the vast church of St George with a grand steeple. Little of the old castle apart from the gateway and moat remains here. The gateway houses a regional museum with a late-Gothic Madonna, a beautiful crucifix and sculptures by Johann Peter Schwanthaler the Elder (1720–95).

Silberzeile, a row of pretty and colourful gabled houses in the Stadtplatz in Schärding

Baroque house façades on Marktplatz in Obernberg

## ❽ Obernberg am Inn

**Road map** D3. 🚶 1,500. 🚌
ℹ Marktplatz 36, (07723) 8555.
🌐 obernberg.at

Until the late 18th century, Obernberg belonged to Bavaria and was ruled by the bishops of Passau. In 1779, it transferred to Austria. The old market town has preserved its lovely **Marktplatz**, the central town square, lined with pretty houses with exceptionally beautiful, richly ornamented stucco façades. Particularly interesting are the façades of the houses at Nos 37, 38 and 57, with decorations attributed to the prominent Bavarian artist Johann Baptist Modler. A fountain in the centre of the square is surrounded by sculptures. When visiting the Anna-kapelle, the parish church of Obernberg, it is worth taking a look at the 16th-century wood-carving of the Holy Family.

A castle, once owned by the bishops of Passau, has stood in Obernberg since the 12th century, but little remains of it.

**Environs:** 15 km (9 miles) southeast of Obernberg is the largest town of the province, **Ried im Innkreis**, an agricultural centre and home of the Schwanthaler family of sculptors. Many members of

the family were outstanding artists, active in the region from 1632 to 1838. The local museum, at No. 13 Kirchenplatz, exhibits some of their works.

## ❾ Braunau am Inn

**Road map** D3. 🚶 16,000. 🚉 🚌
ℹ Stadtplatz 2, (07722) 62 644.
🌐 tourismus-braunau.at

Braunau is a substantial border town on the Inn river and one of the prettiest spots in the entire region. It was built by the dukes of Lower Bavaria, who ruled it for a long time. Originally intended as a bridgehead in their battles with the Turks, the it remained one of the best-fortified towns in this part of Europe until the 17th century. In 1779 it passed to Austria, together with the rest of the province. The Baroque fortifications were dismantled by Napoleon, but some sections survived, includ- ing the remains of several medieval buildings.

The centre of this Gothic town is occupied by the unusually elongated **Stadtplatz**, surrounded by historic houses. At No. 18 Johann-Fischer-Gasse, built in 1385, an old bell-foundry has survived almost intact. Together with the former ducal castle at No. 10 Altstadt, next door, it is now the home of the regional museum, showing art, handicrafts and traditions of the Inn region.

Figure from fountain in Obernberg town square

The town's symbol is the stone tower of the **Stephanskirche** (parish church of St Stephen) which is nearly 100 m (330 ft) tall. Construction of the church began in 1492, but the Baroque cupola dates from a later period. Inside is a lovely stone pulpit. The only surviving parts of the original altarpiece by Michael Zürn are figures of the Madonna with Child and saints Stephen and Laurence. The altar itself dates from 1906; it is a Neo-Gothic copy of Michael Pacher's altar in St Wolfgang (see p209). Among the tombs outside the church is one of Hans Staininger, who is shown with a curly beard that reaches to his toes – and was said to have been the cause of his untimely death.

Braunau was also the birthplace of Adolf Hitler, who lived at No. 15 Salzburger Vorstadt until he was two.

The birthplace of Adolf Hitler in Braunau am Inn

## ❿ Schmiding Zoo

**Road map** E3. 🚉 🚌 **Tel** (07249) 46 272. Haiding: **Open** Mar–Nov: 9am–5:30pm daily. 🐾 ♿ 📷
🌐 zooschmiding.com

Upper Austria's largest zoo, covering an area of some 120,000 sq m (30 acres), is based at Schmiding, 7 km (4 miles) north of Wels. This modern zoo, with giraffes, monkeys, crocodiles, exotic birds and 1,500 other animal species, is famous for its walk-in aviary with birds of prey. A huge tropical house, an African savannah and a large colony

Flamingoes in the zoo at Schmiding

of flamingoes are further highlights of the zoo. Children will love the 5-m- (16-ft-) high platform which allows them to come face to face with the giraffes.

As well as land animals, the zoo features an array of marine life, displayed in an "aqua zoo". Feeding time with the piranhas is particularly popular with visitors.

## ⓫ Lambach

**Road map** D3. 🚶 3,400. 🚌 🚃
ℹ️ (07245) 283550.

Lambach, on the left bank of the Traun river, grew rich in the Middle Ages thanks to the flourishing salt trade. Around 1040, Count Arnold II von Wels-Lambach and his wife Regilinda transformed the family seat into a monastery. Their son, Bishop Adalbero of Würzburg, who was later canonized, invited Benedictine monks here in 1089. In the same year, the Lambach monks established a second monastery at Melk, which was eventually to surpass the mother abbey in terms of status and beauty *(see pp146–7)*. The abbey church was mostly rebuilt in the 17th century; rebuilding of the abbey itself was completed 50 years later.

The Baroque interior of the church is very beautiful, but Lambach owes its fame primarily to its Romanesque frescoes, probably dating from the 11th century. Unique in Austria, they are considered an outstanding example of Romanesque art. At their centre is the Madonna with Child, to the left the Adoration of the Magi, who present gifts to the Holy Infant. The south vault depicts Jerusalem and Herod's palace. The abbey treasury also holds the Romanesque chalice of Bishop Adalbero, and precious monstrances and chasubles. Also on view are ceiling paintings by Martino Altomonte and Martin Johann Schmidt. The musical archives hold a copy of Mozart's *Lambacher Symphonie*, which the composer reputedly created while staying here. Lambach also has a beautifully preserved Rococo theatre.

Romanesque frescoes in Lambach Abbey

## ⓬ Wels

**Road map** E3. 🚶 59,000. 🚌 🚃
ℹ️ Stadtplatz 44 (07242) 67 722-0.
🆆 wels.at

The history of Wels dates back to the Romans, as testified by numerous excavations. Some of the objects discovered are on display in the former Minorites' Abbey, including the famous Wels Venus, a bronze statuette from the 1st–2nd century AD, and the oldest early-Christian epitaph in Austria, from the first half of the 4th century.

Today Wels is a centre of agriculture and industry, and the venue of Agraria, a biennial agricultural fair of international importance. Many historic features have also been preserved. **Stadtplatz**, the main square in the old town, is entered through a Baroque gate, the **Ledererturm**. Many houses in Stadtplatz have attractive façades, such as the Rococo **Kremsmünstererhof** with its arcaded courtyard, which for 400 years belonged to Kremsmünster Abbey. Adjacent to it stands a water tower (1577) and a two-house complex forming the late-Baroque town hall.

Also on Stadtplatz is the Stadtpfarrkirche, the parish church of St John the Evangelist, with an original Romanesque portal and magnificent 14th-century stained-glass windows in the presbytery. **Burg Wels**, the imperial palace, first documented in 776, is now a lively cultural centre and home of the regional museum.

The galleried courtyard of Kremsmünsterhof in Stadtplatz, Wels

## ⑬ Kremsmünster

**Road map** E3. 🚉 🚌 **Tel** (07583) 5275-0. **Open** for guided tours booked in advance only. 🅿️
🖥️ **stift-kremsmuenster.at**

Perched high above the Krems river, on an impressive terrace formed during the Ice Age, is the 8th-century Benedictine abbey of Kremsmünster, its present appearance dating mostly from the 17th century. The abbey was completed by Jakob Prandtauer, to designs by Carlo Carlone. Two of its most remarkable features are the 17th-century fish ponds, surrounded by columns, corridors and sculptural fountains, and the eight-storey **Sternwarte**, or "Mathematical Tower". Completed in 1756, the 50-m- (165-ft-) high observation tower was arguably the highest secular building of its era. Today it holds collections of palaeontology, physics, anthropology, astronomy and zoology. The **Stiftskirche** (abbey church) has rich stucco decorations and angel statues. The abbey museum contains works by Austrian and Dutch masters from the Baroque and Renaissance periods, wood carvings and gold objects. The pride of Kremsmünster

are its earliest exhibits; these include the gilded-copper chalice and candelabras of Duke Tassilo, the legendary founder of the abbey, and the *Codex millenarius* (c.800), an illuminated manuscript.

## ⑭ Steyr

**Road map** E3. 🏔️ 38,000. 🚉 🚌
ℹ️ Stadtplatz 27, (07252) 53 229.

Steyr, one of Austria's largest industrial centres, is also a very attractive town which has managed to preserve its old town almost intact. The townscape is punctuated in the north by the turrets of the castle and in the south by the towers of the Stadtpfarrkirche, the parish church at Brucknerplatz. The centre of town is the elongated Stadtplatz (town square) with most of the historic sights. The **Bummerlhaus** (1497), at No. 32, is a well-preserved Gothic house with a high pitched roof and three arcaded courtyards, that is now a bank. The Rococo **Rathaus** (town hall), with its slender steeple, was designed by Johann Gotthard Hayberger. The inner courtyards of houses around the square are also worth seeing. The **Stadtpfarrkirche**, built in

The Tassilo Chalice in Kremsmünster

1443, was remodelled in the Neo-Gothic style, but it has preserved some elements of its original 15th-century decor, the work of Hans Puchsbaum (builder of the Stephansdom in Vienna), as well as some lovely wrought-iron grilles. The south wall has magnificent 15th-century stained-glass windows; the sculptures in the north portal and the former cemetery chapel of St Margaret (1430), also by Hans Puchsbaum, date from the same period.

The **Schloss** (castle), first mentioned in 10th-century annals, stands in the oldest part of the town. Today it has a Baroque façade and a mostly Rococo interior. The house at No. 26 Grünmarkt, formerly a granary, is now a museum.

**Environs:** In **Gleink**, a northern suburb of Steyr, there is a Benedictine abbey. Some 3 km (2 miles) west of the town centre, in the suburb of **Christkindl**, is the church of the same name (meaning "Infant Christ"), a joint work of Giovanni Battista Carlone and Jakob Prandtauer. In 1695, a sick man placed a wax figure of the Infant Jesus in the hollow of a tree and prayed there every day for a cure. His prayers were answered and soon the crowds of pilgrims drawn to the site of the miracle were so large that, in 1702, the abbot from nearby Garsten

Panorama of Steyr, as seen from the river

decided to build a church. The main object of adoration is a wax figurine of Jesus, kept in a beautifully decorated glass cabinet. The cabinet itself is part of a composition symbolizing the Holy Trinity. Christkindl has its own post office, using the coveted "Christkindl" postmark showing the Infant Jesus. It operates only in the pre-Christmas period, and a huge number of letters, supposedly from the Infant Jesus, are sent around the world from here.

### ⛪ Christkindl Church
Christkindlweg 69. **Tel** (07252) 54 622.

The façade of the Christkindl church, on the outskirts of Steyr

### ⓯ Bad Hall

**Road map** E3. 🚍 4,900. 🚌
ℹ️ Kurpromenade 1, (07258) 7200-0.
🌐 badhall.at

Bad Hall, a health resort between Steyr and Kremsmünster, lies on the so-called "Romantic Route", but the idyllic scenery is just one of its attractions: it also boasts the richest iodine springs in Central Europe. A therapeutic resort surrounds the springs, which are used to treat eye, circulatory and heart diseases. The lovely Kurpark (spa park), with its excellent sports facilities, makes convalescence a real treat. There is also a Rococo church, which belongs to the abbey at Kremsmünster. Another sight worth visiting is

Lovely scenery around the resort of Bad Hall

the fascinating **Forum Hall Museum**, which holds a superb collection devoted to the development of traditional folk handicrafts in Upper Austria, as well as to the history of the local springs.

### 🏛 Forum Hall Museum
Eduard-Bach-Strasse 4. **Tel** (07258) 4888.
**Open** Apr–Oct: 2–6pm Thu–Sun. 🎫
🌐 forumhall.at

### ⓰ Stadl-Paura

**Road map** D3. 🚍 4,900. 🚌 🚌
ℹ️ Marktplatz 1, (07245) 28 011-0.

Stadl-Paura, a small town on the right bank of the Traun river 2 km (1 mile) south of Lambach, has an imposing **Dreifaltigkeitskirche** (church of the Holy Trinity). Construction of the church was started in 1714 in thanksgiving for the sparing of the town from the plague. In its design, the church

The Dreifaltigkeitskirche, pilgrimage church of the Holy Trinity in Stadl-Paura

represents the Holy Trinity – everything is in triplicate. There are three façades, three portals, three towers and three altars. The church was built by the Linz architect Johann Michael Prunner. In the design of the interior decorations some clever false architectural perspectives have been incorporated, creating unusual effects. The paintings on the altarpieces are by Carlo Carlone, Martino Altomonte and Domenico Parodi.

The house at No. 13 Fabrik-strasse, once an orphanage for the children of sailors who lost their lives in the waters of the Traun river, is now a museum of shipping, **Schiffleutmuseum**, which is open on Sundays and holidays in summer.

### ⓱ Schwanenstadt

**Road map** D3. 🚍 4,000. 🚌 🚌
ℹ️ Stadtplatz 54, (07673) 2255.

Schwanenstadt is a typical small upper Austrian town, situated between Lambach and Vöcklabruck. In the centre of town stands a Neo-Gothic parish church with a 78-m (256-ft) spire, built in 1900 on the site of an earlier Gothic church. Worth seeing inside are a late-Gothic statue of the Virgin Mary, a 15th-century relief of the Mourning for Christ and 18th-century Baroque statues of the 12 apostles.

In front of the town hall is a 13th-century well, which is set on an attractive square lined with houses with Renaissance and Baroque façades.

The riverside townscape of the health resort of Gmunden, on the banks of the Traun river

## ⑱ Vöcklabruck

**Road map** D3. 🏙 12,000. 🚗 🚌
ℹ Graben 8, (07672) 26 644.

The name of this town was first
documented in 1134 as Pons
(bridge) Veckelahe. Soon after,
a trading settlement sprang up
on the banks of the Vöckla river.
The only original structures to
have survived from this period
are two medieval towers.

At the centre of town stands
the small, 15th-century, late-
Gothic **St Ulrichkirche** (church
of St Ulrich), which has a Baroque
interior. The site of the 12th-
century hospital and chapel is
occupied by the magnificent
Baroque **St Ägidiuskirche**,
designed by Carlo Carlone, with
sculptures by Giovanni Battista
Carlone. The ceiling frescoes
depict scenes from the
lives of Christ and
the Virgin Mary.

The former parish
house, at No. 10
Hinterstadt, now
houses a regional
museum with a
room devoted to
Anton Bruckner.

The south of the
town is dominated
by the silhouette
of **Wallfahrtskirche
Maria Schöndorf**, a church
of pilgrimage. It has a Neo-
Gothic altarpiece with a
beautiful 15th-century
statue of the Virgin Mary, and
pretty stained-glass windows
behind the main altar from the
same period.

**Environs:** West of Vöcklabruck,
about 12 km (7 miles) away, is
the small town of **Gampern**.
Its Remigiuskirche (church of

A detail from Gmunden
town hall

St Remigius) has an attractive
late-Gothic polyptych (1507)
carved in wood.

## ⑲ Gmunden

**Road map** D3. 🏙 13,000. 🚗 🚌
ℹ Rathausplatz 1, (07612) 65 752.

This lakeside town, on the
northern end of Traunsee,
established itself as a trading
post in the salt trade. Today, it is
a popular and well-run health
resort, and it is also known for
its fine ceramics. Gmunden's
old town centre is situated
between the lake and the left
(western) bank of the Traun
river. Its Hauptplatz boasts a
Renaissance town hall with a
small, arcaded tower and a
carillon that plays regularly.

The **Stadtpfarrkirche**
(parish church) has a
two-fold dedication:
the Virgin Mary
and the Three Kings.
The Magi are also
depicted in the
main altarpiece, one
of the most beautiful
works by Thomas
Schwanthaler.
The figures of saints
Elizabeth and Zacharias were
carved by Michael Zürn. Each
year on Epiphany Eve (5 Jan),
a barge travels along the Traun
river bringing the Three Kings to
town; they then solemnly
proceed to "their" church. A
ceramic fountain decorated
with a figure of a salt miner
stands adjacent to the church.

The **Gmunden K-Hof
Museum**, based in the
Renaissance building of the
former Salt Mines Authorities,
has exhibits on the history of

the town and its salt production,
a room on the astronomer and
mathematician Johannes von
Gmunden, and a section
dedicated to the history of
sanitation, which includes
displays of locally made toilet
bowls and chamber pots.

In Traunsee stands the water
fortress of **Lake Castle Ort**, built
in the 15th and 16th centuries
and rebuilt inn 1634. It has an
enchanting triangular, arcaded
courtyard and remnants of
Renaissance frescoes. A popular
TV series is set in the castle.

🏛 **Gmunden K-Hof Museum**
Kammerhofgasse 8. **Tel** (07612) 794
423. **Open** 10am–5pm Wed–Sun (also
Tue Jun–Aug). 🌐

## ⑳ Traunkirchen

**Road map** D3. 🏙 1,600. 🚌
ℹ Ortsplatz 1, (07617) 2255.

Precariously perched on a rocky
promontory, the small village of
Traunkirchen is one of the most
popular tourist destinations in
Salzkammergut (see p213). It
presents a lovely picture,
clinging to the west shore of

Johannesbergkapelle above Traunsee
in Traunkirchen

Traunsee, Austria's deepest lake, with views of the lake's wild southern shore and the Traunstein peak on the eastern shore, the highest mountain of the region, rising to 1,691 m (5,548 ft). Above the village towers the pretty Johannes-bergkapelle. On the northern end of the headland stands the Jesuit **Pfarrkirche**, rebuilt after a fire in 1632. It has an unusual fishermen's pulpit shaped like a fishing boat, with the apostles drawing nets filled with fish. Since 1632, Traunkirchen has also hosted an annual Corpus Christi boat procession.

## ❷ Salzkammergut Lakes

*See pp210–11.*

The steam mountain railway leading to the top of Schafberg

## ❷ Schafberg

**Road map** D4. Scharfbergbahn: 🛈 (6138) 223 20. 🇼 **scharfbergbahn.at**

One of the most picturesque peaks in the area, Schafberg (Sheep Mountain) rises to 1,783 m (5,850 ft) between Attersee and Wolfgangsee. Austria's steepest cog railway runs old steam trains up to a station only 50 m (164 ft) from the summit for unforgettable views of the most beautiful lakes of the Salzkammergut: Mondsee, Attersee and Wolfgangsee *(see pp210–11).* Visible in the background are the towering mountain ranges running to the Dachstein massif in the south and, beyond Salzburg, you can see the Bavarian Alps on the German-Austrian border.

## ❷ St Wolfgang

**Road map** D4. 🚠 2,800. 🚍 🛈 Au 140, (06138) 8003. 🇼 **stwolfgang.at**

On the northern shore of Wolfgangsee lies the popular town of St Wolfgang. According to legend it arose around a chapel built by Wolfgang (died 994), bishop of Regensburg in Germany and teacher of Emperor Henry II. Although he died a hermit, Wolfgang was an extremely popular figure in his day, and was later canonized. His chapel became a much-visited place of pilgrimage. In the 15th century it was replaced by a church with room for a much larger number of pilgrims. It was around that time that the abbot of Mondsee commis-sioned the famed South Tyrolean artist, Michael Pacher, to create an altar for the **pilgrimage church**.

Pacher's high altar, combining sculpture, painting and archi-tecture, is a late-Gothic masterpiece. The four scenes visible on the wings of the altarpiece when they are closed (on weekdays) depict events from the life of St Wolfgang. The saint is shown holding a model of the church and is flanked by the figures of the saints George and Florian. On Sundays, the wings of the altar are opened to reveal eight painted scenes from the life of Christ. They are striking in their coloration, the dynamics of their life-like figures and, above all, in the architectural perspective employed by the artist. The brightly gilded, sculpted centrepiece depicts the Coronation of the Virgin Mary attended by Christ, St Benedict and St Wolfgang.

The church of St Wolfgang also has a lovely Baroque altar-piece by Thomas Schwanthaler, depicting the Holy Family on their journey to Jerusalem. The three side altarpieces on the north wall and the magnifi-cently ornate pulpit are the works of a Mondsee master, Meinrad Guggenbichler.

St Wolfgang is also popular with tourists who come to see the Weisses Rössl hotel, which inspired the operetta, *White Horse Inn* by Ralph Benatzky.

## ❷ Bad Ischl

**Road map** D4. 🚠 14,000. 🚉 🚍 🛈 Auböckplatz 5, (06132) 27 757-0. Kaiservilla: Jainzen 38, (06132) 23241. 🇼 **badischl.com**

Therapeutic saltwater springs were discovered in this region as early as the 16th century, but Bad Ischl did not become a popular health resort until the early 1800s, when the court doctor ordered saline treat-ments for the infertile Arch-duchess Sophie. Soon, she started producing babies. The most famous of these was Franz Joseph I, the future emperor, who spent all his summer holidays with his wife Elizabeth at the **Kaiservilla**, now a museum, which can be visited on a guided tour. It was also here that he signed the declaration of war with Serbia, on 1 August 1914, signalling the start of World War I.

Many aristocrats and artists have been attracted to the spa, among them the composer Franz Lehár, who lived at No. 8 Franz-Lehár-Kai, which is now a museum devoted to him.

The imposing Spa House in the popular resort of Bad Ischl

*For hotels and restaurants in this region see pp296–7 and pp320–21*

# ㉑ Salzkammergut Lakes

This corner of Austria is one of the country's most-visited regions. With more than 70 lakes surrounded by mountains, it features breathtaking scenery as well as a unique climate. During winter it becomes a hotspot for skiiers, while the summer months serve hikers and those keen to take in the views. This is also one of the few areas in Europe to preserve many original folk customs, including the tradition of placing a crib in front of the house at Christmas.

**Mondsee**
The warmest of the Salzkammergut lakes, at the foot of craggy mountains, is popular with windsurfers. The little town of the same name arose around a Benedictine abbey, which dominates it to this day.

**★ St Wolfgang**
The main attraction in this charming small town and holiday resort is the parish church, with its beautiful altar-piece by Michael Pacher (see p209).

Braunau ↑

St Georgen •

A1 E55 E60

Mondsee

Salzburg ←

154

Mondsee

151

Unterach •

Burggrabenklamm

Wolfgangsee

St Wolfga

St

## Politicians and Artists on Holiday

The shores of the Salzkammergut lakes have seen many famous visitors. The house that witnessed the engagement of Emperor Franz Joseph I to Elisabeth of Bavaria in 1853 is now a museum with memorabilia of famous guests, in Bad Ischl. There were scores of them: crowned heads and high-ranking aristocrats were joined by artists. Franz Lehár, composer of operettas such as *The Merry Widow* and *The Land of Smiles*, had his villa here; so did the actor Alexander Girardi and the actress Katharina Schratt, the long-term mistress of Franz Joseph I. Other regular visitors included the writer and actor Johannes Nepomuk Nestroy, the painter Rudolf von Alt, and musicians Johannes Brahms, Anton Bruckner, Johann Strauss and Imre Kálmán. In the late 20th century, many politicians spent their holidays in St Wolfgang, including both the Austrian and German chancellors.

Franz Joseph I and his hunting party

### Key
▬▬ Motorway
▭▭ Major road
⋯⋯ Minor road
— River
– – Bundesland provincial border

★ **Attersee**
The largest of the Salzkammergut lakes, Attersee is dominated by the Höllengebirge (Mountains of Hell). This popular lake is a great base for boating holidays.

**VISITORS' CHECKLIST**

**Practical Information**
**Road map** D3, D4.
🚹 Salzkammergut Tourism, Salinenplatz 1, A-4820 Bad Ischl.
**Tel** (06132) 26909.
email: info@salzkammergut.at
🎭 "Glöcklerlauf" (Bell walk) Night Procession in many towns Jan 5.
**w** salzkammergut.at

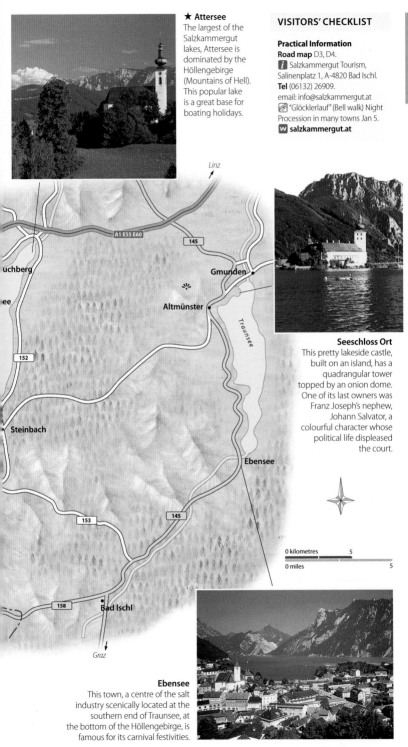

**Seeschloss Ort**
This pretty lakeside castle, built on an island, has a quadrangular tower topped by an onion dome. One of its last owners was Franz Joseph's nephew, Johann Salvator, a colourful character whose political life displeased the court.

**Ebensee**
This town, a centre of the salt industry scenically located at the southern end of Traunsee, at the bottom of the Höllengebirge, is famous for its carnival festivities.

**For keys to symbols** *see back flap*

Bronze-Age finds in Hallstatt's World Heritage Museum

### ㉕ Hallstatt

**Road map** D4. 🏔 800. 🚌 🚉 ⛴
ℹ️ Seestrasse 99 (06134) 8208.
🌐 hallstatt.net

The village of Hallstatt is one of the loveliest tourist destinations in the Salzkammergut. The steep drop of the Dachstein massif provides a scenic backdrop for the town and adjacent Hallstätter See. The houses are clustered together so tightly that many are accessible only from the lakeside, while the old street runs above the rooftops. Even the local Corpus Christi procession is held on the lake, in festive, decorated boats.

Rising above the village on a rocky headland is the pagoda-like roof of the **Pfarrkirche**. Its stepped dome dates from a later period, but the church was built in the 15th century and to this day contains many original features, including a carved wooden altarpiece of the Virgin Mary, sometimes compared to Pacher's altar in St Wolfgang *(see p209)*. The figure of the Madonna at its

Painted skulls in the Beinhaus chapel of Hallstatt's Pfarrkirche

centre is flanked by the saints Barbara, patron of miners, and Catherine, revered by woodcutters. Depicted on the inner wings are scenes from the lives of Mary and Jesus. The altar is guarded by the statues of two knightly saints, George and Florian.

In the cemetery surrounding the church stands the **Beinhaus**, a chapel that serves as a store-house for some very bizarre objects. This former mortuary now holds some 1,200 human skulls, painted with floral designs and in many cases inscribed with the name, date and cause of death of the deceased. Shortage of space in the graveyard meant that some ten years after a funeral, when a body had decomposed, the remains were moved to the chapel to make room for the next coffin to be buried, resulting in this unusual depository.

A short distance below the Catholic Pfarrkirche stands a Neo-Gothic Protestant church, with a slender steeple.

Directly at a height of 500 m (1,640 ft) above the town is **Salzwelten Hallstatt**, one of the oldest known salt mines in the world, which can be reached by cable car. Salt was mined here as early as 3,000 BC and then transported to the Baltic Sea and the Mediterranean.

In 1846, a large cemetery yielding some 2,000 graves was uncovered in Hallstatt. Rich burial objects dated mainly from the Iron Age but some dated even further back, to the Bronze Age. The Hallstatt finds proved so important archaeologically that the Celtic culture of that

period (800–400 BC) was named the Hallstatt civilization. Its influence reached far into France, the Slav countries and Hungary.

Today, Hallstatt treasures can be seen in many Austrian museums, with the bulk of them held at Schloss Eggenberg, near Graz *(see p166)*. The few finds that stayed in Hallstatt are kept in the **World Heritage Museum**. The entire Hallstatt region has been declared a World Heritage Site by UNESCO.

🏛 **Salzwelten Hallstatt**
Lahnstrasse 21. **Tel** (06132) 200 2400. **Open** late Apr–mid-Sep: 9:30am–4:30pm daily; mid-Sep–Oct: 9:30am–3pm daily. 🅿️ 🅲 ♿
🌐 salzwelten.at

🏛 **World Heritage Museum**
Seestrasse 56. **Tel** (06134) 828015. **Open** Nov–Mar: 11am–3pm Wed–Sun; Apr, Oct: 10am–4pm daily; May–Sep: 10am–6pm daily. 🅿️ 🅲
🌐 museum-hallstatt.at

### ㉖ Gosauseen

**Road map** D4. 🚌
ℹ️ Gosau, (06136) 8295.

For pure, natural, unspoilt beauty, this area has few rivals. The Gosauseen are three small mountain lakes – Vorderer Gosausee, Gosaulacke and Hinterer Gosausee. They lie one after the other, surrounded by forest and limestone rocks, and intercut with deep gorges. Vorderer Gosausee lies at an altitude of 933 m (3,061 ft). An undemanding walk around the lake will reward you with superb views of the surrounding mountains and over the Dachstein range, with its many glaciers.

The most picturesque mountain, with zigzag peaks and a sheer drop, is Gosaukamm (2,459 m/8,068 ft). This is the easternmost part of the Alps where the snow stays on the ground all year round. The road to Hinterer Gosausee climbs steeply among thick forest. From this lake, 1,154 m (3,786 ft) high, you can climb some of the adjacent peaks.

Mountain stream racing through a gorge in the Dachstein range

# ➋ Dachsteinhöhlen

**Road map** D4. 🛈 Winkl 34, Obertraun am Hallstättersee, (06131) 351. 🖥
🌐 dachstein-salzkammergut.com

The caves in the slopes of the Dachstein range are among Austria's most beautiful and fascinating natural monuments. The vast Dachsteinhöhlen cave system, one of the largest on Earth and millions of years old, is covered by 500- year-old permafrost. After the last Ice Age, underground waters created strange ice mountains, glaciers and frozen waterfalls. The most interesting of these is the **Rieseneishöhle** (Giant Ice Cave). The caverns in this surreal underground ice-world are named after King Arthur and the Celtic heroes, Parsifal and Tristan. The most arresting cavern formation is the so-called Ice Chapel.

## The Salzkammergut

For centuries, the name Salzkammergut applied only to the area around the Hallstätter See and Traunsee lakes, and to the towns of Bad Ischl, Hallstatt and Gmunden. Salt has been excavated here since prehistoric times, ensuring the long-term wealth and development of the entire region. Salt mines exist in the area to this day. In the second half of the 19th century the area became famous for its therapeutic springs, and with time the term Salzkammergut came to refer to the entire land of lakes and mountains that is now Austria's most popular tourist destination. It includes the eastern part of the Salzburg Alps, with the picturesque mountain ranges of Dachstein (eastern part), Totes Gebirge (Dead Mountains) and Höllengebirge (Mountains of Hell). Between the mountains lie 76 lakes, the largest and most famous of which are Traunsee, Mondsee, Attersee, Hallstätter See and Wolfgangsee. The "land of salt" now straddles three Austrian provinces. The largest part is in Upper Austria, a small area in the south belongs to Styria, whilst almost all of Wolfgangsee and the St Gilgen resort are part of the Salzburger Land.

The much-loved Salzkammergut, land of lakes and mountains

A little further along, also in a limestone wall of Dachstein, is the entrance to a second system of caves, known as **Mammuthöhle** (Mammoth Caves), so named because of their size rather than after the prehistoric mammal. These caves do not have ice formations, but there is a spectacular light show.

Both networks of caves can be reached via paths starting from the first cable-car station. The sightseeing route leads through a labyrinthine network of tunnels, gorges and chambers that stretch over 44 km (27 miles), with a 1,200 m (4,000 ft) change in altitude. Individual caverns have been given evocative names such as the Realm of Shadows or Midnight Cathedral.

Also worth seeing is a third cave, **Koppenbrüllerhöhle**, which has a giant water source and is considered to be the largest water cave in the Dachstein massif.

All caves are open to the public only during the spring and summer seasons (May to Oct; Koppenbrüllerhöhle May to Sep). When visiting the caves, especially the ice caves, make sure you take warm clothing.

Dachstein ice caves in Obertraun

# SALZBURGER LAND

The province of Salzburg, a region of high mountains, covers an area of 7,154 sq km (2,762 sq miles) and has 450,000 inhabitants. Its neighbours are Germany and the Austrian provinces of Tyrol, Upper Austria, Styria and Carinthia. A narrow wedge of land along the peaks of the Hohe Tauern mountains reaches as far as the Italian border in the south.

Salzburger Land is divided into five regions: Flachgau, Tennengebirge, Pongau, Pinzgau and Lungau. History has made them different in character and traditions; all are great for sports.

Colonization of the Salzach valley goes back to prehistoric times. The mineral deposits – copper, precious metals and, above all, salt (*Salz* in German) from which both the town and province take their names – were being exploited as early as 1000 BC. It was salt which created the basis for the development of the so-called Hallstatt civilization that spread from here. The Celtic town of Noricum established in the Alpine region ultimately became a Roman province of the same name. Christianity arrived here early, and its turbulent progress was halted only by the great Migration of Nations in 5th-century Europe. It was not until the 7th century that monks settled in Mönchsburg, the future Salzburg, which became first a bishopric and then an archbishopric. The entire province was an independent principality for many centuries, governed by an ecclesiastical ruler acting as sovereign prince and, depending on political circumstance and personal preference, associating himself with the Holy Roman Empire, the Austrian Habsburgs or Rome. Following the Congress of Vienna in 1815, Salzburg became part of Austria. Today, the beauty of Salzburg, inextricably linked with Mozart, makes this province a visitor magnet second only to Vienna.

Hochkönig Alpine meadows in Salzburger Land

◀ Spectacular domes of the cathedral towering over Salzburg

# Exploring Salzburger Land

Most of the province lies in the Salzach river basin, at a relatively high altitude, offering excellent conditions for both winter sports and summer mountain walks. Austria's most scenic mountain road, the Grossglockner Hochalpenstrasse *(see pp284–5)*, crosses the southern part of the province. The region abounds in mineral springs and waterfalls, and boasts one of the world's largest caves. Salzburg, an administrative centre, is also the cultural and artistic capital of the province, the city of Mozart and home of the annual Salzburg Festival.

Alpine meadows near Lungötz, typical of Salzburger Land

Branau

Oberndorf

15

🅷🅰

SALZBUR

SCHLO
München       HELLBRU
(Munich)
WASSERSCH

178

**20** LOFER

178

GERMAN

Steinernes Meer

311

Saalfelden

SAALBACH **19**

Kitzbühel

Kitzbüheler Alpen

ZELL AM SEE **18**
🏠 🎠

Niedemsill

MITTERSILL **21**           KAPRUN **17**     Bruck

Neukirchen                                                        Taxenbach

165   Salzach                                                      3

KRIMMLER
**22** WASSERFÄLLE                                        S A L Z B U R

108      Kitzsteinhorn            107
3203m
Reichenspitz                                    Mooserboden       Ferleiten
3301m
Grosses Wiesbachhorn   Edelweißspitz
Großvenediger            Lienz          3564m           2572m
3665m

## Sights at a Glance

Eisriesenwelt near Werfen, the largest ice caves on earth

Straßwalchen

Neumarkt
am Wallersee

-see

Seekirchen

Thalgau

Fuschl

Linz

A1

158

ST GILGEN 4

St Wolfgang

Wolfgangsee

158

Bad Ischl

ALLEIN

10

Kuchl

6 GOLLING

Scheffau

Lueg
Pass

162

7 ABTENAU

Lammer

Annaberg

166

8 WERFEN

311

A10

9

BISCHOFSHOFEN

320

10 RADSTADT

Liezen

ST JOHANN IM
11 PONGAU

12 WAGRAIN

99

Schwarzach im
Pongau

Radstadter Tauern

Lessach

A10

MAUTERNDORF 13

15 TAMSWEG

St Michael im
Lungau

99

14 SCHLOSS
MOOSHAM

Bad Gastein

95

ockstein

Spittal

Villach

Königstuhl
2336m

Castle above the town of Moosham, once the property of
the archbishops of Salzburg

Side altar in the church of St Leonard
in Tamsweg

0 kilometres     10

0 miles          10

**Key**

⬛ Motorway

— Major road

⋯ Minor road

— Scenic route

⋯ Main railway

— Minor railway

▬ International border

▬ Province border

△ Summit

✕ Pass

## Getting There

Most major European airlines fly to Salzburg Airport.
Salzburg is also the starting point of the "corridor" – a
railway and motorway system that connects the city
with the east and south of the country, and passes into
Germany. Most major sights are served by buses, and
where there are no roads, you can make use of an
extensive network of mountain railways.

# ❶ Salzburg

Steeped in legend and unrivalled for its Baroque architecture, Salzburg is most famous as the home of Mozart, who was born here in 1756. Founded by Benedictine monks, Salzburg has one of the most evocative old town centres in Europe, as well as one of the most impressive fortresses, Hohensalzburg. Music remains, however, the city's main attraction. The annual Salzburg Festival is the largest of its kind in Europe, while some 300,000 visitors a year enjoy tours of the original locations used in the 1965 film *The Sound of Music*, including Nonnberg Convent and Mondsee Church *(see p335)*.

Tanzmeisterhaus, on the market square, once the home of Mozart

The churches of Salzburg, overlooked by the Hohensalzburg fortress

## Exploring Salzburg

Salzburg is divided into three distinct areas of interest. The first, including the finest churches, the archbishop's residence and Mozart's birthplace, is on the left bank of the Salzach river. The second area, on the right bank, is the New Town. Its most interesting sights are the Mirabell Palace, the Mozart Conservatoire and Kapuzinerberg. The third area is the mighty former fortress of Hohensalzburg to the south.

## Kapuzinerberg

Kapuzinerberg, a hill on the right bank of the Salzach river opposite the historic Old Town, drops almost down to the river. Two hundred and fifty steep steps, known as the Imbergstiege, climb up from Linzer Gasse. At the halfway point stands the church of St Johannes am Imberg, built in 1681. Its main altarpiece has a painting of the Baptism of Christ. Another interesting feature is the carved pulpit by Johann Georg Hitzl. A small castle once stood on top of the hill and formed part of the medieval fortifications; later it was partly incorporated

into the Capuchin monastery complex whose church was completed in 1602. The monastery has a carved oak door made from the medieval stalls of an earlier cathedral. A short distance away stands a villa that was once the home of the Austrian writer Stefan Zweig. Below the church, from the top of an old tower, the Hettwer Bastei, you can enjoy superb views over the many domes and spires of Salzburg.

## 🚋 Makartplatz

**Mozart-Wohnhaus**
Makartplatz 8. **Tel** (0662) 874227-40. **Open** Sep–Jun: 9am–5:30pm daily, July–Aug: 9am–7pm daily. 🎧

This square was given its current name in memory of the Salzburg-born painter, Hans Makart, whose work greatly influenced contemporary fashion, architecture and interior design in the mid-19th century.

The Tanzmeisterhaus at No. 8 was Mozart's home in 1773–87. The original house, destroyed in World War II, was rebuilt, and is a museum (Mozart-Wohnhaus) dedicated to the composer.

The Dreifaltigkeitskirche (church of the Holy Trinity), in the northeast corner of the square, dates from 1694 and is one of the earliest works of Johann Bernhard Fischer von Erlach. Built shortly after his return from Italy, it shows signs of Roman influence. Its façade is crowned with sculptures of Faith, Love, Hope and the Church by Michael Bernhard Mandl. The frescoes in the dome vault are by Johann Michael Rottmayr.

## 🏛 Sebastiansfriedhof

Linzer Gasse 41. **Tel** (0662) 875208. **Open** 9am–4pm daily (until 6:30pm in summer).

The St Sebastian cemetery lies just below the church of the same name. All that remains of the old church is a Rococo portal with the bust of its patron saint, and a wrought-iron grille by Philipp Hinterseer. The present, much more modest building, dates from the early 19th century. The cemetery is older, dating from the 15th century. It was

Guilded figure from the church of St Sebastian

designed along the lines of the Italian *campo santo*, with burial sites surrounded by columns, and has magnificent sculptures and tombstones. Next to the entrance, beside the church, is the tomb of the philosopher, physician and father of pharmacology, Paracelsus, who died in Salzburg in 1541.

At the centre of the cemetery stands the chapel of the Archangel St Gabriel, which doubles as Archbishop Wolf Dietrich von Raitenau's mausoleum. Nearby are the graves of Mozart's wife, Constanze and his father, Leopold.

### 🏠 Schloss Mirabell

Mirabellplatz. **Tel** (0662) 80720. **Open** 8am–4pm Mon, Wed & Thu, 1–4pm Tue & Fri.

The site of the present Mirabell Palace was originally used by Archbishop Wolf Dietrich von Raitenau in 1606 to erect a much more modest mansion, which he intended as a home for his mistress Salome Alt. The daughter of a Jewish merchant,

she is said to have borne the archbishop 15 children. Dietrich referred to her as his wife and loved her to the end of his life. In 1727, Johann Lukas von Hildebrandt rebuilt the palace for Archbishop Franz Anton Fürst von Harrach as a truly royal Baroque home. A fire in 1818 destroyed part of the building, but fortunately the superb Angels Staircase, with sculptures by Georg Raphael Donner, and the gilt-stuccoed Marble Hall, where a young Wolfgang Mozart performed with his sister

**Putti on the Angels Staircase in Mirabell**

Nanneri, were spared. The palace is now a civic administration building, surrounded by attractive gardens filled with groups of sculptures and fountains.

The beautiful gardens of Schloss Mirabell

## VISITORS' CHECKLIST

### Practical Information
**Road map** D3. 🏛 145,000. ℹ️ Mozartplatz 5, (0662) 88987330. 🎭 Salzburger Festspiele (late Jul–late Aug). 🌐 **salzburg.info**

### Transport
✈️ Innsbrucker Bundesstrasse 95, (0662) 85800. 🚉 Hauptbahnhof, Südtirolerplatz, (0662) 930 003161.

## Salzburg City Centre

① Kapuzinerberg
② Makartplatz
③ Sebastiansfriedhof
④ Schloss Mirabell
⑤ Mozarteum
⑥ Haus der Natur
⑦ Salzburg Museum
⑧ Festspielhäuser
⑨ Mozarts Geburtshaus
⑩ Kollegienkirche
⑪ Franziskanerkirche
⑫ Residenzplatz
⑬ Stift St Peter
⑭ Dom
⑮ Stift Nonnberg

0 metres 500
0 yards 500

**For keys to symbols** *see back flap*

# Street-by-Street: Old Town

Salzburg's beautiful Old Town occupies the area between Mönchsberg (Monks' Mountain) and the Salzach river. It has been designated a World Cultural Heritage Site by UNESCO. The town that grew up on the left bank of the Salzach was built almost entirely in the Baroque style and is unusually uniform in appearance. Its ubiquitous Baroque-period designs have been faultlessly and seamlessly blended with both earlier and modern architecture.

★ **Getreidegasse**
One of the longest and busiest streets in Salzburg's Old Town, Getreidegasse accommodates modern-day commerce in medieval settings. No. 9 is the house where Wolfgang Amadeus Mozart was born and lived until he was 17; it is now a museum of the composer's life.

**Kollegienkirche**
The university church is one of the earliest works of Johann Bernhard Fischer von Erlach. The high altar in the transept is the work of Johann Michael Rottmayr.

**Key**

— Suggested route

0 metres     50
0 yards      50

★ **Franziskanerkirche**
The Franciscan church has a Baroque altarpiece by Johann Bernhard Fischer von Erlach, which has as its centre an exquisite figure of the Madonna and Child.

**Altes Rathaus**
The angular tower of the 15th-century Old Town Hall comes into view at the end of a narrow medieval alleyway.

**★ Residenz**
The most opulent building in town, this former home of the archbishop clearly reveals his wealth and power.

RUDOLFSKAI

MOZART PLATZ

RESIDENZ PLATZ

KAPITEL PLATZ

HERRENGASSE

**Kapitelplatz**
The bustling market square has one of Salzburg's most attractive fountains, and offers outdoor games and fun for everyone.

**Dom**
The cathedral church of St Rupert and St Virgil was first built in 774, but has been frequently altered.

**Stift St Peter**
This 12th-century Benedictine church is dedicated to St Peter, whose statue adorns the fountain (1673) in front of the church.

**Hohensalzburg**
The fortress (see pp226–7), on top of the rocky Mönchsberg, is best reached by the funicular from Festungsgasse.

The Mozarteum building, Salzburg's conservatoire

### 🏛 Mozarteum

Schwarzstrasse 26. **Tel** (0662) 88 940-0.
🖪 🗔 **mozarteum.at**

In 1870 the International Foundation of Mozarteum was established here to celebrate the life and works of Salzburg's favourite composer. Today, the Mozarteum stages frequent concerts, is home to a renowned music school and helps manage the Mozart museums: Mozarts Geburtshaus and Mozart-Wohnhaus.

The Mozarteum was built in 1910–14 to a design by architect Richard Berndl. In the grounds stands the cottage in which Mozart wrote the opera *The Magic Flute*, brought here from Vienna. Some departments are housed in the completely rebuilt former palace of Archbishop Lodron next to the foundation's gardens.

### 🏛 Haus der Natur

Museumsplatz 5. **Tel** (0662) 842653.
**Open** 9am–5pm daily. 🖪 🗔 🔄
🗔 **hausdernatur.at**

Enormous fun for all the family, the Natural History Museum has a huge collection of fauna spread across 90 rooms and five floors. As well as exhibitions describing Earth's animals, the museum has a space centre, an aquarium and a reptile zoo.

The museum's galleries are arranged thematically. In "sea world", a gigantic aquarium recreates conditions that closely resemble the natural habitat of various water creatures. The reptile zoo's 33 terraria house some of the most exciting snakes from around the world. There are also huge rooms simulating the natural habitat of Mississippi alligators and the lost worlds of Jurassic creatures,

including firm favourites, the dinosaurs. Other themes include "men and animals in myths and fairy tales", "the cosmos" and "forest animals". Finally, the treasury room displays equipment needed for gold-panning, as well as crystalline forms of precious gems and stones.

### 🏛 Salzburg Museum

Neue Residenz Mozartplatz 1.
**Tel** (0662) 620808-700.
**Open** 9am–5pm Tue–Sun. 🗺
🗔 **salzburgmuseum.at**

This Salzburg Museum was founded in 1834 by the amateur collector and treasury official, Vinzenz Maria Süss, who donated his collections to the town. It was named after the Bavarian Princess Caroline Augusta, who, in 1850 took over the stewardship of the museum's collections.

The most exciting items on display date back to Celtic times and include a Celtic pitcher from the Dürnberg area and a Bronze-Age helmet from the Lueg Pass. The

exhibits from Roman Salzburg, or *Juvavum*, are also interesting; there are fragments of mosaics, including one depicting the abduction of Europa, and numerous architectural features and statues.

Also worth seeing are paintings by the Baroque masters Paul Troger and Johann Michael Rottmayr, as well as those by Hans Makart, who was born in Salzburg in 1840. Separate departments are devoted to handicrafts, coins and musical instruments.

### 🏛 Festspielhäuser

Hofstallgasse 1. **Tel** (0662) 80450.
**Open** 2pm daily for guided tours only.

In 1606, Archbishop Wolf Dietrich von Raitenau started building the palace stables on the site of a former barracks. The north façade was designed by Johann Bernhard Fischer von Erlach. The marble fountain, Pferdeschwemme (horses' trough), in the stable yard, was built in 1695.

In 1917, it was decided that Salzburg should host a theatre and opera festival, and the stables were converted into

Pferdeschwemme (horses' trough) fountain at the Grosses Festspielhaus

*For hotels and restaurants in this region see pp297–8 and pp322–3*

the Small and Grand Festival Theatres. One of Austria's most outstanding architects, Clemens Holzmeister, designed the Small Festival Theatre (now known as Haus für Mozart) during the 1920s, and then from 1956 until 1960 supervised the rebuilding of the Grand Festival Theatre. The building incorporates the original façade of the former stables and is one of the largest opera houses in the world. Its vast stage is 100-m (328-ft) wide and is carved deep into the rock face of Mönchsberg. The auditorium can easily accommodate up to 2,180 spectators.

### 🏛 Mozarts Geburtshaus

Getreidegasse 9. **Tel** (0662) 844313. **Open** Sep–Jun: 9am–5:30pm daily; Jul & Aug: 8:30am–7pm daily. 🌐 📷

Hagenauerhaus, at No. 9 on the narrow Getreidegasse, is the house where Wolfgang Amadeus Mozart was born on 27 January 1756. The composer's family occupied only one floor of the house.

In 1880, the Mozarteum-Stiftung (International Mozart Foundation) helped to establish a museum here, featuring a collection of Mozart's memorabilia, including family portraits, documents and his first instruments. On the second floor is a delightful exhibition on the theatrical staging of Mozart's operas.

### 🏛 Kollegienkirche

Universitätsplatz. **Tel** (0662) 841327. **Open** 9am–dusk daily.

The Collegiate church, consecrated in 1707, is one of Salzburg's finest Baroque structures. It was designed by Johann Bernhard Fischer von Erlach, who achieved fantastic and unusual effects by letting natural light shine through windows of various shapes. The paintings on two side altars of the church are by Johann Michael Rottmayr. Italian artisans produced the beautiful stuccowork which decorates the church walls, to a design by Johann Bernhard Fischer von Erlach. The very ornate main altarpiece shows the university as a temple of art

and science. It features winged figures symbolizing music, poetry, painting, architecture, theology, philosophy, law and medicine.

The Romanesque south portal of Franziskanerkirche

### 🏛 Franziskanerkirche

Franziskanergasse 5. **Tel** (0662) 843629. **Open** 6:30am–8:30pm daily.

The Franciscan church seems somewhat out of place in Baroque Salzburg. Repeated attempts at refashioning it in the Baroque style have failed to disguise its Romanesque origins, mixed with Gothic. The 13th-century Romanesque portal leading to the presbytery is particularly fine, with a figure of Christ on the throne flanked by St Rupert and St Peter. The presbytery, with its tall tower and magnificent star-vault, is Gothic.

In the 16th century, when the Franciscan church was temporarily used as a cathedral, it gained an additional Baroque portal, a ring of chapels and many rich interior furnishings. The creator of the new altar, Johann Bernhard Fischer von Erlach, preserved the central statue of the

Madonna from the earlier Gothic altar made by Michael Pacher, the outstanding artist of the late-Gothic. The St Francis Chapel has frescoes by Johann Michael Rottmayr, with scenes from the life of its patron saint.

On the opposite side of the street are the monastery buildings, which are connected to the church by a bridge.

### 🏛 Residenzplatz

Residenz: Residenzplatz 1. **Tel** (0662) 8042-2690. **Open** Sep–Jun: 10am–5pm Wed–Mon; Jul & Aug: 10am–5pm daily. 🌐 📷 Residenzgalerie: **Tel** (0662) 840451. **Open** same hours as Residenz. 🌐 📷

The **Residenz**, seat of the prince-archbishop, the religious and secular ruler of the entire province, was built for Archbishop Wolf Dietrich von Raitenau. His successors further extended the building. Following secularization, it became the seat of the administration. Now one part of the building houses central government agencies and university offices, while the upper storeys are occupied by the **Residenzgalerie**, which exhibits artworks from the 16th to 19th centuries.

Not much remains of its former exterior decor, but the interior decorations, completed under Johann Lukas von Hildebrandt and carried out by the most prominent artists of the Baroque era, including Johann Michael Rottmayr and Martino Altomonte, still charm visitors to this day.

On the forecourt of the palace is the Baroque Residence Fountain, with Tritons and horses spouting water. On the opposite side of the square stands the Neue Residenz (New Residence), used as a temporary abode while the bishop's seat was being rebuilt. It has a carillon – the bells can be heard at 7am, 11am and 6pm from Mozartplatz, where a statue of the great composer stands.

Statue of Mozart in Mozartplatz

Sculptures decorating the façade of the Dom

### ⬆ Stift St Peter

St Peter Bezirk 1/2. **Tel** (0662) 844576-0.
**Open** 8am–noon, 2:30–6:30pm.

Salzburg's Benedictine abbey was founded in the 7th century by St Rupert, who is said to have resurrected the town after the Great Migration of Nations. It is the only abbey in this part of Europe that has survived intact since then. The present church and monastery complexes were built in the 12th and 13th centuries, but remodelled during the Baroque era, in the 17th and 18th centuries. However, some older sculptures have survived, including the early-15th-century *Beautiful Madonna*. The majority of the Baroque altar paintings are by Kremser Schmidt. The abbey interior is an impressive display of Baroque opulence.

In the cemetery, Salzburg's oldest, are the final resting places of Mozart's sister Nannerl and of Johann Michael Haydn, brother of Joseph.

### ⬆ Dom

Cathedral: Domplatz 1a. **Tel** (0662) 80477950. Cathedral Museum: **Tel** (0662) 80471860. **Open** Jan, Feb & Nov: 8am–5pm Mon–Sat, 1–5pm Sun; Mar, Apr, Oct, Dec: 8am–6pm Mon–Sat, 1–6pm Sun; May–Sep: 8am–7pm Mon–Sat, 1–7pm Sun.

The first cathedral church in Salzburg, the Dom was built in the 8th century. Following several remodellings and a fire in 1598, the archbishops set out to build an almost entirely new church, designed by the Italian architect Santino Solari, on the site of the earlier one. The new cathedral, consecrated in 1628, became a model of Baroque

church architecture north of the Alps. The façade is decorated with the vast sculpted figures of the cathedral's patron saints, Rupert and Virgil, and Saints Peter and Paul. The cathedral was designed to accommodate 10,000 worshippers, more than the entire population of Salzburg at the time. Its monumental interior is still impressive today. Stairs lead from the transept to the crypt, where several prince-archbishops have been laid to rest. Mozart himself played the Baroque organ here. Today, the great Mozarteum choir often holds concerts of his music in the cathedral. The church's treasures are on show in the **Cathedral Museum**.

### ⬆ Stift Nonnberg

Nonnberggasse 2. **Tel** (0662) 841607.
**Open** Summer: 7am–7pm daily; winter: 7am–5pm.

The Benedictine nunnery on the slope of Mönchsberg, also known as Nonnberg (Nuns' Hill),

The pilgrimage church Maria Plain on Plainberg

was founded in 714 by St Rupert, who established his niece, St Erentrude, as Mother Superior. Her tomb lies in the crypt of the church. Emperor Henry II and his wife Kunegunde had the convent and the church extended in the 11th century. A fire in 1423 destroyed most of the buildings and, in the 15th century, a new convent was built on the same site, with a church devoted to the Assumption of the Virgin Mary and to St Erentrude. The Romanesque tympanum above the main door shows the Virgin Mary accompanied by John the Baptist and St Erentrude.

A true jewel of Nonnberg is its late-Gothic main altarpiece, brought from Scheffau and reputedly produced to sketches by Albrecht Dürer. Behind the main altar, in the central window of the apsis, is an interesting stained-glass panel by Peter Hemmel von Andlau, one of

Fresco (1150) in Stift Nonnberg

the most renowned stained-glass artists in the late-Gothic style. Original 12th-century Romanesque frescoes are preserved in the niches. The adjacent chapel of St John has a Gothic altarpiece from the earlier period; its creator was visibly influenced by the school of Veit Stoss.

### Environs

On top of Plainberg, a hill north of Salzburg, stands the pilgrimage church of **Maria Plain**, built by Giovanni Antonio Dario and consecrated in 1674. In 1779, Mozart composed the *Coronation Mass* in celebration of the miraculous picture of the Madonna and Child. The interior was designed by famous Austrian Baroque artists, including Kremser Schmidt and Thomas and Franz Schwanthaler.

Further north, in the village of **Oberndorf**, the carol *Silent Night* was first performed in 1818. Franz Xaver Gruber (see p228), a local teacher and organist, wrote the music, and Joseph Mohr the words.

---

# The Salzburg Festival

The Salzburger Festspiele, the largest and most important opera and theatre festival in Europe, was initiated by three people. The eminent writer Hugo von Hofmannsthal, the composer and conductor Richard Strauss, and the greatest theatrical innovator of the 20th century, the director Max Reinhardt, decided to honour the memory of Mozart by organizing a festival devoted to his work. It was to be held in his home town and be a celebration of theatre and opera. The first festival was held in Salzburg in 1920. Today, it is a more all-embracing event, and the festival programme has become increasingly rich and varied. The former court stables were converted to create two festival theatres and performances are also held in the Makartplatz theatre, in Schloss Mirabell and in many open-air venues around town. Theatre troupes come from all over the world, often with original performances prepared specifically for the festival. Tickets tend to be sold out several months in advance *(see pp334–5)*.

**Herbert von Karajan** (1908–89), born in Salzburg and one of the most outstanding 20th-century conductors of symphonies and operas, was the musical director of the Salzburg Festival for almost 30 years.

**A stage in front of the cathedral** in Salzburg is where the Salzburger Festspiele performances begin each July. Max Reinhardt pioneered the idea of open-air performances at the festival, and theatre troops now play to large audiences.

**The Grosses Festspielhaus** is adorned with a Baroque portal by Johann Bernhard Fischer von Erlach. The modern building of the Grand Festival Theatre was completed in 1960 by Clemens Holzmeister *(see pp222–3)*.

**The Fire Dance** is one of the most beautiful performances staged regularly during the Salzburg Festival. As soon as night falls, the whole town comes alive with the lights of the spectacle.

**Since its very first staging** the festival has opened with a performance of Hugo von Hofmannsthal's morality play *Jedermann* ("Everyman").

# Hohensalzburg Fortress

Hohensalzburg, the fortress perched on the rocky peak of Festungsberg, was built in the 11th century, during the wars between the Holy Roman Empire and the Papacy, and was gradually extended. The castle served as a refuge for Salzburg's archbishops whenever they felt threatened. Archbishop Leonhard von Keutschach gave it its present look in the 16th century; Archbishop Paris von Lodron introduced further architectural changes in the 17th century. A modern funicular provides easy access up the steep hill.

**Early Cannons**
Aimed at the town, many cannons can be seen among the numerous bastions, bulwarks and walkways.

**Salzburg Coat of Arms**
The coat of arms is placed above the wicket leading to the inner courtyard, in front of the old castle.

## KEY

① **The Glockenturm**, through which the castle's residential quarters can be reached, has a bell case created by Hans Reichert in 1505.

② **The well**, dating back to 1539, is an interesting feature in the fortress courtyard.

**Archbishop**
Johann Jakob Khuen von Belasi (1560–86) carried out the final remodelling of the old fortress. His portrait hangs in one of the rooms of the old castle.

### Schulhaus and Kuchlturm
Schoolhouse and Kitchen Tower are the remains of fortifications built outside the castle in the 16th century during a revolt against the archbishops.

### ★ Goldene Stube
The richly ornamented Golden Chamber, with its large tiled stove in Gothic style, is one of the loveliest rooms in the castle.

### Small Courtyard
In a small square on the castle ramparts stand an old salt warehouse (former stables), and two towers, Hasenturm (Hares' Tower) and Schwefelturm (Sulphur Tower).

### ★ Torture Chamber
Reckturm, the corner tower, was once a prison and torture chamber. Prisoners were still being tortured at Hohensalzburg until 1893.

Portrait of Archbishop Marcus Sitticus in Schloss Hellbrunn

## ❷ Schloss Hellbrunn

**Road map** D4. 🚗 🚌 **Tel** (0662) 820372-0. **Open** Apr & Oct: 9am–4:30pm daily; May–Sep: 9am–5:30pm daily (until 6pm Jul–Aug; trick fountains until 9pm). 🅿 🖥 **hellbrunn.at**

Schloss Hellbrunn, once a summer residence of Salzburg's Archbishop Marcus Sitticus, stands about 4 km (2 miles) south of Salzburg. Sitticus was a nephew of Wolf Dietrich von Raitenau, with an Italian mother. He spent most of his life in Italy, and so his small, suburban castle resembles a Venetian villa. It has an interesting state room with architectural paintings and a tall, octagonal music room. However, the most popular feature is its garden, which contains ornamental fountains and scenic grottoes, including a mechanical theatre with trick fountains and moving figures powered by water.

## ❸ Wasserschloss Anif

**Road map** D4. 🏔 4,000. 🚗 🚌 ℹ (06246) 72365.

Another 2 km (1 mile) beyond Hellbrunn, stands the small Neo-Gothic castle of Anif. Once a

suburban residence, it now lies virtually within the limits of the town of Anif. Its earliest historic records date from the 15th century, but it bears signs of an earlier, late-Gothic structure. Once the summer estate of the Salzburg rulers, it belonged to the Chiemsee bishops from 1693 to 1803. After the secularization of the province, it was put up for sale and passed to Count Aloys Arco-Stepperg. This new owner had the summer residence converted into a romantic English-style Neo-Gothic castle that has survived unchanged to this day. Its rectangular turret is proudly mirrored in the waters of the lake; the interior is furnished in the English fashion of the day. At the end of World War I, on 13 November 1918, the last king of Bavaria, Ludwig III, signed his abdication in Anif. As the castle is privately owned, visitors can only see its high outside walls.

## ❹ St Gilgen

**Road map** D4. 🏔 3,800. 🚌 ℹ Mondsee, Bundesstrasse 1A, (06227) 2348.

Set on the western shores of the warm Wolfgangsee, amid mountain scenery, St Gilgen is one of the most picturesque health resorts in the Lake Wolfgang region. St Gilgen was the birthplace of Mozart's mother, Anna-Maria Pertl. Later, the composer's sister, Nannerl, lived here with her husband, a local office worker. These Mozart-related facts are commemorated by a plaque on the court building. In 1927, the Mozart Fountain was erected in the town square.

The local church of St Giles (St Ägidius) shows hints of an earlier structure. It was extended in the 18th century and given three Rococo altars with paintings by Peter Lorenzoni.

St Gilgen is a water sports centre and harbour, with cruises on Wolfgangsee aboard the steamer *Kaiser Franz Josef I*, which has been in continuous service since 1873. Not far from St Gilgen, on the

shores of the neighbouring Fuschlsee, stands **Schloss Fuschl**, a small hunting lodge that now houses a luxury hotel.

## ❺ Hallein

**Road map** D4. 🏔 20,000. 🚗 🚌 ℹ Mauttorpromenade 6, (06245) 85394.

The town of Hallein was founded in the 13th century, but salt was mined here way back in prehistoric times. The long association with the salt trade is apparent from the town's name: *hall* is the Celtic word for "salt". The "white gold", as it was called, brought wealth to the entire region for many centuries, until the 18th-century Counter-Reformation led to the emigration of the predominantly Protestant salt miners.

Hallein's Old Town, on the left bank of the Salzach river, is mainly 18th-century in appearance, following much remodelling. The church of St Antonius has a Gothic presbytery, but the rest is much newer. The painting of the Birth of Christ in the main altarpiece is by the last court painter of the Salzburg rulers, the Neo-Classical Andreas Nesselthaler. Hallein was the home of Franz Xaver Gruber who wrote *Silent Night*, and he is buried here. His house at No. 1 Gruberplatz is now a small museum. The most interesting sight in Hallein, however, is the

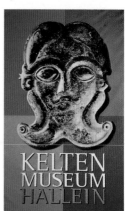

Poster of the fascinating Keltenmuseum in Hallein

**Keltenmuseum**, with its collection of Celtic objects from the La Tene period of the Iron Age.

🏛 **Keltenmuseum**
Pflegerplatz 5. **Tel** (06245) 80783.
**Open** 9am–5pm daily. 🐾♿📧
Ⓦ keltenmuseum.at

**Environs:** From the southern end of Hallein you can drive to the top of Dürrnberg, which has some of the most interesting prehistoric finds in Austria. The remains of the settlements that grew up around the rich local salt deposits can be seen to this day.

The spa of **Bad Dürrnberg** has a show-mine open specifically for tourists, who are offered rides on an under-

Logo of salt mine in Bad Dürrnberg

ground salt lake. In the village stands a 14th-century Marian church, now a Baroque structure. The altarpiece contains a miraculous picture of the Madonna, once visited by pilgrims.

## ❻ Golling

**Road map** D4. 🚹 4,200. 🚇🚌
ℹ (06244) 4356.

South of Hallein lies the small town of Golling. At its centre stands the church of St John the Baptist and St John the Evangelist, with a Gothic main nave and remodelled Baroque side naves. A small medieval castle, devoid of any ornaments and adjoined by a chapel with a Rococo altar, now houses a regional museum.

**Environs:** There are many natural features of interest near Golling, including the **Lueg Pass** with the spectacular 100-m- (328-ft-) deep Salzach river gorge, and the Schwarzbacher Wasserfall, better known as **Gollinger Wasserfall** (100 m/328 ft), much beloved by romantic painters of natural scenes. Also worth a

The Gollinger Wasserfall, a favourite theme for painters

detour are two interesting churches in the vicinty – St Ulrich's in **Scheffau** and the late-Gothic St Nicholas's church near **Torren**, which stands high up on a rocky shelf.

## ❼ Abtenau

**Road map** D4. 🚹 5,600. 🚇🚌
ℹ Markt 165, (06243) 4040.

Abtenau, a summer resort situated in the Salzburg Dolomites, is surrounded by the mighty peaks of the Tennengebirge. The church in the valley was built around 1500. Its main nave is guarded by figures of St George and St Florian. On the north wall, an original late-Gothic fresco can be seen, but the new main altar and side altars are built in the Baroque style. It is worth taking

a walk upstream along the Lammer river, which cuts a scenic valley between the Tennengebirge and the craggy wall of the Dachstein massif.

## ❽ Werfen

**Road map** D4. 🚹 3,000. 🚇🚌

The little town of Werfen has several interesting churches. St James's church is mentioned in 14th-century records, but its present style dates from a 17th-century Baroque conversion. The Marian Church was built in the early 18th century.

**Environs:** There are two fascinating sights near Werfen. **Hohenwerfen fortress**, built on a rocky outcrop, dates back to the 11th century. Today, it is an interactive museum with many displays, including late-Romanesque frescoes and an exhibition of weapons. It also includes Austria's first museum of falconry.

A major attraction for visitors, and likely to be very busy during the summer months, is **Eisriesenwelt** (Ice World), the largest ice cave in the world. Accessed by cable car, there are some 42 km (26 miles) of stalagmites and ice galleries to be explored – all in freezing temperatures.

🏛 **Eisriesenwelt**
Eishohlenstrasse 30. **Tel** (6468) 5248.
**Open** May–Oct: 8am–4pm daily.
🐾🚠📧Ⓦ eisriesenwelt.at

Inside Eisriesenwelt, the world's largest ice cave

## ❾ Bischofshofen

**Road map** D4. 🏔 10,000. 🚉 🚌
ℹ (06462) 2471.
🅆 **bischofshofen.at**

The Celtic settlement that stood on the site of the present Bischofshofen was once a centre of the copper mining trade; the area was also rich in salt mines. Colonization of the region started well before recorded history and traces of ancient cultures can be found everywhere.

The town is dominated by the spire of **St Maximilian's church**, reputedly built on the site of an older church established by St Rupert, founder of Salzburg. The walls are decorated with 15th-century frescoes, and next to the Neo-Gothic side altarpieces stand the original Gothic figures of St Rupert and St Virgil. In the south arm of the transept is a Baroque altar with a picture of St Anna attributed to Lienhart Astl (c.1520) and a relief on the predella of Christ and the 12 apostles dating from the same period. The most valuable historic relic in the church is St Rupert's crucifix. This simple gilded cross, encrusted with precious stones, was given to Bischofshofen in the 12th century by the Archbishop of Salzburg.

Bischofshofen is renowned for its excellent ski-jumping hills. Every year, on 6 January, the final event of the world-famous Four Hills Ski-Jumping event takes place on the largest of the slopes.

*St Rupert's crucifix, Bischofshofen*

## ❿ Radstadt

**Road map** D4. 🏔 4,800. 🚉 🚌
ℹ (06452) 7472.

The small town of Radstadt grew up around a 13th-century fortress on the banks of the Enns river. Its wealth hailed from its propitious location on the road to Venice and its monopoly position in the wine trade. Radstadt also had a licence to stock iron and salt. Its medieval fortifications, built by the archbishops of Salzburg, have remained intact.

The surrounding area boasts many small, beguiling castles, including the Renaissance **Schloss Tandalier**, southwest of the town. **Schloss Lerchen**, in the centre of town, shows some traces of original 13th-century architecture; today it houses a regional museum.

**Environs:** East of Bischofshofen runs **Radstädter Tauernstrasse**, one of the most scenic roads in the Alps. A skiing area extends on both sides. The **Rossbrand** (1,770 m/ 5,807 ft), rising north of Radstadt and accessible by car via the Rossbrand Panorama Street, offers astonishing views of more than 150 Alpine summits on a clear day.

## ⓫ St Johann im Pongau

**Road map** D4. 🏔 11,000. 🚌
ℹ (06412) 6036.

The largest town in the region, St Johann im Pongau is a popular resort, visited for its excellent skiing conditions in winter and its plentiful facilities for swimming and walking in summer.

Little remains of its original buildings due to a series of fires in the 19th century; the present town was almost entirely rebuilt. The Neo-Gothic **Domkirche**, the cathedral of St John the Baptist (1861), is one of the most outstanding works of Neo-Classicism in the Salzburg area. Its architects were Georg Schneider and Josef Wessiken. The charming carved altarpiece (1530) in adjacent St Anna's Chapel has late-Gothic wooden figures of saints. Some 5 km (3 miles) south of the town run the torrential waters of **Grossarler Ache**, a rapid mountain stream that winds through the scenic Liechtensteinklamm.

## ⓬ Wagrain

**Road map** D4. 🏔 3,000. 🚌 🚉
ℹ (06413) 8448. 🅆 **skiamade.com**

Wagrain, situated at an altitude of 800 m (2,625 ft), is part of a family-oriented group of ski resorts called Ski Amadé. This vast terrain extends between the Tennengebirge and Radstädter Tauern mountain ranges, and includes several villages connected by good public transport links, funiculars and buses. The area is further linked to the overall Salzburger Sportwelt skipass area of eight resorts and 270 ski installations, mostly for intermediate skiers.

Year-round fun in the water is guaranteed by the Amadé Water World's all-weather pool. The most interesting place is **Zauchensee**, the highest village in the region (1,361 m/4,465 ft).

View of the town and cathedral in St Johann im Pongau

Grossarler Ache rushing through the Liechtensteinklamm, near Wagrain

It is also worth going inside the Gothic church in **Altenmarkt im Pongau**. Wagrain itself has a museum devoted to Joseph Mohr, who wrote the words for *Silent Night*, and to the popular 20th-century Austrian writer and humorist Karl Heinrich Waggerl.

The views from the tops of Schwarzkopf, Rosskopf and Mooskopf are stunning and worth a detour.

## ⓭ Mauterndorf

Road map D4. 🏔 1,700. 🚌
🛈 (06472) 7949.

Strategically positioned on the road connecting Salzburg with the Hohe Tauern passes, this little town owed its former wealth to the road tolls it was able to collect. Mauterndorf's greatest attraction is its **Burg**, built in the 13th century and extended in the 16th century under Archbishop Leonhard von Keutschach. Scenically located and well proportioned, it is an attractive medieval structure. The rooms are richly decorated with stuccowork and provide interesting interiors. The castle's best feature is the lovely chapel devoted to St Henry (Emperor Henry II), with superb 14th-century frescoes of the Coronation of the

Virgin Mary on the rainbow arch, and a 15th-century carved altarpiece. The castle was well restored in the 20th century, and is now a museum and cultural centre. Mauterndorf also has excellent summer and winter sports facilities.

## ⓮ Schloss Moosham

Road map D4. 🚌 Schloss Moosham: Moosham 13. **Tel** (06476) 305. **Open** for guided tours only; Apr–Sep: 10 am, 11am, 1pm, 2pm, 3pm & 4pm Tue–Sun (Aug daily); Oct & mid-Dec–Mar: 11am & 2pm Tue–Sun. 🅿️

Moosham Castle, near the southern end of Radstädter Tauernstrasse, high above the Mur river, is famous for its ghosts and witch trials, as popularized on American television. The structure probably dates from the 13th century and consists of an upper and a lower castle. After the secularization of the archbishop's principality, the castle fell into ruin, but in 1886 it passed to Count Hans Wilczek, who fully renovated it. Among the remaining original features are the Baroque roadway, Gothic stained-glass windows in the presbytery of the chapel and a collection of local works of art, which are kept in the castle museum. The coach house and the armoury are also of interest. Some rooms are open to the public, such as a torture chamber,

Bedchamber in Schloss Moosham

and a Gothic bedchamber with a panel listing the supposed characteristic traits of various European nationalities.

Below the castle is the popular resort of St Michael, with an interesting Gothic church.

Stained-glass window in the church of St Leonard in Tamsweg

## ⓯ Tamsweg

Road map E4. 🏔 5,600. 🚉 🚌
🛈 (06474) 2145. 🎭 Samson Procession (late Jun, Jul, Aug).

The largest town in the isolated Lungau region, Tamsweg is famous for its curious Samson Procession, when an effigy of Samson and other figures are paraded around town. Tamsweg owes its past wealth to the iron and salt trades. Fine town houses, such as the 15th-century Mesnerhaus and the 16th-century turreted town hall, line the market square. The 18th-century Post House has frescoes by Gregor Lederwasch, who also painted the pictures in Heiliger Jakobus (St James's church), built in 1741 to a design by Fidelis Hainzl. The original Rococo interior has been preserved. The 15th-century church of St Leonard, towering above the town, is an important pilgramage church. It has beautiful stained-glass windows, including the famous Golden Window (created between 1430 and 1450). The interior furnishings are almost entirely late medieval.

# ⑯ Gasteinertal

The therapeutic properties of the radon-rich mineral springs in and around Bad Gastein were known to the Celts and Romans, and this was when the first settlements grew in the valley of the Gasteiner Ache stream. The valley flourished in late medieval times and more recently it has become a popular spa, with a long list of clients including royalty, politicians and artists. Cures are sought by those suffering from cardiac and gastric ailments, rheumatism and allergies. At the same time, the valley has developed into a fabulous winter sports centre, with skiing for all levels and snowboarding.

**Bad Hofgastein**
The late-Gothic parish church was built in the 15th and 16th centuries. The carved tombstones found in its niches show the skills of gold- and silversmiths using locally excavated metals.

**The Gasteiner Ache**
The stream runs along a scenic valley, down from the Hohe Tauern mountains, finishing as a tributary of the Salzach, the principal river of Salzburger Land.

## KEY

① **The summit of Stubnerkogel** has a viewing platform at 2,050 m (6,726 ft), providing panoramic views of the neighbouring peaks. It can be reached by gondola.

② **Gasteinertal**, a well-developed valley surrounded by modest mountains, is a popular skiing, snowboarding and summer walking area.

★ **Sportgastein**
The wide valley near Sportgastein has been transformed into a true mountain gorge, with bridges and viaducts spanning the stream.

Bad Hofgas

② 

Stubnerkogel
① ▲
*2050*

▲
*2461*

▲
*2600*

*Gasteiner Ache*

Spor
gast

**Dorfgastein**
The village of Dorfgastein has preserved many traditional, rural customs.

**VISITORS' CHECKLIST**

**Practical Information**
Road map D4.
⟩ Tauernplatz 1,
Bad Hofgastein.
Tel (06432) 3393-260.
w gastein.com

**Transport**

**★ Bad Gastein**
The most popular resort in Gasteinertal is crossed by the Gasteiner Ache, which runs right through its centre in a series of attractive waterfalls.

**Key**
━━ Major road
━━ Minor road
···· Funicular
══ River

**★ Böckstein**
The altar in the Neo-Classical church of Our Lady of Good Counsel is the work of Johann Baptist Hagenauer. The medieval mine where gold was once excavated now houses a sanatorium.

Bad Gastein

Böckstein

0 kilometres    2
0 miles         2

## ⓱ Kaprun

**Road map** D4. 🚡 3,000. 🚌
🛈 (06547) 8080. 🖥 zellamsee-kaprun.com

Together with its neighbour, Zell am See, Kaprun makes up one of the largest ski regions in Austria. The 140 km (87 miles) of inter-connected ski slopes offer superb modern facilities and spectacular views of the lake below. The slopes are dominated by the Kitzsteinhorn glacier (3,203 m/10,509 ft), which is open for skiing ten months of the year. The region is renowned for its tough runs but there are family and beginner areas. For the adventurous, there are nighttime ski runs on the Schmitten slopes and a number of snowboard parks with jumps, rails and pipes.

In 2000, Kaprun was the scene of a dreadful mountain tragedy when a funicular carrying snow-boarders up to the Kitzsteinhorn caught fire inside a rock tunnel. The incident resulted in 155 deaths, and the tunnel has since been sealed and replaced with cable cars. The disaster was commemorated in the 2003 play *In der Alpen*, written by Austria's Nobel Prize for Literature winner Elfriede Jelinek.

Aside from its renowned ski slopes, Kaprun is also famous for its sophisticated hydroelectric power station, Kapruner Ache. Construction of the power station began in 1938 and was completed in 1951. Acclaimed as an engineering marvel, the power station is not only a technological wonder, it is also a major tourist attraction, offering great views over the towns of Kapun and Zell am See. Artificial lakes, weirs and dams, set amid the rocky limestone peaks of the Hohe Tauern mountain range, create a unique natural environment, with numerous trails and attractive scenery for walkers. The highest artificial lake is Mooserboden, situated at 2,036 m (6,680 ft) and fed by the melting ice of the Pasterze glacier. It was after the building of the power station that Kaprun became one of Austria's foremost sports resorts.

Inside St Hippolytus church in Zell am See

## ⓲ Zell am See

**Road map** C4. 🚡 9,500. 🚍
🚌 **Tel** (06542) 770.

This picture-postcard town on the western shores of Zeller See has a long history. First recorded as the Roman settlement of Bisontio, in medieval times Zell was a mining centre. Among its more interesting historic sights are the 13th-century Vogtturm, and the church of St Hippolytus (St Hippolyte), which once belonged to the Augustinian order. There are some interesting medieval frescoes: the figures of Saints George and Florian in the western gallery are by an artist from the Danube School.

Zell am See, connected to the slopes of Kaprun to form a single skiing region, is considered one of the best-developed sports resorts in Austria, with excellent facilities.

Charming, flower-bedecked houses in Saalbach

**Environs:** South of Zell am See is the **Hohe Tauern** mountain range and national park *(see pp282–5)*, to the north the rugged scenery of the Steinernes Meer (Stone Sea) and to the west the Schmittenhöhe, divided into the Sonnkogel and Hirschkogel regions, with the highest peak rising to over 2,000 m (6,562 ft).

The **Pinzgauer Spaziergang** is one of the most beautiful walking trails in the Austrian Alps, running at an altitude of about 1,000 m (3,280 ft) above the valley floor, from Zell am See to Saalbach via Schmittenhöhe (a 7-hour walk).

## ⓳ Saalbach

**Road map** C4. 🚡 2,900. 🚍 🚌
🛈 Glemmtaler Landesstrasse 550, (06541) 6800-68. 🖥 saalbach.com

At the heart of the Glemmtal lies this small town marking the border between Salzburger Land and Tyrol. A charming winter resort, linked to Hinterglemm, Leogang and Fieberbrunn, with guaranteed snow, it provides access to 200 km (120 miles) of pistes, with beginner and more challenging runs, and facilities for tobogganing and tubing. Exciting as the winter sports are, the resort claims to be the home of *lässig*, an Austrian concept perhaps best translated as "contentment".

To the north of Saalbach the Spielberghorn comes into view, while to the south the Schattberg marks the end of the Pinzgauer Spaziergang. This trail *(see above)* affords breathtaking views over the neighbouring mountain range. The view from Rohrertörl Pass (1,918 m/6,293 ft) embraces the town of Saalbach and the valley.

## ⓴ Lofer

**Road map** C4. 🚡 2,000. 🚍 🚌
🛈 Lofer Nr. 310, (06588) 8321.
🖥 lofer.com

The town of Lofer, in the green Salzach valley, has retained much of the charm of an old mountain village. It is surrounded by the snow-covered rocky summits of the Loferer Steinberge (Stone Mountains). These limestone mountains hide many caves still waiting to be explored. The Lamprechtsofenloch is said to be the deepest aquiferous cave in the world.

**Environs:** A short distance south of Lofer, outside the village of St Martin, is the pilgrimage church **Maria Kirchenthal**, built between 1693 and 1701 by Johann Bernhard Fischer von Erlach. It is one of the greatest works by this outstanding architect, in which he employed some of the ideas that he had developed earlier in Salzburg.

The building is blended into the rocky mountain scenery of the Saalach valley, and two white towers are prominent against the distant snowy mountains. The Neo-Baroque altarpiece includes the 15th-century miraculous picture of the Madonna that was once the destination for pilgrims. On one of the two altars, created by Jakob Zanussi from reddish-pink Salzburg marble, the parents of the Virgin Mary, St Jacob and St Anne, are depicted.

## ㉑ Mittersill

**Road map** C4. 🚠 5,500. 🚃 🚌
ℹ️ Stadtplatz 1, (06562) 4292.
🌐 mittersill-tourismus.at

This summer resort at the main crossroads of the upper Salzach valley sprang up around a

The scenic Krimmler Wasserfälle

castle. The castle was built in the 12th century and since then has been rebuilt many times, following its destruction during the Peasant Wars and numerous fires. Today it is the seat of the International Protestant Youth Community, a cultural centre and a hotel.

The chapel (1533) features an interesting late-Gothic polyptych attributed to an Aussee master. St-Leonhard-Kirche was originally Gothic, but was remodelled in the 18th century to a design by Johann Kleber. It contains a heavily ornamented Rococo pulpit and some remains of the old decorations, including an early 15th-century stone statue of St Leonard.

Mittersill lies at the Salzburg end of a beautiful mountain trail leading from East Tyrol, among the wild scenery of the Hohe Tauern National Park. The road known as Felbertauernstrasse affords lovely views of the rugged slopes of Grossvenediger.

## ㉒ Krimmler Wasserfälle

**Road map** C4. 🚌

In the northwestern part of the Hohe Tauern National Park (see pp282–5), on the border between the provinces of Salzburger Land and Tyrol, are the famous Krimmler Wasserfälle, the waterfalls of the Krimmler Ache, a stream flowing from the glacier of the same name at an altitude of around 3,000 m (9,850 ft). The water falls in three steps, with a total drop of 380 m (1,247 ft).

The journey to the waterfalls can be made by car, but a walk along the Wasserfallweg (waterfall path) will prove a truly unforgettable experience.

The best starting points for the walk are the Gerlos Pass or Krimmel village. In winter, the waterfalls freeze solid.

View of the Hohe Tauern mountains, near Mittersill

# TYROL AND VORARLBERG

Both Tyrol and Vorarlberg lie on a narrow stretch of land
west of Salzburg. Their main attractions is the Alps –
few areas are below 500 m (1,640 ft) – and tourism is
their primary source of income. Tyrol is famous for its
magnificent scenery and world-renowned resorts
such as Kitzbühel, Seefeld and St Anton, while
Vorarlberg draws visitors seeking a more relaxed, rural environment.

Tyrol occupies an area of 12,648 sq km
(4,883 sq miles) and has a population of
722,000. Its neighbours are Bavaria in the
north, Italy in the south, Vorarlberg in the
west and Salzburger Land in the east.
The Inn is the province's main river, winding
its way through the Alpine massifs.

In ancient times Tyrol was inhabited by
Rhaetian and Illyrian tribes; it came under
Roman rule in the 1st century BC, and later
fell to the Bavarians and the Lombards.

In the 13th century, it became an
independent principality of the Reich.
Until 1363, having been a bone of
contention between the Habsburgs and
the Bavarians, it was bequeathed to the
Habsburgs. Tyrol was a domain of the
family's junior line and as such enjoyed a

degree of independence. To this day it has
maintained its unique character, music,
dialect and even fashion, which has
influenced cultural life in the rest of Austria.

The province of Vorarlberg, in contrast,
has for many years been culturally fairly
separate, largely orientating itself towards
its neighbours Germany, Liechtenstein
and Switzerland. After Vienna, it is the
smallest Austrian province, covering an
area of just 2,600 sq km (1,000 sq miles),
with 375,000 inhabitants. It was once
inhabited by Aleman tribes. From the
15th century the area of present-day
Vorarlberg passed gradually into the
hands of the Habsburgs, and in 1919
it finally became a province of
independent Austria.

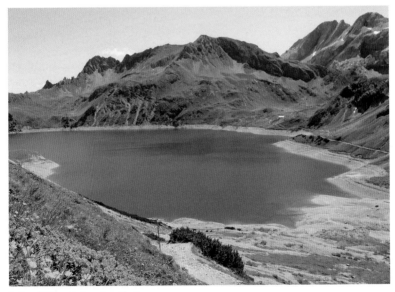

The beautiful Lünersee in the province of Vorarlberg

◀ Lech am Arlberg, a popular ski resort in Vorarlberg

# Exploring Tyrol and Vorarlberg

Both provinces, in the far west of Austria, are predominantly winter sports regions, although they also offer excellent facilities for summer activities. Among the popular and famous tourist centres of Tyrol are Kitzbühel, the area around the Arlberg Pass, and the hinterland of Innsbruck. The latter has twice played host to the Winter Olympic Games, in 1964 and 1976. The capital of the smaller Vorarlberg province is Bregenz, a somewhat sleepy resort located in a romantic spot on the eastern shores of Lake Constance (Bodensee).

Chairlift and ski runs near Zürs

## Sights at a Glance

## Getting There

From Innsbruck-Kranebitten Airport flights arrive from Vienna and many major European cities. Both Tyrol and Vorarlberg are served by the main railway line from Vienna to Bregenz, and the western motorway reaches Bregenz. Austria's first toll road tunnel passes through the Arlberg massif. Both provinces have a good network of bus routes, although many roads may become impassable in winter. From autumn until spring, motorists planning excursions to the mountains need to remember to take winter tyres and snow chains.

The Ballunspitze peak, seen from Paznauntal

**Key**

━━━ Motorway
━━━ Major road
┅┅┅ Minor road
∿∿∿ Main railway
──── Minor railway
▬▬▬ International border
▬▬▬ Province border
△ Summit
⋉ Pass

Coat of arms on the 5th-century town hall, in Hall in Tyrol

Chapel in the snow-covered valley of Stubai

**For keys to symbols** *see back flap*

# ❶ Innsbruck: Street-by-Street

Innsbruck was built at the confluence of the
Sill and Inn rivers and became an important
trading post in the Middle Ages. The present
district of Wilten was once the site of the
Roman camp of Veldidena, but the founders
of the city itself were the counts of Andechs,
who built a settlement here in 1187. Today
Innsbruck is the capital of the province of
Tyrol, one of Austria's most important tourist
regions. In 1964, and again in 1976, Innsbruck
was the host city for the Winter Olympics;
many competitions took place in Axamer
Lizum, 20 km (14 miles) southwest of the city.

**★ Goldenes Dachl**
The symbol of
Innsbruck, the
Golden Roof is
an oriel window
added in 1500 by
Maximilian I to
Friedrich IV's former
residence. It is
covered with 2,657
gilded copper
roof tiles.

**Herzog-Friedrich-Strasse**
The main street of the
old town is lined with
the attractive façades
of numerous Baroque
buildings.

**Key**

— Suggested route

**Stadtturm**
The 15th-century city tower
next to the old town hall
acquired its present Renaissance
look in 1560. The observation
deck affords great views.

**Helblinghaus**
The building with an elegant
Regency façade at No. 10
Herzog-Friedrich-Strasse was
originally a medieval corner
house in the Gothic style.
In 1725 it was decorated with
opulent Rococo stuccowork.

**★ Dom St Jakob**
The Baroque cathedral has
enchanting vault frescoes
by Cosmas Damian Asam
and a picture of the
*Madonna and Child* by
Lucas Cranach the Elder.

## VISITORS' CHECKLIST

**Practical Information**
**Road map** B4. 🚏 125,000.
ℹ️ Burggraben 3, (0512) 59850.
🚉 Tanzsommer Innsbruck (Jun,
Jul) (0512) 561 561, Innsbrucker
Festwochen der Alten Musik
(Festival of Early Music, Jul, Aug)
(0512) 571032.
w innsbruck.info

**★ Hofburg**
The interior of the imperial palace
was extensively rebuilt in Rococo
style during the reign of Maria
Theresa, to designs by Johann
Martin Gumpp the Younger.

Jesuitenkirche

Landesmuseum

**Hofkirche**
The court church
(*see pp246–7*), built in
1553–63 as a mausoleum
for Maximilian I, is guarded
by 28 large bronze
statues (*right*).

0 metres 75
0 yards 75

## Exploring Innsbruck

Innsbruck straddles the Inn river. Its Old Town is situated on the right bank, close to the river. Leading up to it is the broad Maria-Theresien-Strasse with the tall Column of St Anna (1706). The most impressive historic buildings are found on Herzog-Friedrich-Strasse, Stadtplatz, Hofgasse and Rennweg. Other important sights are Schloss Ambras, on the southern outskirts of the city, and the Panorama of the Battle of Bergisel (see p247).

### ⬆ Dom St Jakob

Domplatz. **Tel** (0512) 583902.
St James's Cathedral was originally built in the Gothic style, but was converted to Baroque in the early 18th century by Johann Jakob Herkomer. Severely damaged during World War II, it was rebuilt in the 1950s, when the church finally acquired the figures for the niches, as well as the equestrian statue of St Jakob on top of the building, sculpted by Hans André. The fine Baroque interior is the work of Munich artists, brothers Cosmas Damian (painter) and Egid Quirin (sculptor) Asam. The vault paintings depict scenes from the life of St James (St Jakob). The picture of *Madonna and Child* in the high altar, which miracles are attributed to, is by Lucas Cranach the Elder.

The old town houses with their rich stucco ornaments, reliefs and frescoes provide an enchanting backdrop to the cathedral, which is regarded as the most magnificent Baroque church building in North Tyrol.

### ⬛ Hofburg

Rennweg 1. **Tel** (0512) 587186.
**Open** 9am–5pm daily (Mar–Aug: until 7pm Wed). 📷
In the 1460s, Archduke Sigismund embarked on a project to build a princely residence in Innsbruck. His Gothic castle, extended by Maximilian I, survived for several centuries, and to this day the castle dungeons feature the original late-Gothic vaults. A major remodelling took place in 1755,

under Maria Theresa, when plans for a Rococo south wing were prepared by Johann Martin Gumpp the Younger, who also remodelled the front of the building and the grand staircase. His work was continued by Konstantin Johann von Walter, who is responsible for the palace's uniform, Classicist shape.

The interior of the Hofburg is furnished in Rococo style. The state rooms on the second floor were completed in 1773. The most beautiful of these is the Riesenhalle (the Giants' Hall), embellished with white and gold stucco and a ceiling painting by Franz Anton Maulbertsch, depicting the triumph of the House of Habsburg-Lothringen. The walls are hung with vast portraits of Maria Theresa, her 16 children and other members of the imperial family.

The remaining rooms of the south wing also have original Rococo decorations and furnishings.

Riesenhalle, a state room in the Hofburg

### ⬛ Goldenes Dachl

Herzog-Friedrich-Strasse 15.
**Tel** (0512) 581111. **Open** May–Sep: 10am–6pm daily; Oct–Apr: 10am–5pm, Tue–Sun. 📷

In about 1500 the tall oriel window, with its 2,657 gilded copper tiles, was added to this former residence of the Tyrolean rulers. It created a viewing box from which Emperor Maximilian I could observe street life on the main square of Innsbruck. The two-storey oriel rests on two slender columns. There are six coats of arms under the first-floor windows and the second-floor balustrade is decorated with reliefs; one of these depicts Maximilian I and two of his three wives: Maria of Burgundy and Bianca Maria Sforza; the second shows the emperor surrounded by court jesters. The building behind the Goldenes Dachl houses the small Maximilianeum, a museum of the emperor's life.

### ⬛ Herzog-Friedrich-Strasse

Herzog-Friedrich-Strasse is one of Innsbruck's loveliest streets. Its main historic sights include the Rococo Helblinghaus (No. 10), the Gothic old town hall, dating from the 14th–15th centuries (No. 21), and its adjacent Stadtturm (city tower), with a viewing terrace.

Many of the other houses along the street also warrant a close look. The four-storey Ottoburg at No. 1, close to the Inn river, has four oriels stacked on top of each other and late-Gothic interior vaults.

The richly ornamented pulpit in Dom St Jakob

The Baroque façade of Altes Regierungsgebäude (Old Governmental Building) at No. 3 hides some beautiful rooms including the Claudia-Saal, the Hall of Claudia de Medici, with a late-Renaissance coffered ceiling. At No. 6 is an old inn, Der Goldene Adler (Golden Eagle Inn), and the Katzunghaus (at No. 16) has interesting 16th-century reliefs on its oriels.

### 🏛 Altes Landhaus

Maria-Theresien-Strasse 43.
**Tel** (0512) 5900. **Closed** to visitors.

This 18th-century house, built in 1725–8 by Georg Anton Gumpp and today the seat of Tyrol's provincial government, is one of Austria's most beautiful secular structures. It has an attractive inner courtyard and its colourful elevations were embellished by Alessandro Callegari. The niches lining the walls of the monumental internal staircase are filled with marble statues and busts of Greek and Roman gods. Ceiling frescoes depict the Tyrolean eagle with an open map of the country. The most opulent room is the Rococo conference hall. Along the same street the Annasäule (1706) rises in front of the Neues Rathaus (new town hall).

Georg Anton Gumpp's imposing stairwell in Altes Landhaus

### 🏛 Tiroler Landesmuseum Ferdinandeum

Museumstrasse 15. **Tel** (0512) 59489.
**Open** 9am–5pm Tue–Sun. 🅿 ♿
🌐 tiroler-landesmuseum.at

Together with the former armoury of Maximilian I at No. 1 Zeughausgasse, this 19th-century

The impressive, two-tiered, 16th-century Schloss Ambras

building houses the collection of the Tiroler Landesmuseum (the Tyrol Regional Museum), named after Archduke Ferdinand II (1529–95), a Tyrolean ruler and a passionate collector. The museum has galleries devoted to the natural environment, history, art and handicrafts, and it is also home to a library. Among its most precious exhibits are Gothic panel paintings, sculptures by Michael Pacher, and works by old German and Dutch masters – Lucas Cranach the Elder, Rembrandt, Pieter Bruegel the Younger and others. The museum also exhibits more recent Austrian art, including works by Klimt, Schiele and Kokoschka.

### 🏰 Schloss Ambras

Schlossstrasse 20. **Tel** (01) 52524-4802.
**Open** 10am–5pm daily. **Closed** 25 Dec.
🅿 🌐 schlossambras-innsbruck.at

The castle, on the southeastern city limits, was once the symbol of Tyrol's power and glory. In the 12th century it was the seat of local rulers.

The present 16th-century building consists of a lower castle with entrance gate and spacious courtyard, and an upper castle built on the site of an earlier structure. The two parts are connected by the early-Renaissance Spanish Hall, built by Giovanni Luchese in 1569–72, with original coffered ceiling and inlaid doors.

Archduke Ferdinand II established his own museum at Ambras, but the exhibits ended up being dispersed in various Viennese museums. Nonetheless, there is still plenty to see, including the Rüstkammer (arsenal), the Kunst- und Wunderkammer (chamber of arts and marvels), and the gallery with portraits of members of the Habsburgs by famous artists such as Lucas Cranach, Peter Paul Rubens and Diego Velázquez.

### Andreas Hofer (1767–1810)

Andreas Hofer is regarded as Austria's national hero, widely extolled in its literature and poetry. In 1809, he led the Tyrolean uprising against the Bavarian rulers, who were allied with Napoleon's forces. He succeeded in beating the Bavarians, and forced the French army, led by Marshal Lefebvre, to retreat from Tyrol after their defeat on Bergisel, a hill just outside Innsbruck (see p247). Hofer assumed civilian power in Tyrol, but was soon betrayed and captured, and subsequently executed by the French in the town square of Mantua.

# Hofkirche

Hofkirche, the court church, was built by Ferdinand I to house the cenotaph of his grandfather, Emperor Maximilian I. The cenotaph was designed by Maximilian himself and although his plans were never fully realized the ensuing structure, completed in 1584, is very impressive indeed and ranks as a masterpiece of Renaissance sculpture. It stands in the centre of the church, alongside a kneeling figure of the emperor, and is guarded by 28 larger-than-life bronze statues. Reliefs on the side panels depict scenes from the emperor's life. Maximilian's body was laid to rest in the castle of Wiener Neustadt, in Lower Austria.

**Vaults**
The vaults acquired their present form in the early 17th century, when the church was rebuilt in the Baroque style.

★ **Cenotaph of Maximilian I**
The cenotaph, at the centre of the church, is guarded by 28 giant figures representing members of Maximilian I's family.

**Main Portal**
The grand Renaissance portal leading into the church was built in 1554 as a tribute to the House of Maximilian I.

**Main entrance**

## KEY

① **Kneeling figure of Emperor Maximilian I**

② **An onion dome** crowns the octagonal tower of the church.

★ **Silberne Kapelle**
The silver chapel holds the tombs of Archduke Ferdinand II and his beloved wife, Philippine Welser.

## VISITORS' CHECKLIST

**Practical Information**
Universitätsstrasse 2.
**Tel** (0512) 594 895 10.
**Open** 9am–5pm Mon–Sat,
12:30–5pm Sun & hols.
**W** tiroler-landesmuseen.at

**Charles the Bold**
The statue of Charles the Bold, duke of Burgundy and Maximilian's father-in-law, stands to the right of the cenotaph, closest to the high altar.

## ⌂ Wilten

In the southeastern suburb of Wilten stands a lovely Baroque basilica, built in 1751–6 on the foundations of a former chapel. The church was intended to provide a worthy setting for the picture of *Our Lady at Four Columns,* which miracles were attributed to. It was designed by Franz de Paula Penz and the interior has been kept in the Rococo style. The altarpiece, with its gold, pink and yellow colour scheme, includes a 14th-century painting of the Madonna. It is surrounded by an intricate canopy resting on slender columns. The ceiling paintings are by an Augsburg artist, Matthäus Günther, and show in the presbytery *Saint Mary Our Advocate* and in the nave *Esther and Judith.*

The Romanesque abbey of Wilten has a church built in the 12th century, devoted to St Lawrence. According to legend, the abbey was built by the giant Haymon, in atonement for the murder of another giant, Thyrsus; both are commemorated by statues. Burned and destroyed several times, the abbey was rebuilt in Baroque style in the 17th–18th centuries.

### Bergisel

Das Tirol Panorama and Kaiserjäger-museum: Bergisel 1–2. **Tel** (0512) 5948 9611. **Open** 9am–5pm Wed–Mon (until 7pm Thu Jul & Aug).

On 13 August 1809, Bergisel (Isel Mountain), in the south of the city, was the scene of a battle fought by Andreas Hofer *(see p245)* and his army of insurgent highlanders, who defeated the combined occupying forces of Bavaria and France. The hill is now a popular place for weekend walks among the residents of Innsbruck.

A monument to Andreas Hofer and the Kaiserjäger-museum serve as reminders of the 1809 battle, as well as of later battles by this famous regiment of imperial fusiliers.

**Statue of Andreas Hofer on Bergisel**

In 2011, the *Riesenrundgemälde,* a panoramic painting of the Battle of Bergisel, was moved from its previous home at the bottom of the Hungerburg cable car, to **Das Tirol Panorama**, a museum on top of Bergisel. Painted by Zeno Diemer in 1896, and measuring 10 x 100 m (33 x 328 ft), the panorama is a *trompe l'oeil* depicting an abbreviated version of the entire battle.

The museum also hosts temporary exhibitions alongside its permanent collection of Tyrolean artifacts.

On Bergiselschanze, one of the competitions in the world-famous Vierschanzentournee (four hills' ski-jumping tournament) is held every year on 4 January.

### ⊠ Alpenzoo

Weiherburggasse 37A. **Tel** (0512) 292323. **Open** Apr–Oct: 9am–6pm; Nov–Mar: 9am–5pm.

On the southern slopes of Bergisel is a fascinating Alpine zoo, housing a comprehensive collection of alpine fauna. There are some 2,000 animals here, representing more than 150 species typically found in an Alpine habitat, including the alpine ibex and bear, and many local birds, fish and reptiles. A cable car from Hungerburg Talstation takes you to the zoo; the ride is free with an entry ticket to the zoo.

**An otter in Alpenzoo, which is located above Hungerburg**

The emblematic Mint Tower of Burg Hasegg in Hall in Tirol

## ❷ Igls

**Road map** B4. 🚠 2,000. 🚌
ⓘ Hilberstrasse 15, (0512) 377101.

This small town south of Innsbruck, which had long been popular as a holiday centre and winter-sports resort, was given a new face for the 1976 Winter Olympic Games when modern toboggan and bobsleigh runs were built. The nearby Patscherkofel (2,247 m/7,372 ft) is a popular destination for winter skiing expeditions and summer rambles. It is served by a funicular, a chairlift and five T-bars. An old salt track, Römerstrasse, runs above the Sill valley, providing views of the famous Europabrücke (Europe Bridge; *see p256*), which spans the Alpine gorges and is part of the busy motorway network connecting northern Europe with Italy.

The **Aegidius-kirche** in Igls, the church of St Giles, probably dates back to the 13th century but was remodelled in the Baroque period. It has beautiful vault frescoes by Josef Michael Schmitzer.

Near Igls is the interesting pilgrimage chapel Heiligwasser (1662), with attractive stucco-work created in 1720 as well as a wooden statue of the Virgin Mary dating back to the early 15th century.

Coat of arms of Hall in Tirol

## ❸ Hall in Tirol

**Road map** B4. 🚠 13,000. 🚌 🚌
ⓘ Wallpachgasse 5, (05223) 455440.
ⓦ hall-wattens.at

Hall ranks mostly as a holiday resort, but the Old Town, with much of its original architecture intact, bears testimony to the town's former glory. The symbol of Hall is the twelve-sided tower known as the Mint Tower, or **Burg Hasegg**. This castle, with its beautiful inner courtyard, once formed a corner section of the town's fortifications. It was the seat of the Tyrolean rulers and, in the 16th century, it became the mint. Today the castle houses the town museum.

In the Old Town, the **Town Hall** with its steep Gothic roof consists of two parts: the 1406 Königshaus (Royal House) with a beautiful debating hall with an exposed-beam ceiling; and a large building on the south side of Oberer Stadtplatz, with a Renaissance portal and a balcony from which the town fathers used to make their proclamations. The 14th-century **Nikolauskirche**, the church of St Nicholas, nearby, has a lovely portal featuring the Sorrowful Christ, the Virgin Mary and St Nicholas, and an attractive Baroque interior. Particularly worth seeing is the Waldaufkapelle, which is closed off from the rest

of the church interior by a wrought-iron grille. It houses a collection of reliquaries.

## ❹ Wattens

**Road map** C4. 🚠 7,700. 🚌 🚌 ⓘ
(05224) 455 440. ⓦ hall-wattens.at

At the Swarovski factory and museum of decorative glass and glass jewellery in Wattens you can see the world's largest cut crystal (300,000 carats), and an impressive crystal wall 11 m (36 ft) high, with several tons of glittering semiprecious stones.

🏛 **Swarovski Crystal Worlds**
Kristallweltenstrasse 1. **Tel** (05224) 51080. **Open** 9am–6pm. ♿
ⓦ kristallwelten.swarovski.com

### Environs
**Volders** has an unusual church devoted to St Charles Borromeo, dating from 1620–54, considered a Rococo masterpiece.

The entrance to Swarovski Crystal Worlds in Wattens

## ❺ Schwaz

**Road map** C4. 🚠 13,000. 🚌 🚌 ⓘ
Münchnerstrasse 11, (05242) 63240.
ⓦ silberregion-karwendel.com

During the 16th century, this busy commercial town in the Inn river valley was the second largest in Tyrol. Schwaz suffered extensive damage during the battle of 1809, but it has preserved some lovely historic sights. The most impressive of these is the 15th-century **Pfarrkirche**, with its high

The imposing Renaissance Schloss Tratzberg

copper-shingled tower and beautiful, crenellated gables. The most striking elements inside are the stone balustrade of the gallery with intricate lacework (c.1520) and an impressive Baroque organ enclosure. The figures of St Anne, St Ursula and St Elizabeth on the altarpiece are original Gothic decorations. The statues of St George and St Florian, the patron saints of Austria, were added at a later date.

The double **cemetery chapel** (1504–7) has a lovely covered staircase leading to the upper chapel, which has a carved wooden altar. The lower chapel has original 16th-century frescoes depicting the Crucifixion and the Mount of Olives.

The **Franziskanerkirche**, the Franciscan church and monastery, has retained its original late-Gothic interior, clearly visible despite Baroque additions made in the 18th century. The cloister along the south wall of the church was built in 1509–12 by Christoph Reichartinger; it shows a series of 16th-century paintings with Passion scenes.

Schwaz was once a major centre for the production of silver, and one of the mines, the **Silberbergwerk**, is now open to the public and can be explored by train and a guided tour on foot.

**Ⅲ Silberbergwerk**
Alte Landstrasse 3a. **Tel** (05242) 72 372. **Open** May–Sep: 9am–5pm daily, Oct–Apr: 10am–4pm Wed–Sun.
**w** silberbergwerk.at

## ❻ Schloss Tratzberg

**Road map** C4. **Tel** (05242) 63 566. **Open** Apr–Oct: 10am–4pm daily.
**w** schloss-tratzberg.at

A short way from Schwaz, in the Inn river valley, stands the impressive Renaissance Schloss Tratzberg. This castle was once a frontier fortress which guarded Andechs county against the Bavarians. It changed hands many times and is now the private property of the Enzenberg family, with a small museum.

The castle is entered from the west side through a Renaissance portal. The inner courtyard, with its heavily decorated low arcades, was built in two stages: the first around 1500 and the second in the late 16th century. The most interesting parts of the castle are the armoury, with its tremendous collection of early arms; the Royal Room, with its exposed-beam ceiling, once used by Anna of Bohemia, the widow of Duke Henry of

Tyrol; and finally the Habsburg Hall, with the family tree of Emperor Maximilian I and 148 portraits. The room has a red marble column at its centre and is covered by a coffered ceiling. The emperor's room on the second floor retains its original intricately carved wooden ceiling, and the bedroom is decorated with a series of 16th-century paintings of a knightly tournament created by Hans Schäufelein. The Fugger family room still boasts its original Renaissance decor. Its best feature is the richly inlaid door dating from 1515.

## ❼ Achensee

**Road map** C4. **i** (5246) 530 00. **w** achensee.at

Situated between the Inn and the Isar river basins is Achensee, the largest lake in Tyrol, about 9 km (6 miles) long. Surrounding ski slopes provide great views of the lake. The town also promotes a range of alternative winter sports, including snowshoeing, cross-country trails and tobogganing.

Achensee can be reached by cog-wheel train from **Jenbach**. Worth seeing in this village is the church of St Wolfgang, a late-Gothic structure built in 1487–1500 by Gilg Mitterhofer from Schwaz; its Baroque tower is a later addition. Although repeatedly rebuilt, it still has its late-Gothic side portals and ogival windows. One of the side altars has a late-Gothic statue of the Madonna.

Sailing yachts on Achensee, Tyrol's largest lake

Charming flower displays outside the Alpine houses in Alpbach

## ❽ Alpbach

**Road map** C4. 🏔 2,600. 🛈 (05337) 21200-30. 🌐 **alpbachtal.at**

Proclaimed the most beautiful village in Austria, Alpbach is located in a high mountain valley, 1,000 m (3,280 ft) above sea level. Its charm is undeniable: traditional wooden chalets and Alpine houses, their balconies brimming with colourful flowers, are surrounded by lush cow pastures, unspoilt woodlands and beautiful mountain scenery, making Alpbach a picture-postcard destination.

It is also one of Austria's most popular ski resorts, offering a range of cross-country skiing trails and ski slopes. The terrain is gentle and undulating, making it perfect for beginners and families. During the summer months cycling, hiking and even para-gliding are major attractions.

The little town also has the interesting **church of St Oswald**. Its earliest records date from 1369, although it was altered in 1500 and the Baroque interior dates from 1724. The naves have ceiling paintings by Christoph Anton Mayr (1751); the sculptures in the presbytery (c.1779) are the work of Franz Xaver Nissl.

## ❾ Wörgl

**Road map** C4. 🏔 13,000. 🛈 Bahnhofstrasse 4a, (05332) 76007.

The industrial town of Wörgl, at the fork of Inn river and Brixentaler Ache stream, is an important road and rail hub. The earliest settlement on the site, revealed by archaeological finds on the northeastern outskirts of town, date from the Bronze Age. In later years this was the site of a Roman settlement, and in the 4th century a Christian community was founded in the area. In the 13th century Wörgl belonged to Bavaria; during the reign of Maximilian I it finally became incorporated into Tyrol. Wörgl and its environs were the scene of fierce fighting during

Monument to the Battle of 1809 in Wörgl

the Napoleonic wars, when the Tyrolean highlanders fought for their independence from the Bavarians and the French. A monument commemorating the battle now stands in front of the **church of St Lawrence**. This church, built in 1748, is Baroque in style and has interesting stucco decorations, vault paintings, a main altar with Baroque sculptures and an attractive medieval statue of the Madonna.

Wörgl's location between the two popular tourist regions of Kaisergebirge and the Kitzbühel Alps makes it a convenient base for winter and summer expeditions.

## ❿ Söll

**Road map** C4. 🏔 3,500. 🛈 050509-210.

Söll, a small town in the foothills of the Hohe Salve, part of the Wilder Kaiser (Wild Emperor) massif, grew around the **church of St Peter and St Paul**. Built in 1361 but completely altered in the Baroque style in 1768 by Franz Bock of Kufstein, it contains beautiful vault paintings by Christoph Anton Mayr and, by the same artist, a picture of the Madonna in the main altarpiece. The town has many attractive houses with picturesque façades.

The greatest attraction of Söll, however, is the **Hohe Salve** mountain, rising to 1,828 m (5,997 ft) and visible from every point in the town. Two gondolas provide transport to the summit. There is a small chapel here, and the view over Brixental, the Kitzbühel Alps and the High Tauern Mountains in the distance, is truly majestic.

Söll lies at the centre of a large skiing region, **Skiwelt Wilder Kaiser-Brixental**, in the southern part of Kaisergebirge. It is one of the most extensive ski regions in Europe, and includes the nearby towns of Scheffau and Ellmau.

Visitors sunbathing on Hohe Salve, near Söll

## ⓫ Kufstein

**Road map** C4. ⛰ 18,000. 🚉 🚌
ℹ️ (05372) 62207. 🌐 **kufstein.com**

The remains of a Stone Age settlement have been found in this health resort and tourist centre on the Bavarian border.

On a rocky hill to the north of the town stands the Feste Kufstein, a fortress with a small barbican and the Emperor's Tower. Today it houses a regional museum and the Heldenorgel (Heroes' Organ), built to commemorate all who were killed in World War I. The late-Gothic **church of St Vitus** was rebuilt in the 17th century in the Baroque style, but in the 20th century it was partly returned to its original Gothic appearance. Nearby stands the Holy Trinity Chapel, with a beautiful Baroque altar dating from 1765.

### Environs
Hechtsee and Stimmersee, two small, scenic lakes west of Kufstein, are excellent for water sports enthusiasts. About 30 km (22 miles) northeast of Kufstein, beyond the Kaisergebirge ridge known as Zahmer Kaiser (Tame Emperor), is **Walchsee**, a beguiling town and lake of the same name, with many fine houses with picturesque façades and a good water sports centre. The road from Kufstein along the Sparchenbach river leads to Stripsenkopf, at 1,807 m (5,929 ft)

the highest peak in the Zahmer Kaiser range, with great views of the Kaisergebirge.

## ⓬ St Johann in Tirol

**Road map** C4. ⛰ 9,000. 🚉 🚌
ℹ️ (05352) 63335-0.

St Johann in Tirol is a small winter sports resort, with good downhill runs on the northern slopes of the Kitzbüheler Horn and splendid conditions for cross-country skiing. The town has several Baroque buildings, and the walls of the parish house feature original frescoes from 1480. The first large Baroque church in the area was built in 1728 by Abraham Millauer, on the site of an earlier Gothic structure. Inside **Mariä Himmelfahrtskirche** (church of the Assumption of the Virgin Mary) are magnificent vault paintings by one of the great masters of Baroque art, Simon Benedikt Faistenberger.

## ⓭ Kitzbühel

**Road map** C4. ⛰ 8,500. 🚉 🚌
ℹ️ Hinterstadt 18, (05356) 66660.
🌐 kitzbuehel.com

One of the most charming and upmarket of the Tyrolean ski resorts, the town of Kitzbühel has quaint cobbled streets leading out into gentle summer pastures filled with cows. Every January,

A picturesque snow-covered scene in Kitzbühel

however, the town is filled with daredevils arriving for the Hahnenkammrennen, the most dangerous downhill ski race in the world.

But Kitzbühel is more than a sporting resort; untouched by wartime ravages, it has many historic sights. The **Andreaskirche** was built in 1435 on the site of a Romanesque church; in 1785 it was rebuilt in the Baroque style. Inside are late-Gothic columns and 15th-century traceries and frescoes. There is also an interesting main altarpiece, by Simon Benedikt Faistenberger.

Adjacent to the parish church is **Liebfrauenkirche** (church of Our Lady), with a square tower. The main altar is also by Faistenberger. The 14th-century St Catherine's church in the city centre is now a monument to those killed in the two world wars.

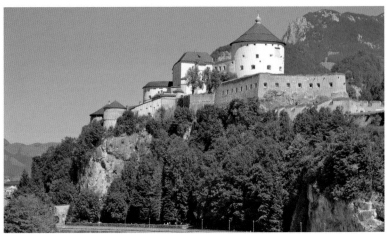

The mighty fortress with its Emperor's Tower in Kufstein

# ⑭ Zillertal

The Zillertal, the valley of the Ziller river, extends from Innau to the border with Italy. Initially a wide upland, beyond Mayrhofen it splits into four narrower valleys that cut into the mountain ranges. Artificial lakes and large dams were built into most of the local rivers to provide a power supply for the entire region. Especially popular with skiers are the Hintertux glacier runs, where snow is guaranteed. Accommodation is of a high quality throughout the region and Mayrhofen has a particularly good nightlife. The well-marked trails in breathtakingly beautiful countryside lure ramblers here in the summer, and there are many attractive cycling routes.

**Zillertaler Alpen**
The Zillertaler Alps, a side range of the High Tauern, are steep crystalline mountains. Their highest peak is the Hochfeiler at 3,510 m/ 11,516 ft.

**★ Tuxertal**
The valley of the Tuxerbach (Tux stream) is picturesque, with many attractive resorts. Tuxer Ferner, the local glacier, offers great year-round skiing conditions.

Lanersbach • L6

*Tuxertal*

2867

Hintertux •

Ginzl

3231 Zemmtal • 169

3250

Zamser Grund •

*Zemmgrund*

3476

Schlegeis-
speicher

3289

3478

## Key

― Major road
― Minor road
- - Cable car, chairlift
― River
⚶ Viewpoint

**Schlegeisspeicher**
The largest artificial lake in the area is scenically situated at the foot of the Hochfeiler massif and the Schlegeis glacier.

| 0 kilometres | 5 |
|---|---|
| 0 miles | 5 |

**★ Zell am Ziller**
This beautiful fresco (1779) by Franz A. Zeiller adorns the church of St Vitus. Another sight to see here is the old gold mine.

*Schwaz*

**Zell am Ziller**

165

• **Hippach**

*Gerlostal*

169

**Mayrhofen**

nkenberg

*Zillergrund*

*2700*

*Stillupp-speicher*

*Stilluppgrund*

▲ *3383*        ▲ *3376*

▲ *3368*

**Stilluppspeicher**
The best views of this lake in its pristine natural environment are gained from the top of the dam at 1,130 m (3,707 ft). Nearby are two waterfalls.

## VISITORS' CHECKLIST

**Practical Information**
Road map C4.
 Bundesstrasse 27d, Schlitters, (05288) 87187.
W **zillertal.at**

**Transport**

**Mayrhofen**
In this picturesque resort, the most popular tourist destination in the Zillertal, the wide valley narrows and divides into four smaller Alpine valleys.

## Tyrolean Traditional Costume

The Tyrolean version of Austria's national costume is not reserved for special occasions – here many people wear it every day. The man's *Tracht* consists of leather shorts (summer) or breeches (winter) held in place by braces and tied under the knees, thick socks and a *Loden* jacket made of thick, woollen cloth, with bone buttons. To this is added a felt hat with a distinctive tuft of coarse animal hair. The woman's *Dirndl* comprises a puffed-sleeve blouse with a bodice and a pleated skirt with an apron.

A young couple dressed in typical Tyrolean outfits

Europabrücke, the highest road bridge in Europe

### ⑮ Brenner Pass

**Road map** B5.

At an altitude of 1,374 m (4,508 ft), the Brenner Pass is the lowest passage across the Eastern Alps, and as such one of the most easily accessible routes connecting northern Europe with Italy. Lying between the Stubai Alps and the Zillertal Alps, the pass was originally used by the Romans as a trade and military route. A highway suitable for carriage traffic was built in 1772, and the first trans-Alpine railway line was opened here in 1867. Today the motorway across the wide saddle of the Brenner also boasts the highest and most impressive road bridge in Europe, the Europabrücke, 815 m (2,674 ft) long.

### ⑯ Stubaital

**Road map** B4. 🚌 🛈 Bahnstrasse 17, Fulpmes, (0501) 881 200.
🌐 **stubai.at**

Travelling on the Brenner motorway from Innsbruck towards Italy you will pass the Stubai Alps to your right, a high ridge massif with few valleys.

The lowest route into the centre of the massif runs along the Stubaital (Stubai valley), with its busy tourist resorts of Fulpmes and Neustift. The highest peak of the Stubai Alps, Zuckerhütl (Little Sugar Loaf), rises to 3,507 m (11,506 ft). The Stubaital is a very quiet place, particularly when compared with the neighbouring Zillertal (pp252–3). The Stubai glacier, the largest glacier ski resort in Austria, provides excellent conditions for skiing.

Fulpmes, a popular tourist centre in the Stubaital

### ⑰ Ötztal

**Road map** B4. 🚉 🚌
🛈 Gemeindestrasse 4, Sölden (05720) 05 00. 🌐 **oetztal.com**

Following the course of the Ötztaler Ache, a tributary of the Inn river, is the long valley of Ötztal. At its southern end, near the border with Italy, rise the Ötztal Alps, with many peaks above 3,500 m (11,500 ft); the Wildspitze, at 3,774 m (12,381 ft), is North Tyrol's highest summit.

Nestling within the Ötztal Alps is also the highest parish in Austria, the ski resort of Obergurgl at 1,927 m (6,322 ft). The largest settlement in the lower part of Ötztal is **Oetz**, an old village with attractive, colourful houses. The paintings on the Star Inn date from 1573 and 1615. On a steep slope stands the church of St George and St Nicholas, which retains some original Gothic features, including a vault and portals.

The largest town at the upper end of the Ötztal valley is **Längenfeld**, where you find the church of St Catherine. It has a 74-m- (243-ft-) high Gothic tower, a decorative west portal and a Baroque interior.

Ötztal's administrative centre is the old Tyrolean village of **Sölden**. The Tiefenbach glacier attracts early and late-season skiers, as do the extensive terrain and hearty après-ski.

In 1991, a frozen human body was discovered on the Italian side of the Ötztal Alps. Although over 5,000 years old, Ötzi, as he was named, was perfectly preserved by the ice, along with some 70 artifacts.

### ⑱ Seefeld

**Road map** B4. 🏔 3,300. 🚉
🛈 Klosterstrasse 43, (05088) 050.
🌐 **seefeld.com**

This small town occupying a large sunny plateau is one of Austria's most fun and fashionable resorts for family-oriented ski holidays, featuring gentle, welcoming runs. In the 1964 and 1976 Winter Olympics, Seefeld was the venue for all the Nordic skiing contests,

◀ View of a man-made reservoir at the foot of the Zillertaler Alps enhancing the town's prosperity and reputation. The local cross-country skiing trails are the longest in the Alps, measuring some 250 km (155 miles).

At the centre of Seefeld stands the huge 15th-century church of St Oswald, while at the western end of the town is a chapel built on the orders of Archduke Leopold V to house a crucifix dating from the early 16th century and said to have miraculous powers. The crucifix stands within the altarpiece of this small, circular building with a Renaissance portal and onion dome.

Visitors to Seefeld can also enjoy a trip to the casino, one of the largest in Austria.

View of Zugspitze from the Ehrwald side

# ⑲ Ehrwald

**Road map** B4. 2,600. Kirchplatz 1, (05673) 20 000-208. zugspitzarena.com

Nestling below the western side of Zugspitze (2,965 m/ 9728 ft), the highest peak of the Bavarian Alps, is the resort village of Ehrwald. On the German side of the mountain is the resort of Garmisch-Partenkirchen, the most popular winter sports centre in that area. Several Austrian and German resorts, including Garmisch-Partenkirchen and Ehrwald, have joined up to form one vast skiing area.

The summit of Zugspitze can be reached from both the German and the Austrian sides. From Ehrwald, you take the cable car from the lower station of Ehrwald/Obermoos. The upper station affords magnificent views. To the south, beyond the mountain ranges

of Kaisergebirge, Karwendelgebirge and Dachstein, you can see the snow-covered peaks of the High Tauern. To the east, there are the Arlberg mountains with Silvretta and Rätikon, with the peaks of the Appenzeller Alpen in between, and the Allgäu mountains in the distance. To the north, Bavaria can be seen.

Clemens Krauss, the founder of the famous Vienna New Year's Day concerts, lived in Ehrwald and lies buried here.

# ⑳ Reutte

**Road map** B4. 6,000. Untermarkt 34, (05672) 62336. reutte.com

Reutte is the largest town in the Ausserfern district, a remote area that was cut off from the world for a considerable time: it is said that the first car arrived here only in 1947. Reutte can be reached from Innsbruck via the Fern Pass, a route first used in Roman times. In the valley of the Lech river, it is today the main town and trade centre of the region. In medieval times it grew rich on the salt trade, and to this day it has some lovely town houses with oriel windows, open staircases and painted façades. Many of the paintings are by Johann

Jakob Zeiller, the best-known member of an artistic family that settled in Reutte in the 17th and 18th centuries – they once lived at No. 1 Zeiller Platz.

The 15th-century convent church of St Anna features several interesting works of art. In the main altarpiece are a picture of the Madonna with Child and St Anna (c.1515) and two vast figures of St Magnus and St Afra dating from the early 18th century.

The **Heimatmuseum** (regional museum) has a fine collection of paintings by outstanding masters of the Baroque, mainly of the Zeiller family members, as well as exhibits associated with transport and salt mining.

Specimens representative of the local flora can be seen in the **Alpenblumengarten**, an Alpine flower garden on top of the Hahnenkamm, at a height of about 1,700 m (5,577 ft) above sea level.

**Heimatmuseum**
Grünes Haus, Untermarkt 26. **Tel** (05672) 72304. **Open** 1–5pm Tue–Sat. museum-reutte.at

**Environs**
A short distance east of Reutte is the beautiful 5-km- (3-mile-) long **Plansee**, where small pleasure boats offer cruises on the tranquil waters. In winter the entire lake freezes over and becomes a giant ice-skating rink.

Plansee, a tranquil, picturesque lake near Reutte

*For hotels and restaurants in this region see pp298–9 and pp323–4*

Warth, a town situated within the most famous winter sports region

### ㉑ Elbigenalp

**Road map** A4. 🚹 850. 🚌
ℹ️ (05634) 621 012.

The Lech river valley, which is parallel to the Inn river valley and snakes between mountain passes, cuts a deep ravine between the Allgäuer Alps and the Lechtal Alps. About halfway between the towns of Reutte and Warth (a popular ski area) lies Elbigenalp, a small village worth visiting for the local **Nikolauskirche** (church of St Nicholas). Built in the 14th century, the church's oldest surviving parts include the Gothic tower, presbytery and font. It was altered in the Baroque style, and the vault and wall paintings as well as the Stations of the Cross are the work of the artistic Zeiller family,

who lived in Reutte. St Martin's cemetery chapel in Elbigenalp has interesting original Gothic frescoes depicting scenes from the life of St Magdalene and the Dance of Death by Anton Falger.

### ㉒ Lech am Arlberg

**Road map** A4. 🚹 1,500. 🚌 🚍
ℹ️ (05583) 2161-0.
🔲 lechzuers.at

This small resort is situated on a large plateau at an altitude of 1,450 m (4,800 ft), not far from the source of the Lech river. Lech is regarded as one of Austria's most beautiful and luxurious mountain resorts and regularly attracts celebrities and royals, who come to spend their winter holidays here. Today, Lech, Oberlech and neighbouring Zürs

are linked by ski lifts to form the formidable Ski Alberg skipass region, with 305 km (190 miles) of runs. Lech is never crowded; once a certain number of ski passes are sold, Lech simply closes the roads.

Summer, too, can be very pleasant here, and there are many beautiful trails for walking or mountain cycling. Sights to see include the 15th-century Gothic **church of St Nicholas**, with an even older tower. In addition, there are swanky hotels, chic shops, smart cafés and restaurants.

### ㉓ St Anton am Arlberg

**Road map** A4. 🚹 2,600. 🚌 🚍
ℹ️ (05447) 55 64.
🔲 stantonamarlberg.com

St Anton is something of a skiing mecca. Consistently ranked as one of the top five skiing resorts in the world, it is certainly number one in Austria, and is one of the most snow-sure resorts in the Alps. Runs range from those for beginners to the challenging Valluga peak, which is restricted to expert skiers accompanied by a guide. The après-ski is enthusiastic, with the nightlife continuing into the early hours of the morning.

The snowy mountain resort of St Anton am Arlberg

The resort is often heralded as the "birthplace of skiing"; it was here that Johann "Hannes" Schneider conceived the "Arlberg method", a step-by-step transition from the snowplough to the Christie. Taught through a series of films and books, the method is still in use today.

Besides snowy slopes, St Anton features a charming village, complete with a 17th-century onion-domed church, a fascinating Alpine museum and a plethora of traditional Alpine houses. In addition, the village has a number of luxurious spas, while on the slopes is the Arberg 1800 hotel resort, which hosts art displays and concerts.

## ㉔ Arlberg

*See pp260–61.*

Ischgl, one of Austria's most attractive skiing resorts

## ㉕ Ischgl

Road map A5. 🏔 1,550. 🚍
ℹ 050990-100. 🌐 ischgl.at

Ischgl, on the Trisanna river at the eastern end of the Silvretta-strasse, may retain the charm of a small farming village, but it is in fact the venue for a distinctly young, affluent and sometimes raucous clientele of skiers and snowboarders. An international ski centre, it provides access to 200 km (120 miles) of ski runs and 40 lifts within the Silvretta range on the Austrian–Swiss border. The town is also an ideal starting point for a drive along the Silvrettahochalpenstrasse, a hairpin mountain road, often

Lünersee, a reservoir lake at the foot of Schesaplana

snow-covered – and therefore closed – from November until late May, which connects the Montafon valley and the Ill river with the Trisanna valley. The road drops by 1,000 m (3,280 ft) over just 15 km (9 miles).

The area around the Silvretta-Stausee, a reservoir on the Bielerhöhe Pass at 2,036 m (6,680 ft), has been made a national park; the ski runs in the Silvretta massif start here. The most beautiful views are to be had from Hohes Rad, at 2,934 m (9,626 ft). The high mountain section of Silvrettastrasse ends in Galtür, a lovely village on the Ballunspitze.

## ㉖ Lünersee

Road map A4. 🚍

Lünersee lies at the foot of the Schesaplana peak (2,965 m/ 9,728 ft), at an altitude of 1,907 m (6,257 ft). Once, this was the largest lake in the Eastern Alps, surrounded by rugged mountains criss-crossed with ravines. The dam built here in 1958 raised the water level by 27 m (89 ft), creating an artificial reservoir that now powers the Lünersee and Rodund power stations.

## ㉗ Bludenz

Road map A4. 🏔 14,000. 🚍 🚍
ℹ Werdenbergerstrasse 42, (05552) 63621-970. 🎪 Chocolate Festival (early Jul). 🌐 bludenz.at

Beautifully situated at the confluence of five Alpine valleys, the town of Bludenz is now a

popular resort with excellent skiing areas in its environs. A 10th-century document survives in which Otto I gives the bishop of Chur a church "in loco Plutenes". During the reign of Friedrich IV the Poor, the town became an administrative centre and power base for the region.

Despite several devastating fires, Bludenz still has some interesting historic sights. The oldest building is **Oberes Tor** (Upper Gate), which houses the local history museum (open in summer). Inside St Lawrence church (1514) are two original altars made from black marble and paintings (1510) showing the Marriage of the Virgin Mary and the Visitation. The seat of the regional authorities is Gayenhofen Castle, a medieval building remodelled in Baroque style in 1643.

Today, the town is permeated by chocolate smells from the Suchard factory, producers of the famous confectionery and organizers of an annual chocolate festival.

The octagonal tower of the Laurentiuskirche in Bludenz

# ㉔ Arlberg

The Arlberg Pass in the Eastern Alps is part of the European watershed between the catchment areas of the North Sea, the Black Sea, the tributaries of the Rhine and the Danube. Arlberg used to be completely cut off from the rest of the country, oriented more towards Germany and Switzerland, until the railway tunnel was built in 1880–84, connecting Vorarlberg with the rest of Austria. The tunnel, at an altitude of 1,310 m (4,298 ft), measures 10,238 m (33,589 ft) in length, and was for many years the longest in Austria. Today, the Arlberg region has some of the country's most exclusive ski resorts.

**⑦ Valluga**
The breathtaking view extending from the summit at 2,809 m (9,216 ft) embraces the Rätikon mountains, the Montafon valley, the Brenner Pass, the Ötztal and the Stubai Alps.

**⑥ Flexenpass**
The pass is surrounded by the Rätikon mountain peaks, including Zimbaspitze and Schesaplana. Thanks to a system of avalanche defences, the road across remains passable in winter.

Lech

Feldkirch

**⑤ Stuben**
This quiet village at the foot of the Albonagrat (2,334 m/ 7,658 ft) has ski runs leading to St Anton. The name ("cosy living room") refers to the cabins from where travellers set off on the mountain trails.

**④ Arlbergtunnel**
The road tunnel underneath the Arlberg Pass, 14 km (9 miles) long, was the longest in the world when it opened in 1978.

### ① Landeck

Schloss Landeck, built in about 1200 and rebuilt after a fire, has retained its original grand hall, with its late-Gothic vault, and a chapel with early-16th-century frescoes. Today, the castle is the home of the local folk museum.

## Tips for Drivers

**Length of route:** 45 km (28 miles).

**Stopping-off points:** the hotel by the hospice in St Christoph offers accommodation. There are many restaurants and excellent shops in St Anton am Arlberg.

### Key

Motorway

Suggested route

Scenic route

Other road

River, lake

Tunnel

| 0 km | 5 |
|------|---|
| 0 miles | 5 |

_Innsbruck_

_Davos_

### ③ St Christoph

The small statue of St Christopher, from the old hospice in the town of St Christoph, was replaced with a new sculpture after fire damage in 1957. The hospice itself is today a luxury hotel. Austria's first regular ski-school was founded here in 1901.

### ② St Anton am Arlberg

The largest tourist resort in Arlberg, St Anton is surrounded by numerous ski trails, and good snow conditions are guaranteed throughout the season.

# ㉘ Bregenzer Wald

The Bregenzer Wald (Bregenz Forest) occupies the northern part of Vorarlberg and extends along the Bregenzer Ache valley. This region has maintained much of its individual character. Its inhabitants cherish their traditions, and the architecture, the national costumes and the dialect spoken here differ from those found in the rest of the country. The Bregenz Forest has many picturesque resorts with excellent facilities for visitors. Apart from Bregenz itself, two larger urban centres have become established on its borders – Dornbirn and Feldkirch, the "gateway to Austria", with its beautifully preserved old town.

⑥ **Schwarzenberg**
This was the home town of Angelika Kauffmann, a prominent artist of the Neo-Classical period. Her paintings depicting Christ's apostles and disciples can be seen in the local Holy Trinity church.

⑦ **Ammenegg**
From the forecourt of the Sonnblick Inn in Ammenegg, visitors can enjoy lovely views which, on a clear day, extend as far as Lake Constance and the peaks of the Swiss Alps.

*Lindau*
*Feldkirch*

⑧ **Dornbirn**
The largest town in Vorarlberg, this is a centre for the textile industry. The Inatura museum houses modern displays on the natural environment and the history of the region.

## Angelika Kauffmann

Angelika Kauffmann, a Swiss painter (1741–1807) of idealized portraits in sentimental or Neo-Classical style, was associated with German, English and Italian artistic circles. She left many works in Schwarzenberg, where she had family links. The local church has an altarpiece by her and also a small bust. More works by this celebrated artist can be seen in the Vorarlberger Landesmuseum in Bregenz.

Angelika Kauffmann

⑨ **Rappenlochschlucht**
The road to the Rappenloch gorge runs steeply uphill along the Dornbirner Ache stream, and ends at a reservoir.

### ⑤ Bezau
This picturesque village set among orchards has a lovely church, dating from 1771, and a small but interesting museum devoted to the region's folk art.

### ④ Mellau
A quiet village on the Bregenzer Ache, Mellau is famous for its wooden houses with shingle-clad roofs, characteristically adorned with flowers.

### ③ Bregenzer Ache
The valley of Bregenzer Ache, running from the Lechtaler Alpen, is the main axis of the Bregenzer Forest. The river flows between steep rock faces and gentle hills, past pleasant villages, down a long winding gorge, on its way to Bodensee (Lake Constance).

### ② Schröcken
The church in Schröcken, at the foot of the Widderstein (2,533 m/8,310 ft), has a richly decorated interior and beautiful stained-glass windows.

### ① Hochtannbergpass
The pass between Schröcken and Warth winds its scenic way along the upper Bregenzer Ache, and reaches its highest point near Schröcken at 1,679 m (5,508 ft).

**Au**

*Schoppernau*

### Key
▨ Suggested route
▬ Scenic road
═ Other road
═ River, lake

## Tips for Drivers

**Length of the route:** 63 km (39 miles).
**Stopping-off points:** there are restaurants and accommodation in Dornbirn, the largest town.
**Further attractions:** Angelika Kauffmann Museum, Brand 34, Kleberhaus. **Tel** (05512) 3570.
**Open** May–Oct: 10am–5pm Tue–Sun; Nov–Jan: 2–4pm Fri–Sun. ♿

0 kilometres     3
0 miles     3

# ㉙ Bregenz

The capital of Vorarlberg since 1923, Bregenz is strategically – and attractively – situated on the eastern shore of Bodensee (Lake Constance), at the edge of the Rhine valley and the foot of the Austrian and Swiss Alps. It is a meeting point of four countries: Austria, Germany, Switzerland and the Principality of Liechtenstein. The Romans established the settlement of Brigantium, and later it became the Alemanni town of Brancantia. In 1451 and 1523 Bregenz came under Habsburg rule, and during the Thirty Years' War, it was destroyed by the Swedes. Attractions in Bregenz include walks on the nearby Pfänder massif, and boat trips out on the lake.

Renaissance altarpiece of 1615, in Seekapelle St Georg

View of Bregenz, on the shores of Bodensee

## Exploring Bregenz

Oberstadt (upper town) is the oldest part of Bregenz, with a number of well-preserved historic buildings and the remains of 13th-century fortifications. Innenstadt (inner city) is much newer. It has a theatre and an interesting regional museum. The promenades along Lake Constance, always shrouded in a gentle mist, are worth exploring, as are the grounds of the popular Bregenz summer festivals.

### 🏛 Vorarlberg Museum

Kornmarktplatz 1. **Tel** (05574) 46 050.
**Open** 10am–6pm Tue–Sun (Jul & Aug until 7pm; Thu until 8pm year round).
🖼 **W** vorarlbergmuseum.at

The Vorarlberg Museum holds collections of prehistoric relics, artifacts dating from the Roman time of the settlement of Brigantium and objects from the days of the Alemanni settlers, all found in Bregenz and its vicinity. A separate department is devoted to

regional handicrafts and customs, old weaponry, coins and medals, and regional costumes. One particularly fascinating exhibit is the collection of portable organs. The museum also has an art gallery which holds many beautiful portraits by Angelika Kauffmann (1741–1807), whose family came from Bregenzer Wald (see p262). Other interesting exhibits are early Christian artifacts, Gothic sculptures, paintings, old altarpieces, and beautiful gold and silver ornaments. The jewels of this museum are the 9th-century stone tablet from Lauterach and the early 16th-century crucifix from the collegiate church in Mehrerau.

### 🏛 Rathaus

Rathausstrasse 4.
The former granary built in 1686 became the town's chancellery in 1720 and, in 1810, the seat of the town's authorities. It remains the town hall to this day.

### ⬆ Seekapelle St Georg

Rathausstrasse.
The small chapel of St George, known as the Lakeside Chapel, was built in 1445 and was once lapped by the waters of Bodensee. Today it is separated from the lake by roads and a railway line. In 1690–98 it was moved and rebuilt in the Baroque style by the master bricklayer Kaspar Held. The 1615 Renaissance altarpiece has been preserved. Depicted at its centre is the Madonna at the foot of the Cross; the side niches show scenes from the Passion.

### 🏛 Martinsturm

Martingsgasse 3b. **Tel** (05574) 410 1560.
**Open** May–Oct: 10am–6pm Tue–Sun.
The square St Martin's Tower, the symbol of Bregenz, was

The Martinsturm, topped with a Baroque dome

probably built in the 14th century on earlier Romanesque foundations. Its present look and its staircase date from 1599, while the Baroque cupola was added at a later date. With its Venetian windows and overall muted colour scheme, the tower is reminiscent of Moorish architecture. It houses a city archive which presents changing exhibitions.

In the adjacent St Martin's Chapel, beautiful frescoes can be seen, which date back to 1362 and depict Christ in Mandorla with the symbols of the four Evangelists and portraits of the chapel founders, members of the Monfort family.

### 🎠 Altes Rathaus
Oberstadt.

The Old Town Hall, built in 1662 by Michael Kuen, was the seat of the Bregenz municipal authorities until the 19th century. This solid, half-timbered structure stands in the centre of Oberstadt, close to the former town gate, Unteres Tor (Lower Gate). A relief depicts Epona, the Celtic goddess of agriculture who is shown on horseback, holding a horn of plenty.

### 🏠 St Gallus
Kirchplatz 3.

Opposite the city centre, on the banks of the Thalbach stream, stands the Stadtpfarrkirche St Gallus (the parish church of St Gallus). According to legend, a previous church on this site had been consecrated by Gallus, an Irish missionary who arrived here in the 7th century. The present church was consecrated in 1318, and the sandstone gate tower in front of it was added in the 15th century. Another tower was added in 1672, and in 1738 the church was altered in the Baroque style, to plans by Franz Anton Beer. At that time, the nave was raised and a chapel was added in the transept.

The rather modest interior of the church is typical of Vorarlberg's ecclesiastical style and contrasts sharply with the styles of Tyrol and Bavaria, where Baroque opulence is much more in evidence. The main altarpiece includes statues of the saints Gallus,

Decorative detail on the wall of Stadtpfarrkirche St Gallus

Peter, Paul and Ulrich, while the side chapel has figures of saints Magnus and Nicholas. St Magnus, an 8th-century Benedictine monk from St Gallen, is the patron saint of the Allgäu, the region between Tyrol and Vorarlberg. St Nicholas is said to keep a careful watch over the navigation on Bodensee. The beautiful stalls in the presbytery are made from walnut wood. They have deep inlays and the backrests are decorated on the outside with the effigies of saints.

## Bregenz City Centre

① Vorarlberg Museum
② Rathaus
③ Seekapelle St Georg
④ Martinsturm
⑤ Altes Rathaus
⑥ St Gallus
⑦ Festspielhaus

0 metres 250
0 yards 250

For keys to symbols *see back flap*

Seebühne, the floating stage on Lake Constance

### 🏛 Festspielhaus

Platz der Wiener Symphoniker 1.
**Tel** (05574) 4130.
🌐 kongresskultur.com

This congress and convention centre, situated next to Lake Constance, was created specifically for the Bregenz arts festival that has been held every year since 1946, from late July until late August. The festival events include theatre and opera performances, as well as symphony concerts and fine art exhibitions. Since 1955, shows have been staged at the Theater am Kornmarkt, a building in the city centre, erected in 1838 as a granary and converted into a theatre in 1955. In 1980, this modern festival and congress complex was opened, including show and concert halls, exhibition rooms and a congress centre. The most spectacular of the festival venues is the famous Seebühne, a floating stage extending into the lake. Shows and concerts are staged here and watched by the public on the shore.

The centre hosts all kinds of conferences and events throughout the rest of the year.

### 🏛 Zisterzienserkloster Mehrerau

Mehrerauerstrasse 66. **Tel** (05574) 71461. **Open** for guided tours for groups only.

To the west of the city centre stands the Zisterzienserkloster Mehrerau, a Cistercian monastery that has been a centre

of spiritual and intellectual life since the 11th century. The church and monastery complex, originally built for the Benedictines and subsequently taken over by the Cistercians, was remodelled in 1740 in the Baroque style by Franz Anton Beer; the new tower was built using material from the previous Romanesque basilica. It was destroyed in the Napoleonic wars, rebuilt in 1855 and renovated in the 20th century. Inside, two pictures survive with the Stations of the Cross and two late-Gothic statues of the Madonna. The late-Gothic altar in the capitular room dates from 1582.

Adjacent to the reconstructed church and the Romanesque crypt there is now a secondary school, a monastery and a sanatorium.

### 🏛 Hohenbregenz

The Hohenbregenz fortress, whose ruins stand to this day

on Gebhardsberg, was built in the 10th century. In 1338, the recorded owner of the castle was Hugo de Montfort.

In 1451, following the death of the last ruler of that line, the castle, together with the town and Bregenz province, were bought by Sigismund of Tyrol.

In 1647, the castle was blown up by the Swedish troops of General Wrangel during the Thirty Years' War, leaving only ruins. The original parts still standing today are the gateway, walls, barbican and a single turret.

In 1723, a chapel devoted to the saints Gebhard and George was built on top of Gebhardsberg and it became a popular pilgrimage site. St Gebhard, a 10th-century bishop of Constance, was the son of Ulrich of Bregenz, born in Hohenbregenz.

### Environs

At the foot of the **Pfänder** (1,065 m/3,494 ft), southeast of the current town, stood the Roman settlement of Brigantium. This area is a favourite destination for walkers; you can also reach the top of the mountain by cable car. From this summit, there are magnificent views extending across Bodensee (Lake Constance) and all of Bregenz. Nature trails have information signs on the area's flora and fauna. Far to the south, the Allgäu Alps can be seen on a clear day, as well as the ice-covered Schesaplana massif, the deep Rhine ravine and the Swiss peaks of Altmann and Säntis.

The Hohenbregenz fortress on Gebhardsberg

Serene blue waters of Bodensee, also known as Lake Constance

# 30 Bodensee

**Road map** A4. 🚉 🚌 **ℹ** Bodensee-Alpenrhein Tourismus, Römerstrasse 2, Bregenz, (05574) 43 443-0.
**W** bodensee-vorarlberg.com

Bodensee, or Lake Constance in English, is one of the largest and best-known European lakes. It divides its waters between the three countries surrounding it: Austria, Germany and Switzerland. Austria actually only claims a very small part of it: the total area of the lake is 538.5 sq km (208 sq miles), of which only 38 sq km (14.7 sq miles) is Austrian. Bodensee is 74 km (44 miles) long, the largest lake in the Alps. Once the lake was much larger, but with time, deposits carried by the Rhine have reduced its size. The Rhine flows into the lake in a broad delta, wholly in Austrian territory. Having passed through the entire length of Bodensee, it emerges in a waterfall as a turbulent mountain river near Schaffhausen, in Switzerland. The countryside around the lake benefits from a pleasant, moderate climate.

Today, Bodensee forms not so much a border as a link between the countries that lie on its shores. For Austria it is a highly convenient transport route to western Europe, while for the inhabitants of the surrounding towns and villages, as well as for the visitors that arrive here from neighbouring countries in great numbers every summer, it provides excellent facilities for water sports and relaxation. Once one of Europe's most polluted lakes, Bodensee is now one of its cleanest, after extensive efforts were made over several decades to control pollution.

The mountains around the town of Bregenz extend right up to the water, creating a picturesque setting for the countless artistic events that take place here, such as the Bregenz Spring dance festival (Mar) and the internationally acclaimed Bregenz Festival *(see p334)*. Many performances take place on the famous Seebühne, or floating stage.

A number of interesting towns line the shores of Bodensee, including Lindau, Konstanz with its island of Mainau containing flower-filled gardens, an arboretum and butterfly house, and Friedrichshafen on the German side, which can be reached by ferry or pleasure craft sailing from Bregenz.

# 31 Lustenau

**Road map** A4. 🏔 22,000. 🚉 🚌
**ℹ** Rathausstrasse 1, (05577) 81810.
**W** lustenau.at

A fairly large town, Lustenau lies 5 km (3 miles) north of the mouth of the Rhine as it joins Bodensee, on the border with Switzerland. It is famous for its embroidery and lace-making.

It was at Lustenau that the Romans under the leadership of Emperor Constantine II defeated the Alemanni tribes who had risen up against the empire. The earliest historic records date from 887, when the settlement belonged to the Carolingians. Until 1806, it was a free territory within the Habsbrug Empire. In 1814, after the Congress of Vienna, Lustenau came under Austrian rule.

The **Museum Rhein-Schauen** documents the history of the local people and the Rhine. It is also the terminus of the Rheinbähnle, a narrow-gauge train line that takes passengers along the shores of the Rhine to the outmost point of the Rhine delta in Lake Constance, or to an old depot and quarry where materials for the Rhine dams were once taken. A little electric engine pulls the passenger cars and, on occasion, a steam engine takes its place.

🏛 **Museum Rhein-Schauen**
Höchsterstrasse 4. **Tel** (05577) 20 539.
**Open** 1–5:30pm Thu–Sun.
Rheinbähnle: 3pm Fri–Sun from the museum. **W** rheinschauen.at

17th-century lace in the Rhein-Schauen museum in Lustenau

# CARINTHIA & EAST TYROL

Carinthia and East Tyrol, Austria's two southernmost regions, are bordered by Slovenia and Italy in the south, and Styria and Salzburger Land to the east and north. Between them they have many attractions, including the Carinthian lakes and the Hohe Tauern National Park. East Tyrol is separate from the rest of Tyrol, and has closer transport and cultural links with Carinthia.

The earliest inhabitants of what is now Kärnten (Carinthia) were the Celtic Carnuni. In the 1st century AD it was part of the Roman province of Noricum, and in the 6th century was overrun by the Slav tribe of the Carantani, from whom it probably took its name. Although Carinthia belonged to the Habsburgs from 1335, a Slav national minority has survived in the area to this day. After World War I the newly formed state of Yugoslavia tried to annex part of Carinthia from the defeated Austro-Hungarian Empire, but a plebiscite kept the region with Austria.

The beauty of its landscape and its pleasant, Mediterranean climate attract many foreign visitors to Carinthia, and numerous Austrians also have second homes here. The most scenic route in the Austrian Alps, the Grossglockner Hochalpenstrasse, separates Carinthia from East Tyrol, passing through Salzburger Land. Carinthia's two main towns are its capital Klagenfurt, and Villach.

After World War I, the southern part of Tyrol (Südtirol) became an autonomous province of Italy. Thus, geographically isolated from other parts of Tyrol, East Tyrol (Osttirol) grew closer to its Carinthian neighbour than it was to the Tyrolean administration in Innsbruck. The entire province is surrounded by high mountain ranges and much of it is home to the Hohe Tauern National Park. The administrative centre of East Tyrol is Lienz.

A giant relief model of the province of Carinthia in the Schillerpark pavilion in Villach

◀ Impressive view from the 2,572-m- (8,438-ft-) high Edelweissspitze, Hohe Tauern National Park

# Exploring Carinthia and East Tyrol

High mountain peaks that descend right down to expansive lakes make these southernmost regions of Austria a paradise for visitors. Excellent on-shore facilities attract water sports enthusiasts, while the mountain glaciers enable committed skiers to enjoy the slopes even in summer. The loveliest parts of the region are the scenic route of Grossglockner Hochalpenstrasse and the Hohe Tauern National Park. While Carinthia is a lake district, East Tyrol is an inaccessible region of high mountains. In winter, cars need to be properly equipped, and not all roads are passable.

Hohe Tauern National Park, one of the great attractions of the region

Horse-drawn coach on a Roman relief, Maria Saal Wallfahrtskirche

**Key**

━━━ Motorway

━━━ Major road

⋯⋯ Minor road

━━━ Scenic route

╼╾ Main railway

─── Minor railway

▰▰▰ International border

▰▰▰ Province border

△ Summit

## Getting There

Villach, in Carinthia, is one of Austria's most important road transport hubs. The southern motorway which comes from Vienna passes through Villach and Klagenfurt, Carinthia's capital, which also has a small passenger airport. The easiest way to reach Lienz, in East Tyrol, is via Carinthia. Road and railway tunnels through the mountain ranges provide convenient transport links.

A church in Gratschach, at the foot of Landskron

## Sights at a Glance

The marvellous library in the abbey of St Paul im Lavanttal

Late-15th-century fresco in the abbey church, St Paul im Lavanttal

# ❶ St Paul im Lavanttal

**Road map** E5. 🏘 3,400. 🚇 🚌
ℹ️ Platz St Blasien 1, (04357) 201722.
ⓦ sanktpaul.at

On the banks of the Lavant river stands one of the largest churches in Austria, the **Benedictine Abbey of St Paul**. Within the abbey complex is a well-preserved Romanesque church. The apse is decorated with reliefs showing the Adoration of the Magi and the enthroned Christ. Gothic frescoes behind the main altar depict the abbey founders and various saints.

The abbey museum houses magnificent works of art, including early chasubles, an 11th-century cross-shaped reliquary that once belonged to Queen Adelaide, an art collection with paintings by Peter Paul Rubens and Martin Johann Schmidt, and superb woodcuts by Albrecht Dürer and Rembrandt.

🏛 **Benedictine Abbey of St Paul**
Hauptstrasse 1. **Tel** (04357) 2019-10.
**Open** May–Oct: 10am–5pm daily.
🖼 🖼 🅿️

# ❷ Völkermarkt

**Road map** E5. 🏘 11,000. 🚌
ℹ️ Hauptplatz 1, (04232) 257147.

This town lies on the banks of a reservoir created by damming the Drau river, 25 km (16 miles) east of the Carinthian capital

Klagenfurt. It grew up around the bridge across the Drau and the 12th-century church of St Rupert, whose Romanesque tower still rises above the town.

The **Kirche St Magdalena** (church of Mary Magdalene), built in 1240 and altered in the 15th century, has a lovely late-Romanesque west portal. Its interior is late-Gothic, with some earlier features, such as the 14th-century frescoes next to the entrance. In one of the side chapels and in the presbytery, remains of late-Gothic frescoes can be seen.

In Völkermarkt's Hauptplatz stands a former ducal palace, now the seat of the local authorities, and an arcaded late-Gothic town hall.

The Romanesque portal of Kirche St Magdalena in Völkermarkt

# ❸ Klagenfurt

*See pp274–7.*

# ❹ Maria Saal

**Road map** E5. 🏘 3,800. 🚇 🚌
ℹ️ Am Platzl 7, (04223) 2214.
ⓦ mariasaal.at

The first church was erected at Maria Saal in the 8th century, and a secondary Christianization was conducted from here, which is why it became known as the cradle of Carinthia. The pilgrimage church, built in 1430–56, has a stone statue of the Virgin Mary in the high altar from 1420. On the outer walls of the church are two remarkable Roman reliefs, one depicting the cart of Death, the other showing Achilles pulling the body of Hector behind the chariot. The relief on the south wall, showing the Coronation of the Virgin Mary, is the work of Hans Valkenauer.

Opposite the church is a late-Gothic octagonal mortuary and the cemetery chapel. It has beautiful 15th-century vault frescoes with the family tree of Jesus, as well as a late-Gothic altar with scenes from the life of St Mary and an altar of St George slaying the dragon. The Sachsen-Kapelle (Saxon Chapel) is devoted to St Modestus, who founded the church and whose tomb-stone has survived to this day.

Archaeological excavations near Maria Saal, at the site of the Roman town of Virunum, the capital of Noricum, have yielded relics including the Bronze-Age carved stone throne of the princes of Carinthia (see p42).

# ❺ Burg Hochosterwitz

**Road map** E5. **Tel** (04213) 34597.
**Open** May–Sep: 9am–6pm; Apr, Oct: 10am–5pm. 🖼 🖼
ⓦ burg-hochosterwitz.com

The fortress of Hochosterwitz, a symbol of Carinthia, perches on a rock 160 m (525 ft) high and is clearly visible from afar. Although the origins of the castle can be traced back to Roman times, it was built in the 16th century by Domenico dell'Allio.

The present fortress is the result of Renaissance remodelling of earlier Romanesque and Gothic structures. A fief from the mid-16th century, it later became the property of the Khevenhüller family, who own it to this day. Both fortress and fortifications are open to visitors; the access road runs in a loop between the old walls, passing through 14 gates. There is also a local museum.

The turreted fortress of Hochosterwitz is said to have inspired Walt Disney's animated version of *Snow White*.

The slopes of Magdalensberg, site of fascinating archaeological finds

## ❻ Magdalensberg

**Road map** E5. 🏔 3,300. 🛈 Deinsdorf 10, Pischeldorf, (04224) 2213. 🖵 **magdalensberg.at**

On top of Magdalene mountain, rising 1,056 m (3,465 ft) from the Glan valley, are the remains of a town believed to be ancient Noricum, from the late-Celtic and early-Roman periods. Numerous fragments of statues and the remains of old altars testify to the overlapping nature of Celtic and Roman cultures, with some later Christian additions. Below the summit are the scant remains of a Roman temple

and secular buildings dating from the 1st century AD. In spring and summer, the finds can be viewed in the open-air archaeological park and in the museum.

There is a small church on top of Magdalensberg, with a three-headed stone statue in the nave. This, as well as the hilltop location of the church, indicate the pagan, Celtic origins of the area.

## ❼ St Veit an der Glan

**Road map** E5. 🏔 12,500. 🖵 🚌 🛈 Hauptplatz 23, (0664) 88736032.

From 1174 to 1518, St Veit an der Glan was the seat of the dukes of Spanheim, who ruled Carinthia during the Middle Ages; it later lost its position to Klagenfurt.

Many historic buildings are preserved in the old town around Hauptplatz, including the beautifully decorated **Rathaus** (town hall) of 1468, altered in the Baroque style. It has a lovely 16th-century arcaded courtyard. The 12th-century **Pfarrkirche St Veit** (parish church of St Vitus) contains stone carvings from various periods; the altars are made in the Baroque style.

The most recent symbol of St Veit is the unusual Kunsthotel Fuchspalast, a modern hotel built in 1998 to designs by the artist Ernst Fuchs. It is themed around the signs of the zodiac. Also worth a visit is Museum St Veit, which covers the history of the local railways.

Baroque stuccowork on the Rathaus façade, St Veit an der Glan

## ❽ Gurk

**Road map** E5. 🏔 1,300. 🚌 🛈 Dr. Schnerichstrasse 12, (04266) 812527. 🖵 **gurk.at**

Gurk, the former ecclesiastical capital of Carinthia, is dominated by a cathedral church, built in 1140–1200 by Bishop Roman and one of the most outstanding achievements of Austrian Romanesque architecture. The Gothic vestibule is adorned by stained-glass windows (1340) and Gothic frescoes. The original main portal and door have carved and painted Romanesque medallions. Inside, it is a startling combination of Romanesque and Gothic, with net vaulting and a Baroque main altar. The striking crypt is supported by 100 columns. The cathedral houses the **Diözesanmuseum**, which exhibits a large collection of church furnishings as well as many early sacred art objects.

**🏛 Diözesanmuseum**
Domplatz 11. **Tel** (04266) 8236. **Open** May–Oct: 10am–6pm daily. 📷 at 3pm daily Jul & Aug.

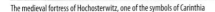

The medieval fortress of Hochosterwitz, one of the symbols of Carinthia

# ❸ Klagenfurt: Street-by-Street

Situated at the eastern end of Wörthersee, the warmest lake in Austria, Klagenfurt, the attractive provincial capital of Carinthia, is an important trade centre and transport hub, founded in the 12th century. In 1544, it was almost entirely destroyed by fire and had to be rebuilt. Reconstruction was undertaken mainly by Italian architects and it is highly reminiscent of Italian towns in style. In the 16th century, Klagenfurt was the centre of the Counter-Reformation. During the Baroque period it was extended and partially rebuilt, although most of its historic buildings date from an earlier era. Its historic centre is the district around Alter Platz (Old Square).

**Stadtpfarrkirche St Egid**
This Baroque church was built on the site of an earlier church destroyed by an earthquake in 1692. Its spire rises to 91 m (299 ft).

URSULINENGASSE

HERRENGASSE

HEILIGEN GEIST PLATZ

WIESBADENER STRASSE

Rathaus

PARADEISERGASSE

**The square** is the site of a modern bus station.

**Heiligengeistkirche**
The church of the Holy Spirit, built in 1355 and altered in 1660, features a beautiful altarpiece by Lorenzo Glaber and an interesting Baroque pulpit.

★ **Landhaus**
The 16th-century Landhaus boasts a lovely galleried inner courtyard and a magnificent heraldic hall with ceiling paintings by Josef Ferdinand Fromiller.

**Key**

— Suggested route

| 0 metres | 75 |
|---|---|
| 0 yards | 75 |

### Altes Rathaus

One of the most attractive sights is the galleried courtyard of the 17th-century former town hall. Once known as Welzer Palace, now as Rosenberg Palace, it was the first seat of the Klagenfurt town authorities.

### Dragon Fountain

In Neuer Platz (New Square) is a fountain with the mythical Lindwurm dragon, created by Ulrich Vogelsang in 1593. A town symbol, it has found its way into the Klagenfurt coat of arms.

### ★ Dom St Peter und Paul

The cathedral of St Peter and St Paul, originally built as a Protestant church, was taken over and altered by the Jesuits in 1604, and in 1727 it was completely rebuilt after a major fire. The high altar (1752) is the work of Daniel Gran.

Market in the historic Old Town of Klagenfurt

### Exploring Klagenfurt

Klagenfurt lies south of the Glan river, 30 km (19 miles) from the Slovenian and 60 km (37 miles) from the Italian borders. Its Old Town, laid out on a rectangular grid, extends between Hauptplatz, Alter Platz and Neuer Platz. It is 4 km (2 miles) from Wörthersee; the road to the lake runs through Europapark and the Minimundus exhibition.

### 🏛 Landhaus

Landhaus. **Tel** (0463) 577570.
**Open** Apr–Oct: 9am–4pm Mon–Fri, 9am–2pm Sat; Nov–Mar: 9am–4pm Thu–Fri, 9am–2pm Sat. 🅿 📷 📹

The Landhaus, the present seat of the Carinthian provincial government, stands on the western side of Alter Platz.

The attractive, galleried courtyard of the Landhaus

Commissioned by the Carinthian estates, it was built in 1574 on the site of a former ducal palace to designs by Antonio Verda of Lugano and Franz Freymann. The resulting structure is Klagenfurt's most important secular building and a Renaissance gem, with two symmetrically spaced spires, beyond which is an open two-storey, galleried courtyard. The domes crowning the two towers and the decorated elevation date from 1740.

The most beautiful room in the Landhaus, the Wappensaal (heraldic hall), dates from the same period. It is almost entirely the work of Josef Ferdinand Fromiller, the foremost Carinthian artist of the day. The walls of the hall display hundreds of Carinthian coats of arms, while the ceiling painting shows Carinthian nobles paying homage to Charles VI; the flat ceiling is made to look vaulted in this *trompe l'oeil*. The north wing houses the remains of the armoury.

Many old buildings have survived in the town centre nearby, including the Old Town Hall with a galleried Renaissance courtyard. The Trinity Column in Alter Platz, heart of the shopping district, dates from 1680; the crescent and cross were added after the victory over the Turks (1683).

### 🏛 Neuer Platz

Neuer Platz.
The square is dominated by Lindwurmbrunnen (Dragon Fountain), whose winged beast has become the symbol and crest of the town. The dragon was carved from a single block of stone by Ulrich Vogelsang, in 1593, while the giant who eventually saved the town was added later by Michael Hönel. The unveiling of this monument in 1636 was a great public event.

In 1764, Neuer Platz was the site of the first monument to be erected to Maria Theresa in Austria. The square is lined on all sides by many 16th- and 17th-century mansions with beautiful façades.

The Town Hall, formerly the Palace of the Rosenberg family, has been the seat of the municipal authorities since 1918. Built in 1582 and altered in 1650, it has an interesting Renaissance stairway. Originally outside the town walls surrounding Spanheim Castle, it became the centre of the new Renaissance town.

The pretty 17th-century Old Town Hall in Alter Platz

### 🏛 Dom St Peter und Paul

Domplatz. **Tel** (0463) 54950.
**Open** 7am–7pm daily.
Klagenfurt's cathedral was built in 1578 as a Protestant church by Klagenfurt's mayor, Christoph Windisch. In 1604, the church was taken over by the Jesuits, and was elevated to the rank of cathedral in 1787, when the bishopric was transferred from Gurk to Klagenfurt. In 1723, following a fire, the late-Gothic interior was rebuilt in the Baroque style. The cathedral was badly damaged in World

War II, during the 1944 bombing raids, but has been restored to its former splendour. Rich stucco decoration on the walls and ceiling blend elements of various architectural styles into one successful composition. The vault frescoes were painted by Josef Ferdinand Fromiller, while the gallery stucco was the work of Kilian Pittner. Daniel Gran painted the main altarpiece in 1752. The vestry holds the last work by Johann Martin Schmidt.

### 🏛 Landesmuseum Kärnten

Museumgasse 2. **Tel** (050536) 30599. **Closed** for refurbishment until late 2018.

The collections of the Regional Museum, founded in 1844, illustrate several centuries of history in Carinthia as well as its art, rooted in Celtic and Roman cultures. The floor mosaic of a young Dionysus surrounded by hedonistic satyrs is a beautiful example of Roman art. One of the museum's curiosities is a "dragon's skull" (in fact a rhinoceros), found nearby, which served as a model for the fountain dragon in Neuer Platz. Its discovery gave credence to the legend that a dragon once tormented the town, demanding the sacrifice of animals and humans. The museum also holds many works of art and handicrafts.

During the renovations, most exhibits are packed away, but the building remains open for limited special exhibitions of Carinthian paintings and photographs.

### 🏛 Minimundus

Villacher Strasse 241. **Tel** (0463) 21194. **Open** Mar–Apr: 9am–6pm daily; May, Jun & Sep: 9am–7pm daily; Jul & Aug: 9am–8pm daily (until 11pm Wed). 🅦 minimundus.at

Europapark, a large green space west of Klagenfurt, is home to this theme park, with over 170 miniature models of the world's most famous buildings. They are

crafted in minute detail to a scale of 1:25, and have been added to since 1959, when a children's charity, *Rettet das Kind*, set up the first architectural miniatures near Wörthersee. All the profits go to the foundation. Among the models from all continents are Rome's St Peter's Basilica, Paris's Eiffel Tower, London's Big Ben, Brussels' Atomium, Agra's Taj Mahal and New York's Statue of Liberty. Not surprisingly, Austria's own historic buildings, such as the Stephansdom in Vienna, are heavily represented. Many other achievements and inventions are also represented by miniature models, for example Austrian watermills, Mississippi paddle steamers and the earliest steam trains.

*Statue on the side altar in the Dom*

**Environs:** The town of Klagenfurt is surrounded by lakes and mountains; the closest is **Wörthersee** (*see pp280–81*), which gave the Carinthian capital its byname, Rose of the Wörthersee. **Viktring Abbey**,

Stained-glass window in the Cistercian abbey in Viktring

6 km (4 miles) southwest of Klagenfurt, belonged to the Cistercian monks who arrived in Viktring in 1142. The many castles and palaces in the vicinity testify to the region's prosperity. Sights worth visiting include the fortified castle of **Mageregg** (1590, altered in 1841), surrounded by a zoological park for local animals. The lovely 12th-century **Schloss Hallegg**, which has preserved its old turret, was remodelled in the 16th century and turned into a Renaissance residence with two inner courtyards.

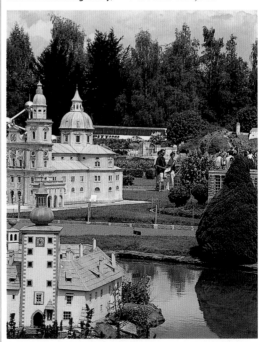
Models of Salzburg Cathedral and Ort Castle, Minimundus

## ❾ Friesach

**Road map** E5. 🏛 5,000. 🚉 🚌
ℹ️ Fürstenhofplatz 1 (04268) 2213-40.

Friesach is Carinthia's oldest town, with a history going back to 860, when the nearby fortress of **Petersberg** was founded. Traces of the town's glorious past have survived to this day, including a moated town wall, 820 m (2,690 ft) long, and several castle towers. Of the fortress itself, only the six-storey keep on Petersberg survives. In the former chapel room, on the fourth floor, the remains of 12th-century frescoes can be seen.

Adjacent to the fortress is **Peterskirche** (church of St Peter), which has a Gothic altar (1525) with a Romanesque statue of the Madonna (c.1200). The **Dominikanerkloster** (Dominican abbey) from 1217 holds a 14th-century Madonna, a wooden crucifix (1300) and other medieval artifacts. The church of St Blaise, built by the Teutonic Knights in 1213 on the ruins of an earlier church, has some original 12th-century frescoes.

## ❿ Around Wörthersee

*See pp280–81.*

## ⓫ Villach

**Road map** E5. 🏛 60,000. 🚉 🚌
ℹ️ Bahnhofstrasse 3, (04242) 205 2900.

Carinthia's second largest town is an important tourist centre, health resort and transport hub. The earliest archaeological finds testifying to the

region's settlement date from Celtic times. In the small old town, **Stadtpfarrkirche St Jakob** (parish church of St Jacob) was built after a powerful earthquake in 1348, and later rebuilt. Its most notable features are the Renaissance chapels of the Görz-Dietrichstein and the Khevenhüller families and the 95-m-(312-ft-) high tower. The **Municipal Museum** (open May–Oct) in a 16th-century building at No. 38 Widmanngasse, covers regional history, archaeology and art. In **Schillerpark** you can see an astonishing 3D-map of Carinthia, at a scale of 1:10,000.

**Environs:** Lovely 14th-century frescoes and a late-Gothic altar (c.1520) can be seen in the church of **Maria Gail**, 3 km (2 miles) southeast of Villach.

## ⓬ Spittal an der Drau

**Road map** D5. 🏛 16,000. 🚉 🚌
ℹ️ Schloss Porcia, Burgplatz 1, (04762) 5650220.

The town of Spittal is dominated by the Goldeck peak (2,142 m/ 7,028 ft). The history of the town began in the 12th century, when Count Ortenburg founded a church and a *Spittal*, or hospice on this site. The town owes its Renaissance character to the vast 16th-century **Schloss Porcia**, which is also known as Salamanca Palace after its builder, the Spanish nobleman Gabriel of

Schloss Porcia's galleries, Spittal an der Drau

Salamanca. The Porcia family, who owned the palace from 1662 until 1918, added to its decor while preserving the original architecture based on Spanish Renaissance palaces. Its most beautiful aspect is the galleried inner courtyard; be sure to have a close look at the rich decorations of its individual storeys. The well-preserved palace now houses a museum of folk art on the two top floors.

**Environs:** On a hill near the village of St Peter in Holz, 5 km (3 miles) northwest of Spittal an der Drau, stand the ruins of an early-Christian church and the **Römermuseum Teurnia** (open May–Oct). The hill was settled first by Celts, then by Romans, and the museum exhibits many small items, scripts and coins.

## ⓭ Millstatt

**Road map** D5. 🏛 3,400. 🚌 ℹ️
Rathaus, Marktplatz 8, (04766) 202 10.
🌐 millstatt.at

The greatest attraction in Millstatt, on the northern shore of Millstätter See, is a **Benedictine abbey** dating from 1070. From then until 1469 it was run by the Hirsau Benedictines; later the monastery and church passed into the hands of the Order of the Knights of St George, and from 1598 until 1773 it was owned by the Jesuits. The most beautiful part of the abbey is its

Thermal bath complex in Villach

*For hotels and restaurants in this region see p299 and p325*

Renaissance courtyard surrounded by two-storey arcades. This was built in the 16th century, when the abbey was run by the Order of St George. The monastery is linked with the church by a 12th-century cloister whose pillars, decorated by medieval carvers, display a grotesque world of animals, plants and faces. Even older, dating back to the Carolingian period, are the magical ornaments on the old buildings, possibly representing some pagan spells. An eye-catching feature inside the church is the Romanesque portal, made by master craftsman Rudger in 1170. In the side chapels are the red marble tombs of the Order's Grand Masters. Also worth seeing is a fresco from 1519, depicting the Last Judgement.

Courtyard of the Benedictine abbey in Millstatt

## ⓮ Gmünd

**Road map** D5. ⛰ 2,600. 🚌
🛈 Hauptplatz 20, (04732) 221514.

In the 12th century, the archbishops of Salzburg, who ruled Gmünd, began to encircle the town with mighty fortifications, many of which survive to this day, including old gate turrets and bastions. Two castles tower over the town: the older one, **Altes Schloss**, was destroyed by a fire in 1886, but was restored and is now used as a cultural centre. It was commissioned in 1506 by Archbishop Leonhard von Keutschach. The **Neues Schloss** (New Castle) was built in 1651–4 by Count Christoph von Lodron. Today

An alley in Gmünd, famous for its former production of Porches

the former castle keep houses a school and a concert hall.

The Austrian-born designer Ferdinand Porsche worked in Gmünd in 1944–50, and 52 of the classic "365" models were hand-made locally. The most famous models and construction frames are displayed in the **Porsche Museum**.

🏛 **Porsche Museum**
Gmünd. **Tel** (04732) 2471.
**Open** 15 May–15 Oct: 9am–6pm, 16 Oct–14 May: 10am–4pm.
ⓦ porschemuseum.at.

## ⓯ Mölltal

**Road map** D5. 🚐 🚌 ⓦ moelltal.at

The Möll river, a tributary of the Drau and overshadowed by Grosses Reisseck peak, runs along the Mölltal, a valley whose upper reaches form a natural extension of the magnificent road known as Grossglockner Hochalpenstrasse (see pp284–5). The river meanders scenically between the high mountain peaks, while the road along the valley winds its way between old mills, waterfalls and huts, blending in seamlessly with its spectacular natural surroundings.

The parish of **Grosskirchheim** was once a major mining district, and the 16th-century **Schloss Grosskirchheim** now houses an interesting museum of local history and gold mining.

In **Döllach** you can see the interesting late-Gothic church of St Andrew, and in **Sagritz** the

originally late-Gothic church of St George. **Schloss Falkenstein**, on a rocky promontory near Obervellach, has an unusual tower with a wooden top.

## ⓰ Lienz

**Road map** D5. ⛰ 12,000. 🚉 🚌
🛈 Europaplatz 1, (050212) 400.
ⓦ tirol.tl

The town has been the capital of East Tyrol since 1919, but its origins date back to the Middle Ages. The **Stadtpfarrkirche St Andrä** (parish church of St Andrew), a triple-nave Gothic basilica, was built in the 15th century; western sections include parts of an earlier Romanesque church. Today, following many alterations, the church is predominantly Baroque in style. Inside are a fresco by Josef Adam von Mölk and a high altar by Franz Engel. The **Franziskanerkirche** (Franciscan church), built around 1350, features original 15th-century frescoes and a Gothic Pietà standing by a side altar.

High above the town sits **Schloss Bruck**, the seat of the Görz counts, built between the 13th and 16th centuries. The castle has a tall Romanesque turret; its main body contains a Romanesque chapel with 13th- and 15th-century frescoes. Today it also houses a regional museum with Gothic and Baroque artifacts and paintings by the local Tyrolean artist Albin Egger-Lienz (1868–1926).

The Romanesque tower of Schloss Bruck in Lienz

# ⑩ Around Wörthersee

Wörthersee is the warmest lake in Austria; in summer, the temperature of its waters can reach 25°C (77°F). Numerous resorts line its shores; the largest of these is the modern, brash town of Velden, with its casino. Krumpendorf and the exclusive resort of Pörtschach lie on the easily accessible northern shore; quiet Reifnitz is on the southern shore. Nearby are other, smaller lakes, including Ossiacher See, in a scenic mountain setting. To the south, the Carinthian lake district extends along the Slovenian border, surrounded by the snowy peaks of the enchanting Karawanken Alps.

### ① Ossiach
The former Benedictine abbey in Ossiach and its church were built in the 11th-century and altered in the early-Baroque style. The oldest monastery in Carinthia, it was burned down by Turkish invaders and is now a hotel.

### ② Schloss Landskron
Not much remains of the original medieval castle, but the ruins are nevertheless impressive. Today, the bird of prey show, held on the slopes of the castle hill, and "Monkey Mountain" are the greatest attractions nearby.

| 0 kilometres | 4 |
| 0 miles | 4 |

### ③ Rosegg
This small village between Wörthersee and Faaker See has a beautiful 19th-century landscaped wildlife park, which attempts to recreate a natural habitat for its resident animals and birds.

### ④ Schloss Velden
The well-known, swanky resort on the shores of Wörthersee boasts an early-Baroque castle, originally built by the Khevenhüller family, which featured as the setting for a popular Austrian TV series. It is now an elegant hotel.

## Tips for Drivers

**Length of route:** 45 km (28 miles).
**Stopping-off points:** There are several resorts around the lake offering restaurants and hotels; Velden is the largest resort.
**Further attractions:** Wildpark in Rosegg. **Tel** (04274) 52357. **Open** Apr–Oct.

**⑤ Maria Wörth**

On a promontory that extends far into the lake stands a 12th-century church built on earlier foundations and featuring original 11th-century Romanesque frescoes.

**⑥ Wörthersee**

Wörthersee is Austria's warmest lake and its shores have become known as the Austrian Riviera. Entertainment here ranges from relaxation to swimming and all sorts of water sports.

**⑦ Reifnitz**

Established as early as 1195, this was once one of the mightiest castles in Carinthia. All that remains today are the main body and the castle keep.

**⑧ Pyramidenkogel**

From the top of the Pyramidenkogel hill, above the lake, there are stunning vistas of the entire area, including Wörthersee itself, with the Karawanken Alps to the south, and several beautiful neighbouring lakes.

**Key**

▬▬▬ Motorway

▬▬▬ Suggested route

▬▬▬ Scenic route

▬▬▬ Other road

▬▬▬ River, lake

❖ Viewpoint

# ⓱ Hohe Tauern National Park

The beautiful area around Austria's highest peak, the Grossglockner, is a national park. The unique landscape, flora and fauna of the region, the Hohe Tauern, is jointly protected by the provincial governments of Salzburger Land, Tyrol and Carinthia. The Hohe Tauern has more than 300 peaks rising above 3,000 m (9,850 ft) and several glaciers – the Pasterze is the longest and most spectacular. This whole national park area is protected by law and visitors are asked to keep to the marked trails. On its edges are many popular tourist resorts, such as Bad Gastein, Kaprun, Zell am See and East Tyrol's capital, Lienz.

**Artificial Lakes**
One of the great attractions of the Hohe Tauern is its many picturesque reservoirs, gathering the crystal-clear meltwaters from the glaciers high above each spring.

**★ Pasterze Glacier**
The largest glacier in the Eastern Alps is 8 km (5 miles) long and covers an area of 18 sq km (7 sq miles). Like many glaciers, however, it is slowly shrinking in size.

**★ Grossglockner**
Austria's highest peak (3,797 m/12,457 ft) towers at the border between Carinthia and East Tyrol, a crucifix marking the summit.

Grossglockner

Traunera

3368

3564

3401

3331

2548

3797

3247

3762

**Key**

━━ Major road
━━ Minor road
⋯⋯ Cable car
–·–· Provincial border
═══ River
☀ Viewpoint

### Edelweissspitze

Edelweissspitze, 2,572 m/8,438 ft high, is the central peak of the Fusch-Rauriser range. There are amazing views from the viewing tower at the summit.

**Alpine Flora**
An impressive range of Alpine plantlife, such as this aromatic Alpine tansy (Tanacetum) can be seen in the park at different altitudes.

**Gondola to Schareck**
Schareck peak (2,606 m/8,550 ft) in the Goldberggruppe (Gold Mountains) can be reached by gondola, with one change en route. Schareck is an excellent starting point for excursions into the upper mountains.

**Alpine Ibex**
This protected species inhabits the upper regions of the Alps. It is easiest to see them in the Ferleiten Reserve (see p284).

# ⑱ Grossglockner Hochalpenstrasse

Traversing the Hohe Tauern National Park is the Grossglockner High Alpine Road, regarded as one of the world's most beautiful mountain routes. Completed in 1935, the road was built along the old mountain passes between Bruck in Salzburger Land and Heiligenblut in Carinthia. Measuring 47.8 km (29.7 miles) long, it forms part of a north–south route from Bavaria to Italy. A road branching off from the main road leads to two spectacular viewpoints. The highest point of the route is Hochtor, at 2,505 m (8,218 ft), the lowest is Bruck, at 755 m (2,477 ft). With the 1.5 km (1 mile) rise in altitude, the flora also changes.

⑤ **Hochtor**
The Hochtor (High Gate) is the highest point along the Grossglockner Hochalpenstrasse. Here the road runs through a tunnel measuring 2.3 km (1.5 miles) in length.

⑥ **Fuscher Törl**
The road winds its way above steep ravines, offering splendid views on both sides of this ridge to the Goldberggruppe (Gold Mountains).

⑦ **Viewing Tower on Edelweissspitze**
The tower built on top of Edelweissspitze (2,572 m/8,438 ft) affords fantastic views of the Grossglockner to the west and the Goldberggruppe to the east.

⑧ **Alpine Naturschau Museum**
Situated at an altitude of 2,260 m (7,415 ft) is a small museum of the local flora, fauna and ecology, offering free admission to visitors. In Ferleiten, to the north, is an Alpine animal reserve.

**Key**

■■ Suggested route
══ Other road
· · · Cable car
═ River, lake
·▬ Provincial border
✼ Viewpoint

## ④ **Schareck**

The Schareck peak, part of the Goldberg massif, was once mined for gold. From here visitors can see the Schildberg peak and the looming Grossglockner massif to the west, as well as the superb high-altitude ski slopes.

Zell am See

● **Ferleiten**

● **Piffkar**

107

8

Lienz

### Tips for Drivers

**Length of the route:** 40 km (25 miles).

**Stopping-off points:** You can stay at one of the mountain hostels, and many restaurants also offer accommodation.

**Additional information:** The route is a toll road, open to cars only from May to November.

## ③ **Observatory**

The William Swarovski Observatory, built in 1998 above Franz-Josefs-Höhe, enables visitors to view the magnificent Alpine landscape using the latest optical equipment.

0 kilometres 2

0 miles 2

## ① **Heiligenblut**

The church in Heiligenblut was built in the 15th century by monks from Admont. Inside is a beautiful altar from the workshop of Michael Pacher, and a richly carved tabernacle said to house a phial of Christ's blood.

## ② **Franz-Josefs-Höhe**

Along the Gletscherstrasse (Glacier Road) is a viewing terrace at 2,369 m (7,772 ft), giving fabulous views of both Grossglockner and the Pasterze Glacier.

# TRAVELLERS' NEEDS

# WHERE TO STAY

Austria has a plethora of accommodation options, including enchanting medieval castles, charming family-run guesthouses and traditional Alpine chalets tucked away on the mountain hills. On these four pages, the types of hotels on offer are summarized alongside tips on what to expect. The hotel listings *(see pp292–9)* describe some of the best hotels around the country in every price category and style. Alternatively, you could opt for self-catering: pitching up with a tent or camper van is ever popular, and farm stays provide the chance to get to know rural Austria. For those hiking in the Alps, there is also information about the many mountain hostels and shelters dotted along the trails.

A hotel complex in Kampl, in a typically scenic location

## The Range of Hotels

Hotels and pensions are awarded between one and five stars, as in other countries, with the number of stars depending on the facilities offered by the hotel. However, small hotels and pensions often have a more inviting atmosphere despite fewer overall facilities.

The choice of hotel is usually determined by what one intends to do while visiting Austria. Visitors who are mainly interested in sightseeing and are likely to be constantly on the move may prefer to stay in modest private guesthouses or pensions. Winter sports enthusiasts need to look for hotels that offer the appropriate facilities. Alternatively, for peace and quiet, or personal health and wellbeing, visitors can choose from numerous, well-equipped spa hotels. Whatever the plan, there is always a perfect accommodation option available here.

## Booking

Austria offers such a diverse amount of accommodation that it is possible – if moving from place to place for example – to find accommodation as you travel. The Austrian National Tourist Office will help find a hotel, as will any regional or local tourist office.

However, to get the best prices and the most appropriate accommodation, booking ahead is crucial. These days, most people book online, either through a hotel booking site (such as booking.com) or directly via the hotel's own website; both tend to offer discounts throughout the year.

## Prices

The price of hotel accommodation is dictated not only by the category of the hotel, but also by its location and the local events at the time. Accommodation in Vienna, Salzburg and Graz is often expensive, and many hotels and pensions in prime locations are overpriced. It is possible to cut costs by staying outside the main town centres; in Vienna, for example, staying just outside the Ringstrasse brings a significant

Part of the penthouse suite at Augarten Art Hotel, Graz *(see p296)*

reduction in room rates. Staying in provincial towns tends to be somewhat cheaper, though prices really are variable.

Accommodation will be less expensive for visits outside the main tourist season. For example, visiting a resort specializing in winter sports during the summer months is cheaper. In the cities, it is also possible to negotiate discounted room rates for weekend visits or longer stays.

The impressive grand lobby of the Imperial Hotel, Vienna *(see p294)*

◀ Café in the Cupola Hall of the Kunsthistorisches Museum, Vienna

## Hidden Extras

When booking a room, check in advance if any additional charges, such as *Kurtaxe* (health spa tax) or for cleaning on departure, will be levied. Generally, prices are inclusive of taxes such as *Mehrwertsteuer* (VAT), but occasionally these are separate. Breakfast is included in all but the five-star hotels. Other extras to watch out for are charges for off-road parking, especially in the larger cities. Some places still charge for Internet access. For full-board accommodation in a pension, you will need to take the additional cost of lunch and dinner drinks into account, and also allow for a small tip. In ski and some country resort areas, smaller hotels may insist on half-board accommodation.

## Hotels in Historic Buildings

Visitors looking for something special beyond the usual hotel experience should consider a stay at one of the many medieval castles that have been converted into hotels. These are denominated by the name *Schlosshotel* and include former palaces and royal hunting lodges. Some excellent examples of such converted fortresses or palace hotels are Schloss Hotel Dürnstein *(see p295)* in the Wachau region, the 12th-century Burg Deutschlandberg in Styria *(see p296)* and Schloss Mönchstein *(see p298)* in Salzburg. Each of these offers up-to-date accommodation facilities in luxurious surroundings. Health-spa resort Schloss Fuschl *(see p297)*, for example, is a set in a sumptuous former palace near Salzburg.

Prices at such historic establishments are, not surprisingly, often higher than those charged by other

Opulent furnishings at the Hotel Bristol in Vienna *(see p293)*

well-known hotels. Check out the **Schlosshotels und Herrenhäuser** website, the booking association for *Schlosshotels*, or go directly to the individual hotel's website.

## Chain Hotels

Austria's hotel chains provide a reliable, and often cheap and cheerful, choice for some visitors. In addition to well-known and popular hotel chains, such as **Mercure, Best Western** and **Marriott**, Austria has its own groups of hotels, including **Austria Trend**.

Sign of the Golden Eagle in Innsbruck *(see p298)*

Almost all of these will offer the usual conveniences, dependable good service and free Wi-Fi access.

There are also associations grouping hotels under a themed banner. **Romantik Hotels** lists a variety of accommodation choices, while **Relais & Château** champions luxury hotels.

## Pensions and Gasthöfe

Pensions are widespread and popular in Austria. Less formal than a hotel, they are typically run by a family and usually provide modest accommodation, breakfast and a pleasant ambience – guests often meet the owners, who are usually friendly and willing to help with travel plans. Most rooms have an en-suite bathroom, some have telephone, TV and a balcony as well. In smaller towns and villages, the owners often invite their guests to social evenings with music, dancing or a barbecue.

A *Gasthof* is a traditional inn typically with a restaurant on the ground floor and rooms to rent on the floor above. A wide range of establishments are covered under this category, from small, inexpensive, family-run hotels with modestly equipped rooms, to exquisitely restored country inns offering luxurious furnishings, facilities and surroundings.

A charming rustic pension in the mountainous region of Lech

The lakeside Hotel Sacher, in Salzburg *(see p298)*

## Inexpensive Accommodation

Austria has a long tradition of renting out rooms in private homes. Vacancies are generally indicated by the sign *Zimmer frei* (rooms available). The standard varies, but by and large these rooms tend to be inexpensive and with simple furnishings. Breakfast may or may not be included in the room price. More upmarket rooms will be found in homes signposted as "bed and breakfast" (in English). These typically offer more amenities and en-suite bathrooms. Private rooms and homes, most at reasonable prices, are also available on Internet booking sites such as **Airbnb**.

There are plenty of back-packer-friendly hostels and *Jugendherbergen* (youth hostels) throughout Austria. Many of them offer double rooms and family rooms as well as simple bunk beds in dorms. Some "backpacker hotels" in the cities and at resorts have recreation rooms, free Wi-Fi and laundries.

## Farm Stays

In rural Austria, most holiday accommodation takes the form of rooms in working *Bauernhöfe* (farms), offering high service standards in traditional and rustic surroundings. Some provide self-catering facilities; in others, meals are provided by the farmer, on a similar basis as in pensions, usually *Zimmer mit Frühstück* (bed and breakfast), *Halbpension* (half-board) or *Vollpension* (full-board). The number of rooms available in a *Bauernhof* and the prices charged vary but the rooms are of a perfectly acceptable standard. For children from towns and cities it is an ideal opportunity to observe the daily workings of a farm and to have contact with farm animals. There may also be the opportunity to go horse riding, or hire a bike, boat or fishing tackle, so that a full programme of outdoor activities can be enjoyed by the whole family.

Booking one of 625 farms located around the country can be done via the **Farm Holidays** website or through local tourist offices, which often have detailed brochures with pictures and price lists.

## Mountain Hostels and Shelters

Mountain hostels and shelters, known as *hütte*, can be found across Austria, from the flatlands to high up in the Alps. The country's highest accommodation, in fact, is the Erzherzog-Johann hut, at 3,454 m/11,332 ft. Some private mountain inns can be quite luxurious but, on the whole, mountain shelters are kept simple. There are usually rooms for two or three, and sometimes more on a sharing basis; people sleep on simple mattresses, often in bunks, and there are limited washing facilities. Higher in the mountains and in more remote regions, the huts are basic. Despite this, each has an authentic charm.

If you're planning to hike for several days, book huts through the **Österreichischer Alpenverein (ÖAV)** well in advance. Hostels can provide information on the local hiking trails, current climbing conditions and the weather forecasts.

Depending on the popularity of an area and the season, hostels will be open either all year round or only during the summer months, usually until the end of September or October. Some open only at the weekend, even in summer, or by appointment. Some hostels are closed one day in the week, on the *Ruhetag* (rest day). The ÖAV or the local tourist bureau will be able to advise on timings.

## Camping

Travelling with a camping trailer, camper van or just a tent is popular in Austria, and there are dedicated campsites in all the larger towns and popular resorts. Generally of a high standard, sites are equipped with washrooms and kitchens.

A caravan site on the shores of Ossiacher See in Carinthia

Tents pitched at a campsite in Salzkammergut

Traditional campsites charge €25–50 per unit. In addition to the Austrian **Camping Club** site, there is a UK **Camping and Caravanning Club** site offering discounted bookings in Austria.

There are a handful of "glamping" (glamorous camping) sites around the country, offering a range of unusual accommodation: Ikuna Tipidorf in Natternbach has Native American-style teepees *(see p297)*, while Nature Resort Natterer See has lodges raised off the ground with panoramic terraces.

## Travelling with Children

A lot of hotels and pensions in Austria specifically offer facilities for children, with play areas, toys and child-minding services available to guests. Many of these hotels advertise themselves as *Baby und Kinderhotels* (Baby and Child Hotels) in their promotional literature. Local tourist offices will have details on where the nearest ones are.

Some pensions, particularly those aimed at families with children, organize special activities to keep young people engaged. These might include all sorts of sports activities, ranging from skiing, skating and tobogganing to horse riding, tennis, canoeing, swimming and cycling.

## Recommended Hotels

The lodging options featured in this guide have been selected across a wide price range for their excellent facilities and unique value. They are all representative of their context, be it bustling Vienna, fairytale Salzburg or the placid mountain resorts of the Tyrol. The hotels are listed by area and then by price. They cover a diverse array of accommodation, from simple **pensions** to stunning **boutique** options. There are **family-friendly** guesthouses for those who seek a homely atmosphere and **luxury** hotels that offer all the comfort one needs. Alternatively, one may opt for a **spa** hotel to unwind in style or a **contemporary** hotel for all the modern comforts. For those looking to get a taste of the traditional there are always **country** guesthouses. The places highlighted as DK Choice are the very best of the pack, chosen for being outstanding in some way. They may be set in historically important buildings, stand in beautiful surroundings, have particularly eco-friendly policies or may just be incredibly charming.

## DIRECTORY

### Accommodation Information

**Austrian Tourism Board**
W austriatourism.com

**Carinthia Information**
W carinthia.at

**Lower Austria Information**
W lower-austria.info

**Styria Information**
W steiermark.com

**Tyrol Information**
W tyrol.com

**Upper Austria Information**
W oberoesterreich.at

**Vienna Information**
W wien.info

### Hotels in Historic Buildings

**Schlosshotels und Herrenhäuser**
W schlosshotels.co.at

### Hotel Chains

**Austria Trend**
W austria-trend.at

**Best Western**
W bestwestern.com

**Marriott**
W marriott.com

**Mercure**
W mercure.com

**Relais & Châteaux**
W relaischateaux.com

**Romantik Hotels**
W romantikhotels.com

### Inexpensive Accommodation

**Airbnb**
W airbnb.com/austria

**Backpacker Hostels**
W hostels.com
W hostelworld.com

**Österreichischer Jugendherbergsverband (ÖJHV)**
W oejhv.at

### Farm Stays

**Farm Holidays**
W farmholidays.com

### Mountain Hostels and Shelters

**Österreichischer Alpenverein (ÖAV)**
W alpenverein.at

### Camping

**Camping and Caravanning Club (UK)**
W campingandcaravanningclub.co.uk

**Glamping**
W glamping.com

**Österreichischer Camping Club**
W campingclub.at

# Where to Stay

## Vienna

### Inner City

**Domizil** €
Pension                    Map 2 C4
*Schulerstrasse 14, 1010*
**Tel** *(01) 513 31 99*
W *hoteldomizil.at*
Clean, contemporary rooms in a
great central location close to all
the main historic sights. There's a
generous breakfast buffet of cold
meats, cheeses, pastries and fruit.

**Graben Hotel** €
Boutique                   Map 2 B4
*Dorotheergasse 3, 1010*
**Tel** *(01) 512 15 31-0*
W *kremslehnerhotels.at*
Although a bit on the small
side, the rooms in this quaint
hotel are comfortable and well
cared for. The location, right by
Stephansdom, couldn't be better.

**Hotel Am Parkring** €
Contemporary              Map 3 D4
*Parkring 12, 1015*
**Tel** *(01) 514 80-0*
W *schick-hotels.com*
With spectacular views from
floors 11–13 that take in the city's
major landmarks, this hotel is
remarkably good value for money.

**Kaiserin Elisabeth** €
Luxury                    Map 2 C4
*Weihburggasse 3, 1010*
**Tel** *(01) 515 26-0*
W *kaiserinelisabeth.at*
An elegant hotel set in a historic
building dating back to the 14th
century. Beautifully appointed
rooms, friendly staff and an
exceptional location right in
the historic centre.

**Pension Nossek** €
Pension                   Map 2 B4
*Graben 17, 1010*
**Tel** *(01) 533 70 41-0*
W *pension-nossek.at*
Charming, family-run pension set
in a historic building that was
occupied by Mozart for several
months in 1781. The rooms are
decorated with chintzy floral prints.

**Best Western Plus Hotel
Das Tigra** €€
Contemporary              Map 2 B3
*Tiefer Graben 14–20, 1010*
**Tel** *(01) 533 96 41-0*
W *hotel-tigra.at*
The bright, modern rooms and
helpful staff at this hotel attract
both tourists and business exe-
cutives alike. Excellent facilities
and a convenient central location.

### DK Choice

**Hollmann Beletage** €€
Boutique                  Map 2 C3
*Köllnerhofgasse 6, 1010*
**Tel** *(01) 961 196-0*
W *hollmann-beletage.at*
With its sleek tangerine and
granite decor and 25 spacious
rooms boasting an array of
luxury amenities and thoughtful
details, this quirky hotel is a real
find. Mammoth breakfasts,
friendly staff and a sauna are
just some of the many perks
of staying here. The hotel also
has a pretty courtyard – the
perfect place to enjoy a snack or
drink from the hotel delicatessen.

**Hotel Capricorno** €€
Contemporary              Map 3 D3
*Schwedenplatz 3–4, 1010*
**Tel** *(01) 533 31 04-0*
W *schick-hotels.com*
A buzzing metropolitan hotel
located close to the city's best
bars and restaurants. It offers
single, double and family rooms,
decorated with vibrant colours and
furnishings. A hearty breakfast is
served until 11am.

**Hotel Am Stephansplatz** €€
Contemporary              Map 2 C4
*Stephansplatz 9, 1010*
**Tel** *(01) 534 05-0*
W *hotelamstephansplatz.at*
Staff go out of their way to ensure
you enjoy your time at this chic
design hotel. Request a room on
one of the upper floors for the
great views of Stephansdom and
minimal noise.

A cosy library with stylish furnishings at
Hollmann Beletage

### Price Guide

Prices are based on a standard double
room per night, inclusive of breakfast,
service charges and taxes:

€        under €150
€€       €150 to 250
€€€      over €250

**Imperial Riding School
Renaissance Vienna** €€
Historic                  Map 3 E5
*Ungargasse 60, 1030*
**Tel** *(01) 711 75-0*
W *marriott.com*
This former military riding school,
built in 1850, has been sensitively
converted into a hotel with first-
class facilities. The opulent rooms
hark back to the building's history
but boast all the usual mod cons.

**K&K Palais** €€
Historic                  Map 2 C3
*Rudolfsplatz 11, 1010*
**Tel** *(01) 533 13 53*
W *kkhotels.com*
This handsome imperial building
has a stylish interior with
66 contemporary guest rooms
and a bistro decorated in
subdued tones.

**König von Ungarn** €€
Luxury                    Map 2 C4
*Schulerstrasse 10, 1010*
**Tel** *(01) 515 84-0*
W *kvu.at*
Founded in 1746, this hotel has
welcomed heads of state, artists
and other luminaries. Some
rooms are decorated in a classic
style inspired by the history of
the building and some in a
contemporary style.

**Radisson Blu Style Hotel** €€
Boutique                  Map 2 B4
*Herrengasse 12,1010*
**Tel** *(01) 227 80-0*
W *radissonblu.com*
A first-rate boutique hotel with a
great range of amenities. Chic,
contemporary rooms with plenty
of space and large bathrooms.
The breakfast buffet is excellent.

**Schlosshotel Römischer
Kaiser** €€
Luxury                    Map 2 C5
*Annagasse 16, 1010*
**Tel** *(01) 512 77 51-0*
W *gshotels.de/roemischerkaiser*
Set in a Baroque palace dating
back to 1684, this sumptuous
hotel retains much of its former
splendour. All of the 24 rooms
have Baroque-style furnishings,
chandeliers and antiques, but
with all the modern amenities
you'd expect of a first-rate hotel.

### DO & CO Hotel Vienna
€€€
Contemporary     **Map** 2 C4
*Stephansplatz 12, 1010*
**Tel** *(01) 241 88*
**w** doco.com
This top luxury hotel offers discerning travellers beautifully designed rooms with a range of personal touches, such as toys for children and safes that can accommodate laptops.

### Palais Coburg
€€€
Luxury     **Map** 3 D5
*Coburgbastei 4, 1010*
**Tel** *(01) 518 18-200*
**w** palais-coburg.com
Steeped in six centuries of history, this refined hotel is set in a majestic former palace. Enjoy beautifully appointed guest rooms, impeccable service and world-class facilities.

### Palais Hansen Kempinski Vienna
€€€
Luxury     **Map** 2 B2
*Schottenring 24, 1010*
**Tel** *(01) 236 100-0*
**w** kempinski.com
Elegant contemporary rooms and suites in a grand hotel originally built for the World Exhibition in 1873. Fantastic central location and state-of-the-art facilities.

## North of Mariahilfer Strasse

### Altstadt Vienna
€
Contemporary     **Map** 1 B5
*Kirchengasse 41, 1070*
**Tel** *(01) 522 66 66*
**w** altstadt.at
A stylish boutique hotel combining period features with contemporary furnishings. Opt for a room on the mezzanine level with pretty stucco-work on the ceilings.

### Harmonie
€
Contemporary     **Map** 2 A1
*Harmoniegasse 5–7, 1090*
**Tel** *(01) 317 66 04*
**w** harmonie-vienna.at
Located in one of the trendiest parts of town, this well-designed hotel is known for its extensive complimentary breakfast buffet, which includes cooked items and good quality organic produce.

### Hotel Alpha
€
Contemporary     **Map** 1 C3
*Buchfeldgasse 8, 1080*
**Tel** *(01) 403 52 91*
**w** gerstner-hotels.at
A no-frills hotel with clean, comfortable rooms in a quiet but central location. The staff are very helpful.

### Hotel-Pension Museum
€
Pension     **Map** 1 C4
*Museumstrasse 3, 1070*
**Tel** *(01) 523 44 26*
**w** hotelmuseum.at
A charming hotel, with parquet floors throughout, in a historic building. Ask for a room with a view; some of the back rooms can be on the small side. The communal areas, decorated with period-style furniture, are stunning.

### Hotel Rathaus Wine & Design
€€
Boutique     **Map** 1 B3
*Lange Gasse 13, 1080*
**Tel** *(01) 400 11 22*
**w** hotel-rathaus-wien.at
An unusual hotel with a wine theme that extends to the decor, artworks and (of course) the bar. Guests can enjoy wine tastings at the hotel and regular excursions to vineyards.

### The Levante Parliament
€€
Boutique     **Map** 1 C4
*Auerspergstrasse 9, 1080*
**Tel** *(01) 228 28-0*
**w** thelevante.com
Bold modern decor pervades at this hotel. The communal areas are especially eye-catching, and include a bar made of glass and a courtyard with clever lighting.

### Sans Souci
€€€
Luxury     **Map** 1 C5
*Burggasse 2, 1070*
**Tel** *(01) 522 25 20*
**w** sanssouci-wien.com
A trendy hotel in a historic building with chic, contemporary furnishings and original art dotted throughout the communal areas. There's an exceptionally large swimming pool.

## South of the Ring

### Hotel Beethoven
€
Contemporary     **Map** 4 B1
*Papagenogasse 6, 1060*
**Tel** *(01) 587 44 82-0*
**w** hotel-beethoven.at
Enchanting hotel owned by the Ludwig family, who sponsor many cultural institutions. Guests may find themselves invited to sip champagne and enjoy a free art show or concert in the lobby.

### Hotel Daniel Vienna
€
Contemporary     **Map** 5 F4
*Landstrasser Gürtel 5, 1030*
**Tel** *(01) 901 31-0*
**w** hoteldaniel.com
Chic hotel with quirky rooms and an in-house bakery that emits the seductive smell of freshly baked bread in the morning. Vespa hire is available to all guests.

Hotel Beethoven, perfect accommodation for culture lovers

### Hotel am Konzerthaus
€
Boutique     **Map** 5 E1
*Am Heumarkt 35–37, 1030*
**Tel** *(01) 716 16-0*
**w** accorhotels.com
A well-run hotel in a convenient central location. The rooms have pretty Klimt-inspired furnishings and a range of modern amenities.

### Hotel Kaiserhof Wien
€€
Historic     **Map** 4 C2
*Frankenberggasse 10, 1040*
**Tel** *(01) 505 17 01*
**w** hotel-kaiserhof.at
This grand property dates back to the early 1900s. Among the elegant period features is the original lift. Enjoy afternoon tea in the refined Kaiserhof bar.

### Lindner Hotel Am Belvedere
€€
Contemporary     **Map** 5 F2
*Rennweg 12, 1030*
**Tel** *(01) 794 77-0*
**w** lindner.de
Popular with business travellers, this hotel has comfortable, modern rooms. The excellent facilities include a spa and sauna.

### Le Méridien Vienna
€€
Design     **Map** 2 B5
*Robert-Stoltz-Platz 1, 1010*
**Tel** *(01) 588 90-0*
**w** lemeridienvienna.com
This hip hotel appeals to the young, cultured and well-off with contemporary art, scooter rental, a champagne bar and special "art experience" suites.

### Bristol
€€€
Luxury     **Map** 5 D1
*Kärntner Ring 1, 1010*
**Tel** *(01) 515 16-0*
**w** bristolvienna.com
Opulent, grand and imposing, the five-star Hotel Bristol is steeped in history and rich in antiques. It's also home to one of the city's best restaurants *(see p314)*.

**For more information on types of hotels** see p291

## DK Choice

**Hotel Sacher**                          €€€
Luxury                          Map 2 B5
*Philharmonikerstrasse 4, 1010*
**Tel** *(01) 514 56-0*
W sacher.com
Mix with the city's elite at this
family-run landmark hotel,
which was founded by the son
of the inventor of *Sachertorte*.
Today, it offers some of the most
sumptuous accommodation in
Vienna. Toys and bathrobes are
provided for kids.

**Imperial**                          €€€
Luxury                          Map 2 B5
*Kärntner Ring 16, 1015*
**Tel** *(01) 501 10-0*
W imperialvienna.com
Opulent accommodation in the
former palace of the Prince of
Württemberg. Transformed into a
hotel in 1873, this place is now a
byword for luxury, with personal
butlers serving the suites.

## DK Choice

**The Ring**                          €€€
Boutique                          Map 2 B5
*Kärntner Ring 8, 1010*
**Tel** *(01) 22 122*
W theringhotel.com
Set in a historic building, this
boutique hotel has an elegant
interior that blends old-world
charm with modern design
and comforts. Attentive staff go
the extra mile. Guests dine on
top-notch cuisine at Eight *(see
p313)*, and enjoy fantastic views
of the skyline while being
pampered in the spa.

## Further Afield

**A&O Wien Stadthalle**                          €
Hostel
*Lerchenfelder Gürtel 9–11, 1160*
**Tel** *(01) 493 04 80-3900*
W aohostels.com
Great-value accommodation in
this clean, stylish hostel, which
is part of a large chain. There
are some wonderfully quirky
communal areas, including a
stylish bar in a vaulted cellar and
a book-lined reading corner.

**Das Capri**                          €
Contemporary                          Map 3 E3
*Praterstrasse 44–46, 1020*
**Tel** *(01) 214 84 04*
W dascapri.at
A comfortable hotel with a range
of well-appointed rooms, suites
and apartments. Appeals to a mix
of weekenders and business
travellers on longer trips.

**Flemings Deluxe Hotel**                          €
Contemporary
*Josefstädter Strasse 10–12, 1080*
**Tel** *(01) 205 99-0*
W flemings-hotels.com
Nothing is too much trouble for
the staff at this unpretentious,
inexpensive and central hotel.

**Hotel Bellevue**                          €
Historic
*Althanstrasse 5, 1090*
**Tel** *800 9733 4226 (within the EU)*
W bellevue-hotel-vienna.com
Behind the 19th century façade
this hotel focuses on business
travellers. The common rooms
are in the period style but
conference facilities are available.

## DK Choice

**Hotel Boltzmann**                          €
Boutique
*Boltzmanngasse 8, 1090*
**Tel** *(01) 354 50-0*
W hotelboltzmann.at
Named after the Viennese
physicist Ludwig Boltzmann, this
family-run hotel has spacious,
well-cared-for rooms. In summer,
enjoy a hearty breakfast buffet in
the peaceful courtyard garden.
The friendly staff are eager to
ensure your visit is as pleasant
as possible. Book ahead.

**Hotel Korotan**                          €
Contemporary
*Albertgasse 48, 1080*
**Tel** *(01) 403 41 93*
W korotan.com
This modern glass-fronted hotel
offers good views of the city. The
comfortable rooms are decorated
in a monochrome colour scheme,
with big, bold modern artworks
imparting splashes of colour.

Tastefully decorated, comfortable room
at the Ring

**Hotel Mozart**                          €
Family-friendly
*Julius-Tandler-Platz 4, 1090*
**Tel** *(01) 317 15 37*
W hotelmozart-vienna.at
This family-run hotel has a great
location for those keen to explore
the city's bike trails. Solar power
heats the water for the hotel's
bathrooms. Note that Internet
access costs extra.

**Hostel Ruthensteiner**                          €
Hostel
*Robert Hamerlinggasse 24, A-1150*
**Tel** *(01) 893 42 02*
W hostelruthensteiner.com
Opened in 1968, this friendly,
laid-back place remains a firm
favourite with backpackers and
makes a great choice for families.
iPads and a selection of DVDs are
available for hire.

**Hotel Stefanie**                          €
Historic
*Taborstrasse 12, 1020*
**Tel** *(01) 211 50*
W schick-hotels.com
Pleasant, modern rooms are
offered at this excellent four-star
hotel that claims to be the oldest
hotel in Vienna. Continuously
run by the Schick family, who
take pride in having offered good
old-fashioned friendly service
ever since they purchased the
hotel in 1880.

**Landhaus Fuhrgassl-Huber**                          €
Family-friendly
*Rathstrasse 24, Neustift am
Walde, 1190*
**Tel** *(01) 440 30 33*
W landhaus-fuhrgassl-huber.at
Overlooking vineyards on
Vienna's outskirts, this lovely
country house is a relaxing base
from which to explore the city.
Designed by a former stage
designer at the Vienna Opera
House, it has country-style
parlours and pretty leafy patios.

## DK Choice

**Boutiquehotel Stadthalle**    €€
Boutique
*Hackengasse 20, 1150*
**Tel** *(01) 982 42 72*
W hotelstadthalle.at
Claiming to be the world's first
zero-energy city hotel, this
place promotes green living by
only using renewable energy
sources. The courtyard garden
is an oasis of calm and in June
the lavender – watered from
the hotel well – blooms. Staff
harvest and dry the lavender,
using it in the hotel's lotions,
potions, soaps and oils.

## Lower Austria and Burgenland

### DK Choice

**DÜRNSTEIN: Schloss Dürnstein** €€
Luxury          Road map F3
*Dürnstein 2, A-3601*
**Tel** *(02711) 212*
🆆 schloss.at
This dreamy castle is the ultimate romantic address, with four-poster beds, silver-service dining and indoor and outdoor pools. It opens seasonally, from May to October.

Lobby and bistro-bar at the Hotel Metropol in St Pölten

**EGGENBURG: Stadthotel Eggenburg** €
Pension        Road map F2
*Kremserstrasse 8, A-3730*
**Tel** *(02984) 35 31*
🆆 oppitz.at
This family-run hotel is located in the centre of medieval Eggenburg. It offers quiet, traditional rooms with modern amenities.

**EISENSTADT: Hotel Ohr** €
Family-friendly     Road map G3
*Rusterstrasse 51, A-7000*
**Tel** *(02682) 62 46-0*
🆆 hotel-ohr.at
A friendly hotel some distance from the centre, with basic, modern rooms and an excellent breakfast buffet. Horse-riding excursions are on offer.

**GÖSING: Alpenhotel Gösing** €
Spa         Road map F3
*Gösing an der Mariazellerbahn 4, A-3221*
**Tel** *(02728) 217*
🆆 goesing.at
This large chalet-style hotel aims to provide respite from the everyday. The rustic rooms have original wooden beams, and the hotel has spa facilities.

**LOIPERSDORF: Pension Krainz** €
Family-friendly     Road map G4
*Henndorf-Therme 1, A-8282*
**Tel** *(03329) 46 611*
🆆 krainz-loipersdorf.at
Set in the quiet countryside, near the thermal spa centre of Loipersdorf and its golf course, this family-oriented hotel has bright, spacious rooms.

**MAUERBACH: Berghotel Tubingerkogel** €
Contemporary     Road map F3
*Tulbingerkogel 1, A-3001*
**Tel** *(02273) 73 91*
🆆 tulbingerkogel.at
Every room boasts floor-to-ceiling windows with forest views.

There's an infinity lap pool and sauna, and walking and cycling trails run nearby. The restaurant has a 1,200-bottle wine cellar.

**NEUHAUS AM KLAUSENBACH: Pferdehof Pfaffenriegel** €
Family-friendly     Road map F5
*Panoramastrasse 33, A-8385*
**Tel** *(3329) 22 78*
🆆 farmholidays.com
The Ludwig family horse farm has horses, goats, a lake for swimming and a nearby thermal spring. Guests can enjoy some traditional home cooking.

**NEUSIEDL AM SEE: Hotel Wende** €€
Family-friendly     Road map G3
*Seestrasse 40, A-7100*
**Tel** *(02167) 81 11*
🆆 hotel-wende.at
Set in beautiful countryside, this child-friendly hotel offers an indoor pool, extensive grounds and guest rooms with balconies.

**RUST: Hotel Sifkovits** €
Pension       Road map G3
*Am Seekanal 8, A-7071*
**Tel** *(02685) 204 60*
🆆 sifkovits.at
A lovely little hotel in the perfect spot for exploring Rust. There's a good organic breakfast buffet and a pretty garden with sun loungers.

**ST PÖLTEN: Hotel Metropol** €
Contemporary     Road map F3
*Schillerplatz 1, A-2680*
**Tel** *(02742) 7070-0*
🆆 hotel-metropol.at
This centrally located business hotel, part of a large chain, offers well-equipped rooms.

**SEMMERING: Belvedere** €
Family-friendly     Road map F4
*Hochstrasse 6, A-2680*
**Tel** *(02664) 22 70*
🆆 belvedere-semmering.at
The pretty, traditional-style Belvedere hotel has bags of

character, spacious, comfortable rooms, and superb pool and spa facilities.

**WEISSENKIRCHEN/WACHAU: Donauwirt** €
Traditional     Road map F3
*Wachaustrasse 47, A-3610*
**Tel** *(02715) 22 47*
🆆 donauwirt.at
This cheerful family-run hotel is set right on the edge of the Danube, with wonderful views. The restaurant is exceptional.

**ZWETTL: Schwarz-Alm** €
Family-friendly     Road map F2
*Almweg 1, A-3910*
**Tel** *(02822) 53173-0*
🆆 schwarzalm.at
A traditional country hotel surrounded by a large alpine forest. It has a wellness centre and a wide range of hiking and biking activities right on the doorstep.

## Styria

**BAD AUSSEE: Hotel Erzherzog Johann** €€
Spa         Road map D4
*Kurhausplatz 62, A-8990*
**Tel** *(03622) 525 07-0*
🆆 erzherzogjohann.at
A modern hotel with comfortable, spacious rooms and spectacular views of the Alps. The fabulous spa and attentive staff ensure a thoroughly relaxing stay.

**BAD BLUMAU: Rogner-Bad Blumau** €€€
Spa         Road map F4
*Bad Blumau 100, A-8283*
**Tel** *(03383) 5100-0*
🆆 blumau.com
Designed by Friedensreich Hundertwasser *(see p31)*, this eccentric building is made up of irregular undulating forms, with a maze of tunnels and pools, and brightly coloured mosaics.

For more information on types of hotels *see p291*

**BAD GLEICHENBERG:
Hotel Stenitzer** €€
Spa **Road map** F5
*Schulstrasse 19, A-8344*
**Tel** *(03159) 22 50*
w hotel-stenitzer.com
An elegantly furnished four-star
hotel with extensive spa facilities
and pretty formal gardens.

**BAD RADKERSBURG:
Thermenhotel
Radkersburger Hof** €€
Spa **Road map** F5
*Thermenstrasse 22, A-8490*
**Tel** *(03476) 3560-0*
w radkersburgerhof.at
Advertised as a health and
rehabilitation resort, this hotel
offers group fitness classes and
sports, as well as specific therapies.

**DEUTSCHLANDSBERG: Burg
Deutschlandsberg** €€
Luxury **Road map** F5
*Burgplatz 1, A-8530*
**Tel** *(03462) 565 60*
w burg-deutschlandsberg.at
This 12th-century castle, with
tower and turret, overlooks the
river Lassnitz and the rolling
vineyards of southwest Styria.
There are 50 rooms, a small spa
and a lauded restaurant.

**FOHNSDORF: Hotel Schloss
Gabelhofen** €€
Luxury **Road map** E4
*Schlossgasse 54, A-8753*
**Tel** *(03573) 55 55-0*
w gabelhofen.at
Splendidly atmospheric castle
hotel with beautifully decorated
rooms, some of which are in the
castle towers.

**DK Choice**

**GRAZ: Augarten Art Hotel** €
Boutique **Road map** F4
*Schönaugasse 53, A-8010*
**Tel** *(0316) 20 80-0*
w augartenhotel.at
A trendy, minimalist design hotel
featuring bespoke furnishings
and contemporary art from the
private collection of the hotel's
owner, Helmut Marko. The
building combines curving
surfaces and glass to provide a
feeling of light and space.

**GRAZ: Hotel Zum Dom** €
Boutique **Road map** F4
*Bürgergasse 14, A-8010*
**Tel** *(0316) 82 480-0*
w domhotel.co.at
This unique boutique hotel is
set in a historic building. The
stylish rooms are individually
decorated, combining modern
luxuries with period features.

**GRAZ:
Palais-Hotel Erzherzog Johann** €
Historic **Road map** F4
*Sackstrasse 3–5, A-8010*
**Tel** *(0316) 811 616*
w erzherzog-johann.com
This charming hotel right in the
town centre was as an inn in the
16th century. All the rooms are
richly furnished with antiques.

**KAPFENBERG: Bohlerstern** €
Contemporary **Road map** F4
*Friedrich-Böhler-Strasse 13, A-8605*
**Tel** *(03862) 206 375*
w boehlerstern.at
The classical exterior belies the
modern, albeit basic, design
inside. Events, including
weddings, are often held here.

**MARIAZELL:
Hotel Schwarzer Adler** €
Pension **Road map** F4
*Hauptplatz 1, A-8630*
**Tel** *(03882) 28 63-0*
w hotelschwarzeradler.at
Traditional and cheerfully painted
hotel with comfortable rooms in
the town centre. A great place for
those hiking or skiing in the area.

**RAMSAU:
Alpengasthof Peter Rosegger** €
Traditional **Road map** D4
*Ramsau 233, A-8972*
**Tel** *(03687) 81 223-0*
w alpengasthof-peter-rosegger.at
Comfortable rooms with natural
pine furniture and stunning views
of the Dachstein mountains.
There's also a reading room and
a pretty garden.

**RAMSAU-KULM: Almfrieden** €
Family-friendly **Road map** D4
*Leiten 47, A-8972*
**Tel** *(03687) 81 753*
w almfrieden.at
Child-friendly resort hotel with
a playground and a range of
beautifully decorated rooms.

Light-filled modern room at the boutique
design-hotel Augarten Art Hotel in Graz

**SCHLADMING: Posthotel** €€
Pension **Road map** D4
*Hauptplatz 10, A-8970*
**Tel** *(03687) 22 571*
w posthotel-schladming.at
This attractive 400-year old inn
has a superb restaurant and small
but well-appointed rooms. The
staff are exceptionally friendly
and helpful.

**TURRACHER HÖHE:
Schlosshotel Seewirt** €€
Family-friendly **Road map** D4
*Turracher Höhe 33, A-8864*
**Tel** *(04275) 82 34*
w schlosshotel-seewirt.com
This cosy 19th-century
guesthouse with original timber
features offers a range of facilities,
including a good-sized indoor
pool and a sauna.

# Upper Austria

**BAD GOISERN/ST AGATHA:
Landhotel Agathawirt** €
Pension **Road map** D4
*St Agatha 10, A-4822*
**Tel** *(06135) 83 41*
w agathawirt.at
Built in 1517, this historic hotel
offers a comfortable and cosy
base for those heading out on
mountain-biking excursions. Relax
in the garden in summer or by a
wood-burning stove in winter.

**BAD ISCHL: Goldenes Schiff** €
Contemporary **Road map** D4
*Adalbert-Stifter-Kai 3, A-4820*
**Tel** *(06132) 24 241*
w goldenes-schiff.at
This attractive four-star hotel has
been an inn since the 17th century.
Rooms are modern and spacious,
and the breakfast is excellent.

**BAD LEONFELDEN:
Kurhotel Bad Leonfelden** €€
Spa **Road map** E3
*Spielau 8, A-4190*
**Tel** *(07213) 63 63*
w daskurhotel.at
A stunning hotel in a resort with
a long spa history. Therapies
include massage, mud baths and
beauty treatments. The staff are
friendly and hospitable.

**GMUNDEN: Seehotel Schwan** €
Historic **Road map** D3
*Rathausplatz 8, A-4810*
**Tel** *(7612) 633 910*
w seehotel-schwan.at
Run by the same family for six
generations, this impressive
19th-century hotel is situated
in the town square, right on the
shore of Lake Traunsee. Rooms
are simple yet tasteful.

**GRUENAU IM ALMTAL:**
**TreeHouse Backpacker Hotel** €
Hostel　　　　Road map D3
**Tel** *(7216) 8499*
🆆 treehousehotel.net
A Backpacker Hotel of the Year,
this hostel is surrounded by
woodland, countryside and
snowy mountains. Homecooked
meals, horse riding, bike rental
and close proximity to the slopes
add to the attraction.

**LINZ: Arcotel Nike** €
Contemporary　Road map E3
*Untere Donaulände 9, A-4020*
**Tel** *(0732) 76 26-0*
🆆 arcotelhotels.com/Nike
This high-rise is close to the
Danube and offers great views.
Most rooms follow a red-and-
white colour scheme.

**LINZ: Hotel Schillerpark** €
Contemporary　Road map E3
*Rainerstrasse 2–4, A-4020*
**Tel** *(0732) 695-0*
🆆 austria-trend.at
This cube-like glass-and-steel
building has a casino in house.
Part of the Austria Trend chain,
the rooms are pleasant and
modestly priced.

**MONDSEE: Lackner** €€
Contemporary　Road map D3
*Mondseestrasse 1, A-5310*
**Tel** *(06232) 23 59-0*
🆆 seehotel-lackner.at
A lovely inn with spectacular lake
views and a first-rate restaurant. It
has well-designed spacious rooms
with balconies overlooking the
lake, and warm, friendly staff.

**NATTERNBACH:**
**Ikuna Tipidorf** €
Family-friendly　Road map D3
*Naturpfad 1, A-4723*
**Tel** *(7278) 208 00*
🆆 Ikuna.at
An eco-friendly tepee village in
the woods with totem poles.
There's an adventure park – with
animals – for kids and bike tours.
Tepees have electricity and
modern bathrooms.

**ST WOLFGANG:**
**Landhaus zu Appesbach** €€
Luxury　　　Road map D4
*Au 18, A-5360*
**Tel** *(06138) 22 09*
🆆 appesbach.com
This former private mansion, akin
to an English manor house, has
been converted into an exclusive
hotel with beautiful rooms and
apartments. The idyllic setting
right on the lake provides plenty
of scope for relaxation. Book the
Windsor Suite, where the Duke of
Windsor once stayed.

## DK Choice
**ST WOLFGANG:**
**Weisses Rössl** €€€
Luxury　　　Road map D4
*Markt 74, A-5360*
**Tel** *(06138) 23 06*
🆆 weissesroessl.at
This famous lakeside hotel,
celebrated in an operetta by
Ralph Benatzky and Robert
Stolz, embodies traditional
Austrian style and hospitality.
Consisting of several historic
houses clustered together,
it offers a range of elegant,
romantic rooms, many with
17th-century wooden ceilings.
Excellent facilities include an
outdoor swimming pool with
spectacular views over the lake.

**SCHÄRDING: Stiegenwirt** €
Pension　　　Road map D3
*Schlossgasse 2–6, A-4780*
**Tel** *(07712) 30 70-0*
🆆 stiegenwirt-schaerding.at
Set in a pretty Baroque building,
this hotel has been owned by
the same family since 1910 and
offers large, comfortable rooms.
Excellent regional cuisine is
served in the hotel restaurant.

**TRAUNKIRCHEN:**
**Symposionhotel Post** €€
Contemporary　Road map D3
*Ortsplatz 5, A-4801*
**Tel** *(07617) 23 07*
🆆 hotel-post-traunkirchen.at
Comfortable, modern four-star
hotel on the shores of the
Traunsee. Room overlooking the
lake also take in the peaks of
Johannesberg – a stunning view.

## Salzburger Land

**BAD GASTEIN:**
**Hotel Weismayr** €€
Spa　　　　Road map D4
*Kaiser-Franz-Josef-Strasse 6, A-5640*
**Tel** *(06434) 25 94*
🆆 weismayr.com
Built at the turn of the 19th
century, this grand four-star hotel
retains all the glamour of the
Austrian *belle-époque* and offers
great views of the Gastein valley.

**BAD GASTEIN:**
**Haus Hirt** €€€
Spa　　　　Road map D4
*Kaiserhofstrasse 14, A-5640*
**Tel** *(06434) 27 97-0*
🆆 haus-hirt.com
A stylish, contemporary spa resort
offering trendy, modern rooms
and plenty of pampering in the
wellness centre.

High-rise hotel Arcotel Nike, located near
the Danube in Linz

**EUGENDORF: Holzlnerwirt** €
Pension　　　Road map D3
*Dorf 4, A-5301*
**Tel** *(06225) 82 05*
🆆 holzlnerwirt.at
Atmospheric hotel in a traditional
chalet. The charming rooms,
many of which have four-poster
beds, include special touches
such as down duvets and quaint
clay stoves.

**FILZMOOS: Tannenhof** €
Pension　　　Road map D4
*Filzmoos 84, A-5332*
**Tel** *(06453) 82 020*
🆆 sieberer-filzmoos.at
A delightful guesthouse nestled
in the mountains, Tannenhof is
perfect for families on hiking or
skiing holidays. Friendly, hospitable hosts. Apartments available.

**FUSCHL: Seewinkel** €€
Resort　　　Road map D4
*Seestrasse 31, A-5330*
**Tel** *(06226) 83 44*
🆆 seewinkel.com
This picturesque hotel offers a
splendid panorama over the
Fuschlsee. Facilities include a
private bathing beach, sailing
and windsurfing facilities, and a
small spa and sauna.

**FUSCHL: Schloss Fuschl** €€€
Luxury　　　Road map D4
*Schloss Strasse 19, Hof bei
Salzburg, A-5322*
**Tel** *(06229) 22 530*
🆆 schlossfuschlsalzburg.com
This stately hotel set in a 15th-
century castle overlooks the lake
and has spa facilities and a nine-
hole golf course. Refined, elegant
rooms both in the main castle
and in lakeside cottages.

**For more information on types of hotels** *see p291*

Charming hotel complex of Berghof, next to the Hintertux Glacier, Hintertux

**KLEINARL: Vienhof**
Family-friendly        Road map D4
*Viehhofstrasse 15, A-5603*
**Tel** *(06418) 240*
W pension-viehhof.at
Traditional chalet-style guesthouse with pine furnishings, family apartments and a children's playroom. Convenient for hiking and skiing.

**SAALBACH: Hotel Bauer**        €€
Contemporary        Road map C4
*Oberdorf 232, A-5753*
**Tel** *(06541) 62 13-0*
W hotel-bauer.at
Located a stone's throw from the lifts and ski slopes, this hotel has well-appointed rooms and a superb restaurant.

**ST GILGEN:**
**Parkhotel Billroth**        €€
Contemporary        Road map D4
*Billrothstrasse 2, A-5340*
**Tel** *(06227) 22 17*
W billroth.at
This calm lakeside retreat is a perfect base for long walks around the edge of Wolfgangsee. The bedrooms are only surpassed in grandeur by the opulent dining and social areas.

**SALZBURG: Berglandhotel**        €
Contemporary        Road map D3
*Rupertgasse 15, A-5020*
**Tel** *(0662) 872 318*
W berglandhotel.at
About a 10-minute walk from the Old Town, this efficiently run family-owned hotel offers neat rooms at reasonable prices.

**SALZBURG: Auersperg**        €€
Boutique        Road map D3
*Auerspergstrasse 61, A-5020*
**Tel** *(0662) 889 440*
W auersperg.at
With sleek contemporary decor, a garden setting and organic food at breakfast time, this place is ideal for a weekend away.

**SALZBURG:**
**Goldener Hirsch**        €€€
Luxury        Road map D3
*Getreidegasse 37, A-5020*
**Tel** *(0662) 80 840*
W goldenerhirsch.com
Set in a 15th-century building, this charming hotel is decked out with pretty hand-crafted furnishings and antiques that complement the historic surrounds. It also boasts a truly exceptional restaurant.

**DK Choice**

**SALZBURG:**
**Hotel Sacher Salzburg**        €€€
Luxury        Road map D3
*Schwarzstrasse 5–7, A-5020*
**Tel** *(0662) 889 770*
W sacher.com
Sister to the Viennese hotel of the same name, this place offers traditional luxuries such as marble bathrooms, richly furnished rooms and the famous *Sachertorte* chocolate cake in the hotel café. Pets and children welcome – the latter provided with toys and games.

**SALZBURG:**
**Schloss Mönchstein**        €€€
Luxury        Road map D3
*Mönchsberg Park 26, A-5020*
**Tel** *(0662) 848 555-0*
W monchstein.at
An enchanting 14th-century castle with its own park and spa. It offers unparalleled views of the city and high standards of comfort and service.

**STROBL: Bergrose**        €
Spa        Road map D4
*Weissenbach 162, A-5350*
**Tel** *(06137) 54 31*
W bergrose.at
A family-run hotel surrounded by mountains and meadows. The rooms are spotlessly clean and beautifully decked out in vintage fabric and wooden furniture. The spa facilities are in keeping with the hotel's serene, relaxing atmosphere.

## Tyrol and Vorarlberg

**AU: Hotel Rössle**        €€
Traditional        Road map A4
*Lisse 90, A-6883*
**Tel** *(05515) 22 16*
W roessle-au.at
This traditional village hotel offers spacious rooms with balconies and panoramic mountain views. Guests can hire mountain bikes and there is also an excellent spa.

**BREGENZ: Weisses Kreuz**        €€
Luxury        Road map A4
*Römerstrasse 5, A-6900*
**Tel** *(05574) 49 88-0*
W hotelweisseskreuz.at
Service is exceptional at this hotel, which has been hosting guests for some 100 years. The rooms feature exposed beams and ornate cornices.

**FONTANELLA/FASCHINA:**
**Alpenresort Walsertal**        €€
Family-friendly        Road map A4
*Faschina 55, A-6733*
**Tel** *(05510) 224*
W alpenresort-walsertal.at
A comfortable mountain retreat featuring wood-panelled interiors and a fully equipped spa. The on-site restaurant serves excellent food.

**FULPMES: Waldhof**        €€
Family-friendly        Road map B4
*Gröbenweg 19, A-6166*
**Tel** *(05225) 62 175*
W waldhof-stubaital.at
This charming mountain hideaway with traditional Tyrolean decor offers a wide range of luxurious amenities, including a spa. The comfortable rooms have panoramic views of the Stubai Alps.

**GOING: Bio-Hotel Stanglwirt**        €€€
Resort        Road map C4
*Kaiserweg 1, A-6353*
**Tel** *(05358) 2000*
W stanglwirt.com
Play a round of golf, book a lesson at the ski school or simply gaze at the outstanding views of the Wilder Kaiser peaks at this uniquely Austrian chalet-style holiday village.

**HINTERTUX: Berghof**        €€
Luxury        Road map C4
*Hintertux 754, A-6293*
**Tel** *(05287) 85 85*
W berghof.at
This luxurious modern hotel is at the foot of the Hintertux Glacier, which is open all year round. Excellent facilities, impeccable service and a good hotel restaurant.

**INNSBRUCK: Goldener Adler**        €€
Historic        Road map B4
*Herzog-Friedrich-Strasse 6, 6020*
**Tel** *(0512) 571 111-0*
W goldeneradler.com
Part of the Best Western chain, this elegant 14th-century inn sits in the heart of the Old Town, and boasts European royalty and Mozart among its former guests. The rooms offer panoramic views of the city and the mountains beyond.

**INNSBRUCK:**
**Schlosshotel Igls** €€€
Luxury **Road map** B4
*Viller Steig 2, A-6080*
**Tel** *(0512) 377 217*
Guests are treated like royalty at this luxurious and discreet mountain castle. Rooms are beautifully appointed and boast superb views of the surrounding Alps.

**KIRCHBERG: Sportalm** €€
Contemporary **Road map** C4
*Brandseitweg 26–28, A-6365*
**Tel** *(05357) 27 78*
w hotel-sportalm.at
Amid the rolling foothills of the Kitzbühel Alps, this hotel focuses on providing good food. Sleek, modern rooms pay homage to traditional Tyrolean style.

**KITZBÜHEL: Goldener Greif** €€€
Luxury **Road map** C4
*Schulgasse 3/Hinterstadt 24, A-6370*
**Tel** *(05356) 64 311*
w hotel-goldener-greif.at
This hotel dates from the 13th century and has a pretty flower-covered façade. Rooms have beautiful wood-panelled interiors and ceiling frescoes.

**KRAMSACH:**
**Camping Seeblick Toni** €
Family-friendly **Road map** C4
*Moosen 46, A-6233*
**Tel** *(5337) 635 44*
w camping-seeblick.at
This campsite is located right by the sea. As well as plots for tents and camper vans, there are bungalows and caravans to rent. A playroom, park and activities keep children entertained.

**LERMOOS: Mohr** €€€
Spa **Road map** B4
*Innsbruckerstrasse 40, A-6631*
**Tel** *(05673) 23 62*
w mohr-life-resort.at
Built entirely with traditional materials, this bold, contemporary building frequently stars in design magazines. The ultra-stylish rooms are decked out with iconic design pieces and free-standing bath tubs. Choose from a full range of spa-resort facilities.

**MAYRHOFEN/FINKENBERG:**
**Sporthotel Stock** €€€
Spa **Road map** C4
*Dorf 142, A-6292*
**Tel** *(05285) 67 75*
w sporthotel-stock.com
A destination resort hotel with romantic rooms, indoor and outdoor pools, wellness facilities and numerous sports activities. The food in the hotel restaurant is excellent.

**OBERLECH: Montana** €€€
Luxury **Road map** A4
*Oberlech 279, A-6764*
**Tel** *(05583) 24 60*
w montanaoberlech.at
A hotel of top-notch ski pedigree, owned by the family of former world ski champion Patrick Ortlieb. Located on the edge of the piste, in a large chalet-style building, it is ideal for skiers in search of a luxury base. Everything is beautifully designed and well thought through, keeping the needs of the skier in mind. There is baby-sitting and a children's ski school. Half-board is mandatory.

# Carinthia and East Tyrol

**BAD BLEIBERG:**
**Der Bleibergerhof** €€
Spa **Road map** D5
*Drei Lärchen 150, A-9530*
**Tel** *(04244) 22 05*
w bleibergerhof.at
This spa hotel offers thermal waters, modern design and state-of-the-art facilities, including indoor and outdoor pools and numerous saunas.

**BODENSDORF: Stofflwirt** €
Family-friendly **Road map** E5
*Deutschberg 6, A-9551*
**Tel** *(04243) 69 20*
w stofflwirt.at
An attractive hotel that combines traditional materials with modern style. Guests can enjoy the garden, mountain views and spa facilities.

**KLAGENFURT: Palais Porcia** €€
Boutique **Road map** E5
*Neuer Platz 13, A-9020*
**Tel** *(0463) 511 590-0*
w palais-porcia.at
An elegant hotel set in a historical palace with opulently decorated rooms, plush carpets and a

Roaring log fire at the luxurious Schlosshotel Igls, Innsbruck

wide range of modern amenities. Truly exceptional service.

**LIENZ: Traube** €€
Spa **Road map** D5
*Hauptplatz 14, A-9900*
**Tel** *(04852) 64 444*
w hoteltraube.at
An elegant and romantic hotel located in the centre of town, featuring wonderful views of the Alps. Rooms are beautifully furnished, some with antiques.

**MILLSTATT: See-Villa** €€
Spa **Road map** D5
*Seestrasse 68, A-9872*
**Tel** *(04766) 21 02*
w see-villa.eu
An award-winning countryside hotel and spa decked out in traditional style and set amid well-tended grounds. Very warm and hospitable hosts.

**OSSIACH:**
**Strandgasthof Seewirt** €
Pension **Road map** E5
*Ossiach 2, A-9570*
**Tel** *(04243) 22 68*
w seewirt-ossiach.at
A charming guesthouse with a lovely garden located on the shores of Ossiacher See. Perfect for lakeside strolls, boating and fishing.

**DK Choice**

**PORTSCHACH:**
**Schloss Leonstain** €€
Boutique **Road map** E5
*Leonstainerstrasse 1, A-9210*
**Tel** *(04272) 28 16*
w leonstain.at
This place so enchanted Brahms that he wrote a violin concerto here. Built in 1492, Schloss Leonstain offers the perfect balance between old-world charm and contemporary facilities.

**VELDEN:**
**Casino Hotel Velden** €€
Luxury **Road map** E5
*Am Corso 10, A-9220*
**Tel** *(04274) 51 233*
w casino-hotel.at
Uniquely designed rooms in a classic Wörthersee hotel, with a casino and private beach.

**VILLACH: Holiday Inn** €€
Boutique **Road map** E5
*Uropaplatz 1–2, A-9500*
**Tel** *(04242) 22 522*
w hi-villach.at
This is a hotel of genuine flair and individuality, offering a range of pretty rooms with enormous bathrooms. Great service.

**For more information on types of hotels** *see p291*

# WHERE TO EAT AND DRINK

Austrian cooking forms one of the classic European schools of cuisine, incorporating many elements, such as *Wiener Schnitzel*, that have become standard across the continent. Traditional Austrian fare such as breaded chicken, boiled beef and *Gulasch* soup is served in almost all establishments. Freshwater fish is a feature of Austria's many lakes and rivers, while hearty dumplings and noodle dishes are common in the south and west. Larger cities are also home to Italian, Greek, Turkish and Chinese restaurants.

The restaurants listed on pages 310–25 have been selected from the best on offer, across all price ranges. They are organized by region and price. The phrase book on page 380 will help you order a meal, although most restaurants will have English menus.

Display of pastries and rolls at the charming Café Mozart *(see p310)*

## What to Eat and When

For breakfast, Austrians tend to eat a roll or two with butter and jam, accompanied by coffee. Most hotels offer a self-service buffet breakfast, which generally includes a variety of meats and eggs. Even small bakeries usually have a few tables for sitting and enjoying a breakfast pastry.

Most restaurants serve lunch from noon to 2 or 3pm. Many offer a *Tagesmenü* (fixed-price menu of the day), or a *Tagesteller* (dish of the day), as one of the best-priced options. This is usually displayed on a blackboard outside the restaurant.

.Austrians are very health-conscious and fiercely dedicated to local ingredients, which are often emphasized in restaurants and cafés located in the countryside or by a lake. Menus often show in detail the country of origin of meats, fish and even mushrooms. It is increasingly common to see allergy information on the menu as well.

## Opening Hours

A few small grocery stores, bakeries and coffee houses open as early as 7am, but most open between 8am and 10am.

Restaurants are usually open from around 11am to 10pm, although many establishments take a break after lunch (around 3pm) and then reopen at around 6pm for dinner. Rural restaurants often serve as meeting points for locals and may remain open until the early hours, although the kitchen may close much earlier. At a country inn it may be difficult to order a meal after 9pm. Many places close for the *Ruhetag* (day off set aside for rest), and may also be closed on public holidays.

## Types of Restaurants and Snack Bars

A wide range of restaurants, bars and snack bars offer modest or grand meals at any time of day. There are a large number of upmarket restaurants, often located within the luxury hotels, which offer first-class international menus prepared by top chefs.

A *Wirtshaus* is a country inn and a *Gasthaus* is a slightly more sophisticated restaurant – both typically concentrate on local cuisine. A *Beisl* is something like a local pub serving drinks alongside hot meals. Many old-fashioned, richly furnished, traditional cafés in Vienna and Salzburg are tourist attractions in themselves, and serve light meals.

One uniquely Austrian culinary establishment is the *Heuriger*, a simple wine bar in the wine-growing villages, offering light meals at low prices. Here, wine is served at your table in a glass mug, and food is available from a buffet. If fir branches are displayed outside it means that the *Heuriger* is open and is serving the fresh home-pressed vintage.

Formal dining at the celebrated Vestibül in Vienna *(see p312)*

The stylish interiors of Motto, a restaurant in Vienna *(see p315)*

In cities, pubs and bars often have quite extensive menus of sandwiches, burgers and other hot food. One Austrian classic snack that should be tried at least once is the hot sausage, traditionally served at an *Imbissstube* (snack bar) or a *Würstelstand* (sausage stand). Such stands usually offer a variety of sausages and frankfurters, served with bread and mustard or sometimes freshly grated horseradish.

## Reservations

Reservations are always advisable at any popular eatery, and are easily made by phone or email. During the high season and in busy tourist areas it is often essential to book ahead. Even a simple *Gasthof* or *Beisl* may have a faithful local clientele and you may be disappointed if you wander in and expect to find a free table. If you are going to a *Heuriger* in a group, you will definitely need to book a table in advance.

## Prices and Tips

It is difficult to generalize about prices. Lunch at an average restaurant should cost about €20–30 per person. For an evening meal you need to allow two or three times that price, or more if drinks are included. Most of the self-service establishments usually charge by the size of the plate.

In the more expensive restaurants, the bill may also include *Gedeck*, the cover charge, or a cover charge may be levied for the bread served at the table.

Although a service charge is almost always included in the bill, you are expected to leave an additional sum of up to 10 per cent for service.

Credit cards are accepted in most luxury and hotel-restaurants, but the majority of rural establishments and snack bars accept only cash.

## Vegetarians

Austrians are well-known meat eaters but vegetarians need not worry they might go hungry. Few Austrian towns are without a dedicated vegetarian restaurant, and most menus in tourist restaurants offer a choice of meatless meals.

Austrians have embraced the organic food movement, as well as cuisine from Asia, but Austrian traditional cuisine actually includes a number of meat-free dishes. In the Alps, especially in ski resorts in Vorarlberg, one of the most filling and popular meals is *käseschnitte*, a variation of cheese on toast, with bread soaked in white wine. Many other traditional dishes are made from potatoes, spinach and mushrooms, including the famous *Kärntner Nudeln*, the signature dish of Carinthia. Many *Heurigen* offer buffets with a wide selection of vegetarian dishes to choose from.

## Recommended Restaurants

The restaurants featured in this guidebook have been selected for their good value, food, location and atmosphere. A wide range of establishments has been included, all representative of their setting. Each one stands out and has earned a noteworthy reputation.

The listings cover a vast variety of eateries, from the simple *Heuriger* wine tavern to the family-run *Gasthaus*, historic Viennese cafés and smart gourmet restaurants. Particular attention is devoted to regional specialities, from the freshwater fish of the Neusiedler See to the sumptuous sweets of Salzburg.

Those establishments labelled DK Choice have been highlighted in recognition of an exceptional feature – celebrity chef, exquisite food, inviting ambience or simply great value. Most of these eateries are quite popular among locals and visitors, so be sure to make reservations well in advance to avoid waiting.

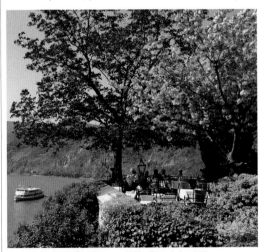

Diners enjoying the view from the terrace of Schloss Dürnstein *(see p316)*

# The Flavours of Austria: Savoury Dishes

Austrian cuisine is a direct legacy of the country's imperial past, when culinary traditions from many parts of Europe influenced Viennese cooks. As a result, it is far more varied and flavoursome than most people realize. There are Italian and Adriatic influences, Polish- and Hungarian- inspired dishes, and even a rich seam of Balkan flavours running through much of the Austrian kitchen repertoire. *Schnitzel*, for example, is an import from Milan, which was once under Austrian control, while *Gulasch* is the Austrian version of the Hungarian dish that became popular in Vienna in the 19th century.

Chanterelle mushrooms

Cheese stall at a local Austrian farmers' market

## Meat, Poultry and Dairy

Beef is narrowly ahead of pork as the nation's favourite meat. Austrian cattle farmers have a long and proud heritage of producing fine beef, which is used in many dishes, such as paprika-rich *Gulasch*. That most famous of Austrian dishes, *Wiener Schnitzel*, is traditionally made with veal. Pork is used primarily to make hams and sausages. The classic Austrian way with pork is to cure it, smoke it and leave it to mature for months in the clean air of the high Alpine pastures. The result is called *Speck*. Lean *Speck* is similar to Italian *prosciutto*, though with a distinctive smoky tang, while fattier cuts are more like *pancetta* or streaky bacon.

*Bratwurst*, made with beef, pork and veal, are Austria's preferred sausages, but other types such as *Frankfurters* are also common. Chicken is almost always served breaded, but *Grillhendl* is a whole chicken roasted over an open fire, or on a spit. Duck *(Ente)* is often served with sweet sauces, but sometimes with

Frankfurters
Bierwurst
Frankfurters
Bratwurst
Lean Speck
Speck

Selection of typical Austrian cured pork, sausages and salami

## Austrian Dishes and Specialities

While most classic Austrian dishes (especially those originating in Vienna) are found all over the country, there are some regional differences. *Knödel* (dumplings) are more popular in the east, as are carp, game and pork, while beef and lamb appear more often the further west (and higher up the mountains) you travel. Beef is essential for *Tafelspitz*, often called the national dish. *Speck* is used to make *Speck Knödel*, small, dense dumplings, but the one part of the pig that Austrians love to eat uncured is the knuckle, called *Stelze*, roasted and served chopped with heaps of sauerkraut. *Fischgröstl* is a mix of fish and seafood, fried together with onion, potato and mince (usually leftovers). It is rarely found on menus, but you may be lucky enough to try it in an Austrian home.

Paprika

**Tafelspitz** is silverside of beef, boiled with root vegetables and served thickly sliced with gherkins and sauerkraut.

Spectacular array of vegetables on display in a Viennese market

sour accompaniments such as pickled red cabbage. Roast goose (Gänsebraten) is also popular, as are goose livers. The milk of Austrian dairy cows, grazed on sweet Alpine pastures, produces some excellent artisan cheeses, such as fruity Wälder.

## Fish

While not great seafood-lovers, Austrians have developed a number of their own fish dishes. Trout (Forelle) is the most popular fish, usually served grilled with boiled potatoes. Herring (Hering) is pickled and eaten as an appetizer. Heringsschmaus, a smoked herring and apple salad, is hugely popular at Easter. Carp (Karpfen) is a favourite Christmas dish, but is eaten all year, as is plaice (Scholle or Goldbutt), which is often served with a rich vegetable-based sauce.

## Vegetables

Vegetables in Austria are of the highest quality and so, while imported produce is available all year round, seasonality is still important to Austrians. That is truest of all for the nation's favourite vegetable, asparagus (Spargel).

Bunches of pale spears of Austrian Spargel (asparagus)

Only local asparagus is used, and so it is found on menus only during the harvesting season, which runs from the end of April to early July. Austrians use asparagus in every way imaginable at this time of year. Wild mushrooms are another seasonal prize, especially chanterelles (Eierschwammerl).

Potatoes (Erdäpfel) feature widely, sometimes in the form of Knödel (dumplings, which may be savoury or sweet). Cabbage (Kohl) is popular: the white variety is often pickled (Sauerkraut), and the red (Rotkraut) served with venison and game dishes.

### SAVOURY SNACKS

**Liptauer:** Goat's or sheep's milk cheese is mixed with paprika, caraway seeds, capers, mustard, chives and onions to create this paste, a staple of Austrian wine bars.

**Maroni:** Roast chestnuts are a winter treat; the aroma of them, toasting over a brazier on a snowy day, is somehow quintessentially Viennese.

**Saure Blunzen:** Blood sausage is marinated in vinegar, thinly sliced and served with brown bread. A popular "beer snack".

**Schmaltzbrot:** Brown bread spread thickly with beef or pork dripping, and eaten with onions and pickles.

**Wiener Schnitzel** should classically be veal, breaded and fried. In Austria it is never served with sauce.

**Rindsgulasch** is the beef version of Hungarian goulash, a rich stew flavoured with paprika and caraway.

**Forelle Blau**, literally "blue trout", is made by poaching an unscaled fish in stock, which gives it a blueish hue.

# The Flavours of Austria: Cakes and Pastries

Few cities in the world can rival Vienna's devotion to all things sweet. The Viennese enjoy cakes mid-morning or afternoon, and set aside time for between-meal snacks. The finest *Torten* (gâteaux), pastries and cakes tend to be found in *Konditoreien*. Traditional Viennese desserts can be found in all good restaurants, and are typically rich. From the classic Viennese *Apfelstrudel* to *Gugelhupf* from Tirol, Austrian desserts carry a regional influence. In Vienna, pastries take pride of place while, to the west, the Italian influence is strong and cakes, ice creams and meringues are preferred.

Poppy seeds

Relaxing over coffee and cake in an elegant Viennese café

## Cakes

The Austrian tradition of cake-baking goes back centuries, with competition fierce between towns and cities to produce the finest. Even in small villages, bakeries try to outdo each other with their sweet creations. Almost every Austrian city now has its trademark cake, with its citizens quick to boast that theirs is the best. The most famous Austrian cake is a Viennese creation, the *Sachertorte*, a rich chocolate cake invented by chef Franz Sacher for Chancellor Metternich in 1832. The signature dish of many an Austrian chef, it should be the first cake the visitor tries – with so much choice on offer, it will be difficult to decide on the second. While the Viennese rave about *Sachertorte*, over in Linz the locals revere their own *Linzertorte* – an almond-based cake usually topped with raspberries. The people of Linz also say that the *Linzertorte* is older, dating back – legend has it – to the 17th century. Around the Hungarian border, they are proud of their *Dobostorte*,

Stollen  Sachertorte  Dobostorte  Esterházytorte
Linzertorte
Some of the many mouthwatering Austrian cakes available

### Viennese Desserts

From *Topfentascherl* (curd cheese envelopes) to *Kastaniereis* (chestnut purée), Vienna's dessert cuisine uses rich and varied ingredients. Fruits such as plums and apples fill featherlight dumplings, pancakes, fritters and strudels, and although *Mehlspeisen* (puddings) translates literally as "dishes with flour", ground hazelnuts or almonds can be used in its place. Nuts play a key role, especially hazels and pine nuts, the latter often featuring in *Apfelstrudel*. More unusual desserts include sweet "pasta" served with poppy seeds to create *Mohnnudeln*, and *Böhmische Omeletten* (Bohemian omelettes) served with whipped cream and prune sauce. Conversely, *Palatschinken* may also be a savoury snack.

Hazelnuts

**Mohr im Hemd**, a hazelnut and chocolate pudding, is served with chocolate sauce and whipped cream.

Display of traditional pastries and cakes in a *Konditorei*

named after the Budapest chef who created it in the 19th century. Its layers of biscuit and chocolate butter cream are topped with a caramel glaze. In Salzburg, the cake of choice is baked meringue, known as *Salzburger Nockerl*, or Salzburg soufflé. *Esterházytorte* also features meringue, layered with a rich hazelnut cream. Stollen is a marzipan-filled fruit cake originally from Germany and now an integral part of an Austrian Christmas. Regional or not, you'll now find all these classic cakes in Vienna and across the country.

## Pastries

In the perfect global village, a place on the main street would always be reserved for an Austrian pastry and coffee shop. That the French collective name for sweet pastry is *Viennoiserie*

underlines the noble Viennese tradition of sweet baking. Austrian legend has it that the nation's café habit began when the Turks left all their coffee behind as they abandoned Vienna after the failed siege of 1529. The *Kipfel*, a light, crescent-shaped pastry (which later became famous as the croissant) also dates from the

Entrance to one of the world-famous Mozart chocolate shops

time of the Turkish siege, its shape being based on the crescent moon in the Ottoman flag. While such symbolism is often lost today, the importance of the café in Austrian society is not. Modern-day Austrians view cafés as extensions of their home, and spend hours reading, chatting and even watching television in them. Treats on offer in cafés will generally include a classic *Apfelstrudel*, *Cremeschnitte* (slices of puff pastry filled with custard and glazed with strawberry fondant), and *Punschkrapferl*, a calorie-packed, pink-fondant-topped pastry laced with rum.

### MOZARTKUGEL

Fine chocolates, presented in colourfully decorated boxes carrying the portrait of Mozart, are probably the quintessential Austrian souvenir. Known in Austria as *Mozartkugel*, the chocolates originated in Salzburg, where Mozart lived while composing *Cosi fan Tutti*, the opera in which he worships chocolate. In 1890, master confectioner Paul Fürst made the first Mozart chocolates by forming small balls of marzipan which he coated in a praline cream and then dipped in warm chocolate. Viennese confectioners soon adopted the technique and even today producers vie with one another as to whose *Mozartkugel* are the best and most authentic.

**Apfelstrudel** rolls paper-thin pastry with apple, sultanas, cinnamon and sometimes pine nuts or poppy seeds.

**Palatschinken** are fat, fluffy crêpes that may be filled with fruit or jam, or served with vanilla or chocolate sauce.

**Topfenknödel** are light curd cheese dumplings rolled in breadcrumbs, fried and served with fruit compôte.

# Cafés and Bars in Vienna

A stalwart of Viennese culture, cafés have played many roles over the centuries and continue to attract a loyal clientele of locals and visitors alike. More than just a place to drink coffee, they are somewhere to linger over a light lunch, or perhaps relax with a newspaper or book. Temples to the Habsburg era, traditional cafés can be found throughout the city and rank highly on visitors' must-see lists. Joining these coffee houses are sleek new cafés and bars serving a range of beverages to quench all thirsts.

The spacious Café Central with its fine Neo-Gothic vaulted ceiling

## The Viennese Café

It may be an exaggeration to call Vienna's cafés the heart of the city, but they are certainly one of its lifelines. Following the Turkish invasions of the 16th and 17th centuries, cafés in Vienna have been important meeting places, and have traced the history of this remarkable city. In Vienna's oldest café, **Café Frauenhuber**, Mozart himself once performed; in **Café Central**, once a gathering spot for writers and free thinkers, Leon Trotsky made revolutionary plans for Russia; Sigmund Freud often took therapy breaks at the traditionally elegant **Landtmann Café**; and the Bohemian-esque **Café Bräunerhof** provided inspiration for renowned writer Thomas Bernhardt.

## Café Culture

An advantage of Vienna's cafés is that you can linger at your table for several hours by ordering just one cup of coffee. Patrons can read newspapers and magazines, provided free of charge, or use their laptops or tablets with the free Wi-Fi. Some establishments have their own

unique selling point: at **Café Prückel**, for example, the bridge tables are set up, while **Café Sperl** is ideal for billiard playing. Literary readings are a favourite at the 200-year-old **Café Dommayer**.

Architecture and design are important elements of café culture, too. **Café Museum**, built in 1899, shows off the talent of Art Nouveau functionalist Adolf Loos. The **Kleines Café** (*Kleines* meaning "little") is a wonder with its nearly Lilliputian proportions. And the splendidly painted Neo-Gothic vaulting is the main feature of Café Central.

At Café Prückel diners can enjoy a game of bridge with their coffee

## Types of Coffee

In most of Vienna's finer cafés, a tuxedoed waiter will serve your coffee, along with a glass of water, on a silver metal tray. But ordering coffee in the first place may be no easy task, as there are at least 20 different types to choose from. Some variations are:
**Kleiner Brauner:** small coffee with milk
**Grosser Brauner:** large coffee with milk
**Kleiner Schwarzer:** small espresso
**Grosser Schwarzer:** double espresso
**Melange:** light Grosser Brauner with steamed milk
**Mokka:** strong black coffee
**Kapuziner:** black coffee with frothed milk
**Franziskaner:** lighter version of the Kapuziner
**Milchkaffee:** half coffee, half milk
**Verlängerter:** espresso with a dash of hot water
**Einspänner:** large glass of Mokka with whipped cream on top and sometimes sprinkled with cocoa
**Eiskaffee:** cold, black, with vanilla ice cream and topped with whipped cream

Coffee is elegantly served on a silver tray with a glass of water

## What to Eat

Café fare ranges from sausages and soups to cakes and pastries. Lunch at Landtmann Café and the mirror-laden **Café Schwarzenberg** can include traditional *Wiener Schnitzel*, while **Demel**, formerly the confectioners to the Habsburg court, offers fancy salads and an array of tantalizing sweets. **Café Diglas** never runs out of over-sized portions of strudels and cream cakes, while **Café Leopold Hawelka** is famous for its *Buchteln* (jam-filled buns), served late into the evening.

The elegant interior of the sophisticated Blaue Bar

## Vienna's Bars

Vienna has an exciting bar scene, with numerous modern bars serving as buzzing alternatives to the more traditional establishments. Fabulous views of the Stephansdom, plus fine mixed drinks, can be had at the rooftop **Skybar** on the pedestrian Kärntner Strasse. Cocktails, including tasty martinis, are served just down the street

at the sophisticated **Loos Bar**. For sumptuous elegance there is nothing like the **Blaue Bar** inside the venerable Hotel Sacher. For a taste of old-fashioned 1950s nightclub glamour, **Eden Bar** is the place to go.

## Austrian Wines in Vienna

Today, Austria produces some world-class wines, from whites such as Grüner Veltliner and Riesling from the Wachau and Kamptal regions, to reds– including Blaufränkisch from Mittelburgenland and Zweigelt from Neusiedlersee – and luscious dessert wines (in styles such as Eiswein and Trockenbeerenauslese) from around the towns of Illmitz and Rust.

Vienna, a wine-growing area in its own right, produces excellent Gemischte Satz, a traditional dry white varietal blend. Most bars in Vienna

feature Austrian wines. **Weinbar Coburg** in Palais Coburg offers a fine range by the glass as does **Wein & Co**, which has several branches around the city.

## Austrian Beers

A large number of beers are produced in Austria, with the light-bodied Märzen the most common. There is also Weissbier (wheat beer), and even an alcohol-free beer, Null Komma Josef, which is made by Vienna's Ottakringer brewery. Also produced by this brewery is the soft Gold Fassl brand, plus a pilsner and an unfiltered Zwickl beer.

The cosy, vaulted-ceiling **Bierhof** serves these and other fine Austrian beers. Most order either a *Seidl* (0.3 litre glass) or the half-litre *Krügel*, but there is also the tiny 0.2 litre *Pfiff*, which is a must served with the single-face sandwiches at **Trześniewski**.

## DIRECTORY

### Cafés

**Café Bräunerhof**
Stallburggasse 2,
1010 Vienna.
**Tel** (01) 512 38 93.
**Map** 2 B4.

**Café Central**
Palais Ferstel,
Herrengasse 14,
1010 Vienna.
**Tel** (01) 533 37 24/61.
**Map** 2 B3.

**Café Demel**
Kohlmarkt 14, 1010
Vienna.
**Tel** (01) 535 17 17-0.
**Map** 2 B4.

**Café Diglas**
Wollzeile 10,
1010 Vienna.
**Tel** (01) 512 57 65.
**Map** 2 C4.

**Café Dommayer**
Dommayergasse 1,
1130 Vienna.
**Tel** (01) 877 54 650.

**Café Frauenhuber**
Himmelpfortgasse 6,
1010 Vienna.
**Tel** (01) 512 53 53.
**Map** 2 C4.

**Café Leopold Hawelka**
Dorotheergasse 6, 1010
Vienna. **Tel** (01) 512 82 30.
**Map** 2 B4.

**Café Museum**
Friedrichstrasse 6, 1010
Vienna.
**Tel** (01) 214 00 620.
**Map** 4 C1.

**Café Prückel**
Stubenring 24, 1010
Vienna.
**Tel** (01) 512 61 15.
**Map** 2 D4.

**Café Schwarzenberg**
Kärntner Ring 17, 1010
Vienna.
**Tel** (01) 512 89 98.
**Map** 4 D1.

**Café Sperl**
Gumpendorferstrasse 11,
1060 Wien.
**Tel** (01) 586 41 58

**Kleines Café**
Franziskanerplatz 3, 1010
Vienna. **Map** 2 C4

**Landtmann Café**
Universitätsring 4, 1010
Vienna. **Tel** (01) 241 001 00.
**Map** 2 A3.

### Bars

**Bierhof**
Naglergasse 13, 1010
Vienna. **Tel** (01) 533 44 28.
**Map** 2 B4.

**Blaue Bar im Sacher Hotel**
Philharmonikerstrasse 4,
1010 Vienna.
**Tel** (01) 514 56 842.
**Map** 2 B5.

**Eden Bar**
Liliengasse 2, 1010
Vienna.
**Tel** (01) 512 74 50.
**Map** 2 C4.

**Loos Bar**
Kärntner Durchgang 10,
1010 Vienna.
**Tel** (01) 512 32 83.
**Map** 2 C4.

**Skybar**
Kärntner Strasse 19,
1010 Vienna.
**Tel** (01) 513 171 20.
**Map** 2 C4.

**Trześniewski**
Dorotheegasse 1, 1010
Vienna.
**Tel** (01) 512 32 91.
**Map** 2 B4.

**Wein & Co**
Jasomirgottstrasse 3–5,
1010 Vienna.
**Tel** 05 07 06-3122 (bar);
05 07 06-3121 (shop).
**Map** 2 C4. (One of several branches)

**Weinbar Coburg**
Coburgbastei 4, 1010
Vienna.
**Tel** (01) 518 18 130.
**Map** 2 D5.

**Wiener Rathauskeller**
Rathausplatz 1,
1010 Vienna.
**Tel** (01) 50 876-1001.
**Map** 1 C3.

# What to Drink in Austria

Austria is a source of excellent wines and good rich beers. Austrian wine is mainly white, though there are excellent local red wines. The wine is drunk before it has finished maturing: *Most*, available from late summer, is the product of the first fermentation of the grapes. In early autumn, this is followed by *Sturm*, a gently fizzing, low-alcohol drink produced by the next stage of grape fermentation. Finally, the *Heuriger*, new-vintage wine, is served. Sweet *Eiswein* is made from grapes left on the vines until the first frosts. Some first-class brandies are also produced – fruit brandies and *Schnaps* are typical drinks.

Vineyards to the north and west of Vienna, producing *Heuriger* wines

Chardonnay from Styria and sparkling wine from Lower Austria

## Austrian Wines

The most popular wine in Austria is Grüner Veltliner *(see below)*; a grape variety that also makes an excellent *Eiswein*. Other varietal wines include superb dry Rieslings, especially from the Wachau, and rich Weissburgunders (Pinot Blanc), Chardonnays and Traminers. Red wines tend to be soft and lush; robust reds come from the Blaufränkisch and Zweigelt grapes.

**Riesling** from the Wachau can be light or full-bodied in style.

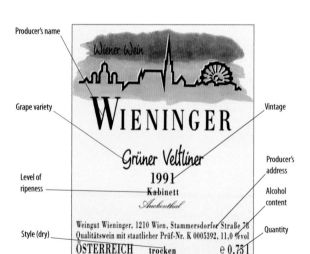

Producer's name

Grape variety

Level of ripeness

Style (dry)

Vintage

Producer's address

Alcohol content

Quantity

**Grüner Veltliner** is a fresh, fruity white grape. It makes a dry wine that is widely available.

**St Laurent** is a soft red wine from the Neusiedler See region; it is rich and stylish.

**Blaufränkisch** is a quality red wine – the best is produced in Burgenland.

*Krügel* or 0.5-litre tankard

*Seidl* or standard 0.3-litre measure

*Krügel* or 0.5-litre of pale beer

*Pfiff*, the smallest measure of beer, a 0.2-litre glass

## Austrian Beers

Good malty beers have been produced in Austria for centuries. The most popular beers are made by the Gösser brewery in Styria – light Gösser Gold, stronger Gösser Spezial and dark, sweet Gösser Stiftsbräu. In Vienna, beer from the local brewery in the Ottakring district, the pale sweet Gold Fassl, is popular although Bavarian-style wheat beers such as Weizengold are also available. The most popular alcohol-free beer in Austria is Null Komma Josef.

Kaiser is a light beer

Weizengold wheat beer

Gösser Spezial, a rich beer

**Bierhof** beer mat advertising a pub in the Haarhof.

**Null Komma Josef** (Nought Point Joseph), an alcohol-free beer.

## Other Austrian Drinks

Austria offers a good range of non-alcoholic fruit juices such as *Himbeersaft* (raspberry juice) and *Johannisbeersaft* (blackcurrant juice). *Almdudler* ("Alpine pasture yodler"), a herbal lemonade, is also a speciality. Fruit is the basis of many types of schnaps (sometimes called *Brand*). This powerful eau-de-vie is distilled from berries such as juniper or fruits such as apricots *(Marillen)* and quince *(Quitten)*. It is worth paying the extra to sample the schnaps from specialists. Mixer drinks are popular: they include *Radler* ("cyclist"), a beer with lemonade. An innkeeper is said to have invented this drink on a hot day when, almost out of beer, he served it to thirsty cyclists.

Apricot schnaps

Wiener Rathauskeller, a popular beer-drinkers' haunt *(see p307)*

# Where to Eat and Drink

## Vienna

### Inner City

**Beaulieu** €
French **Map** 2 B3
*Herrengasse 14–18, 1010*
**Tel** *(01) 532 11 03*
The seafood risotto with saffron
is a popular draw at Beaulieu.
Or go for a plate of delectable
Austrian cheese and breads,
paired with local wines.

**Café Bräunerhof** €
Café **Map** 2 B4
*Stallburggasse 2, A-1010*
**Tel** *(01) 512 38 93*
A lovely red-fronted café offering
standard Viennese delicacies.
The fascinating clientele of
intellectuals and academics
testifies to the café's status as
a cultural icon.

**Café Central** €
Café **Map** 2 B3
*Herrengasse 14, 1010*
**Tel** *(01) 533 37 24 or 61*
This place was once a gathering
point for luminaries in art,
literature, politics and science.
The top-notch two-course lunch
is recommended.

**Café Demel** €
Café **Map** 2 B4
*Kohlmarkt 14, 1010*
**Tel** *(01) 535 17 17-0*
Oozing with style, this venerable
institution is blessed with finesse
and grandeur. Come here to
sample glorious cakes, scones,
sweets and pastries.

**Café Frauenhuber** €
Classic Austrian **Map** 2 C5
*Himmelpfortgasse 6, A-1010*
**Tel** *(01) 512 53 53*
Come here for simple, old-
fashioned Viennese cooking in
a venue that found fame as the
setting of Mozart´s last public
performance in 1791.

**Café Hofburg** €
Café **Map** 2 B4
*Hofburg-Innerer Burghof, 1010*
**Tel** *(01) 24 100-420*
This grand café, attached to the
Sisi Museum, is a great stop-off
point for a coffee or lunch after a
visit to the imperial palace. Classical
piano music every afternoon.

**Café Leopold Hawelka** €
Café **Map** 2 B4
*Dorotheergasse 6, 1010*
**Tel** *(01) 512 82 30*
A meeting point for post-war
writers, this family run eatery
won fame for its desserts, espec-
ially *Buchteln* (Austrian sweet roll).

**Café Prueckel** €
Café **Map** 3 D4
*Stubenring 24, A-1010*
**Tel** *(01) 512 61 15*
A much-loved Viennese café,
with 1950s style decor, offering
excellent coffee, meals and
pastries. A cool, arty crowd.

**Gasthaus Pöschl** €
Gasthaus **Map** 2 C5
*Weihburggasse 17, 1010*
**Tel** *(01) 513 52 88*
Sit down with a crisp chicken
*Schnitzel* with parmesan potatoes

and a glass of Austrian beer in
this laid-back restaurant.

**Gasthaus Reinthaler** €
Gasthaus **Map** 2 B4
*Gluckgasse 5, 1020*
**Tel** *(01) 512 33 66* **Closed** *Sat & Sun*
Locals flock to this friendly
*Gasthaus* for delicious Viennese
lunches such as cabbage rolls
followed by apricot dumplings.

**Konditorei Gerstner** €
Café/Patisserie **Map** 2 B5
*Kärntner Strasse 13–15, 1010*
**Tel** *(01) 526 13 61*
One of the city's greatest pastry-
makers and chocolatiers, and
former supplier of the royal court.
Indulge in heavenly macaroons,
delectable cupcakes or
scrumptious poppy-seed pie.

**Oberlaa** €
Patisserie **Map** 2 B4
*Neuer Markt 16, 1010*
**Tel** *(01) 513 29 36-0*
A treasure trove for the sweet-
toothed, this lovely patisserie
dishes out gorgeous cakes and
fruit-topped pastries. One of
several branches across the city.

**Restaurant Figlmüller** €
Classic Austrian **Map** 2 C4
*Wollzeile 5, 1010*
**Tel** *(01) 512 61 77*
This tiny, cosy restaurant calls
itself the home of *Schnitzel* and
has been serving up huge plates
of Austrian fare for over a century.
Wine only to drink, and no
pastries on offer.

**Trześniewski** €
Café **Map** 2 B4
*Dorotheergasse 1, 1230*
**Tel** *(01) 512 32 91* **Closed** *Sun*
Follow your nose to find this really
popular bakery. Trzesniewski
offers a superb range of local
breads, delicious pastries,
muffins, bagels and cakes.

**Café Mozart** €€
Café **Map** 2 B5
*Albertinaplatz 2, 1010*
**Tel** *(01) 24 100*
Quaint, popular café with an
inexpensive lunch menu. In 1947,
Graham Greene worked on the
screenplay of *The Third Man* here.

Terrace tables at the popular Café Mozart

### Café Sacher
€€
Café      **Map** 2 B5
*Philharmonikerstrasse 4, 1010*
**Tel** *(01) 51 456 661*
One of the city's swankiest addresses is also the authentic home of the *Sachertorte*. A great place to enjoy exquisite coffee and people watch.

### Griechenbeisl
€€
Classic Austrian      **Map** 3 D3
*Fleischmarkt 11, A-1010*
**Tel** *(01) 533 19 77*
Enjoy a *Schnitzel* meal and a few drinks in Vienna's oldest inn. Superb beef fillet and a long wine list. Framed images of such figures as Beethoven and Schubert seem to nod their approval.

---

## DK Choice

### Ilona Stüberl
€€
Classic Austrian      **Map** 2 B4
*Bräunerstrasse 2, 1010*
**Tel** *(01) 533 90 29*
Founded in 1957, this family-run Austro-Hungarian restaurant is a well-respected part of Vienna's culinary scene. A menu in eight languages covers veal, pork, fish, beef and vegetarian dishes. The restaurant also serves salads, pastas, soups and a few hearty desserts. The waiters are amateur historians, well versed in the 1867 unification history of Austria and Hungary under Emperor Franz Josef.

---

### Landtmann Café
€€
Café      **Map** 2 A3
*Universitätsring 4, 1010*
**Tel** *(01) 24 100 100*
Dating from 1873, this is Vienna's most elegant café. Tuck into a full meal or sample a traditional Viennese dessert like stuffed yeast dumplings.

Shady outdoor seating at Oberlaa, a patisserie and confectionery *(see p310)*

The opulent dining area at Café Sacher

### Lebenbauer
€€
Vegetarian      **Map** 2 A3
*Teinfaltstrasse 3, 1010*
**Tel** *(01) 533 55 56*    **Closed** *Sat & Sun*
This upmarket vegetarian restaurant uses mainly organic produce and avoids fat, eggs or flour. Don't miss the pumpkin risotto.

### Ofenloch
€€
Classic Austrian      **Map** 2 B3
*Kurrentgasse 8, 1010*
**Tel** *(01) 533 88 44*    **Closed** *Sun*
Traditional menu with all the usual soups, potato dumplings and *Schnitzel*. The service is a cut above the rest.

### Oswald & Kalb
€€
Classic Austrian      **Map** 2 C4
*Bäckerstrasse 14, 1010*
**Tel** *(01) 512 13 71*    **Closed** *Sun*
Owned by arty patrons, this exciting eatery is set within a vaulted medieval house. Offers some unusual home-made breads and herb-infused oils.

### Palmenhaus
€€
European      **Map** 2 B5
*Burggarten 1, 1010*
**Tel** *(01) 533 10 33*
One of Vienna's plushest venues with a menu to match. Opt for a Carpe Diem breakfast – fresh pineapple, honeycracker, rye bread and jam, and a goat's-cheese omelette.

### Plachutta
€€
Classic Austrian      **Map** 3 D4
*Wollzeile 38, 1010*
**Tel** *(01) 512 15 77*
With several brances across town, this Plachutta plays host to numerous Austrian soap stars and other celebrities. Savour Viennese dishes such as the famous *Tafelspitz* (boiled beef).

### Regina Margherita
€€
Italian      **Map** 2 B4
*Wallnerstrasse 4, 1010*
**Tel** *(01) 533 08 12*
Large choice of organic pizzas and pastas, as well as gluten-free,

vegetarian and lactose-free dishes. There's a good choice of Italian wines.

### Restaurant Kanzleramt
€€
Classic Austrian      **Map** 2 B4
*Schauflergasse 6, 1010*
**Tel** *(01) 533 13 09*
Located next to the Hofburg imperial palace, this place serves traditional fare. Choose from a wide range of specialities such as pork steak with cream sauce.

### Sapori Restaurant
€€
Mediterranean      **Map** 2 B4
*Herrengasse 12, 1010*
**Tel** *(01) 227 80-0*    **Closed** *Sat & Sun*
Tasty, modern takes on delicious Mediterranean fare. The beetroot and anchovy salad with dijon mustard and braised lemon chicken are truly delicious.

### Teahouse Haas & Haas
€€
European      **Map** 2 C4
*Stephansplatz 4, 1010*
**Tel** *(01) 512 26 66*
A 25-year-old institution, this friendly teahouse is known for its inviting courtyard. It expertly delivers a wide selection of small dishes – there are no full meals or dinners.

### Tian
€€
Vegetarian      **Map** 2 C5
*Himmelpfortgasse 23, 1010*
**Tel** *(01) 890 46 65*    **Closed** *Sun & Mon*
This self-proclaimed gourmet restaurant has six- and ten-course tasting menus. All dishes make use of produce grown in the restaurant's own organic garden.

### Trattoria Martinelli
€€
Mediterranean      **Map** 2 B3
*Freyung 3/Palais Harrach, 1010*
**Tel** *(01) 533 67 21*
This beautiful courtyard restaurant in a historic Baroque palace with high arched ceilings offers wonderful food and flawless service. The steak is unbeatable.

**For more information on types of restaurants** *see p301*

## DK Choice

### Vestibül €€
Modern Austrian    **Map** 2 A3
*Universitätsring 2, 1010*
**Tel** *(01) 532 49 99*    **Closed** *Sun*
This accolade-winning kitchen
specializes in seasonal dishes
with everything made from
scratch, be it home-made
stock or elderberry juice.
Great food, reliable service
and a superb location just a
stone's throw from Vienna's
fine cultural venues.

### Walter Bauer €€
Classic Austrian    **Map** 3 D4
*Sonnenfelsgasse 17, 1010*
**Tel** *(01) 512-98 71*    **Closed** *Sat*
Exuding old Viennese charm, this
Michelin-starred restaurant is
famed for its modern
interpretation of local culinary
classics. The smoked eel and
venison dishes are a delight to
the tastebuds.

### Wrenkh €€
Modern Viennese    **Map** 2 C3
*Bauernmarkt 10, 1010*
**Tel** *(01) 533 15 26*    **Closed** *Sun*
Emphasis is placed on regional
food and healthy vegetarian
dishes. Try the mango and
quinoa salad. Lessons are
available in the cooking salon.

### Zum Schwarzen Kameel €€
Classic Austrian    **Map** 2 B3
*Bognergasse 5, 1010*
**Tel** *(01) 533 81 25 11*    **Closed** *Sun*
Step inside this century-old
*Jugendstil* building and be wowed
by an 800-strong wine list. Choose
from dozens of cheeses on a first-
class menu. The wild boar with
red wine is particularly good.

### Fabios €€€
Mediterannean    **Map** 2 B4
*Tuchlauben 4–6, 1010*
**Tel** *(01) 532 22 22*    **Closed** *Sun*
Stunning architecture and dramatic
use of glass and orange-tinted
lighting impress at this restaurant.
The food is outstanding – try the
venison with sage gnocchi.

### Nobu Pop-Up €€€
Japanese    **Map** 2 B5
*Kärtner Ring 1, 1010*
**Tel** *(01) 515 16 553*
Austria's first "new style" Japanese
restaurant opened at the Hotel
Bristol to rave reviews. Traditional
Japanese dishes are infused with
South American flavours:
examples include yellowtail
sashimi with jalapeno, and
Wagyu steak with Peruvian
anticucho sauce.

### Paul €€€
French    **Map** 3 D5
*Johannesgasse 16, 1010*  **Map** 3 D5
**Tel** *(01) 9744 788*    **Closed** *Sun*
As befitting the brasserie motif,
the menu is not extensive. The
decor, too, is rather simple and
modern, unlike many Viennese
traditional establishments. But
the meat and fish dishes are
exquisite, the service attentive
and the reviews positive.

### Le Siècle €€€
Mediterranean    **Map** 3 D5
*Parkring 16, 1010*
**Tel** *(01) 515 17 34 40*
This award-winning restaurant,
located within the Radisson Blu
hotel, is renowned for decadent
dining. Patrons can feast on a
range of delicious dishes,
from caviar and suckling pig
to herb-rubbed roasted lamb
and Chateaubriand.

Café in the magnificent Cupola Hall of
the Kunsthistorisches Museum *(see p313)*

## North of Mariahilfer Strasse

### Amerlingbeisl €
Classic Austrian    **Map** 1 C5
*Stiftgasse 8, 1070*
**Tel** *(01) 526-16 60*
Experiment with the speciality
cocktails and daily specials on
the tiny seasonal menu featuring
excellent dishes such as pasta with
smoked salmon and white wine
cream. The lovely shaded courtyard is ideal for alfresco dining.

### Café Bellaria €
Café    **Map** 2 A5
*Bellariastrasse 6, 1010*
**Tel** *(01) 523-53-20*
At this typical Viennese café,
located behind the Natural
History Museum, the owner
runs operetta and *Lieder*
evenings. The menu offers
traditional Austrian food and
the service is charming.

### Café Eiles €
Café    **Map** 1 B4
*Josefstädter Strasse 2, 1080*
**Tel** *(01) 405 34 10*
This local café remains a favourite
haunt of playwrights and stage
actors. Enjoy great food in an
unassuming setting – faded
black-and-white photographs
chronicle a fascinating past.

### Café Europa €
Classic Austrian    **Map** 4 A1
*Zollergasse 8, 1070*
**Tel** *(01) 526 33 83*
A fixture of the Vienna "scene",
usually filled with dancers and
DJs. Excellent breakfast served for
16 hours a day. The late-night
*Wiener Schnitzel* is delicious.

Vestibül's spacious and airy dining room with marble pillars and arches

Pretty interior at Café Sperl, one of the finest coffee houses in Vienna

### Café Leopold €
Mediterannean **Map** 2 A5
*Museumsplatz 1, 1070*
**Tel** *(01) 523 67 32* **Closed** *Tue & Wed*
Traditional Viennese café that serves innovative dishes. Try the asparagus rocket salad or the green chilli chicken wrap.

### Café Schottenring €
Café **Map** 2 B2
*Schottenring 19, 1010*
**Tel** *(01) 315 33 43*
This coffee house first threw open its doors 130 years ago. Order a *Melange* (an Austrian speciality coffee with steamed milk) rather than a *caffè latte* to avoid the waiter's disapproval.

### Centimetere II €
Classic Austrian **Map** 1 C5
*Stiftgasse 4, 1070*
**Tel** *(01) 470 060 642*
Part of a burger chain (Roman numerals denote each branch), this place also serves huge steaks and sausages.

### La Delizia €
Italian **Map** 1 A3
*Florianigasse 19, 1080*
**Tel** *(01) 406 37 02* **Closed** *Sun*
The pizzas at this Neopolitan-themed restaurant are among the best in the city. Save room for the delicious Neapolitan *gelato* served here.

### Pizzeria Osteria Da Giovanni €
Italian **Map** 1 C5
*Sigmundsgasse 14, 1070*
**Tel** *(01) 523 77 78* **Closed** *Sun*
Cosy Italian pizzeria also serving bruschetta, soups, salads and pastas. Delicious Italian desserts.

### Restaurant Braubräu €
Classic Austrian **Map** 4 A1
*Mariahilfestrasse 47, 1060*
**Tel** *(01) 941 23 32* **Closed** *Sun*
The fun decor of this diner belies the serious regard it holds for its food – try the breaded cheese with plum compote or venison ragout with potato dumplings.

### Schnitzelwirt €
Classic Viennese
*Neubaugasse 52, 1070*
**Tel** *(01) 523 37 71* **Closed** *Sun*
This friendly place serves *Schnitzel* in just about every way imaginable. Large servings and traditional decor.

---

### DK Choice

**Café & Restaurant, Kunsthistorisches Museum** €€
Classic Austrian **Map** 2 B4
*Burgring 5, 1010*
**Tel** *(01) 50 876 10 01*
Enjoy fine dining in the stunning Cupola Hall of the Kunsthistorisches Museum. Beautiful, opulent and grand, the hall provides an idyllic setting for a Sunday brunch or a romantic supper.

---

### Österreicher im MAK €€
Classic Austrian **Map** 3 D4
*Stubenring 5, 1010*
**Tel** *(01) 714 01 21*
Daily set lunches at this stylish restaurant, within the Austrian Museum of Applied Arts, are good value for money. Hugely popular is the elaborate Sunday brunch spread, which includes a guided tour.

### Schnattl €€
Classic Austrian **Map** 1 B3
*Lange Gasse 40, 1080*
**Tel** *(01) 405 34 00* **Closed** *Sat & Sun*
Discerning gastronomes come here for the extensive three- or nine-course tasting menu, which include an array of traditional dishes. Dining in the courtyard is a treat.

### Ulrich €€
Classic Austrian **Map** 1 B5
*Sankt-Ulrichs-Platz 1, 1070*
**Tel** *(01) 96 12 782*
Across from the Baroque church of St Ulrich and perfect for a leisurely brunch, this hip, lively place serves up generous plates of omelettes, eggs and *Schnitzel* until late. Superb desserts.

### Zu ebener Erde und erster Stock €€
Classic Austrian **Map** 1 C5
*Burggasse 13, 1070*
**Tel** *(01) 523 62 54* **Closed** *Sat & Sun*
Charming Viennese café offering the whole range of experiences: from candlelit dinners to set-price meals of classics such as *Schnitzel* and potato dumplings.

## South of the Ring

### Café Museum €
Classic Austrian **Map** 4 C1
*Operngasse 7–Karlsplatz, 1010*
**Tel** *(01) 24 100-620*
Lovely 1800s café that hosted famous artists such as Gustav Klimt and Egon Schiele. Enjoy good Austrian food and evening piano music on weekends.

### Café Schwarzenberg €
Café **Map** 2 C5
*Kärntner Ring 17, 1010*
**Tel** *(01) 512 89 98*
Discover dozens of tea varieties plus great coffee. The glass-fronted cabinet is full of tempting sugar-frosted buns, shiny *Torten* and scrumptious fruit pies.

### Café Sperl €
Classic Austrian **Map** 4 B1
*Gumpendorferstrasse 11, 1060*
**Tel** *(01) 586 41 58*
An ideal place to visit for a simple Austrian breakfast of ham, eggs and freshly baked breads. Lip-smacking lunches, snacks and dinners also available.

### Salm Bräu €
Classic Austrian **Map** 5 E1
*Rennweg 8, 1030*
**Tel** *(01) 799 59 92*
A very popular and good-value eatery with colour-washed walls and good atmosphere. Huge copper brewing vats sit right in the middle of the room.

### Opus €€
Classic Austrian **Map** 5 D1
*Kärntner Ring 16, 1010*
**Tel** *(01) 501 10 389* **Closed** *Mon*
The Opus Restaurant is located in the grand luxury Hotel Imperial, where Austrian monarchs gaze down from gilt frames. Guests are treated like royalty in the plush yet understated dining room and the tables are laden with crystal. An imperial indulgence to savour.

---

### DK Choice

**Restaurant at Eight** €€
Classic Austrian **Map** 5 D1
*Kärntner Ring 8, 1010*
**Tel** *(01) 221 22 38 30*
This slick eatery has a dual personality – light, airy and bustling by day, as well as lively, vibrant and atmospheric by night. The menu changes daily but patrons can expect to see heavy Austrian classics trans-formed into chic, beautifully presented, bite-sized morsels bursting with flavour. Absolutely flawless service.

---

**Anna Sacher** €€€
Classic Austrian **Map** 2 B5
*Philharmonikerstrasse 4, 1010*
**Tel** *(01) 51 456 840* **Closed** *Mon*
One of Vienna's best-loved
high-end traditional dining
venues. The dining room is
adorned with a huge chandelier.
A good selection of wines and
impeccable service.

### DK Choice
**Bristol Lounge** €€€
Classic Austrian **Map** 2 B5
*Kärntner Ring 1, 1010*
**Tel** *(01) 515 16 553*
The gourmet dining room of
the Hotel Bristol, opposite the
Vienna Staatsoper, exudes Art
Deco charm. Open non-stop,
from 7am until midnight, it serves
traditional favourites like venison
*Gulasch* plus international dishes
such as red coconut curry. Dress
up to the nines and revel in
finely honed service.

**Steirereck** €€€
Classic Austrian **Map** 3 D5
*Am Heumarkt 2A/Stadtpark, 1030*
**Tel** *(01) 713 31 68* **Closed** *Sat & Sun*
Steirereck' offers an incredible
seven-course tasting menu –
a luxurious feast of seafood,
poultry and game with such
unusual ingredients as
nasturtium root and goat's liver,
accompanied by honey, rye and
lavender bread.

## Further Afield
**Cafe An-Do** €
Café
*Brunnenmarkt 169*
**Tel** *(01) 308 75 76* **Closed** *Sun*
This lively café serves a variety of
breakfasts all day, with inexpensive
snack-style dishes of chicken
and fish for those who want just
a little something.

**Café Cuadro** €
Café
*Margaretenstrasse 77, 1050*
**Tel** *(01) 544 75 50*
Chrome, beech and opaque glass
lend this café a Scandinavian feel.
Popular with the locals, who come
for the great burgers and beer.

**Café Dialog** €
Café
*Renweg 43, 1030*
**Tel** *(01) 544 75 50*
Eat and drink while reading the
newspapers at this authentic
coffee house, where umpteen
refills are offered. Liquor is served
20 hours a day.

**Café Dommayer** €
Café
*Dommayergasse 1, 1130*
**Tel** *(01) 877 546 50*
This popular café has been taken
over by a chain (which has
resulted in slightly higher prices)
but the cakes are still tasty.

**Café Goldegg** €
European
*Argentinierstrasse 49, 1040*
**Tel** *(01) 505 91 62*
This fine Viennese café near the
Belvedere has leather chairs and
a pool table. The brass beer
pumps are polished to perfection.

**Café Ritter** €
Café
*Ottakringer Strasse 117, 1160*
**Tel** *(01) 486 12 53*
Choose from a range of
breakfasts as well as snacks,
lunches, afternoon teas and dinner.
Special dishes include a delectable
grilled bream with spinach.

**Café Weimar** €
Classic Austrian
*Währinger Str 68, 1090*
**Tel** *(01) 317 12 06*
Traditional and undeniably
charming, with live piano music

and chandeliers. No one is in a
hurry to leave this place. There's
a deli for simple sandwiches
or you can order traditional fare.

**Dellago** €
Italian
*Payergasse 10, 1160*
**Tel** *(01) 95 747 95*
This lovely Italian eatery offers
excellent breakfasts that draw
crowds with fresh fruit, big jugs
of juice, coffee and baskets of
freshly baked Viennese breads
and pastries. For lunch, try the
salmon fettuccine.

### DK Choice
**Kunst-Cafe im
Hundertwasserhaus** €
Café
*Lowengassestrasse 41, 1030*
**Tel** *650 713 86 20*
This small family-run café is
highly praised for its apple
strudel and chai latte. It
displays art objects in the
Hundertwasser style, which
are for sale.

**Das Moped** €
Modern Austrian
*Salmgasse 23, 1030*
**Tel** *(01) 966 11 44*
Extremely popular with a local
young crowd, who enjoy the
modish variations of classic
Viennese favourites – and all at
reasonable prices.

**Rasouli** €
Mediterranean
*Payergasse 12, 1160*
**Tel** *(01) 403 13 47* **Closed** *Mon*
Arrive early for a breakfast of
feta cheese omelette or pancake
stacks, or opt for a lunch of
sausages with chickpeas. The
chicken couscous is heavenly.

**Rote Rübe** €
Vegetarian
*Zieglasse 37, 1070*
**Tel** *(01) 507 9138 60* **Closed** *Mon;
Nov–Apr: Sun*
An art café with a distinct
white- and-red decor, Rote
Rube boasts a completely
meat-free menu. Crêpes and
frittatas fuse Greek flavours
with local produce.

**Strandcafé** €
Classic Austrian
*Florian-Berndl Gasse 20, 1220*
**Tel** *(01) 203 67 47*
Popular Viennese waterfront
food joint. Choose a table
out on the deck or inside,
and enjoy traditional fare at
modest prices.

Pretty façade of the Restaurant Cobenzl *(see p315)*, known for its spectacular views

Stylish dining and bar area at Motto

### Tewa   €
International
*Naschmarkt 672*
**Tel** *(01) 676 847 741*   **Closed** *Sun*
The food here is fresh, exciting and organic. The menu is influenced by Middle Eastern and Indian flavours. Very popular and refreshingly inexpensive.

### Vegetasia   €
Vegetarian
*Ungargasse 57, 1030*
**Tel** *(01) 713 83 32*   **Closed** *Mon & Tue*
This place serves an amazing all-you-can-eat lunchtime buffet – a utopia for hungry vegetarians. Other meal options available.

### Wetter   €
Italian
*Payergasse 13, 1160*
**Tel** *(01) 406 07 75*
This former launderette has been transformed into a busy little eatery. Visit for tasty wholesome northwestern Italian dishes and Ligurian wines.

### Xu's Cooking   €
Vegetarian
*Kaiserstrasse 45, 1070*
**Tel** *(01) 523 10 91*
Nutrition is taken very seriously at Xu's, where vegetarian dishes are rich in proteins, vitamins and minerals and free from mono-sodium glutamate. The buffet is superb value for money.

### Flatschers Restaurant & Bar   €€
Steakhouse
*Kaiserstrasse 113–115, 1070*
**Tel** *(01) 523 42 68*
Popular steak house where smoked meats, beef tartar, chilli steak wrap and decon-structed burgers with umpteen toppings wow a loyal clientele. Do not miss the signature dish – Argentine fillet.

### Le Loft   €€
International
*Praterstrasse 1, 1020*
**Tel** *(01) 906 168 110*
Impressive decor plus dazzling views across the lights of the city, ensure a great atmosphere to go with the excellent French-Austrian menu. Incredible selection of wines.

### Meieri am Stadtpark   €€
International
*Am Heumarkt 2A, 1030*
**Tel** *(01) 713 31 68*
Well-prepared meals are elegantly presented on clear glass plates on white linen tablecloths. Open for breakfast, lunch and late dinners.

### Motto   €€
Classic Austrian
*Schönbrunnerstrasse 30, 1050*
**Tel** *(01) 587 06 72*
The trendy Motto endeavours to emulate an old-fashioned speakeasy, with marble, green leather and low arched ceilings. Guests enter through a plain steel door.

### Palabio Culinaria   €€
Russian
*Annagasse 12, 1010*
**Tel** *(01) 890 22 74*   **Closed** *Sun*
One of seven upmarket Russian eateries in Vienna, this one remains somewhat undiscovered. Organic dishes include bulgur wheat mushroom blinis. The menu features some Italian dishes.

### Restaurant Cobenzl   €€
Classic Austrian
*Am Cobenzl 94, 1190*
**Tel** *(01) 320 51 20*
This historic eatery is in the bright yellow Schloss Cobenzl, where Mozart lived for a time in 1781 and enjoyed the splendid views. The old-fashioned menu features the Viennese delicacy of boiled beef fillet with mustard and herbs.

> ### DK Choice
>
> #### Saint Charles Alimentary   €€
> Vegetarian
> *Gumpendorferstrasse 33, 1060*
> **Tel** *650 97 00 350*   **Closed** *Sun*
> Located in a pharmacy with medicine jars, pill bottles and apothecary gear lining the walls, this quirky eatery focuses on wellness cuisine. The restaurant uses herbs, plants, nuts and seeds with healing properties. Try an aromatic wild root soup or spelt with roast pumpkin and walnuts for a meal that is truly healthy. Book ahead; there are only ten seats.

The elegant interior, complete with an open fireplace, of Bristol Lounge

**For more information on types of restaurants** *see p301*

Guests enjoying the alfresco dining area at Loibnerhof, Dürnstein

**Servitenwirt** €€
Classic Austrian
*Servitengasse 7, 1090*
**Tel** *(01) 315 23 87*
The outdoor seating at wooden
slatted benches and tables is
popular once spring arrives –
so arrive early for lunch here.
The menu changes daily, but is
the usual Viennese fare.

**Split** €€
Croatian
*Hetzendorferstrasse 165, 1130*
**Tel** *(01) 804 09 15* **Closed** *Mon*
Seafood, including lobster, cala-
mari and mussels, is prepared
Croatian-style. Mediterranean
dishes also feature on the menu.

**Mraz und Sohn** €€€
European
*Wallensteinstrasse 59, 1200*
**Tel** *(01) 330 45 94* **Closed** *Sat & Sun*
A creative kitchen serving
beautifully seasoned saddle of
lamb with barley, celery and
capers, as well as a nine-course
menu with a wine pairing.

## Lower Austria and Burgenland

**AMSTETTEN: Stadtbrauhof** €
Classic Austrian **Map** E3
*Hauptplatz 14, A-3300*
**Tel** *(07472) 628 00*
Cheerful bar and restaurant
serving standard wok-fried
dishes, steaks and daily specials.
Wash it all down with locally
brewed beer. It's a popular
place with a young crowd.

**BADEN: Herwig Gasser** €
International **Map** G3
*Hauptplatz 17, A-2500*
**Tel** *(02252) 266 026*
Located right in the middle of
Baden, Herwig Gasser is famous
for its pastries. Pastry-making

lessons are on offer for those
who want to recreate the sweet
treats at home.

**BADEN: Primavera** €€
Gourmet **Map** G3
*Weiburgstrasse 3, A-2500*
**Tel** *(02252) 855 51* **Closed** *Sun–Tue;*
*mid-Jul–mid-Aug*
An award-winning gourmet
restaurant that attracts a
discening clientele of foodies.
The beef and lamb dishes are
particularly popular.

**DÜRNSTEIN: Loibnerhof** €€
Regional **Map** F3
*Unterloiben 7, A-3601*
**Tel** *(02732) 828 900* **Closed** *Mon*
*& Tue*
Family-run restaurant set in a
17th-century house; offers
superb regional dishes, delicious
desserts and excellent wines.

**DÜRNSTEIN:**
**Schloss Dürnstein** €€
International **Map** F3
*Schloss Dürnstein, A-3601*
**Tel** *(02711) 212* **Closed** *Nov–Mar*
It is difficult to imagine a place
more scenic than the terrace of
this castle restaurant overlooking
the blue Danube. International
cuisine and impeccable service.

**GAADEN: Meierei Gaaden** €
Classic Austrian **Map** G3
*Anningerstrasse 5, A-2531*
**Tel** *(02237) 81 43* **Closed** *Mon–Thu*
Light meals feature on the menu
at this popular coffee house and
*jausenstation* (snack bar). Enjoy
sausages and delicious strudels
on the sunny terrace.

**GÖTTELSBRUNN: Jungwirt** €
Wine Tavern **Map** G3
*Landstrasse 36, A-2464*
**Tel** *(02162) 89 43* **Closed** *Mon, Tue*
*& Wed*
Outstanding example of the new
generation of wine taverns in

Lower Austria, with its own
vineyard and vintages. The rustic
high-ceilinged dining room has
a warming central fireplace,
and the cuisine is imaginatively
presented. Try the boiled beef
or the veal.

**GÖTTELSBRUNN:**
**Bittermann Vinarium** €€
Wine Tavern **Map** G3
*Abt Bruno Heinrich Platz 1, A-2464*
**Tel** *(02162) 811 55* **Closed** *Mon*
*& Tue*
Smart wine bar that deals in all
the popular local vintages and
offers innovative cuisine. Ideal
place to sample local delicacies.

**GRAFENEGG:**
**Schlosstaverne Grafenegg** €€
International **Map** F3
*Grafenegg 12, A-3485*
**Tel** *(02735) 26 160* **Closed** *Mon &*
*Tue; Dec–Mar*
A mix of international and
Austrian cuisine with excellent
presentation and service. Just
sitting in the castle dining room
is a treat. When the weather is
fine, dine on the patio.

**HALBTURN:**
**Wieser Knappenstöckl** €€
Classic Austrian **Map** G3
*Schloss Halbturn, 7131*
**Tel** *(02172) 823 90* **Closed** *Mon*
Sample fine Austrian cuisine in
the Schloss Halbturn dining
room. The emphasis is on locally
sourced ingredients, organically
reared cattle and seasonal game.

**HINTERBRÜHL BEI MODLING:**
**Hexensitz** €€
Regional **Map** G3
*Johannesstrasse 35, A-2371*
**Tel** *(02236) 229 37* **Closed** *Mon*
*& Tue*
The best of Austrian country
cuisine prepared and served
by devoted staff in a simple
single-storey building.

**KLOSTERNEUBURG:**
**Poseidon** €
Greek **Map** G3
*Kierlingerstrasse 47a, A-3400*
**Tel** *(02243) 336 43*
Popular Greek restaurant with
authentic fare, which you can
follow with a glass of retsina or a
shot of ouzo. Great decor with
big garden-facing windows.

**KLOSTERNEUBURG: Redinger** €
Wine Tavern **Map** G3
*Agnesstrasse 23, A-3400*
**Tel** *(02243) 379 21* **Closed** *Tues*
A typical *Heuriger* or wine tavern
offering the best of local wines
and a good choice of regional
food. Friendly service.

## KREMS: Kloster Und €€
International **Map** F3
*Undstrasse 6, A-3500*
**Tel** *(02732) 747 45* **Closed** *Sun & Mon*
Atmospheric dining inside the walls of a historic 17th-century monastery, with lovely courtyard seating, a wide-ranging international menu and an extensive wine list.

## KRUMBACH: Triad €€
Gourmet **Map** G4
*Ödhöfen 25, Bad Schönau, A-2851*
**Tel** *(02646) 83 17* **Closed** *Mon & Tue*
Lovely rustic-style restaurant set in an old stable, serving superb-quality modern Austrian cuisine. Ecological and locally sourced ingredients are a priority at this restaurant.

## LACKENDORF:
**Wirtshaus zum Royznyak** €
Classic Austrian **Map** G4
*Hauptsrasse 18, A-7321*
**Tel** *(02619) 673 51* **Closed** *Mon*
You can't mistake the red exterior of this simple and inexpensive bistro-style restaurant. Traditional Austrian dishes are cooked up with creative flair.

## LANGENLOIS:
**Heurigenhof Bründlmayer** €€
Wine Tavern **Map** F3
*Walterstrasse 14, A-3550*
**Tel** *(02734) 28 83* **Closed** *Mon & Tue*
Upmarket *Heuriger* serving the best of the local Grüner Veltliner and Riesling, accompanied either by cold cuts or gourmet dishes featuring game and fish. Lovely courtyard seating.

Simple and understated decor at Heurigenhof Bründlmayer, Langenlois

Impressive Baroque dining space at Nikolaihof Wachau, Mautern

## MARIA TAFERL: Donauterrasse €
Classic Austrian **Map** F3
*Maria Taferl 24, A-3672*
**Tel** *(07413) 63 55*
This restaurant of the Krone & Kaiserhof hotel has an outdoor terrace offering magnificent views over the Danube. The menu celebrates all things classically Austrian.

### DK Choice

## MAUTERN:
**Nikolaihof Wachau** €€
Wine Tavern **Map** F3
*Nikolaigasse 3, A-3512*
**Tel** *(02732) 829 01* **Closed** *Sun–Tue; Dec-Apr*
This historic wine estate with Baroque dining rooms and a historic garden serves delicious local food. The smoked ox-tongue, boiled beef and *saumaise* (a regional meatloaf speciality) are exceptionally well made. The owners use local organic ingredients wherever possible.

## MAYERLING: Gasthof zum Alten €
Classic Austrian **Map** F3
*Mayerling 13, A-2534*
**Tel** *(02258) 22 72* **Closed** *Thu & Fri*
Liver dumpling soup, roast venison and home-made traditional desserts bring locals in their droves to this simple and amazingly inexpensive dining room. There is a garden and flowered terrace.

## MICHELBACH:
**Landgasthof Schwarzwallner** €€
Regional **Map** F3
*Untergoin 6, A-3074*
**Tel** *(02744) 82 41* **Closed** *Tue & Wed*
Home-style food in a farmhouse where guests can dine in the garden in summer or conservatory in winter. Local specialities include *blunzl* (fried black pudding).

## MÖDLING: Babenbergerhof €€
Classic Austrian **Map** G3
*Babenbergergasse 6, A-2340*
**Tel** *(02236) 222 46*
Restaurant, café and bistro attached to the upmarket Hotel Babenbergerhof, where the emphasis is on natural ingredients. A great place to try Austrian classics.

## NECKENMARKT: Zur Traube €
Classic Austrian **Map** G4
*Herrengasse 42, A-7311*
**Tel** *(02610) 422 56*
Lamb, local beef and game feature on the menu at this convivial family restaurant. A garden with picnic tables is available in the summer.

## NEUSIEDL AM SEE:
**Landgasthaus am Nyikospark** €€
Gourmet **Map** G3
*Untere Hauptstrasse 59, A-7100*
**Tel** *(02167) 402 22* **Closed** *Mon & Tue*
Regional gourmet cooking in a contemporary ambience. Enjoy a modern twist on classic dishes such as *Tafelspitz* and freshwater fish. Fine service.

## NEUSIEDL AM SEE: Mole West €€
Gourmet **Map** G3
*Seegelände 9, A-7100*
**Tel** *(02167) 202 05*
A stunning restaurant on the timber-decked lakeshore overlooking the water. Call ahead, as opening hours are determined by the weather.

## PODERSDORF: Dankbarkeit €
Wine Tavern **Map** G3
*Hauptstrasse 39, A-7141*
**Tel** *(02177) 22 23* **Closed** *April–Nov: Wed & Thu; Jan–Mar: Mon, Tue, Wed & Thu*
A country restaurant with its own vineyards, and a menu featuring locally sourced fish, lamb and goose. The summer garden is a perfect setting for a relaxed meal.

**For more information on types of restaurants** *see p301*

**PÖTTSCHING: Der Reisinger** €€
Regional                          Map G3
*Hauptstrasse 83, A-7033*
**Tel** *(02631) 22 12*  **Closed** *Mon–Thu*
This stylish local restaurant offers
good-value regional cooking
with an haute-cuisine flair. The
Sunday buffet brunches are
very popular.

**PURBACH: Kloster am Spitz** €€
International                    Map G3
*Waldsiedlung 2, A-7083*
**Tel** *(02683) 55 19*  **Closed** *Mon–Wed*
Part of a complex that includes
a restaurant, vineyard and hotel,
the Kloster offers a classy menu,
with dishes planned according
to the best seasonal ingredients.

**RUST:**
**Mooslechners Rusterhof** €€
Seafood                          Map G3
*Rathausplatz 18, A-7071*
**Tel** *(02685) 607 93*  **Closed** *Wed*
*& Thu*
Country restaurant and hotel
that serves freshwater fish
from the Neusiedler See, and
regional delicacies such as the
popular, and fiery paprika-fuelled
fish soup.

**SCHÜTZEN AM GEBIRGE:**
**Taubenkobel** €€€
Gourmet                          Map G3
*Hauptstrasse 31–33, A-7081*
**Tel** *(02684) 22 97*  **Closed** *Mon*
*& Tue*
This place, fast featuring on lists
of the world's best restaurants,
presents haute cuisine with flair
and imagination. The menu care-
fully cultivates local produce and
changes according to the best
seasonal ingredients available.
The house wines are first rate.

# Styria

**BAD RADKERSBURG:**
**Romantik Hotel im Park** €€
International                    Map F5
*Kurhausstrasse 5, A-8490*
**Tel** *(03476) 25 710*
Lavish spa hotel offering
top-quality Austrian food in
the gourmet restaurant, and
light bites in the poolside
bar. There is also a restaurant
serving Mediterranean food.

**BAD WALTERSDORF:**
**Safenhof** €€
Classic Austrian              Map F4
*Hauptstrasse 78, A-8271*
**Tel** *(03333) 22 390*  **Closed** *Mon*
Feast on locally sourced beef,
duck and game at this highly
rated, popular restaurant that
mixes the best of Austrian
tradition with international
inventiveness.

**DEUTSCHLANDSBERG:**
**Alpengasthof Koralpenblick** €
Regional                         Map F5
*Rostock 15, Trahütten, A-8530*
**Tel** *(03461) 210*
Lovely guesthouse with a cosy
restaurant that serves organic
Styrian beef, local game, mountain
trout and home-baked bread.

**ETMISSL: Hubinger** €€
Regional                         Map F4
*Etmissl 25, A-8622*
**Tel** *(03861) 81 14*  **Closed** *Mon &*
*Tue, except hols*
Set in an ancient house in the
foothills of the Hochschwab. The
menu here features home-
grown vegetables, naturally
reared cattle and local game.

**FISCHBACH: Zum Forsthaus** €€€
Gourmet                          Map F4
*Fischbach 2, A-8654*
**Tel** *(03170) 201*  **Closed** *Mon & Tue*
Award-winning restaurant
within a wood-panelled 17th-
century house. Come here to
experience the best of local
cuisine, cooked in a creative
way with a light touch.

**GAMLITZ: Jaglhof** €
Wine Tavern                     Map F5
*Sernau 25, A-8462*
**Tel** *(03454) 66 75*  **Closed** *Jan*
*& Feb*
Right in the heart of wine country,
this hotel-restaurant boasts
contemporary design and has a
scenic terrace to woo diners when
the weather is right. Choose from
a great selection of wines.

**GAMLITZ: Sattlerhof** €€€
Gourmet                          Map F5
*Sernau 2a, A-8462*
**Tel** *(03453) 44 54* **Closed** *Sun & Mon;*
*Dec–Feb*
A highly rated Styrian restaurant
that offers an imaginative take on
locally reared meats and home-
grown vegetables.

**GRAZ: Frankowitsch** €
Café                             Map F4
*Stempfergasse 2/4, A-8010*
**Tel** *(0316) 822 212*  **Closed** *Sun*
Downtown patisserie with
a popular pavement terrace.
Serves deli sandwiches, pastries
and typically extravagant
Austrian cakes. Good service.

**GRAZ: Der Steirer** €
Regional                         Map F4
*Belgiergasse 1, A-8010*
**Tel** *(0316) 703 654*
Sample traditional Austrian dishes
and Styrian tapas with local
wines by the glass. Try the fried
chicken. The traditional Sunday
roast meal is a treat.

**GRAZ: thomawirt** €
International                    Map F4
*Leonhardstrasse 40, A-8010*
**Tel** *(0316) 328 637*
Bare-brick bar-restaurant serving
Austrian, fusion and vegetarian
food to a young, professional
crowd. Frequent live music and
DJs in the evenings.

**GRAZ: Anna** €€
Gourmet                          Map F4
*Sackstrasse 3–5, A-8010*
**Tel** *(0676) 969 11 44*  **Closed** *Sun &*
*Mon*
Spectacular atrium restaurant
built into the courtyard of the
Erzherzog Johann hotel. Serves
classic Austrian cuisine with a
Mediterranean twist.

Bright and tasteful interior at Bruno, Graz

**GRAZ: Bruno** €€
Mediterranean **Map** F4
*Sackstrasse 27, A-8010*
**Tel** *(0316) 829 109* **Closed** *Sun*
A central café-restaurant with
pleasant outdoor seating and a
mainly Mediterranean menu.
Good list of international wines.

**GRAZ: Häuserl im Wald** €€
Classic Austrian **Map** F4
*Roseggerweg 105, A-8044*
**Tel** *(0316) 391 1650*
Come here for classic Austrian
dishes at reasonable prices. There
is a playground and petting zoo
in the grounds to keep kids happy.

**GRAZ: Landhauskeller** €€
Classic Austrian **Map** F4
*Schmiedegasse 9, A-8010*
**Tel** *(0316) 830 276* **Closed** *Sun*
This long-established restaurant
is highly rated for its classic
Austrian *Schnitzel* and boiled
beef dishes. Choose from a wide
range of inexpensive set lunches.

## DK Choice

**GRAZ: Magnolia** €€€
International **Map** F4
*Schönaugasse 53, A-8010*
**Tel** *(0316) 823 835* **Closed** *Sat &
Sun*
Located in the Augarten
design hotel, Magnolia has
an outstanding reputation for
contemporary creative cooking.
It has an inexpensive set
lunchtime menu.

**GRÖBMING:**
**Landhaus das Georg** €€
Classic Austrian **Map** E4
*Kulmweg 555, A-8962*
**Tel** *(03685) 227 40*
Modern family hotel with a
restaurant offering a good choice

of local Styrian fare and Adriatic
seafood. Besides the usual meat
dishes, this place also has a
good vegetarian selection.

**GRUNDLSEE: Alpengasthof
Max Schraml** €
Classic Austrian **Map** E4
*Bräuhof 14, 8993*
**Tel** *(03622) 86 42*
This popular *Gasthof*, serving a
wide range of Austrian staples,
has amazing views from its
terrace over Grundlsee and the
Tote Gebirge (Dead Mountains).
The wood-panelled interior is
warm and inviting. Booking
ahead is recommended.

**GRUNDLSEE: Fischkalter** €€
Seafood **Map** E4
*Mosern 19, A-8993*
**Tel** *(0676) 960 59 83* **Closed** *Thu*
Relish delicious fish soup, mountain
trout and freshly caught Grundlsee
fish in this charming wood-
panelled lakeside house.

**HART BEI GRAZ:
Hirschenwirt** €€
Regional **Map** F4
*Rupertistrasse 115, A-8075*
**Tel** *(0316) 465 600* **Closed** *Sun
& Mon*
Popular with Graz residents for
its mix of traditional Austrian
cooking and Styrian specialities.
Enjoy hearty meals in the
summer garden. Dogs are
permitted in the restaurant.

**HOHENTAUERN: Passhöhe** €€
Gourmet **Map** E4
*Hohentauern 110, A-8785*
**Tel** *(03618) 219* **Closed** *Wed*
**This family-run hotel-restaurant
has a loyal clientele and is
renowned for combining
local Styrian cuisine with
Mediterranean influences.**

Stylish seating at the highly rated
Magnolia in Graz

**KITZECK: Kirchenwirt** €€
Regional **Map** F5
*Steinriegel 52, A-8442*
**Tel** *(03456) 22 25* **Closed** *Sun–Tue;
Dec–mid Mar*
Cottage-style restaurant set among
some of Europe's highest vine-
yards. Sample organic Styrian fare
with seasonal delicacies such as
asparagus and pumpkins.

**LEBRING/LEIBNITZ:**
**Gollner** €€
International **Map** F5
*Grazerstrasse 36, Lebring-St
Margarethen, A-8403*
**Tel** *(03182) 25 21* **Closed** *Thu*
A smart family-friendly hotel-
restaurant that dishes out classic
Austrian and international
dishes. It has a lovely garden for
outdoor dining.

**MARIAZELL:**
**Brauhaus Mariazell** €
Classic Austrian **Map** F4
*Wienerstrasse 5, A-8630*
**Tel** *(03882) 25 23* **Closed** *Mon & Tue*
This restaurant serves local,
organic products, accompanied
by palatable light and dark Girrer
beers brewed on the premises.

**MURAU: Hotel Gasthof
Lercher** €€
Classic Austrian **Map** E4
*Schwarzenbergstrasse 10, A-8850*
**Tel** *(03532) 24 31*
Modernized 18th-century hotel-
restaurant in the village centre.
The menu focuses on Styrian
beef dishes and fresh trout from
the local rivers.

**PISTORF: Zur Hube** €€
Gourmet **Map** F5
*Sausal 51, A-8443*
**Tel** *664 221 12 42* **Closed** *Fri & Sat*
Creative cuisine in a rustic
location, with the Austrian–
Central European menu
changing according to season.
Advance booking necessary.

Subtle lighting and romantic interior of Landhauskeller in Graz

For more information on types of restaurants *see p301*

**RAMSAU AM DACHSTEIN:**
**Pehab-Kirchenwirt**                    €
Classic Austrian            Map D4
*Ramsau 62, A-8972*
**Tel** *(03687) 817 32*
Family-run establishment
with farmhouse style decor
offering classic Austrian cuisine.
The emphasis is on seasonally
fresh produce. Also has
a popular beer cellar.

**ST SEBASTIAN/MARIAZELL:**
**Lurgbauer**                          €€
Regional                    Map F4
*Lurg 1, A-3224*
**Tel** *(03882) 37 18*      **Closed** *Mon &*
*Tue May–Oct; Mon–Thu Nov–Apr*
Home-raised beef is the star
item on the menu of this unique
farm-restaurant. Boiled beef
or steak are the standard mains,
followed by home-grown
vegetables. Excellent service.

---

### DK Choice

**TURNAU: Steirereck**            €€
Gourmet                     Map F4
*Pogusch 21, A-8625*
**Tel** *(03863) 20 00*     **Closed** *Mon–*
*Wed*
Located in a gorgeous
ensemble of farm buildings
deep in rural Styria, Steirereck
is renowned throughout the
country for turning the natural
bounty of rural Austria into
haute cuisine. Expect free-range
fowl, locally sourced meats and
freshwater fish, all prepared with
an inventive edge. Steirereck
also offers a good choice of
vegetarian dishes, and some
irresistible traditional desserts.
There is a summer garden
and terrace.

---

# Upper Austria

**AIGEN-SCHLAGL:**
**Bärnsteinhof**                      €€
Regional                    Map E2
*Marktplatz 12, A-4160*
**Tel** *(07281) 62 45*      **Closed** *Wed*
Family-run hotel-restaurant
with a country house ambience.
Offers a blend of Viennese and
rustic Austrian cuisine. Plenty of
vegetarian options as well.

**ATTERSEE:**
**Seegasthof Oberndorfer**       €€
Seafood                     Map D3
*Hauptstrasse 18, A-4864*
**Tel** *(07666) 78 640*      **Closed** *Jan*
Freshwater fish and classic
Austrian *Schnitzel*-type dishes
are the order of the day at this
lakeside hotel-restaurant with
a wonderful terrace.

**BAD GOISERN: Agathawirt**     €
Classic Austrian            Map D4
*St Agatha 10, A-4822*
**Tel** *(06135) 83 41*
A 16th-century hotel-restaurant
with an atmospheric dining
room, the Agathawirt focuses
on fresh ingredients and a
seasonally changing menu
of local meat and poultry.

**BAD ISCHL: Konditorei Zauner** €
Café                        Map D4
*Pfarrgasse 7, A-4820*
**Tel** *(06132) 233 10-20*
In the cake-baking business
since 1832, Zauner is Bad Ischl's
must-visit location for anyone
with a sweet tooth. Study the
display cabinet brimming
with treats before taking a seat
among the chandeliers and
house plants.

---

**EFERDING:**
**Landgasthof Dieplinger**        €
Seafood                     Map E3
*Brandstatt 4, A-4070*
**Tel** *(07272) 23 24*      **Closed** *Thu*
A lovely countryside inn serving
organically raised beef and
lamb with fresh local vegetables.
The house schnapps is particularly
good. Great range of fish dishes.

**GMUNDEN:**
**Seehotel Schwan**               €€
Regional                    Map D3
*Rathausplatz 8, A-4810*
**Tel** *(07612) 633 910*
The menu explores the variety of
the Salzkammergut region, from
fish to free range meat. In fine
weather, dine out on the dock;
inside, the 19th-century rooms
have arched windows.

**GRIESKIRCHEN: Waldschänke** €€
Regional                    Map D3
*Kickendorf 15, A-4710*
**Tel** *(07248) 623 08*     **Closed** *Mon*
*& Tue*
With a seasonally changing menu
overseen by a creative team, this
is a great place to sample rustic,
well-prepared Austrian fare.

**KEFERMARKT: Schlossbrauerei** €
Classic Austrian            Map E3
*Weinberg 2, 4292*
**Tel** *(07947) 71 11*      **Closed** *Mon*
Enjoy beer brewed on the
premises and hearty Austrian
veal and poultry dishes at this
enjoyable castle-restaurant.

**LINZ: Brandl**                       €
Café                        Map E3
*Bismarckstrasse 6, A-4020*
**Tel** *(0732) 773 635-2*   **Closed** *Sun*
This long-standing Linz bakery
also has a sit-down section

Delightful and cosy interior of Konditorei Zauner in Bad Ischl where you can munch your way through a dizzying range of crusty-bread sandwiches, crisp croissants and brioches.

### LINZ: Klosterhof €
Classic Austrian     Map E3
*Landstrasse 30, A-4020*
**Tel** *(0732) 773 373*
Solid Austrian cuisine from sausages to *Gulasch* soup to *Schnitzel* served in a beer-hall restaurant that offers the full range of Stiegl beers.

### LINZ: Cook €€
Fusion     Map E3
*Klammstrasse 1, A-4020*
**Tel** *(0732) 781 305*    **Closed** *Sat & Sun*
Wok-fried salmon and curried herring are on the menu at this inventive Scandinavian-Asian restaurant. An impeccable dining experience is guaranteed.

### LINZ: Royal Bombay Palace €€
Indian     Map E3
*Goethestrasse 34, A-4020*
**Tel** *(0732) 658 605*    **Closed** *Mon*
This centrally located Indian restaurant makes good use of its tandoor oven and has a longer than usual list of vegetarian options as well. Respectable wine list.

### MONDSEE: Jausenstation Holzingerbauer €
Classic Austrian     Map D3
*Oberburgau 12, A-5310*
**Tel** *(06232) 38 41*    **Closed** *Wed, Sat & Sun*
Walk into this traditional wooden-bench *Gasthof* and sample wine, schnapps, cheese-and-sausage cold cuts, home-baked bread and simple Austrian dishes. Outdoor seating under fruit trees.

---

## DK Choice

### MONDSEE: Seehotel Lackner €€
Gourmet     Map D3
*Mondseestrasse 1, A-5310*
**Tel** *(06232) 23 59*    **Closed** *Wed*
This seaside hotel-restaurant on the Mondsee is a wonderful spot for outdoor eating in the summer. There is a lakeside terrace, which has its own barbecue grill and offers fantastic mountain views. The inventive Austrian–French cuisine makes use of the best local ingredients with lamb, venison and freshwater fish featuring prominently on the menu. Kitchen supremo Martin Lackner is a sommelier as well as a chef, ensuring a well-chosen cellar.

Diners enjoying a meal at Austria's first Scandinavian-Asian restaurant, Cook, Linz

### NUSSDORF AM ATTERSEE: Hotel Aichinger €€
International     Map D3
*Am Anger 1, A-4865*
**Tel** *(07666) 80 07*
A hotel-restaurant set in a former brewery offering a wide-ranging menu of Austrian and Mediterranean flavours, with locally raised meat and poultry being the highlights.

### SCHÄRDING: Stiegenwirt €
Classic Austrian     Map D3
*Schlossgasse 2–6, A-4780*
**Tel** *(07712) 307 00*    **Closed** *Thu; Jan–Apr*
A family-run guesthouse and restaurant in a Baroque square, featuring classic Austrian dishes such as *Wiener Schnitzel*, boiled beef and duck.

### ST FLORIAN: Landgasthof zur Kanne €
Classic Austrian     Map E3
*Marktplatz 7, A-4490*
**Tel** *(07224) 42 88*    **Closed** *Mon*
Tucked away in a quiet spot on a cobbled street, this former bakery serves classic Austrian dishes with several vegetarian choices and seasonal game options.

Outdoor tables in the beer garden of Klosterhof, Linz

### ST WOLFGANG: See-Eck €
International     Map D4
*Markt 92, A-5360*
**Tel** *699 1091 6481*    **Closed** *Mon*
Run by a husband-and-wife team, this place is hugely popular with locals. The menu changes regularly but expect a mixture of Italian-inspired and classically Austrian dishes.

### STEYR: Wirtshaus Knapp am Eck €
Classic Austrian     Map E3
*Wehrgrabengasse 15, A-4400*
**Tel** *(07252) 762 69*    **Closed** *Sun & Mon*
The menu here features typical Austrian meat and game dishes presented in modern style in a contemporary-rustic interior. The summer garden is one of Steyr's nicest. Great value for money.

### STEYR: Mader €€
Classic Austrian     Map E3
*Stadtplatz 36, A-4400*
**Tel** *(07252) 533 58*
Austrian staples are handled with flair at this restaurant that is part of a historic city hotel. Guests can choose from a range of dining areas, including an atmospheric vaulted wine cellar.

### TRAUNKIRCHEN: Symposionhotel Post €€
Classic Austrian     Map D3
*Ortsplatz 5, A-4801*
**Tel** *(07617) 23 07*
This classy restaurant set in a traditional coaching inn offers the best of Austrian cuisine and local lake fish. The menu changes according to what is fresh and seasonal.

### WEYREGG AM ATTERSEE: Kaisergasthof €€
Classic Austrian     Map D3
*Weyreggerstrasse 75, A-4852*
**Tel** *(07664) 22 02*
A former imperial post station, this lovely restaurant delivers a blend of Austrian fare and Adriatic seafood. Local freshwater fish and game specialities are also offered.

**For more information on types of restaurants** *see p301*

## Salzburger Land

**ANIF: Schlosswirt zu Anif** €€
Classic Austrian **Map** D4
*Salzachtalbunesstrasse 7, A-5081*
**Tel** *(06246) 721 75* **Closed** *Mon &
Tue Sep–mid-Jul*
A 17th-century house with a shady
summer garden, this traditional
restaurant serves Austrian classics
such as *Schnitzel* with seasonal
game dishes.

**BERGHEIM: Gmachl** €€
International **Map** D3
*Dorfstrasse 35, A-5101*
**Tel** *(0662) 452 124-0*
This hotel-restaurant and spa has
five dining rooms, each with a
slightly different menu. The
emphasis is on Mediterranean
cuisine. Great for vegetarians too.

**FILZMOOS:**
**Johanna Maier & Sohne** €€€
Gourmet **Map** D4
*Am Dorfplatz 1, A-5532*
**Tel** *(06453) 82 04*
Housed in the Relais & Chateaux
Hotel Hubertus, this cooking
school and temple to all things
gourmet is presided over by
Austria's most famous female chef.

**FUSCHL AM SEE: Brunnwirt** €€
Regional **Map** D3
*Wolfgangseestrasse 11, A-5330*
**Tel** *(06226) 82 36* **Closed** *Sun & Mon*
Picture-perfect 15th-century
farmhouse in an idyllic lakeside
setting. Come here to sample
Salzburg cuisine cooked with
locally sourced ingredients.

**FUSCHL AM SEE: Schlick** €€
Seafood **Map** D3
*Seestrasse 12, A-5330*
**Tel** *(06226) 82 37*
Lakeside hotel-restaurant,
Schlick is a good place to sample
Austrian freshwater fish. Large
summer garden for outdoor dining.

**GOLDEGG AM SEE: Hecht** €€
Modern Austrian **Map** D4
*Hofmark 8, A-5622*
**Tel** *(06415) 81 37 0*
Expect top-quality cooking at
this hotel-restaurant. Old-
fashioned cuts such as calf
sweetbreads and brains are
given a modern twist here.

**GOLLING AN DER SALZACH:**
**Döllerer's**
**Geniesserrestaurant** €€€
Gourmet **Map** D4
*Markt 56, A-5440*
**Tel** *(06244) 42 20* **Closed** *Sun & Mon*
Highly regarded gourmet
restaurant that elevates local fare
into the realm of haute cuisine.

Popular dishes include lamb and
beef bred on Alpine pastures as
well as local trout.

---

### DK CHOICE

**HALLWANG/SALZBURG:**
**Pfefferschiff** €€€
Gourmet **Map** D3
*Söllheim 3, A-5300*
**Tel** *(0662) 661 242* **Closed** *Sun
& Mon*
One of Austria's most cele-
brated restaurants, the "Pepper
Ship" serves Austrian and inter-
national cuisine in an elegant
dining room with an antique
ceramic oven.

---

**KAPRUN: Zur Mühle** €
Regional **Map** D4
*Nikolaus Gassner Strasse 62, A-5710*
**Tel** *(06547) 82 54*
This hotel-and-campground
restaurant serves up the standard
Salzburger fare, including plenty
of meat and dumplings, in a
farmhouse-style dining room.

**MAISHOFEN:**
**Schloss Kammer** €€
Regional **Map** D4
*Kammererstrasse 22, A-5751*
**Tel** *(06542) 68202-0*
Relaxed dining in the wood-
panelled rooms of a historic castle.
Local specialities plus Austrian
classics make up the menu.

**MITTERSILL:**
**Meilinger Taverne** €€
Classic Austrian **Map** C4
*Stadtplatz 10, 5730*
**Tel** *(06562) 42 26*
Housed in an 18th-century build-
ing, the Meilinger Taverne is a lively

Signature chocolate *torte* at Hotel Sacher
in Salzburg*)*

local meeting place, thanks to its
emphasis on typically Austrian
dishes at reasonable prices.

**SALZBURG: Bärenwirt** €
Classic Austrian **Map** D3
*Müllner Hauptstrasse 8, A-5020*
**Tel** *(0662) 422 404*
An unpretentious restaurant
popular with the locals and
always reliable for inexpensive
staples such as *Gulasch*, *Schnitzel*
and fried chicken.

**SALZBURG: Pauli Stubm** €
Classic Austrian **Map** D3
*Herrengasse 16, A-5020*
**Tel** *(0662) 843 220* **Closed** *Sun*
This rustic, wood-panelled den
serves comfort food, such as
cheese-and-sausage platters, at
modest prices. Note that it only
opens in the evenings.

**SALZBURG: Pescheria Backi** €
Seafood **Map** D3
*Franz-Josef-Strasse 16b, A-5020*
**Tel** *(0662) 879 778* **Closed** *Sun*
A snug old-fashioned restaurant
set in a shed-like setting, Backi is
dedicated to fresh fish. Good
selection of fruity Slovenian wines.

**SALZBURG: Alt Salzburg** €€
Classic Austrian **Map** D3
*Burgerspitalgasse 2, A 5020*
**Tel** *(0662) 841 476*
A popular and atmospheric
restaurant with a reputation for
quality Salzburg food at reasonable prices. Three dining areas,
including one carved out of rock.

**SALZBURG: Braurestaurant**
**Imlauer** €€
Classic Austrian **Map** D3
*Rainerstrasse 14, A-5020*
**Tel** *(0662) 877 694*
A laid-back restaurant with a
lovely beer garden and bar. This
place has long been favoured for
its traditional Austrian dishes and
locally brewed Stiegl beer.

**SALZBURG: Hölle** €€
Classic Austrian **Map** D3
*Dr-Adolf-Altmann-Strasse 2, A-5020*
**Tel** *(0662) 820 760-0*
Popular and attractive hotel-
restaurant with three beautiful
wood-panelled dining areas
serving Austrian cuisine with
plenty of fowl and game.

**SALZBURG: Hotel Sacher**
**Salzburg** €€
Café **Map** D3
*Schwarzstrasse 5-7, A-5020*
**Tel** *(0662) 889 770*
Sister to the Viennese café of the
same name, Hotel Sacher is home
of the chocolate *Torte (see p304)*
plus many other irresistible cakes.

Homely and intimate setting at Zum Hirschenwirt, Salzburg

**SALZBURG: Triangel**     €€
Classic Austrian     **Map** D3
*Wiener Philharmonikergasse 7,
A-5020*
**Tel** *(0662) 842 229*     **Closed** *Sun
& Mon*
The full range of classic Austrian
culinary repertoire is served here
with contemporary pizazz, in a
modern bistro setting. The daily
specials are worth trying.

**SALZBURG:
Zum Hirschenwirt**     €€
Regional     **Map** D3
*St-Julien-Strasse 21–23, A-5020*
**Tel** *(0662) 872 581*     **Closed** *Sun*
An intimate and traditional hotel-
restaurant that concentrates on
the region's rustic cuisine,
prepared and served with finesse.

**SALZBURG: Esszimmer**     €€€
Gourmet     **Map** D3
*Müllner Hauptstrasse 33, A-5020*
**Tel** *(0662) 870 899*     **Closed** *Sun
& Mon*
Exquisite modern-European
cuisine in a Michelin-starred,
stylishly furnished restaurant.
The three-course lunch menu
is very affordable.

**WERFEN: Obauer**     €€€
Gourmet     **Map** D4
*Markt 46, A-5450*
**Tel** *(06468) 521 20*
An award-winning restaurant
renowned for inventive and
stylish variations of Austrian and
European classics, backed up by
a broad selection of wines.

**ZELL AM SEE:
Steinerwirt 1493**     €€
Classic Austrian     **Map** D4
*Dreifaltigkeitsgasse 2, A-5700*
**Tel** *(06542) 725 02*
At this charming 15th-century
guesthouse, Austrian classics are
prepared with attention to detail.
Most of the traditional features of
this place have been preserved.

# Tyrol and Vorarlberg

**BEZAU: Post**     €€
Gourmet     **Map** A4
*Brugg 35, A-6870*
**Tel** *(05514) 22 07-0*     **Closed** *Tue,
Wed & Thu*
Indulge the senses at this
gourmet restaurant in Hotel Post.
Local lamb is on the menu, and
the beef is served with the
freshest ingredients available.

**BRAZ BEI BLUDENZ: Rössle**     €€
Classic Austrian     **Map** A4
*Albergstrasse 61, A-6751*
**Tel** *(05552) 281 050*     **Closed** *Mon
& Tue*
Charming village guesthouse
with low-ceilinged dining room.
The menu features regional
Bregenzerwald specialities and
set-piece Austrian mains such as
boiled beef and *Schnitzel*.

**BRAZ BEI BLUDENZ: Traube**     €€
Classic Austrian     **Map** A4
*Klostertalerstrasse 12, A-6751*
**Tel** *(05552) 281 03*
A golf-resort hotel with very
traditional wood-panelled
dining rooms serving Vorarlberg
specialities and Austrian classics.

**BREGENZ: Gebhardsberg**     €€
European     **Map** A4
*Gebhardsberg 1, A-6900*
**Tel** *(05574) 425 15*
Stately castle-restaurant with
great views overlooking Bregenz.
Try the Vorarlberg beef, local
fish and suckling pig.

**BREGENZ: Stadtgasthaus**     €€
Gourmet     **Map** A4
*Römerstrasse 5, 6900*
**Tel** *(05574) 4988-0*     **Closed** *Sat
& Sun*
Traditional Austrian dishes are
given a contemporary twist in
the formal dining room of the
Weissen Kreuz Best Western.

**DORNBIRN: Hirschen**     €€
Regional     **Map** A4
*Haselstauderstrasse 31, A-6850*
**Tel** *(05572) 263 63*     **Closed** *Sun*
Quaint guesthouse with
contemporary furnishings. Hirschen
offers good-value meals with a
choice of local specialities and
Austrian standards.

**DORNBIRN: Rickatschwende**     €€
Classic Austrian     **Map** A4
*Dornbirn, A-6850*
**Tel** *(05572) 253 50-408*     **Closed** *Mon*
Modern dining room in a spa
hotel serving Austrian classics
such as *Schnitzel*, boiled beef and
freshwater fish, plus a selection of
vegetarian options.

**EBBS: Der Unterwirt**     €€€
Gourmet     **Map** C4
*Wildbichlerstrasse 38, A-6341*
**Tel** *(05373) 422 88*     **Closed** *Tue
& Wed eve*
Lovingly restored 15th-century
inn with vaulted ceilings, offering
a range of excellent regional and
international dishes – all prepared
with great skill.

**EICHENBERG/BODENSEE:
Schönblick**     €€
Regional     **Map** A4
*Dorf 6, 6911*
**Tel** *(05574) 459 65*     **Closed** *Mon*
Beautiful chalet-style building
offering a well-chosen mixture
of traditional Austrian staples and
local specialities. Well-stocked
wine and cheese cellar.

**ELLMAU: Der Bär**     €€
Gourmet     **Map** C4
*Kirchbichl 9, 6352*
**Tel** *(05358) 23 95*
This Alpine hotel-restaurant
presents a wonderful blend
of Tyrolean tradition and
contemporary European
cooking style. The dining
rooms mix modern and folk
design themes perfectly.

**For more information on types of restaurants** *see p301*

**ELLMAU: Kulimarium** €€€
Gourmet **Map** C4
*Harmstätt 8, A-6452*
**Tel** *(05358) 20 22* **Closed** *Sun–Tue*
Among five eating options in the
Kaiserhof resort hotel, this is the
best. The menu is dictated by the
seasons and local produce.

**FELDKIRCH: Gutwinski** €€
Modern Austrian **Map** A4
*Rosengasse 4–6, A-6680*
**Tel** *(05522) 721 75* **Closed** *Sun*
*& Mon*
The chef here uses regional ingre-
dients for his exquisitely light
creations based on traditional
dishes. In the summer eat in the
courtyard beneath lime trees.

**HIPPACH: Sieghard** €€
Classic Austrian **Map** C4
*Johann-Sponring-Strasse 83, A-6283*
**Tel** *(05282) 33 09* **Closed** *Mon*
An attractive eatery with a
growing reputation for its rustic
cuisine. A balanced menu of
locally raised meats, fowl and
freshwater fish.

**INNSBRUCK: Der Bierwert** €€
Classic Austrian **Map** B4
*Bichlweg 2, A-6020*
**Tel** *(0512) 342 143* **Closed** *Sun*
This traditional restaurant is
located in a chalet-style
guesthouse. The bright dining
room is panelled in pine and has
a menu that changes with the
season, offering asparagus in
spring and game in autumn.

## DK Choice

**INNSBRUCK: Chez Nico** €€
Vegetarian **Map** B4
*Maria-Theresien-Strasse 49,*
*A-6020*
**Tel** *(0650) 451 06 24*
**Closed** *Sun & Mon lunch*
Chez Nico projects itself not
only as a restaurant but an
"arts-workshop", where the
aesthetics of the dining
experience and the quality of
the food are equally satisfying.
Vegetarian cuisine, using
seasonal produce, is accorded
an haute-cuisine approach by
chef Nicolas Curtil, who has
worked in Paris and London.

**INNSBRUCK: Goldener Adler** €€
Classic Austrian **Map** B4
*Herzog-Friedrich-Strasse 6, A-6020*
**Tel** *(0512) 571 11 10*
Located in one of the oldest inns
in Europe, the Golden Eagle serves
traditional Austrian *Schnitzel*,
poultry and game dishes in
rooms where Mozart is believed
to have eaten.

**INNSBRUCK:**
Schwarzer Adler €€
Classic Austrian **Map** B4
*Kaiserjägerstrasse 2, A-6020*
**Tel** *(0512) 587 109*
Locally sourced meat and fish is
elegantly presented and served
in a variety of different rooms at
this rooftop terrace restaurant.
Great views and excellent service.

**ISCHGL: Paznaunerstube** €€€
Gourmet **Map** A5
*Dorfstrasse 95, A-6561*
**Tel** *(05444) 600*
One of two gourmet dining
rooms overseen by Martin Sieber
at the Trofana Royal resort hotel,
and considered the best anywhere in Tyrol. The cellar contains
over 25,000 bottles of wine

**KELCHSAU: Fuchswirt** €€
Classic Austrian **Map** C4
*Oberdorf 11, A-6361*
**Tel** *(05335) 406 30* **Closed** *Tue*
A traditional timber chalet
in an Alpine village offering
Tyrolean dishes as well as
standard Central-European fare.
There is a playground for kids
outside and a large summer
garden dining area.

**KIRCHBERG: Rosengarten** €€€
Gourmet **Map** C4
*Aschauerstrasse 46, A-6365*
**Tel** *(05357) 42 01* **Closed** *Tue & Wed*
Dine in smart and elegant
surroundings at the Rosengarten.
Creative modern-European
cuisine with a pronounced
Mediterranean slant – the menu
changes according to season.

Sleek and sophisticated decor at the
Rosengarten in Kirchberg

**KITZBÜHEL: Kupferstube** €€€
Gourmet **Map** C4
*Griesenauweg 26, A-6370*
**Tel** *(05356) 631 81* **Closed** *Mon*
*& Tue*
Classic Austrian fare meets
European haute cuisine in the
elegant dining room of this
highly acclaimed gourmet
restaurant, presided over by
award-winning chef Stefan Lenz.

**LANDECK: Schrofenstein** €€
Classic Austrian **Map** B4
*Malserstrasse 31, A-6500*
**Tel** *(05442) 623 95*
Historic hotel-restaurant with a
nice blend of Austrian dishes.
Features locally sourced veal and
pork, as well as Mediterranean-
influenced meals.

**LECH: Gasthof Post** €€€
Gourmet **Map** A4
*Dorf 11, A-6764*
**Tel** *(05583) 220 60*
Highly rated traditional ski-resort
with several dining areas. Come
here to enjoy Austrian classics
including the *Kalbs Beuscherl* (a
veal offal dish).

**OBERGURGL: Hohe Mut Alm** €€
Classic Austrian **Map** B5
*Obergurgl, A-64556*
**Tel** *(05256) 6396 32* **Closed** *Oct*
*& Apr*
Tyrolean regional specialities,
Austrian classics and a few
Mediterranean dishes served
with real panache in this
charming Alpine chalet located
at the top of the ski lifts.

**ST CHRISTOPH AM ARLBERG:**
Hospiz Alm €€€
Gourmet **Map** A4
*St Christoph, A-6580*
**Tel** *(05446) 26 11*
One of the very finest dining
establishments in the Alps,
famous for its superbly stocked
wine cellar, great food and
stunning location.

**SÖLL: Söllerstuben** €
International **Map** C4
*Dorf 120, A-6306*
**Tel** *(05333) 53 60*
A welcoming place in the middle
of Söll village offering a broad
range of food, from Austrian
*Schnitzel* to Italian pizza and pasta.

**STUMM: Landgasthof Linde** €€
Regional **Map** C4
*Dorf 2, A-6275*
**Tel** *(05283) 22 77*
One of the best places in the
Zillertal to sample regional
Tyrolean fare prepared and
served with contemporary flair.
Lovely garden dining area.

# Carinthia and East Tyrol

**BAD BLEIBERG:**
**Der Bleibergerhof** €€
Gourmet **Map** D5
*Drei Lärchen 150, A-9530*
**Tel** *(04244) 22 05*
Swish hotel-restaurant serving traditional hearty fare, with a good range of vegetarian and gluten-freen options. It also brews its own beer.

**FELD AM SEE: Lindenhof** €€€
Gourmet **Map** D5
*Kirchenplatz 2, A-9544*
**Tel** *(04246) 22 74*
Lakeside hotel-restaurant offering an eclectic mix of Carinthian and Mediterranean cuisine, with an emphasis on "slow food".

**HERMAGOR: Barenwirt** €
Regional **Map** D5
*Hauptstrasse 17, A-9620*
**Tel** *(04282) 20 52* **Closed** *Mon*
Small-town guesthouse with rustic interiors, serving excellent Carinthian cheese dumplings, fresh vegetables from the garden and seasonal game.

**KLAGENFURT: Felsenkeller** €
Classic Austrian **Map** E5
*Feldkirchner Strasse 141, A-9020*
**Tel** *(0463) 420 130* **Closed** *Sun*
A tunnel-like bar-restaurant burrowed into a small cliff, offering hearty Austrian meat and poultry dishes accompanied by locally brewed Schleppe beer.

**KLAGENFURT: Pumpe** €
Classic Austrian **Map** E5
*Lidmanskygasse 2, A-9020*
**Tel** *(0463) 571 96* **Closed** *Sun*
Popular local tavern in the Gasthaus zum Grossglockner with wood-panelled interiors. The *Gulasch* is legendary.

## DK Choice

**KLAGENFURT:**
**Zum Augustin** €€
Regional **Map** E5
*Pfarrhofgasse 2, A-9020*
**Tel** *(0463) 513 992* **Closed** *Sun*
A speciality beer hall and restaurant, Zum Augustin is the ideal place to sample traditional Carinthian fare such as *Kärntner Nudeln* (ravioli-like parcels stuffed with cheese or potato) or boiled beef. The young crowd keeps the atmosphere upbeat. The Landhaushof room at the back is more formal.

Seating at the popular Parkhotel Tristachersee in Lienz

**KLAGENFURT: Dolce Vita** €€
Mediterranean **Map** E5
*Heuplatz 2, A-9020*
**Tel** *(0463) 554 99* **Closed** *Sat & Sun*
Creative cuisine in contemporary bistro surroundings with an emphasis on Mediterranean cuisine and seafood.

**KRUMPENDORF: Hudelist** €€
Austrian/Scandinavian **Map** E5
*Wieningerallee 12, A-9201*
**Tel** *(04229) 26 81*
This attractive family inn has a wide menu that incorporates a range of Carinthian and Finnish-Scandinavian dishes.

**LIENZ: Gasthof Goldener Fisch** €€
Seafood **Map** D5
*Kärntner Strasse 9, A-9900*
**Tel** *(04852) 621 32*
This 15th-century guesthouse serves fresh trout and pikeperch. In the summer, enjoy a barbecue in the garden with live music.

**LIENZ:**
**Parkhotel Tristachersee** €€
Seafood **Map** D5
*Am Tristachersee 1, 9900*
**Tel** *(04852) 676 66*
On the edge of lake Tristachersee, this eatery offers tranquility, a touch of romance and superb freshwater fish. Large outdoor terrace.

**MATREI: Rauter Stube** €€€
Gourmet **Map** C5
*Rauterplatz 3, A-9971*
**Tel** *(04875) 66 11*
Cosy hotel-restaurant in an idyllic setting. The award-winning chef successfully fuses haute cuisine and East Tyrolean comfort food.

**MILLSTATT: Hotel See-Villa** €€
Classic Austrian **Map** D5
*Seestrasse 68, A 9872*
**Tel** *(04766) 21 02*
A fortified house right by the water, with a lakeside garden

makes this the perfect spot for dining. Sample the freshwater fish and Carinthian staples, or simply enjoy strudel and coffee.

**PÖRTSCHACH: Leon** €€€
Gourmet **Map** E5
*Leonstainerstrasse 1, A-9210*
**Tel** *(04272) 28 16*
Occupying the colonnaded courtyard of the Schloss Leonstain Hotel, this restaurant prepares Carinthian dishes with haute-cuisine flair and imagination.

**PÖRTSCHACH: La Terrasse** €€€
Gourmet **Map** E5
*Töschling 1, A-9210*
**Tel** *(04272) 23 77* **Closed** *Mon*
One of three restaurants in the Schloss Seefels luxury hotel, the award-winning La Terrasse offers fine Austrian–international cuisine and superb lakeside views.

**RADENTHEIN: Die Gartenrast** €
Classic Austrian **Map** D5
*Gartenrastrasse 9, A-9545*
**Tel** *(04246) 20 17*
Charming farmhouse inn famous for its locally reared breaded chicken, although there is other seasonal produce on offer too. Good value for money.

**SPITTAL/DRAU: Edlingerwirt** €
Classic Austrian **Map** D5
*Villacherstrasse 88, A-9800*
**Tel** *(04762) 51 50* **Closed** *Mon & Tue*
A largely local clientele come here to enjoy regional cooking that relies heavily on Carinthian-sourced produce and lots of local game.

**VELDEN: Goritschniggs** €€
Steakhouse **Map** E5
*Seecorso 6, 9220*
**Tel** *(04274) 24 75*
Highly regarded steakhouse run by a family of butchers. As well as organic home-aged beef, pork, veal and grilled chicken feature.

**VELDEN: Landhaus Kutsche** €€
Regional **Map** E5
*Göriacherstrasse 2, 9220*
**Tel** *(04274) 29 46* **Closed** *Wed*
Traditional Carinthian fare in rustic, yet elegant surroundings. Special emphasis on local beef and good service.

**VILLACH: Essbar Caldarium** €€
International **Map** E5
*Hausergasse 27, A-9500*
**Tel** *(0664) 213 91 31* **Closed** *Sat & Sun*
A quiet out-of-town spot near the Leonharder See offering pizzas, seafood and Mediterranean fare. Good value for money.

**For more information on types of restaurants** *see p301*

# SHOPPING IN AUSTRIA

Beyond the elegant designer stores of the capital *(see pp116–17)* are local markets, ceramic factories and craft fairs selling all manner of Austrian wares. In most villages and towns, markets set up in the main square, offering local produce, antiques, knick-knacks and clothes. Craft workshops and factories are scattered throughout the country, creating decorated porcelain, crystal glass and embroidered items, all must-buys for those seeking souvenirs from their trip. Foodies need go no further than the local supermarkets to pick up high-quality treats and decent alcoholic beverages, though wine connoisseurs will enjoy a trip to one of Austria's vineyards. Whether you're after the kitsch, the traditional or something to eat or drink, Austria has something for everyone.

## Opening Hours

Hours are determined by law, not convenience. In general, shops must restrict opening to 66 hours per week, and most places don't open on Sundays at all. As a guide, shops usually open at 8:30 or 9am and close at 6pm or later. Supermarkets open from 8am to 7pm, and until 5pm on Saturdays; The Mercur and Billa supermarkets open until 7:30pm on Fridays.

Smaller shops close at lunchtime for an hour or so. In provincial towns opening hours may vary from those in Vienna and be more suited to local needs.

## Markets and Fairs

Markets and fairs are a firm part of tradition in Austria. The country hosts many international fairs, where anything from household items and construction machinery to modern jewellery or Austrian folk art, wines and spirits are exhibited. For holiday-makers there are countless charming street markets, which are often held

A colourful souvenir glass bauble from Vienna

in the main square of small villages. On Friday and Saturday mornings, some streets close to traffic and fill with market stalls offering produce straight from the farm, including fruit, vegetables, flowers, meat products and freshly baked goods. The market is often surrounded by historic buildings, allowing you to combine shopping and sightseeing.

The Naschmarkt near Karlsplatz in Vienna is the biggest street market in Austria, and besides food and clothes, there is also a flea market on Saturdays. The dates and venues for other flea markets or antiques fairs are published in the daily papers.

## VAT Refunds

With the exception of citizens of other EU countries, visitors to Austria are entitled to reclaim *Mehrwertsteuer* (abbreviated as MwSt), the equivalent of VAT, on their purchases. To claim, each purchase must cost more than €75 and you must tell the vendor that the goods will be exported. Ask for the appropriate refund form and ensure it is signed by the vendor. At customs, present this form, along with your receipt and the goods in their original packaging. It is possible to get an immediate refund at the airport but, if not, you can mail the forms from your home destination. Administrative fees are levied, which makes the average reimbursement no more than 13 percent.

## Smart Shopping

Twice a year, the shopping scene is enlivened by seasonal price reductions; the *Winterschlussverkauf* (winter sales) start in the last week of January, and the *Sommerschlussverkauf* (summer sales) at the end of July. This is a good time to

Wine shop at a private vineyard in Mörbisch

A typical market selling a wide range of goods in Deutschlandsberg

buy clothes, sports equipment and shoes.

Austrians have taken to online shopping in a big way. Those looking for a bargain utilize price comparison websites, like pricerunner.at, which spark keen competition among providers of electronic goods and appliances. Amazon.de is far and away the biggest online site in the country, but universal.at, otto.de and zalando.at are all hugely popular for everything from fashion to fridges. The EU single market and the possibility of delivery within a day or two mean that even visitors spending less than a week in the country can save money shopping online, though it does take the fun out of scouring the stores.

In 2016, the Interspar food chain opened the largest online grocery in Austria. Wine can also be ordered online.

## Ceramics and Crystal Glass

Austria is famous for its beautiful porcelain from the Augarten factory, based in the Viennese park where Johann Strauss once played his waltzes. The decorations on vases, jugs, boxes and tableware reflect the artistic trends of past centuries, from Baroque through Neo-Classical and Biedermeier right up to the present day. Porcelain goods can be purchased in the shop in Graben or from the factory, which is open to visitors. Also worth buying is the attractive hand-painted pottery from Gmunden, with colourful Biedermeier-style flowers, dots and other ornamentation.

Glassware – including superb chandeliers and delicate tableware – tends to be highly original and of high quality, although expensive. Many people also collect imaginative crystal ornaments such as dogs and cats made by Swarovski.

Billa supermarket logo

## Crafts and Folk Art

Hand-embroidered items, such as tablecloths, are also in great demand. The true works of art in this field are ladies' evening purses, miniature pictures and even jewellery, embroidered in *petit point* with 300 to 2,500 stitches per sq cm (2,000 to 16,000 stitches per sq inch). This work, carried out with the aid of a magnifying glass, is so exhausting that it can be done only for a maximum of three hours a day.

Folk costumes are another popular purchase. They vary in the detail, but the woman's *Dirndl* always consists of a skirt with an apron, a waistcoat and a white, often embroidered, blouse, while the man's *Tracht* includes short or calf-length leather trousers and a distinctively cut felt jacket. All this is topped by a jaunty hat adorned with feathers or goats' beard.

## Alcoholic Drinks

Most supermarkets stock a good selection of Austrian wines, but if you head to one of the vineyards you can try before you buy. Visit one of the many vineyards in the Wachau Valley or among the hills of Burgenland, and you can sample the wine, and even buy direct. One of the stronger drinks would also be a good souvenir – try *Weinbrand* (cognac), *Slivovitz* (plum brandy), *Obstler* (fruit brandy) or *Marillenbrand* (apricot brandy).

## Speciality Foods

The most popular purchases from the food counter are Austrian chocolates in their many guises. *Café-Konditorei* (cake shop and café) may post cakes back home for you. You can buy good-quality confectionery at most supermarkets; popular chains include Billa, Merkur, Interspar, Zielpunkt and Hofer, with the latter charging the lowest prices. There are also smaller food stores, especially in the large cities, but these are generally more expensive.

Sweets and confectionery in front of a shop in Salzburg

# What to Buy in Austria

The range of souvenirs available to buy in Austria is vast, ranging from the unashamedly kitsch to the exquisite and delicate. The most typical purchases are chocolates and all kinds of alcoholic drinks, which are often attractively packaged. Quality purchases include Tyrolean costumes and warm winter coats made of loden, as well as attractive Austrian porcelain or glassware, including stunning Swarovski crystal chandeliers.

**Sissi Figurines**
The Austrian people's love for "Sissi", Emperor Franz Joseph's unhappy wife, knows no bounds. It is evident to this day from the many statuettes of the Empress Elisabeth, on sale all over the country.

## Souvenirs

*In a country as reliant on tourism as Austria, the souvenir industry naturally plays an important role, with market stalls, shops and motorway service stations all offering an enormous selection of* Andenken *(souvenirs) designed to help you remember your stay in one of Austria's provinces – and hopefully make you come back for more.*

**Glass Snowstorms**
Glass snowstorms with swirling snowflakes may be considered kitsch by some, yet they remain very popular with tourists, and children are particularly keen on them. Inside, you can see any number of famous Austrian landmarks, such as the Ferris Wheel in the Prater, a symbol of Vienna.

**Wanderhut**
The Tyrolean "walker's hat" is popular with mountain walkers. In winter it protects against the cold; in summer it provides shade from the sun, which can be surprisingly fierce in the mountains.

**Augarten Figurines**
An attractive souvenir from the Augarten porcelain-makers are the delicate, hand-finished porcelain figurines of the famous white Lipizzaner stallions and riders from the Spanish Riding School in Vienna.

**Bells**
In the autumn, the cattle of Tyrol and Vorarlberg are driven down from the Alm, the summer mountain pastures, and the bells around their necks have always fascinated visitors. The bells come in all shapes and sizes, often highly decorated..

**Saddles**
One of the more unusual gifts you can find are intricately made miniature horses with tack and saddles, often copies of items seen in the collections of armouries and arsenals.

**Handicrafts and Folk Art**
Austria is deservedly proud of its local crafts traditions. In specialist shops and markets you can find delicate embroidery and lacework or great wood carvings, such as this mask.

## Ceramics

*Austria is famous for its traditional and modern ceramics. Whether you choose a fine porcelain figure from Augarten or a hand-painted, ornamental faience from Gmunden, it will add elegance to your home. Many factories also produce less costly items, such as busts of famous figures.*

### Modern Ceramics
This curiously shaped tea service, produced at the Provincial College for Ceramics at Stoob, would make a great addition to any tea-time table.

### Bust of Mozart
Mozart memorabilia such as this bust are sold all over Salzburg, a city devoted to marketing the memory of Wolfgang Amadeus Mozart.

### Dinner Service
Attractive ceramic tableware, such as this colourful dinner service from Klagenfurt, will brighten up any kitchen or dining room.

## Confectionery

*Austrian confectioners, of whom many were suppliers to the imperial court, look back with pride on centuries of tradition. The* Sachertorte *has a particularly distinguished history, but there are numerous other specialities worth bringing back for friends and family – if you can bear to share.*

### Mozartkugeln
This speciality chocolate from Salzburg, produced in various shapes and wrapped in silver foil, always bears the portrait of the famous composer.

### Gingerbread
Gingerbread hearts are decorated with a variety of mostly romantic messages and intricate patterns in coloured icing. This one says "Because I love you".

Christmas decorations in a confectionery shop window

## Alcoholic Drinks

*Many Austrian wines have come a long way and are now highly regarded by connoisseurs. The country produces some excellent white dry and dessert wines, as well as the heavier Rieslings. Among the reds, Styrian Schilcher and Blaufränkisch from Burgenland can both compete with Italian and Spanish wines. Austria also produces other alcoholic beverages, including fruit brandies and liqueurs.*

Glass tankards, an excellent present for beer-lovers

### Wine
Specially sealed and bottled at the vineyard where it is produced, a bottle of Austrian wine makes an unusual but welcome present.

### Beer
Although they are little known abroad, Austria produces some very fine beers. Try some of the local brands and take home a few bottles – you won't easily find them elsewhere.

# ENTERTAINMENT IN AUSTRIA

Witty, fun-loving and charming, the Austrians manage to defy pretty much every cliché of what it means to be Germanic. Their sense of *Gemütlichkeit*, or good times, comes alive in the music, festivals, cafés and bars that pulse across the country. *The Sound of Music* may be one of the country's icons, but you are sure to find more than a few of your favourite things in Austria, from a lederhosen-lined folk dance in an old-world village, to extreme sports on mountain tops, to a classical music concert beneath the stars, or the spectacle of a grand opera. Against the setting of breathtaking lakes and mountains, a wide choice of entertainment awaits, both formal and informal. Inevitably, excellent regional cuisine, wine and the ubiquitous beer are also part of the experience.

Mozart's opera *Apollo Et Hyacinthus*, performed at the Salzburg Festival

## Information Sources

Austria is an information-friendly destination. Each province, city and indeed nearly every village of any size boasts a full-service tourist bureau at the ready for walk-in and online information. Here you can find events calendars and back-ground information on anything and everything taking place in the way of music, theatre, festivals and holiday events. Posters announcing current events from concerts to exhibitions are widely displayed in town squares and café windows. For any kind of event in and around Vienna the online guide **eventful** is comprehensive.

For personalized tours, Austria's superb network of professionally accredited English-speaking tour guides, **austriaguides**, is highly recommended. Before travelling, be sure to look at www.austria. info, the website of the **Austrian National Tourist Office**. The website is packed with useful information, including listings of free events and suggestions for saving money.

## Booking Tickets

All the big music festivals offer online booking for seats. Some of them, like the Salzburg Festival, sell out months in advance. It is also possible to buy tickets, sometimes last minute, from ticket agencies.

Money-saving discount cards are available for sightseeing and public transport in all the major cities, including Innsbruck, Linz, Salzburg and Vienna. For a small price, these cards offer significant discounts, or in some cases completely free access to public transport, sights, shopping, dining, and museums. The cards can be purchased upon arrival at your destination, and if you are planning to travel around a lot and take in many of the sights, they can prove to be very economical.

## Free Events

While particular museum and gallery exhibits may charge an entrance fee, access to most churches, markets and galleries in Austria is free of charge, offering a wealth of great architecture, art and history at no cost whatsoever. Attending an organ recital or choir-led mass at one of the country's many Baroque cathedrals is an unforgettable experience. Many churches also offer complimentary guided tours; a small tip for the guide at the end of the tour is customary.

## Facilities for the Disabled

By law, all of Austria's entertainment venues must be accessible to those with mobility problems. Many music and theatre venues also provide help for those with hearing difficulties. To access special facilities and zones, including those for people with hearing problems, it is essential to book in advance.

You will find information on barrier-free access on the Austria National Tourist Office

Guided tour of Salzburg Cathedral, with its fine Baroque architecture

website, as well as on each of the **regional tourism authority websites**. For more information on facilities and information for disabled travellers see pp344–5.

## Religious Celebrations

A predominantly Catholic country, Austrian religious celebrations are pageants of colour in which everyone can participate. Starting at the end of November through to Christmas Day, Christmas markets spring up in towns and cities, offering handicrafts, seasonal foods, mulled wine and heaps of atmosphere. On 5 or 6 December, you may see St Nikolaus wandering the streets accompanied by a scary devil figure, Krampus, who threatens to beat naughty children. Austria's biggest Krampus festival is held in Schladming, Styria, each November.

*Fasching* is the Austrian version of Carnival, and is a let-loose party that takes place just before Lent, with masked balls and socially sanctioned outrageousness.

At Easter, real eggs are hand-painted and hung on plants or twigs called *Palmskatzerln*. At Palm Sunday processions, children carry tall sticks decorated with streamers and pretzels.

## Traditional Music and Dance

When your neighbour lives on the next mountaintop, communicating is a challenge – hence the rise of yodelling as an art form. The melodic throat singing relies on echo and yips and yells, which are impressive performed solo, and mesmerising when sung *en masse*.

Traditional folk celebrations often include the *Schuhplattler*, a lively Austro-Bavarian men's dance with plenty of stamping and clapping.

The *Ländler*, an adaptation of which was performed in *The Sound of Music*, is danced by couples amid much clapping and spinning. The Polka and, ever the pride of Vienna, the Waltz, are classic dances

Local brass band playing at an Austrian beer festival

performed both professionally and at private celebrations.

## Salzburg Festival

Each summer since 1920, the twisting cobblestone streets of Salzburg swell with the thousands attending the **Salzburg Festival**. Around 220,000 spectators attend the 170 performances of classical music, opera and drama.

The main festival halls are located in a prime site in the old town. From Shakespeare and Molière, to Mozart and Beethoven, the Salzburg Festival represents the pinnacle of high culture in Austria. Booking ahead is imperative, and that includes accommodation.

## Casinos

More than 20 casinos across the country, from Bad Gastein to Vienna, offer an assortment

of games of chance – from traditional roulette, blackjack and baccara, to modern day Texas Hold 'em. The minimum age for entrance is 18 years. Blackjack, poker and even slot-machine tournaments are held regularly. The elegant and atmospheric architecture in **Bad Gastein** and **Baden** add a distinctly James Bond element to the thrill.

## Nightlife

Austrian nightlife does not start and stop in Vienna by any means. The provincial capitals certainly hold their own in the party department. There is a wide choice of relaxed pubs, trendy bars, discos and nightclubs that stay open till 4am. For world-class clubbing, DJs Kruder & Dorfmeister have put Austrian electronic music on the map.

Linz boasts some 80 night spots open until well after midnight; its "Bermuda Triangle" bars stay open until the small hours. University towns like Innsbruck and Graz have a young, vibrant feel.

In the countryside there is also action, especially in summer, at the discos and bars around Austria's lakes. All the best late nights culminate in a snack at a Würstlstand, where the party crowd congregate alongside late-night truck drivers.

Viennese Christmas Market, capturing the essence of Christmas spirit

Beer garden and restaurant by Wolfgangsee

## Beer Gardens and Cafés

Café culture is its own form
of entertainment and the
Austrians are rightfully proud
of theirs. People-watching,
reading newspapers mounted
on wooden sticks and chatting
with friends are the norm – all
accompanied by strong coffee
and tasty cakes.

*Kaffee und Kuchen* hour falls
between lunch and dinner,
and precedes a visit to the
*Heurige* (taverns where young,
"early" wine is served).

Drinkers sit comfortably out
in the open under trees drinking
a glass of wine or a *G'spritzn*, a
mixture of wine and soda water.
As a point of etiquette, when
toasting, Austrians always look
each other directly in the eyes;
those failing to do so risk
seven years of bad sex or bad
weather – take your pick.

Cattle decorated with flowers and bells for
the Almabtrieb

## Festivals

From spring to autumn,
hundreds of festivals celebrate
food, wine and the harvest up
and down the country. Austrians
are proud of their traditional
farming methods, and its resulting quality organic products,
which are proudly labelled "bio".

Winemakers of Lower Austria's
**Wine Route** offer local wine,
food and culture at various
regional wine festivals throughout the summer, with live
music, exhibitions, children's
programmes and wine tastings.
Similarly, a variety of summer
festivals are devoted to an
assortment of pumpkins,
cheeses, hams, chocolate,
even a **dumpling festival**,
Knödelfest, in St Johann in Tirol,
where the world's longest
dumpling table takes centre
stage. The Gail Valley hosts a
**Speck festival** in June and a
**cheese festival** in September.

Among the most charming of
the autumn traditions are the
annual **herding festivals**, or
*Almabtrieb*, an annual procession of cows brought down to
their winter barns from the high
summer pastures. The animals
are paraded through the
villages festooned with flowers
and bells. In Styria, the famous
**Lipizzaner Horse Procession**
brings down the horses from
their mountain pastures in this
way to the delight of onlookers.

Not to be outdone by the
animals, humans as performance
art are the focus of the **World
Body Painting Festival** at Poert-
schach. The annual **European**

**Bike Week at Faaker See**, for
Harley-Davidson riders, attracts
its fair share of tattooed bodies.

## Spectator Sports

As national interests go,
skiing and snowboarding take
bronze, silver and gold in the
hearts of Austrians. Don't let
the possibility that you're not
actually taking part stop you
from getting in on the excite-
ment. The ski season kicks
off with the **FIS World Cup
Opening** race at Sölden in late
October, which attracts
thousands of enthusiasts.

The most famous ski race in
the world is held in Kitzbühel
each January. The **Hahnenkamm**
features the dangerous downhill
race, the Streif, and a weekend
of uninhibited partying. More
than 10,000 people come to the
major ski season-ending bash at
Ischgl for the **Top of the
Mountain** concert. In past years,
the free April outdoor concert
has featured Elton John, Tina
Turner, Sting, Lionel Richie, Jon
Bon Jovi, Alanis Morisette, Bob
Dylan and Enrique Iglesias.

While it definitely plays
second fiddle to skiing, soccer
is still a popular sport. As co-
host of the 2008 UEFA European Championships, the cities
of Vienna, Klagenfurt, Salzburg
and Innsbruck all have state-
of-the-art stadiums, and the
opportunity to watch a professional match should not
be missed. The Ernst Happel
Stadion in Vienna is home
to Austria's national team.

Ski contestant on the Hahnenkamm,
in Kitzbühel

## Spas

Part entertainment, part just what the doctor ordered, spa holidays are more than a mere indulgence; they have real health benefits, too. Austria's history of healing waters dates back to the Middle Ages and today there are more than 100 health and wellness spas, treating illness as well as promoting health and beauty treatments. Treatments range from taking the natural Radon mineral water in **Bad Gastein** to aromatherapy, mud plasters and enzyme baths.

The clean, cool lines of the post-modern **Alpen Parks Resort** in Maria Alm is a stylish venue for classic sports massage. In Leogang's **Krallerhof Wellness**

Rogner Bad Blumau spa, designed by Friedensreich Hundertwasser

**Hotel** a full menu of cool and warm, wet and dry saunas and pools bubble and simmer.

Many wellness hotels are located in the mountains, like the five-star spa at **Hospiz** in

St Christoph. High-tech, architecturally ambitious waterworlds are sprouting up across the country: the post-modern minimalism of Langenfeld **Aqua Dome**, two thermal slopeside baths at **Römerbad** and **St Kathrein-Therme** in Carinthia, and the spectacular **Felsentherme** in the Gastein Valley. The dreamscape of Friedensreich Hundertwasser's **Rogner Bad Blumau** thermal spa resort is unforgettable.

## Water Parks

Family fun can be had at **Aquapulco Pirate World** in Bad Schallerbach and **Sonnentherme** at Lutzmannsburg.

# DIRECTORY

## Information Sources

**austriaguides**
🔳 austriaguides.at

**Austrian National Tourist Office**
🔳 austria.info

**eventful**
🔳 vienna.eventful.com

## Booking Tickets

**Concerts Online**
Tel (01) 512 3457.
🔳 concertsonline.com

**oeticket.com**
Tel (0900) 9496 096.
🔳 oeticket.com

**Vienna Classic**
Tel (01) 890 5555.
🔳 viennaclassic.com

**Vienna Ticket Office**
Tel (01) 513 1111
🔳 viennaticketoffice.com

## Facilities for the Disabled

**Austrian Guide to Assisted Holidays**
🔳 barrierefreieurlaub.at

**Regional Tourism Authority Websites:**
Tirol
🔳 handicap.tirol.at

## Upper Austria
🔳 barrierefreies-oberoesterreich.at

## Salzburg Festival

**Salzburg Festival**
Tel (0662) 8045 500.
🔳 salzburger festspiele.at

## Casinos

**Baden Casino**
🔳 casinos.at

**Bad Gastein Casino**
🔳 badgastein.casino.at

## Festivals

**Cheese Festival**
Tel (04715) 8516.
🔳 kaese-festival.at

**Dumpling Festival**
Tel (05352) 633350.
🔳 knoedelfest.at

**European Bike Week at Faaker See**
🔳 europeanbikeweek.com

**Herding Festivals**
🔳 austria.info

**Lipizzaner Horse Procession**
🔳 austria.info

**Speck Festival**
Tel (0650) 428 2000.
🔳 speckfest.at

## Wine Route
🔳 weinstrassen.at

**World Body Painting Festival**
🔳 bodypainting-festival.com

## Spectator Sports

**FIS World Cup Opening**
🔳 skiweltcup.soelden.com

**Hahnenkamm**
🔳 kitzbuehel.com

**Top of the Mountain**
🔳 ischgl.com

## Spas

**Alpen Parks Resort**
Am Gemeindeplatz 2, 5761, Maria Alm. Tel (06584) 2100. 🔳 alpenparks.at

**Aqua Dome**
Oberlängenfeld 140, Langenfeld. Tel (05253) 6400. 🔳 aqua-dome.at

**Bad Gastein**
Sen W Wilflingplatz 1, 5630 Bad Hofgastein. Tel (06432) 33930.
🔳 gastein.com

**Felsentherme**
Bahhofplatz 5, Bad Gastein. Tel (06434) 22230.
🔳 felsentherme.com

## Hospiz
St Christoph 1, 6580 Sankt Christoph am Arlberg. Tel (05446) 2611.
🔳 arlberghospiz.at

**Krallerhof Wellness Hotel**
Rain 6, 5771 Leogang. Tel (06583) 82460.
🔳 krallerhof.com

**Rogner Bad Blumau**
Bad Blumau 100, 8283 Bad Blumau. Tel (03383) 510 00. 🔳 blumau.com

**Römerbad**
Dorfstrasse 74, Bad Kleinkirchheim 9546. Tel (04240) 8282-201..
🔳 thermen.at

**St Kathrein-Therme**
Dorfstrasse 47, Bad Kleinkirchheim 9546 . Tel (04240) 8282301.
🔳 www.badklein kirchheim.com

## Water Parks

**Aquapulco Pirate World**
Promenade 1, 4701 Bad Scallerbach. Tel (7249) 440 610. 🔳 piratwelt.at

**Sonnentherme Lutzmannsburg**
Thermengelände 1, 7361 Lutzmannsburg. Tel (2615) 871 71
🔳 sonnentherme.at

# Live Music and Concerts

It's true: the hills are alive with the sound of music. However, there is much more to be enjoyed musically in this tuneful land than the Rogers and Hammerstein song with angel-voiced siblings. Austria's annual classical music festivals attract the world's premier artists and musicians to stunning venues where the music was often originally performed. Whether in Mozart's Innsbruck or Haydn's Eisenstadt, the settings are as spectacular as the melodies. Also, it is possible to leap out of the cradle of classical music and straight into a leather-lined folk evening, a vibrant electronic music scene or club DJs who are famous across Europe, such as DJ Ötzi. Music programmes vary each year but each of the following summer festivals is an annual extravaganza of sound.

## Opera and Operetta

Though Vienna's reputation for opera is renowned, the rest of the country's operatic contribution should not be overlooked. There is no better example of a perfect harmony of space and sound than the **Bregenz Festival**. Its dramatic 20 m (66 ft) stage floats atop the dark waters of Lake Constance. Past audiences have enjoyed the strains of Puccini's *Tosca* and Verdi's *Il Trovatore*. As well as the headline performance, other musical works are performed in the Festival Hall.

Also on a floating stage, the **Mörbisch Festival on the Lake** celebrated its 50th anniversary of operetta in the open air with *Vienna Blood* by Johann Strauss in 2007.

In Upper Austria, opera-lovers flock in large numbers to Bad Ischl, the former summer hunting retreat of Emperor Franz Josef, for the **Lehár Festival**. Also nearby is the extraordinary Roman quarry of St Margarethen – the backdrop for the **Burgenland Opera Festival**, with productions like Verdi's *Nabucco*.

The **Tiroler Festspiele Erl** is held in the lowlands of Tyrol every July. Founded by the conductor Gustav Kuhn, the festival features a mix of opera and chamber music.

Lighter fare is also on the menu for those new to opera. The **Steyr Music Festival** has staged the musical *Les Misérables* and the Gluck's opera *Orfeo ed Euridice*.

## Classical Concerts and Festivals

The concert halls of Austria are the mainstay of classical music in the country, and you will find concerts in both small towns and the grand provincial capitals. Perhaps most famous is the **Salzburg Festival** (*see p331*), the internationally recognized festival celebrating classical music, opera and drama. Every summer thousands come from around the world to listen to the world's greatest plays and music. The main *Festspielhaus* (festival hall) has been impressively refurbished.

Lesser known is the small **Salzburg Whitsun Festival**, inaugurated by Herbert van Karajan in 1967. It includes delightful comic opera pieces and chamber concerts. The festival takes place annually over four days.

The **Haydn Festival** in Eisenstadt each September is a high point of the concert season calendar. The works of Joseph Haydn are performed against the works of other composers to show contrast in programmes expertly selected by artistic director Dr Walter Reicher.

In September a splendid series of concerts dedicated to the works of Johannes Brahms takes place in Styria, home to the Brahms Museum and the **International Brahms Festival**.

Many festivals guarantee a feast for the ears and eyes. **Allegro Vivo**, Lower Austria's most traditional music festival, opens its doors every summer to thousands of music-lovers who revel in the beautiful castles and Baroque abbeys which form the backdrop for the events. Matinees at Schloss Esterházy offer a wonderful chance to experience the music of Haydn in the very rooms where the composer himself worked and where many of his compositions were first performed. In Radstadt's Renaissance palace of Höch near Flachau, **Paul-Hofhaimer Days** offers early music and new sounds. Past festivals have provided a mixed bag of the oratorios, varying from *The Four Seasons* by Haydn to *King David* by Honecker. Since 1978, the **Innsbruck Festival of Ancient Music** has delighted concert-goers with its grand halls and diverse programmes.

In addition to mixing music with grand architecture, other pleasing combinations are on offer. **Schloss Grafenegg** music festival, the brain child of top contemporary pianist Rudolf Buchbinder, combines tastings from Austria's top vineyards with musical programmes. Similarly, the **Brucknerfest Linz** features a dynamic combination of classical music and modern media art.

The rural charm of the Bregenzerwald region goes well with the music of Schubert and his contemporaries. The annual **Schubertiade** in Schwarzenberg boasts some 70 events, including chamber concerts, song evenings, readings and master classes, attended by more than 70,000 Schubert fans. The little sister to this is Steyr's Schubert Festival, offering a smaller cross-section of Schubert and his contemporaries.

For lovers of something a little edgier, Nikolaus Harnoncourt's Styrian festival of classical music in Graz, **Styriarte**, is one of Austria's leading festivals and is probably the most avant-garde the country has to offer outside Vienna. "Old masters, newly interpreted" is the description often heard.

## Rock, Pop, Jazz and Alternative

Outdoor rock is surrounded by outdoor rocks at the mountain-ringed city of Salzburg's massive **Frequency Festival**. The annual Salzburg outdoor music fest – a full camping experience – means 3 days, 3 stages and 40 bands' worth of rock and alternative music. Previous headliners have included Parov Stelar, the Prodigy and the Kaiser Chiefs.

Heavy metal fans and punk rockers congregate each June in Nickelsdorf for the annual **Novarock** festival, featuring bands like Green Day and Linkin Park.

Blues and boogie are the vibe at the **Kitzbühel Summer Concerts** on five stages across this pretty medieval mountain resort town. A few dozen peaks over in Montafon, the cultural **Montafon Summer** festival comprises some 20 events, including concerts ranging from opera to jazz to classical music, as well as children's entertainment. The best of the international jazz scene meets at the **Jazz Fest in Saalfelden** amid the excellent acoustics of the Congress Center main stage, plus "short cuts" at the Kunsthaus Nexus and free concerts in the town square.

The **Ramsau Festival** stages a pick and mix of culture. Previous years have welcomed the Vienna State Opera Ballet, choreographed by Renato Zanella; the Bratislava Symphonic Orchestra, conducted by Mario Kosik; the L'Orfeo Baroque Orchestra, with light installations by Stefan Knor; Austria's best accordion player Otto Lechner, and many others.

Of course, no discussion of Austrian popular music is complete without mention of **Hansi Hinterseer**, former World Cup ski racer turned aging pop idol. He plays venues across Austria year round, with the stamina one expects of a ski racer.

## Folk Music

You'll find many folk music concerts in Austrian towns and villages throughout the year. Of the annual ones, St Anton's **Folk Music Time** is a favourite. The charming mountain town's pedestrian zone provides the perfect setting for authentic Alpine music, attracting traditionally costumed ensembles from Austria, South Tyrol, Bavaria and Switzerland.

## The Sound of Music

It has been more than 40 years since actor Julie Andrews put Salzburg on the (modern) musical map. The Von Trapp odyssey has become an industry in Salzburg, yet most Austrians have never heard of it. **Sound of Music** tours (of which there are many every day in Salzburg) take in all the big backdrops, and a musical dinner theatre plays all the favourites live.

# DIRECTORY

## Opera and Operetta

**Bregenz Festival**
Tel (05574) 4076.
W bregenzerfestspiele.com

**Burgenland Opera Festival**
Tel (02680) 42042.
W ofs.at

**Lehár Festival**
Tel 43 6132 23839.
W leharfestival.at

**Mörbisch Festival on the Lake**
Tel (02682) 662 100.
W seefestspiele-moerbisch.at

**Steyr Music Festival**
Tel (07252) 53229-0.
W musikfestivalsteyr.at

**Tiroler Festspiele Erl**
Tel (05373) 81000.
W tiroler-festspiele.at

## Classical Concerts and Festivals

**Allegro Vivo**
Tel (02982) 4319.
W allegro-vivo.at

**Brucknerfest Linz**
Tel (0732) 775 230.
W brucknerhaus.at

**Haydn Festival**
Haydn & Esterházy.
Tel (02682) 61866.
W esterhazy.at
W haydnfestival.at

**Innsbruck Festival of Ancient Music**
Tel 01 88088.
W altemusik.at

**International Brahms Festival**
Tel (03852) 3434.
W brahmsmuseum.at

**Paul-Hofhaimer Days**
Tel (06452) 7150.
W radstadt.com

**Salzburg Festival**
Tel (0662) 8045 500.
W salzburger festspiele.at

**Salzburg Whitsun Festival**
Tel (0662) 8045 500.
W salburger festspiele.at

**Schloss Grafenegg**
Tel (02735) 5500.
W grafenegg.com

**Schubertiade**
Tel (05576) 72091.
W schubertiade.at

**Styriarte**
Tel (0316) 825 000.
W styriarte.com

## Rock, Pop, Jazz and Alternative

**Frequency Festival**
W frequency.at

**Hansi Hinterseer**
W hansi-hinterseer.at

**Jazz Fest in Saalfelden**
Tel (06582) 70660.
W jazzsaalfelden.com

**Kitzbühel Summer Concerts**
Tel (05356) 777.
W kitzbuehel.com

**Montafon Summer**
Tel (05556) 722530.
W montafon.at

**Novarock**
W novarock.at

**Ramsau Festival**
Tel (03687) 81833.
W ramsau.com

## Folk Music

**Folk Music Time**
Tel (05446) 22690.
W stantonamarlberg.com

## The Sound of Music

**Sound of Music**
Tel (0662) 883 2110.
W panoramatours.com

# OUTDOOR ACTIVITIES

With its snow-covered mountains, rolling hills and countless lakes, Austria is a veritable adventure playground for sports enthusiasts. Snow sports, naturally, dominate: both Alpine and Nordic skiing prevail, with snowboarding, cross-country skiing and sledging also popular. Some 14,000 km (9,000 miles) of walking trails across the country's pictur-esque hills and mountains are well-trodden by ramblers, while the Tyrolean Alps are a paradise for rock climbers and mountaineers. In a landlocked country, water-lovers head to the lakes, which are perfectly suited for water-skiing, sailing and windsurfing. Throughout Austria there are also superb facilities for more unusual sports, such as glacier climbing, snowshoe walking, bungee jumping and paragliding.

## Skiing

No nation is more serious about its skiing than Austria, the home of racing legends like Franz Klammer and Toni Sailer. From week-long "ski safaris" through wild terrain and nighttime skis, to "bunny runs" down the gentlest of manicured pistes, there are slopes, resorts and ski schools to suit the needs of every visitor.

Austria leads the world in glacier skiing resorts, guarantee-ing some of the best snow in Europe. The best areas are in Upper and Lower Austria and in Styria. Around Innsbruck, one of Austria's largest winter sports areas, year-round skiing is poss-ible, for example on the Stubaital, Glungezer, Axamer Lizum and Mutterer Alm. Pitztal, Sölen and Hintertux all attract World Cup teams training outside of the normal winter season.

Across the county, villages are linked together by ski lifts to form huge, interconnected ski areas, all sharing one lift pass. Saalback-Hinterglemm, for example, has 270 km (168 miles) of groomed slopes.

Taking the lifts, from swift six-person chairlifts to quaint funiculars, can be an adventure in itself. The cable car from St Anton am Arlberg to Valluga only holds five skiers and you must be accompanied by a mountain guide.

*Langlauf*, Nordic or cross-country skiing, is also well catered for in Austria, with numerous attractive routes, called *Loipe*. Almost all cross-country routes have sprint sections, where you can try out your steps.

Austria's real charm comes out in the lower-altitude family-orientated resorts, most of which are found in farming villages. Here, slopes are gentle and rolling, and largely uncrowded, and are perfect for first-time skiers taking their first steps in the snow.

A skier studying an information board in the mountains

## Snowboarding

Snowboarding is one of the most popular winter activities in Austria, after skiing. The sport arrived in Europe from the United States and was originally no more than a teenage craze. It has long since turned serious – Austria was one of the first countries to hold contests in the discipline, and the annual event in Seefeld, Tyrol, has become a meeting ground for the world's snowboarding elite, and something of a snowboarding paradise.

Young people from all over the world come to participate in the Powder Turns, in Kaprun or Saalbach-Hinterglemm. Fun parks, as snowboard "play-grounds" are known, abound and Ischgl has one of the best, with areas for both pros and beginners, not to mention a nearby obstacle course. "Carving", where boarders don stiff boots and gouge out deep ruts at high speeds down hard-packed pistes, is a popular spin on the sport.

Downhill skiing – Austria's most popular sport

## Alternative Snow Sports

As well as skiing, almost all Austrian winter sports centres have facilities for bobsleigh and toboggan rides. Resorts such as Ischgl, in western Tyrol, are famous for their excellent tobogganing facilities. One of, if not the longest prepared runs is the 14-km (9-mile) Wildkogelbahnen, above Neukirchen in the Zell am See region.

If you're not too keen on racing down the mountain, you could try snowshoeing. Most resorts offer guided snowshoe tours far into the high Alps, as well as short walks for the less ambitious. The activity requires very little training and, apart from the cost of snowshoe hire, is relatively inxpensive.

## Mountaineering

Wherever there are mountains you will always find rock climbers and mountaineers. In Austria, the largest organization for climbers is the **Österreichischer Alpenverein**. It has more than 190 regional divisions all over Austria, with its headquarters in Vienna. Besides selling maps, books and guides, the association also runs a library and hires out equipment; maintains mountain hostels and walking trails; organizes skiing courses; and runs a school of mountaineering. Members of the Alpenverein enjoy many discounts, for example on

Mountaineering – a sport for the brave and determined

Ramblers on one of the many mountain trails in summer

accommodation in mountain huts. There is also a meteorological phoneline, giving information about current and expected weather conditions, including any avalanche warnings, which allows rock climbers to make the appropriate arrangements for their expedition.

Fans of scaling rocky heights can also try their hand at ice climbing, in the wild or on artificial ice towers.

## Walking

Rambles on the mountain trails are a popular activity, enjoyed by Austrians and visitors alike. The Rosengartenschlucht, a ravine northwest of Imst whose sides reach 100 m (328 ft) in height, is a particularly attractive walk; you walk along the valley of the Ötz river and get to see the Stuibenfall, Tyrol's tallest waterfall, created by a fallen rock. Many rambling trails can also be found in the region of Eben im Pongau. In Kleinarl, one of the attractions are the *Fackelwanderungen*, nighttime walks with torches. In the Salzkammergut, a lift takes visitors to the top of the Grünberg or Feuerkogel mountains, where many long tourist trails grant walkers views of the fairytale landscape of the Alpine lakes.

There are walking trails all over the country, and they are all clearly signposted and marked on tree trunks by black-and-white signs. As with ski runs, the level of difficulty is indicated by a colour. Local tourist offices have detailed maps of the area. And, if you

don't trust your map-reading skills, you can always hire a mountain guide or join a rambling group.

## Cycling

On the flat, bicycles are an ideal and inexpensive way of getting around. In the mountains, cycling becomes more of an endurance test. Nonetheless, mountain biking is popular and every holiday resort and most hotels offer bikes for hire. Among the most attractive areas for cyclists are the Lake Constance area, the Alpine passes, along the Danube and the Salzburg lakes. Cycling routes are well signposted and appear on most maps.

E-biking, where a normal mountain bike is fitted with a battery, reduces the hard work for those with lower fitness levels. There are specific E-bike regions around the country; Kitzbühel's E-Bike World offers 1,000 km (620 miles) of marked trails.

Visitors on a winter mountain-biking expedition

Yachting marina in Mörbisch

Even in Vienna you can enjoy water sports – along the Old Danube many places hire out water skis, and rowing or sailing boats, without the need to prove any special expertise.

Lastly, the lakes and rivers are perfect for fishing. Local tourist offices will be able to advise you on where the best spots are, and sell you a licence.

Hang gliding – a spectacular sport, enjoyed in Stubaital

## Water Sports

Snow is not the only element that attracts sports enthusiasts to Austria – an abundance of rivers and lakes offer much to the summer visitor, whether it's in the form of relaxation or active holidays. The lovely lakes in the Salzkammergut, especially, are worth exploring.

Austrian lakes come in all shapes and sizes, but most are suitable for swimming and sailing. The largest and most famous are Bodensee (Lake Constance) and Neusiedler See. The latter, easily accessible from Vienna, is a 40-km- (25-mile-) long lake on the Hungarian border, and the venue every weekend for an Olympic-standard regatta. There are sailing and windsurfing schools on many Austrian lakes, and on the larger ones water-skiing and para-skiing are also on offer.

Scuba-diving is also possible at certain times of the year and in designated areas of some lakes, particularly in the Salzkammergut.

Many mountain rivers, particularly those in the western part of Austria, flow through narrow ravines and tumble down in numerous waterfalls. Canoeing, kayaking and rafting expeditions in these regions are offered by adventure firms. An especially popular rafting event takes place along a gorge, the Imster Schlucht, in Tyrol.

## Horse Riding

Horse riding, while not as popular as skiing, also has many followers. Lower Austria has a number of studs which offer a variety of riding holidays. Some hotels, too, own their own horses or have an arrangement with a local riding centre which allows guests to use its facilities. In many resorts, riding lessons can also be booked in indoor arenas, which is especially useful during bad weather or in the winter months.

Even if your visit only takes you to Vienna, you don't have to forego the pleasures of horse riding – the Prater funfair, once the favourite riding course of the Empress Elisabeth, is open to this day to lovers of the sport.

Horse riding is one of the more costly activities, but it is not exorbitant; in Tyrol, for example, 1 hour's riding in winter costs about €15 per person – about the same as you would have to pay for hiring a tennis court.

## Tennis

Indoor tennis courts, which are also open in winter, can be found in many of the larger resorts and hotels; outdoor courts are available in most cities. They are less common in the mountain resorts, which specialize in other sports. Courts tend to be clay rather than grass.

## Extreme Sports

So-called extreme sports, such as rafting, canyoning, speed-boat racing, paragliding, hang gliding, bungee jumping or free climbing, are all well represented in Austria. New companies open every day, offering equipment hire and organized events to tempt the adventurous who are seeking an adrenaline kick. Bungee enthusiasts will enjoy Europe's longest dive at the Europa bridge near Innsbruck, with a jump of 192 m (630 ft).

Horse riding along the shores of Neusiedler See

# DIRECTORY

## Skiing, Snowboarding, Tobogganing

**Ischgl Fun Park**
Tel (50990) 100.
☒ ischgl.com

**Österreichischer Bob- und Skeletonverband**
Haus des Sports,
Stadionstrasse 1, 6020 Innsbruck.
Tel (0512) 20 02 50.
☒ bobskeleton.at

**Tourismusverband Ötztal Arena**
Gemeindestrasse 4,
6450 Sölden.
Tel 057 200 200.
☒ oetztal.com

**Tourismusverband Pitztal**
Unterdorf 18,
A-6473 Wenns im Pitztal.
Tel (05414) 869 99.
☒ pitztal.com

**Tourismusverband Stubai Tirol**
Stubaitalhaus, Dorf 3,
6167 Neustift, Tirol.
Tel (0501) 8810.
☒ stubai.at

**Wildkogelbahn**
Tel (0720) 710 730.
☒ wildkogel-arena.at

**Zell am See/ Kaprun Information**
Bruckner Bundesstrasse 1a, 5700 Zell am See.
Tel (06542) 770.
☒ zellamsee-kaprun.com

## Mountaineering

**Österreichischer Alpenverein**
Olympiastrasse 37, 6010 Innsbruck.
Tel (0512) 595 47.
☒ alpenverein.at

**Österreichischer Touristenklub**
Bäckerstrasse 16, 1010 Vienna. Tel (01) 51 23 844.
☒ oetk.at

**Verband Alpiner Vereine Österreichs**
Bäckerstrasse 16, 1010 Vienna. Tel (01) 512 54 88.
☒ vavoe.at

## Walking

**Europa-Wanderhotels**
Stresweg 8,
9773 Irschen.
Tel (04710) 2780.
☒ wanderhotels.com

## Cycling

**E-Bike World**
Tel (05356) 66660.
☒ e-bikewelt.com

**Mountain Bike Holidays**
Saalfeldnerstrasse 14 ,
5751 Maishofen.
Tel (06542) 80 480-22.
☒ bike-holidays.com

**Radtouren in Österreich**
Freistädterstrasse 119,
4041 Linz.
Tel (0732) 221022.
☒ radtouren.at

## Water Sports

**Austrian Water Ski Federation**
Schottenring 17/3/6,
A-1010 Vienna.
Tel 00151 4624.
☒ oewsv.at

**Österreichischer Segelverband**
Seestrasse 17b,
A-7100 Neusiedl am See.
Tel (02167) 40243-0.
☒ segelverband.at

## Horse Riding

**Reiten in Österreich Reitarena Austria**
Urzenweg 14
A-4121 Altenfelden.
Tel (0664) 424 8036.
☒ tiscover.com

**Urlaub am Bauernhof**
Gabelsbergerstrasse 19,
5020 Salzburg.
Tel (0662) 88 02 02.
☒ farmholidays.com

## Extreme Sports

**Action Club Zillertal**
Hauptstrasse 458,
6290 Mayrhofen.
Tel (05285) 62977.
☒ actionclub-zillertal.at

**Adventure Club Tuxertal**
Lanersbach 376,
A-6293 Tux.
Tel (05287) 87287 or (0676) 307 0000.
☒ natursport.at

**Aktiv-Zentrum**
Neugut 43,
6882 Schnepfau.
Tel 0676 7837878.
☒ aktiv-zentrum.at

**AOS Adventures**
Friedau 1a,
8940 Liezen.
Tel (03612) 253 43.
☒ rafting.at

**Austria-Adventure Sportagentur Raab**
Mairenben 30,
4452 Ternberg.
Tel (0664) 503 13 72.
☒ austria-adventure.at

**Ballonhotel Thaller**
Hofkirchen 51,
8224 Kaindorf.
Tel (03334) 2262.
☒ ballonhotel.at

**Club Aktiv Mölltal**
Flattach 25,
9831 Flattach.
Tel (04785) 410.
☒ cam.at

**Club Montée Adventure Center**
Wolfgangseestrasse 26,
5322 Hof bei Salzburg.
Tel (06228) 30008.
☒ montee.com

**Feelfree**
Platzleweg 5,
6430 Ötz.
Tel (05252) 60350.
☒ feelfree.at

**Flugschule Salzkammergut**
Flachbergweg 46,
4810 Gmunden.
Tel (07612) 730 33.
☒ paragleiten.net

**Freelife**
8923 Palfau 102.
Tel (07230) 79160.
☒ freelife.at

**Jauntal Bungy & Event**
Eis 81, 9113 Ruden.
Tel (04234) 222.
☒ bungy.at

**Österreichischer Aero Club**
Prinz Eugen-Strasse 12,
1040 Vienna.
Tel (01) 505 10 28.
☒ aeroclub.at

**Perschlingtal Ballooning**
Weisching 70,
3071 Böheimkirchen.
Tel (0664) 400 8491.
☒ perschlingtal ballooning.at

**Rupert Hirner Bungy Jumping**
Fressnitzstrasse 31, 8101.
Tel (0316) 688 777.
☒ europabruecke.at

**Salzburg Adventures**
Mehr Abenteuer für Salzburg, Halberstätten 21, 5201 Seekirchen.
Tel (0680) 326 6767.
☒ salzburg adventures.com

# SURVIVAL GUIDE

# PRACTICAL INFORMATION

Austria is a fantastic holiday destination, for both winter and summer. It features numerous attractions, from well-equipped Alpine skiing centres to quaint and charming villages, from fascinating historic sights in the towns to the superb collections of its museums – there is something on offer for every taste and budget. Visitors will have no problems finding suitable accommodation, interesting restaurants or enjoyable cultural events, and the tourist offices in most towns and villages will be only too pleased to furnish you with all the information you require. Alternatively, you can find useful details on the Internet. Many larger towns and all major sights have their own websites with detailed practical and other information.

Visitors crowding around a cable car station in Ischgl

## When to Go

There is no such thing as a low season in Austria – the tourist season continues virtually all year round. The winter season peaks at Christmas and again from the end of January to the beginning of March. Only small hotels and pensions far from winter sports facilities close for the winter. Ski enthusiasts can enjoy the Alps from Christmas until Easter, while walkers are best advised to visit in the spring, when there is a breeze in the air and the mountain slopes are rich with colourful flowers.

The peak of the summer season is between June and August, and this period coincides with the greatest number of cultural events, festivals and village fairs all over the country. At any time of the year you will be able to discover and explore new sides of this multi-faceted country.

## Visas and Passports

Nationals from most European and many overseas countries do not need a visa to enter Austria. Austria is a member of the Schengen agreement, which means that visitors who have a passport valid for a minimum of six months can enjoy stays of up to 90 days, for business or leisure. Exceeding this Schengen limit can lead to a fine. Citizens of EU countries can stay as long as they like.

Dogs and cats require a current rabies vaccination certificate; and motorists need a green card as proof of third-party insurance.

## Travel Safety Advice

Visitors can get up-to-date travel safety information from the **Foreign and Common-wealth Office** in the UK, the **State Department** in the US and the **Department of Foreign Affairs and Trade** in Australia.

## Customs Information

Nationals of EU countries, including Britain and Ireland, may take home unlimited quantities of duty-paid alcoholic drinks and tobacco goods as long as these are intended for their own consumption, and it can be proven that the goods are not intended for resale.

Citizens of the US and Canada are limited to a maximum of 200 cigarettes (or 50 cigars) and 1 litre of spirits (or 2¼ litres of wine or 3 litres of beer). Regulations for residents of Australia and New Zealand vary slightly from these guidelines. Consult the customs offices in your own country or seek advice at airport duty-free shops.

Up-to-date information including details on what may be brought into Austria can be found online at www.bmf.gv.at and in the *Zollinfo* brochure, which is available at the border.

A useful orientation board and map of the local area in Zell am See

## Embassies and Consulates

The embassies for all countries, including the UK, are based in Vienna *(see p344)*. Some larger cities have consulates where you can turn for help.

## Tourist Information

There are many local tourist offices all over Austria, offering useful advice to visitors on accommodation, restaurants, excursions and cultural events *(see p291)*. Offices are sign-posted with the white letter "i" against a green background. Every province also has its own tourist information centre, where you can turn for advice. Tourist offices offer their services free and can supply free leaflets, maps and useful information booklets.

You can plan your trip in advance by getting in touch with travel agencies or the representatives of **Österreich Werbung** (the Austrian National Tourist Office) directly. For cheaper accommodation and information about youth hostels, the multilingual team at **WienXtra-Jugend-Info** in Vienna and **Österreichische Jugend Infos** for the rest of Austria will provide assistance.

## Opening Hours

This guide provides the opening times for each individual sight. Most tourist attractions are closed for Christmas, New Year and Easter holidays as well as the national holiday for workers, May Day. Most businesses start work at around 8am and close at about 4pm. On Fridays, many close early and, even if they do not, it may be hard to get anything done. Most shops are open from Monday to Friday, 8am to 6pm (sometimes 7:30pm) and on Saturdays from 8am until 5pm (in larger cities). Shops are closed on Sundays and public holidays, and in the rural areas some close on Wednesday afternoons.

Banks in many towns are open from 8am until 3pm (5:30pm Thursdays); smaller branches close at lunchtime. All banks are closed at weekends, but cash can be obtained from a *Bankomat* – ATM machine – at any time. Railway stations and hotels should be able to exchange currency.

## Museums and Historic Monuments

The national list of palaces, castles and ruins comprises a staggering 2,000 sights, and this does not even include Austria's countless churches, monasteries or abbeys. Vienna alone has more than 60 museums, and Styria over 200. Of these only 58 are state-owned; the rest belong to church associations, companies or private individuals. Opening hours vary and depend on the local tourist seasons. Museums are generally open from 10am until 4pm or 7pm. Once a week they stay open longer, some until 9pm or even midnight. Some museums close for one day in the week, usually on Monday.

A group of sightseers admiring historic buildings in Innsbruck

Sign of a pension in Lofer

Check times, special events and arrangements for guided tours locally. For groups of 10 people or more it is often possible to arrange the time of the visit in advance – and you may be eligible for a group discount. At the end of a guided tour it is customary to give a small tip.

## Admission Prices

Museum entrance fees can vary from €2 to €8. Admission to historic houses costs about €10–15. Children up to the age of 6 (in some museums, up to the age of 7) are admitted free, and 6–15 year-olds generally pay half price, as do senior citizens (60 and over). There are also reductions for students. Some museums offer family tickets (admitting for example two adults and three children); a few allow free admission on a particular day in the week.

An adult cinema ticket costs around €7–10. Some cinemas sell tickets at lower prices at the beginning of the week.

For theatre tickets you will need to set aside €30–40 or more; musicals cost upwards of €40. Concert tickets start at around €14. The three-day *Wien-Karte* entitles you to unlimited use of all public transport facilities for 72 hours as well as reduced admission to some museums, and discounts in selected shops and restaurants.

Signposts help visitors find the way to Alpine huts

A range of foreign-language newspapers and magazines on a street stand

## Information for Disabled Visitors

Austria is better prepared to receive disabled visitors than most other countries. Accessibility laws mean that allocated parking spaces, ramps and lifts are found almost everywhere. In addition, most forms of transport and attractions will have discounted tickets for those with disabilities. Special parking spaces set aside for disabled drivers are clearly marked as such; if your car displays the appropriate sticker, parking is also free of charge.

For a directory of accessible travel services check the website of the Europe-wide organization **Pantou**. There is also information on barrier-free travel on the Austria National Tourist Office website, as well as on regional tourism authority websites.

**Österreichische Bundesbahn** (ÖBB), the Austrian Federal Railway, offers assistance at railway stations and a 50 per cent discount on tickets for travellers who have an Austrian certificate of disability. Those requiring wheelchairs or special assistance should complete an online form or call 05 171 75 in advance (no certificate is required for this service). Elderly or frail travellers can also request assistance under the ÖBB "barrier free" programme.

## Travelling with Children

Many hotels offer a free stay or reduced rates for children under the age of 12 who share a room with their parents. Children up to the age of 15 pay half fare on public transport; on Sundays, public holidays and during the summer vacations they travel for free. They are also entitled to reduced admission when visiting museums and historic sights. Large supermarkets and also chemists have a department with essential items for babies, as do the Drogeriemarkt and Bipa stores.

## Senior Travellers

Austrians are extremely respectful of older people. Senior travellers are often given priority seating on public transport and many theatres, cinemas, museums and a number of hotels offer generous discounts to travellers with senior ID.

## Information for Students

Students holding an international student card and a valid college ID are entitled to discounts on railways and municipal public transport, as well as reduced admission to cinemas, museums and sports events. They will also be offered accommodation in a *Jugendherberge* (youth hostel) at a lower price. Up-to-date information on accommodation in student dormitories and youth hostels can be obtained from any tourist office.

## Religion

Austria is a predominantly Catholic country – as is apparent from the large number of Catholic churches; Protestants make up just 5 per cent of the population. There is also a fair-sized immigrant population from various national backgrounds and following various religious faiths. Islam is the fastest growing faith, with followers accounting for 6 per cent of the population; this is expected to grow to 10 per cent by 2030. In Vienna, there is a sizeable Jewish community, which has its own synagogues. Cemeteries are communal.

Information board on a building in Innsbruck

## Language

Although all Austrians officially speak German, in reality they speak "Austrian". While this variety of Low German does not differ from High German as markedly as Swiss German, its pronunciation and even some rules of grammar and vocabulary make it quite distinctive. Added to this are several Austrian dialects, which differ from province to province. Austrians are the first to admit that it would be impossible to learn them all in their countless regional varieties. For instance, visitors who know a little German find *Tirolerisch*, the dialect spoken in Tyrol, completely incomprehensible.

You will have few problems making yourself understood in English. Austrians learn the language in school and it is understood throughout the country, especially in the larger cities and main tourist centres.

## Etiquette

Peace and quiet are highly valued by Austrians who live outside the cities. They are friendly and easy-going people who tend to keep up their traditions, especially in the mountainous regions. Austrians, especially the older generation, tend to be very courteous, and they expect the same from visitors.

When asked for directions, Austrians will always do their best to help. The Austrians like polite formalities, though hand-kissing is no longer the norm. It is the exception to go on to first-name terms immediately. Formal forms of address such as Herr Doktor and Herr Ober (head waiter) are often used liberally.

It is worth knowing a few phrases, too, such as, when meeting someone, *Wie geht es Ihnen?*, to enquire after their health. In the morning, *Guten Morgen* is the standard greeting, at lunchtime *Mahlzeit*, later in the day *Guten Tag*. Everywhere and at any time *Grüss Gott* is used, literally "greet God".

## Responsible Tourism

Austria is one of the world's leading destinations for sustainable tourism. About 70 per cent of energy is generated from renewable sources and about 60 per cent of all waste is recycled. In Vienna, recycling bins are

The eco-friendly Hotel Stadthalle in Vienna

located throughout the city and there are numerous organic restaurants, food shops and even clothes stores that promote sustainable fashion.

The *Österreichisches Umweltzeichen* (Austrian Eco-Label) is a seal of approval awarded to hotels and restaurants that meet high environmental and waste-reduction standards. The Stadthalle hotel, near to Westbahnhof station, was the first hotel in Vienna to be awarded the *European Ecolabel* for its green credentials *(see p294)*. This innovative hotel uses solar panels to heat up water and collects rainwater to flush its toilets.

## Electrical Adaptors

The voltage in Austria is 220V AC and the current is 50 Hz. Like the rest of Europe, plugs have two small round pins. It is a good idea to buy a multi-adaptor.

## Time

Austria uses Central European Time (GMT plus 1 hour). Clocks move forward 1hour on the last Sunday in March and back on the last Sunday in October.

# DIRECTORY

## Embassies and Consulates

### Australia
Mattiellistrasse 2–4, 1040 Vienna.
w austria.embassy.gov.au

### Canada
Laurenzerberg 2, 1010 Vienna.
w kanada.at

### Ireland
Rotenturmstrasse 16–18, 1010 Vienna.
w embassyofireland.at

### New Zealand
Mattiellistrasse 2-4/3, A-1040 Vienna.
w nzembassy.com

### United Kingdom
Jauresgasse 12, 1030 Vienna.
w british-embassy.net

### United States of America
Boltzmanngasse 16, 1090 Vienna.
w usembassy.at

## Travel Safety Advice

### Australia
w dfat.gov.au/smartraveller.gov.au

### UK
w gov.uk/foreign-travel-advice

### US
w travel.state.gov

## Tourist Offices

### Österreich Werbung – Austrian National Tourist Office
Margaretenstrasse 1, 1040 Vienna. w austria.info

### Österreichische Judend Infos
Lilienbrunngasse 18/2/41, 1020 Vienna
w jugendinfo.at

### Wiener Tourismusverband
Albertinaplatz & Mayseder-gasse, 1010 Vienna.
w wien.info

### WienXtra-Jugend-Info
Babenbergerstrasse 1, 1040 Vienna.
w jugendinfowien.at

## Tourist Offices Abroad

### London
w austria.info

### New York
w austria.info/us

### Sydney
w austria.info.au

## Information for Disabled Visitors

### Österreichische Bundesbahn
Tel 05 171 75.
w oebb.at

### Pantou
w pantou.org

# Personal Security and Health

Austria is one of Europe's safest countries. Tourists are unlikely to encounter any violence (though there has been an increase in petty crimes such as pickpocketing in busy tourist areas), and the police and emergency services are easy to contact. Visitors should take the normal precautions, such as not leaving baggage unattended. Pharmacists are respected and their advice is often sought by locals. A visit to a pharmacy, unless the problem is serious, is probably the easiest choice if you are feeling unwell.

Typical SOS sign seen on a regular U-Bahn platform

Uniformed police officers (Polizei) in front of a police patrol car

## Police

In Vienna, in the provincial capitals, and in all the larger towns, public order is maintained by the *Polizei*. The police also run lost property departments *(Fundbüro)*, which can be found in any district police station. In the provinces, policing is carried out by the *Gendarmerie*.

## Personal Security and Property

Most areas of Austria are very safe. However, it is always a good idea to consult hotel concierges or speak to your host for local advice. In Vienna, the police has reported a rise in petty crime, such as pickpocketing, at city train stations and on-board trains. There have also been incidents around St Stephen's Cathedral.

In case of a theft, report it without delay to the nearest *Polizeiwache* (police station). Credit and debit card thefts should be reported immediately to your credit card company or bank. Contact your consulate if you lose your passport, or if it is stolen. As a precaution, it is a good idea to leave your passport in your hotel safe and carry a photocopy with you.

## Lost Property

Go to the nearest police station in the first instance. If they do not succeed in restoring your property within seven days, then try the **Lost Property Office**. For property lost on railways or the Schnellbahn, go to the Westbahnhof in Vienna and enquire in person.

## Accidents and Emergencies

Britain has a reciprocal arrangement with Austria whereby emergency hospital treatment is free if you have a British passport. Visits to doctors, dentists or outpatient depart-

ments are also free of charge, but getting free treatment can involve a lot of bureaucracy. Britons should be sure to get a European Health Insurance Card (EHIC), available from post offices or the Internet, before travelling. It is also a good idea to take out full health insurance.

Visitors from other countries should establish what is required to cover their medical treatment, either with their home embassy or with their medical insurance company.

If you are ill, it is best to go to a clinic at a state hospital. In Vienna, the main hospital (and the largest in Europe) is the **Allgemeines Krankenhaus** (General Hospital) in the ninth district. People without insurance or money to pay for medical services are cared for at the **Krankenhaus der Barmherzigen Brüder** (Brothers of Mercy Hospital), which also runs a free emergency dental clinic. In a medical emergency, call an ambulance *(Rettungsdienst)*.

## Health Precautions

In Austria, as everywhere in western Europe, tick-borne encephalitis is a possible danger wherever there are

Policeman riding a motorcycle

Fire engine

Police van

Ambulance

hours. As well as medicines, pharmacies also sell some herbal remedies. *Reformhäuser* specialize in such products and natural healthcare.

## DIRECTORY

### Hospitals

**Allgemeines Krankenhaus**
**Map** 1 A1. Währinger Gürtel 18–20, 1090 Vienna.
**Tel** (01) 404 00-0.

**Krankenhaus der Barmherzigen Brüder**
(Brothers of Mercy Hospital), Johannes von Gott-Platz 1, 1020 Vienna. **Tel** (01) 211 210.

### Important Numbers

**International Pharmacy**
**Map** 5 D1. Kärntner Ring 17, Vienna. **Tel** (01) 512 28 25.

**Lost Property Office**
**Map** 4 A5.
Siebenbrunnenfeldgasse 3, 1050 Vienna.
**Tel** (01) 4000-8091.

**Pharmacy Information Line**
Vienna. **Tel** 1445.

### Emergency Telephone Numbers

**Ambulance**
**Tel** 144.

**Emergency Medical Assistance**
**Tel** 141.
Can be consulted evenings, nights, Saturdays, Sundays and public holidays.

**Fire Service**
**Tel** 122.

**Flying Ambulance Service**
**Tel** 401 44-0.

**Mobile Telephone Emergency Line – can be used without a SIM card**
**Tel** 112.

**Police**
**Tel** 133.

**Roadside Assistance**
**Tel** 120.

deciduous trees. Travellers may experience mild altitude sickness if exercising – be that walking, skiing or montain-eering – above 3,000 m (9,849 ft). Dehydration can compound the problem. Descending to a lower altitude is the only cure. There is a danger of avalanches in some snow-covered areas.

## Pharmacies

If it is not an emergency, it is best to go to an *Apotheke* (pharmacy) for advice on medicines and treatment. Pharmacies display a red "A" sign and operate a night rota

system. Any closed pharmacies will display the address of the nearest one open, and the **Pharmacy Information Line** also has details of opening

Façade of a typical *Apotheke* (pharmacy) in Vienna

# Banking and Currency

Every town, no matter how small, will have an ATM, known in Austria as a *Bankomat*, which accepts international credit and debit cards. Cash is dispensed in euros. Debit and credit cards are accepted by almost all shops and restaurants, though sometimes not for very small purchases. Cards equipped with the contactless function can be used for amounts under €25. The use of traveller's cheques is steadily being phased out – so cash or card is recommended.

## Money Exchange

The best place to change money is at a bank. Bank Austria and Erste Bank charge 3 per cent commission or a minimum handling fee of €5.50. Although you can use travel agents and hotels, the banks give you a better rate and charge less commission. Railway station *Wechselstuben* (bureaux de change) charge 4 per cent on the exchanged sum. Exchanging a larger amount of money at one time can save on commission. You can also exchange sterling or US dollars for euros at an automatic money-changing machine.

Most banks are open from 8:30am until 12:30pm and from 1:30pm to 3pm Monday to Friday (to 5:30pm on Thursdays). A few, such as the main Creditanstalt bank in Vienna, Bank Austria and some banks in the provincial capitals, as well as those in the busier tourist resorts or close to railway stations and airports, have extended opening hours. Banks are not open on Saturdays and Sundays.

## ATMs

A convenient and easy way to change money is at an ATM. Austria's banks operate a large network of ATMs, most of which accept foreign credit and debit cards with 4-digit PIN codes (check with your bank before travelling that you don't have the older 6-digit code). This facility will be clearly stated on the front of the machine – just look for the logo of your card. Visa and MasterCard are generally accepted but few machines take American Express. Instructions are generally given in English and some other languages. Be aware that money drawn out using a credit or debit card often incurs a considerable fee. Depending on your location, *Bankomats* will have different limits of how much cash they can dispense; sometimes it's as little as €300.

*Bankomats* can be found outside all banks or within the bank lobby; these are usually accessible 24 hours a day. In skiing areas, they are often located near ticket offices. Train and bus stations, as well as hotels, usually have an ATM in the vicinty. The website bankomatfinder.at is a handy way of finding your nearest ATM.

## DIRECTORY

### Bureaux de Change (Wechselstuben)

**Vienna**
Airport.
**Open** 5am–11:15pm daily.
Erste Bank: Rauhensteingasse 1.
UniCredit Bank Austria: Stephansplatz 7a.

**Graz**
Bank Austria Creditanstalt AG: Herrengasse 15.
BAWAG PSK Filiale und Post: Europaplatz 4, Objekt 1.

**Innsbruck**
BAWAG PSK Filiale und Post: Südtirolerplatz 10–12.

**Melk**
BAWAG PSK: Wiener Strasse 85 (in the post office).

**Salzburg**
Airport, Terminal 1.
Österreichische Verkehrskreditbank AG: Main station, Südtiroler Platz.
Salzburger Sparkasse: Bundesstrasse 95.

### Automatic Money-Changing Machines

**Vienna**
Kärntner Strasse 23.
Kärntner Strasse 51.
Graben 21.
Operngasse 2.
Tegetthoffstrasse 1.
Schottenring 1.
Stephansplatz 2.

**Feldkirch**
Sparkassenplatz 1.

**Krems**
Obere Landstrasse 19.

**Kufstein**
Georg-Pirmoser-Strasse 2.
Oberer Stadtplatz 1.

**St Wolfgang**
Markt 106.

**Salzburg**
Getreidegasse 1.

**Velden**
Am Korso.

A typical *Bankomat*, found throughout the country

Currency conversion machine accepting foreign banknotes

## The Euro

The euro (€) is the common currency of the European Union. It went into general circulation on 1 January 2002, initially for 12 participating countries. Austria was one of those 12 countries taking the euro in 2002, with the Austrian schilling phased out in the same year.

EU members using the euro as sole official currency are known as the Eurozone. Several EU members have opted out of joining this common currency.

Euro notes are identical throughout the Eurozone countries. The coins, however, have one side identical (the value side), and one side with an image unique to each country, though they can be used throughout the Eurozone.

### Banknotes

Euro banknotes have seven denominations. The grey €5 note is the smallest, followed by the pink €10 note, blue €20 note, orange €50 note, green €100 note, yellow €200 note and purple €500 note. All notes show the stars of the European Union and architectural motifs.

€5 note

€10 note

€20 note

€50 note

€100 note

€200 note

€500 note

5 cents

2 cents

1 cent

€2 coin

€1 coin

50 cents

20 cents

10 cents

### Coins

The euro has eight coin denominations: €1 and €2; 50 cents, 20 cents, 10 cents, 5 cents, 2 cents and 1 cent. The €2 and €1 coins are both silver and gold in colour. The 50-, 20- and 10-cent coins are gold. The 5-, 2- and 1-cent coins are bronze.

# Media and Communications

As an industrialized European country, Austria has a highly sophisticated communications system. Mobile telephone coverage extends to all areas, even ski slopes and remote villages, and reduced or non-existent EU roaming fees now make it more cost-effective to use your phone. In spite of the popularity of mobile phones, public telephone boxes are still widely found, and in an emergency, international phone calls can be arranged at a post office. Most urban areas have high-speed fibre-optic broadband and free Wi-Fi access is offered at most tourist attractions, cafés and bars, and public spaces and buildings. The postal system, run by Osterreichische Post, is very efficient and reliable. Newspapers and magazines, both hard copy and online, are readily available – many, particularly in Vienna, have excellent listings sections.

## International and Local Telephone Calls

Despite the dominance of mobile phones, public tele-phones are easy to find. Called *Telefonzelle*, they accept either coins or prepaid cards, known as *Telefonwertkarte*, which can be purchased in shops, at post offices or from kiosks. Coin-operated telephones accept 10-, 20- and 50- cent as well as 1- and 2-euro coins – the minimum charge for a local call is 30 cents. The cheap-rate calling time for international calls from Austria is between 6pm and 8am and at weekends; for domestic calls, it is between 8pm and 6am, and weekends. Diall 1611 for directory assistance for calls inside Austria, and 1613 for help with international calls. Be warned that calling from a hotel can be prohibitively expensive.

T-Mobile logo

## Mobile Phones

Mobile phone coverage is generally excellent throughout the country and Austria has a number of mobile operators, the main ones being **A1**, **BOB**, **Tele.Ring** and **T-Mobile**. Before travelling, it is advisable to check roaming rates with your mobile provider. EU roaming laws brought into effect in 2016 mean that visitors to Austria from within the EU can use their phones at minimal cost; coverage varies from provider to provider, so check before you travel, and those that exceed their data allowance will still incur additional charges. For those outside of the EU, roaming can still be expensive.

Alternatively, regular or long-term visitors are advised to purchase a prepaid SIM card, or an Austrian mobile phone with a prepaid card – such phones can be bought for under €50. A SIM card typically costs around €15 and includes around €10 credit; you can then purchase additional credit from phone shops, supermarkets and the post office. Note, though, that your phone will need to be unlocked; visitors from North America may find that Austrian SIM cards are not compatible with their phones.

Austrian mobile numbers are identified by the range 0650 to 0699. Some numbers that are advertised as toll-free,

Coin-operated phone

Emergency phone sign

Sign for cardphone

## Reaching the Right Number

- The international dialling code for Austria is +43. When calling from abroad, omit the initial 0 from the area code.
- For directory enquiries, dial 118877.
- Railway timetable information: 05 17 17.
- Road conditions and snowfall: 0800 400 12 400.
- Central Post Office Information (Zentrale Postauskunft): 0800 010 100.
- To ring home from Austria, dial the appropriate country code, followed by the number and omit the 0 from the local area code.
- For the **UK** dial 0044.
- For the **Irish Republic** dial 00353.
- For the **USA** dial 001.
- For **Australia** dial 0061.
- For **New Zealand** dial 0064.

such as 0180 and 0190, may actually incur charges. A phone call to a "toll-free" international number, such as 0800 in the United States, will be charged at the normal international rate.

## Internet

Vienna has a smattering of dedicated Internet cafés, but, as elsewhere, these are a dying breed as just about every café or coffeehouse now has Wi-Fi – which you are free to use yourself, just so long as you make a purchase. Where you do find an Internet café, expect to pay around €3–6 per hour. Increasingly, many public areas in the bigger towns and cities offer free Wi-Fi; in Vienna, for example, there are hotspots all over the city, as well as the train and subway stations – a full list of these is available at **freewave.at**. Many tourist offices offer Wi-Fi and/or a terminal, though you may need a password from the staff. Otherwise, nearly all hotels (and many hostels) have Wi-Fi, and often a terminal for guests to use.

## Postal Services

Österreichische Post, Austria's postal service, is, unsurprisingly, very efficient. There are approximately 15,300 yellow postboxes around the country, and 1,800 post offices. Stamps (*Briefmarken*) can be bought from post offices (which also have vending machines), as well as tobacconists (*Tabak Trafiken*). International post is sent either as "priority" or "economy", with rates to countries within the European Union costing less than those to the rest of the world. Parcels sent internationally require a customs form, which is available at the post office. You will also need to fill in a form when sending registered or express mail.

You can collect correspondence marked *Postlagernd* (*poste restante*), but you will need proof of identity.

Most post offices in Vienna and larger towns and cities are open Monday to Friday 8am–6pm, while some (such as those at train stations) stay open until 8 or 10pm. Post offices in smaller resorts are likely to close between noon and 2pm, or may even only be open in the mornings. Larger branches are also open on Saturdays between 8am and 10pm.

A typical signboard indicating a post office

## Newspapers and Magazines

Quite a few newsagents and kiosks in Vienna and other major towns and cities stock English-language newspapers, sometimes on the day of publication – typically the *Guardian International*, *Financial Times*, *USA Today* and the *International Herald Tribune*. In addition, you'll find weekly news magazines such as *Time* and *Newsweek*. Online newspapers include *Austria Today*, though its full content is only available via subscription. Austria's most well-regarded broadsheet – and one of the oldest still-published newspapers in the world – is *Wiener Zeitung*, while other reputable dailies include the right-of-centre *Die Presse*, and the left-leaning *Der Standard*; the tabloid brigade, meanwhile, is led by *Kronen Zeitung*.

In Vienna, the best read is *Der Falter*, which also has weekly listings. Well worth consulting is the excellent *Vienna In Your Pocket*, a fun online magazine with comprehensive, irreverent, and up-to-date information and listings for the city.

## Television and Radio

ORF, the state service broadcaster, offers two channels, ORF1 and ORF2, while the main commercial channels are ATV and TW1. Inevitably, German channels like SAT1 and RTL are prominent on Austrian TV. The majority of hotels have satellite or cable TV, providing the ubiquitous English-language channels CNN and BBC World News, and occasionally one or two others. The main public radio stations are O1 for

Range of international newspapers on sale at a kiosk in Vienna

news and culture (97.7 FM), O3 for popular music (103.9 FM) and FM4, which offers a more alternative musical slant. Radio Austria International (ROI) presents Austria-related news in various languages. BBC World Service frequencies and listings can be found on their website: bbc.co.uk/worldservice.

Yellow post- or mailbox used for sending letters

# TRAVEL INFORMATION

As a popular tourist destination, Austria is well served by both air and rail. The major cities – Vienna, Linz, Graz, Innsbruck, Salzburg and Klagenfurt – have international airports and there are direct flights from main European cities as well as from the USA, Canada, Japan and Australia. Vienna is a key transit point in Europe, and about eight million passengers a year pass through its Schwechat airport. There are good rail and coach links, too, but from Britain this involves a long journey, often overnight, and is not significantly cheaper than air travel. The motorway network throughout Austria and motorway links between Austria and the rest of Europe are extensive; the roads are clearly signposted and well maintained.

Check-in counters at the international airport in Vienna

## Air Travel

There are several flights a day between London's Heathrow and Vienna's Schwechat airport, operated by **British Airways** and by Austria's national airline **Austrian Airlines**. Austrian Airlines also serves Innsbruck from London Heathrow and Vienna from Manchester. Of the "low-cost" airlines **Ryanair** tends to be good value for money and flies from London Stansted to Linz and Salzburg; **easyJet** flies from several UK airports to Vienna, Salzburg and Linz; and **Flybe** flies from Birmingham and London Gatwick to Salzburg and Vienna.

If you wish to fly from the United States, the only carrier offering direct flights is Austrian Airlines, with a choice of departure cities including Miami, New York and Washington. There are also direct flights from Toronto with Austrian Airlines

Thanks to its central location, **Vienna International Airport** (Flughafen Wien-Schwechat) is a major European transit airport, and serves more than 85 airlines. The airport is located 19 km (12 miles) from Vienna's city centre, and is easily accessible by train or bus. A modern airport, Schwechat is very easy and quick to use.

**Busse nach: / Busses to:**
| City Air Terminal | 11:10 |
| Süd-/Westbahnhof | 11:40 |
| Vienna Int. Centre | 12:50 |
| Bratislava | 13:20 |

Bus transfer information board

## Domestic Flights

Domestic flights within Austria are operated by Austrian Airlines. There are daily flights from Vienna to Graz, Klagenfurt, Innsbruck, Salzburg and Linz. Air travel in Austria is expensive and, with extra time needed for checking in, the journey to and from the airport and for retrieving your luggage, it is not the fastest and best way of getting to another destination in Austria.

## Special Deals

Any savvy traveller knows that it's not necessary to pay full price for a scheduled ticket. A number of web-based flight booking sites offer price comparisons, showing the dates and times of days when flights are cheaper; prices really do vary from one day or even one time to the next, so it's worth doing a bit of homework. "Budget" airlines, such as Ryanair and easyJet, offer sales throughout the year, particularly post-Christmas. Ski season is always expensive, regardless of who you book with, so budget airlines may not be that cost-effective in comparison to national carriers like British Airways or Austrian Airlines.

Regular travellers may enjoy privileges if they join frequent fliers' programmes, which may include priority for upgrades to business class. Such programmes also often award points for car hire from major companies such as Avis, Europcar, Hertz or Sixt, as well as overnight stays at major hotel chains.

Travellers with special requirements, for example those with mobility issues, should notify the airlines of their situation. Children up to and including the age of two travel free (or at 10 per cent of the price). Children aged three years and over pay the same price for flights as adults on all airlines.

The modern building of Schwechat International Airport near Vienna

## Austrian Airports and Transfers

Many business travellers to Vienna never leave the airport: opposite the terminal building is the five-star luxury hotel Astron, and next to it the vast World Trade Centre, where many companies have their head offices. Vienna's airport has all the facilities that a traveller might need: information desks, service desks, shops, automatic money-exchange machines, bureaux de change and banks (though the rates for exchanging money at the airport are less favourable than elsewhere).

The CAT (City Airport Train: www.cityairporttrain.com) leaves every half hour and takes you to Wien-Mitte Station. The journey time is 16 minutes and the fare (one way) is around €11. Buses go to Schwedenplatz and Westbahnhof. They depart every 25 minutes and the 30-minute journey costs about €8 one way.

The cheapest means of transport into the city is the suburban railway line, the *Schnellbahn*, which operates a half-hourly service.

The taxi journey from the airport to the centre of Vienna costs around €35. Vienna Airport Taxi provides a taxi service (Tel 664 366 1 660). Alternatively, you can hire a car at the airport, from companies such as **Avis**, Budget, Europcar, **Hertz** or Thrifty. All you need when hiring a vehicle is a driver's licence, a passport and a credit card for the deposit.

Salzburg Airport, which is at No. 95 Innsbrucker Bundesstrasse, is situated extremely close to the town centre, a mere 4 km (2 miles) to the west. It can be reached by bus or taxi.

Innsbruck Airport is also located near the town centre (4 km/2 miles) and the transfer by taxi or bus "F" takes 10–15 minutes. Buses from Klagenfurt Airport run every 30 minutes

Logo of Austrian Airlines

and take approximately 15 minutes to reach the centre of town.

## DIRECTORY

### Airport Information

**Vienna International Airport**
Tel (01) 7007-22233.
W viennaairport.com

### Airlines

**Air Canada**
Tel 1888 247 2262 in Canada; 069 27115 111 in Austria.
W aircanada.com

**Austrian Airlines**
Marxergasse, at corner of Invalidenstrasse 1030 Vienna.
Tel (05176) 61000. W aua.com

**British Airways**
Tel 0845 7733377 in UK; (01) 7956 7567 in Austria.
W britishairways.com

**easyJet**
Tel 0330 365 5000 in UK; 0820 320 950 in Austria.
W easyjet.com

**Flybe**
Reservations for UK passengers:
Tel 0371 700 2000 in UK; 01392 683 152. W flybe.com

**Ryanair**
Tel In Ireland: 0818 303030. In the UK: (0871) 246 0000.
W ryanair.com

### Car Hire

**Avis**
Tel (01) 587 6241 or 7007 32700.
W avis.at

**Hertz**
Tel (01) 512 8677 or 7007 32661.
W hertz.at

Shopping centre inside Vienna's Schwechat International Airport

# Travelling by Train

Situated in the heart of Europe, Austria is a rail transport hub. Comfortable, clean and safe, a train departs every 12 seconds, one of 570 running at any given moment on almost 5,000 km (3,100 miles) of track. The largest railway line is the Österreichische Bundesbahnen (ÖBB), Austrian Federal Railway Lines, and there are also 12 small mountain and regional rail companies. Protecting the environment is a prime concern and an impressive 92 per cent of locomotive energy comes from renewable resources and hydroelectricty. The service receives continuous investment, ensuring high levels of comfort, shorter travelling times and reductions in emissions.

*Hauptbahnhof*, the main railway station in Vienna

## Trains

Österreichische Bundesbahnen (ÖBB) runs several types of service. The high-speed Railjet trains, which operate at speeds of up to 230 kph/ 143 mph, run the breadth of the country, from Salzburg to Vienna. The service offers business-, first- and second-class seating; business class costs €15 more than a first-class ticket. Business- and first-class carriages feature reclining leather chairs, an extensive choice of magazines and newspapers, and meals served at your seat. Free Wi-Fi is available throughout each train, and there are electrical sockets at every seat. A second high-speed train, called the Intercity-Express (ICE), runs between main cities. Eurocity (EC) and

Intercity (IC) trains run respectively to international and major Austrian destinations. Since 2015, Cityjet trains are gradually being introduced on over 100 major routes across the country. The luxury Nightjet service runs to destinations within and beyond Austria, including Italy, Switzerland and Germany. Choose from a variety of cabins including a 6-bed bunk and a deluxe single with bathroom.

Bundesbahn logo

### Seat Reservations

Unlike in some other European countries, it is not necessary to reserve a seat, except for overnight sleeper trains. If you do want to, seats on any train can be reserved up to three months in advance, at a minimum charge of €3; there is no extra charge for business- or

first-class tickets. Reservations can be made at railway ticket offices, at ÖBB Reisebüros (ÖBB travel agencies), or online at www.oebb.at.

If special facilities are required, such as space for wheelchairs, it is highly advisable to make an advance booking. Alert the ÖBB Mobility Centre on 05-1717-5 or via the form on the ÖBB website. Requests are usually handled in as little as 3 hours.

### Railway Stations

The German word for a railway station is *Bahnhof*, and the main railway station is *Hauptbahnhof*. The latter are found in cities, like Vienna, and usually have more than one rail terminal. Many stations are also information hubs, with shops, bureaux de change, luggage deposits and help desks, with English-speaking staff. If there is no ticket office, you can buy a ticket from machines, which accept credit cards.

### Arriving from Britain

Rail travel from Britain to Austria has achieved new levels of speed and comfort with the introduction of the ÖBB's high-speed Railjet and luxury Cityjet trains. It is possible to leave London St Pancras at around 7am and step off the train in Vienna no later than 9pm on the

High-speed Railjet trains

same day (this trip involves taking the Eurostar to Brussels, and changing there and in Frankfurt). Other routes, for example travelling via Paris and Munich, are slower but enjoy the same level of service. The travel agency *(Reisebüro)* at Westbahnhof in Vienna is open from 8am to 7pm on weekdays and 8am to 1pm on Saturdays; staff will be able to provide information.

The main train station in Vienna, Hauptbahnhof Wien, is located on Südtirolerplatz and opened in 2014. It serves all international routes and is connected to line U1 on the underground. Many trains from Germany, as well as some domestic services, terminate at Westbahnhof in the western part of the city. You can access this train station from the U-Bahn underground lines U3 and U6. Trains from the

A railway viaduct near the small town of Mattersburg

north arrive at Franz-Josefs-Bahnhof; this is served by the Schnellbahn and the cross-city tram "D", which takes you to the Ringstrasse in the centre.

## Tickets

Austrians are among the highest users of trains in Europe. In general, tickets in Austria cost half the price of the equivalent in the United Kingdom, and a quarter of the price of the EU average. To find the best price for a particular journey, the ÖBB provides online price comparisons; changing your journey time by an hour can reduce the ticket price dramatically. The ÖBB also offers huge reductions with their *Sparscheine* scheme; a limited number of reduced-price tickets for each journey are available when booking online in advance. A journey from Vienna to Linz, for example, can be as little as €9,

Schnellbahn, Vienna's suburban train line

while a journey across the length of the country can be obtained for just €29. Look out, too, for ÖBB Plus online offers, where ski tickets and entry to tourist attractions are added free to selected destinations. If you are planning frequent train journeys throughout Austria, it is worth investing in a *Vorteilscard*. Used by most Austrians, this card provides a 45–50 per cent discount on all travel; the best discounts are available for tickets purchased online or via ticket machines. The card costs €99 a year but those aged under 29 can purchase a young person's *Vorteilscard* for just €19; those over 62 for €29. The card can be purchased in Austria or in advance on the ÖBB website. You can also download the card onto a smartphone app.

Tickets for travel inside Austria and to all international destinations are best bought online on the ÖBB website (www.oebb.at). Alternatively, you can purchase tickets through travel agents. Tickets can be bought at railway stations, at ticket windows or from ticket machines on train platforms. Dial 05-1717-3 to book by phone or 05-1717 for general questions. The free ÖBB app for Android and iOS is another handy way of booking tickets.

## Railway Network Map

**Key**

— Main railway routes

0 kilometres 100

0 miles 100

# Travelling by Car

Austria's dramatic scenery and varied landscape make driving a real pleasure. Crisscrossing the country, passing snow-capped mountains and winding along country lanes, are motorways *(Autobahns)*, long-distance roads and country roads. Motorways are marked with the letter "A", for *Autobahn*, while European motorway routes are marked with "E". Throughout, the road surfaces are in good condition and routes are well-signposted. Fuel – both gas and diesel – is less expensive than in France or Britain, and traffic is generally calm.

The spectacular Grossglockner Hochalpenstrasse *(see pp284–5)*

## Driving in Austria

Visitors arriving by car can use any of a number of border crossings. There are no border checks; Austria is within the Schengen Area (26 European countries that have abolished border controls) and is surrounded by other Schengen states.

A toll is charged on the motorways and some other fast-traffic roads (in urban areas as well as the countryside). It is collected via a pre-paid disc, known as a *vignette* or *Autobahnpickerl*, which can be bought online at tolltickets.com before you travel. Short-term visitors can buy a sticker for a ten-day period for around €9; a sticker for two months costs around €26; and an annual pass about €86.

Stick the sticker to the top-left corner of your car windscreen. It will allow free access to all national motorways and urban freeways. There are limitations: it does not entitle the driver to use any private pay-roads, of which, fortunately, there are very few; usually such roads are situated at high altitudes. You will also be asked to pay a separate charge for going across Alpine passes and through tunnels.

## What to Take

Visitors travelling by car in Austria need to carry a valid passport and driver's licence as well as their vehicle's registration document and insurance policy. Non-EU drivers need an international driving licence. The vehicle must be equipped with a first-aid box, a safety triangle and a fluorescent safety vest; the latter two must be deployed, by law, at the scene of an accident. In winter, it is obligatory to have winter tyres and snow chains, which are essential for driving on the mountain roads.

## Roads and Signposts

Motorways *(Autobahnen)* and the slip roads leading to them are signposted with white lettering on blue boards; on official maps in Austria, motorways are shown as yellow lines between two thinner lines. An inn near a junction is indicated by a short sign with black lettering on white background.

*Fernstrassen* (long-distance roads) and *Bundesstrassen* (federal roads) are marked in red, and *Landstrassen* (country roads) in yellow. On the road, traffic signs are black-and-white. The written ones you may need to know are: *Stau* – traffic jam, *Schnee* – snow, *Umleitung* – diversion, and *Baustelle* – road works. All other road signs follow the European standard.

## Road Traffic Regulations

In Austria, motorists drive on the right-hand side of the road. The speed limit on motorways is 130 km/h (81 mph), and on other roads 100 km/h (62 mph). In towns and built-up areas the limit is 50 km/h (31 mph), but only 30 km/h (19 mph) in Graz. Cars with caravans are restricted to 100 km/h (62 mph) on motorways. Speeding

A toll station at the entrance to a pay-road in the mountains

violations and using a mobile phone while driving are just two of the infractions that can incur on-the-spot fines, which are payable in cash.

Drivers and passengers are obliged to wear seatbelts at all times. Children under 12 are not allowed to sit in the front seat. Holders of foreign driving permits are not allowed to drive in Austria if under 18 years of age.

Drivers must yield to traffic coming from the right. Be aware that traffic lights will flash green for several seconds before changing to amber.

A road hugging the edge of the Seidewinktal valley

## Driving in Towns

Finding a place in which to park is not easy, especially in the centre of the larger towns; it is often best to use a multi-storey car park, which is indicated by the word *Parkhaus*. *Frei* means that parking spaces are available.

Cars left in a controlled parking zone, indicated by blue lines on the road, must display a parking ticket or be parked validly near a meter. Parking discs, or clock discs, allow free parking in zones clearly marked with the blue disc symbol. Set the time of your arrival on your disc and return within the time allowed within that zone. Discs are available from shops and petrol stations, and discs from other countries are not

Sign informing motorists of the need to fit wheelchains

permitted. In most parts of Vienna, parking is restricted to resident permit holders.

## Car Hire

Airports and garages in most towns will offer car hire. Major car-hire firms, such as Avis, Europcar and Hertz, all have offices in Austria. It is advisable to book your car hire in advance, as even the choice at airports can be limited, especially during the holiday season. Car hire is likely to be more expensive at the airport.

To hire a car you must be 19 or over, and for some car companies the age limit is 25. You must hold a valid passport and a driver's licence as well as a credit card or charge card from an approved company. A car may be hired for any

duration and dropped off at any agreed point, to be collected by the hire company. Not all destinations, however, have suitable drop-off points. Cars may be taken outside Austria to approved EU countries. Be warned, however: dropping a car off in a different location to the one you hired it from can add to the cost considerably.

## Arriving by Coach

Flixbus, National Express and Regiohet run coaches from London Victoria to Wien Mitte. This is also the terminal station for routes to major European cities such as Bratislava, Budapest, Zurich, Paris, Brussels, Milan and Copenhagen, plus domestic routes from eastern Austria.

Coaches are equipped to the European standard and tickets may be cheaper than rail travel, but the journey from the UK is long – over 24 hours – and fares are not particularly cheap – usually between €65 and €100. Often, budget airlines offer a more convenient way to travel at a comparable cost (*see p352*).

## Travelling by Coach

The entire country is served by an excellent coach network, allowing you to reach almost any destination, including some remote places not connected to the rail network. Prices are similar to those charged for rail travel.

Coaches lined up outside Vienna International Airport

# Getting Around Towns

Austria has an excellent urban public transport system. Most towns generally have a network of buses and, in most cities, trams. Vienna also has an underground subway *(U-Bahn)* – the quickest way to reach any destination. One type of ticket can be used across the transport system, and tickets for unlimited travel for specific time periods can be purchased. One-way traffic systems and pedestrianized areas make driving more troublesome than using trams and buses, or setting out on foot. Especially in historic, compact city centres, where most of the main sights are to be found, walking is the most efficient and satisfying mode of transport.

## Walking

Pedestrians have priority, even on roads – but you should never rely on this. Try to use subways or crossings where there are signals, especially when crossing wide roads with fast-moving traffic. Visitors should note that motorists drive on the right. Do not cross a road when the red signal shows, even if there is no traffic – you may be spot-fined for jay walking. Watch out for cycle lanes and cyclists who share the pavement with pedestrians.

In larger cities, guided walking tours in English are organized by tourist offices. These will take you past all the sights, with entry to some included. Some tours are themed – exploring Baroque architecture or Vienna 1900, for example – while others combine city highlights with interesting anecdotes.

Tourists strolling through a mountain village

## Bicycles

All Austrian cities have dedicated cycle paths, clearly marked. When such paths run onto pavements, the cyclist has right of way. Where there is no cycle route, cyclists join the road traffic and are obliged to adhere to all normal traffic rules – though they can cycle against one-way systems. There are a number of city bike rental schemes, most usually free for the first hour. Bikes may also be hired from some stations, at a discount if you have a train ticket. In Vienna, bike paths take you around the Ringstrasse and past many of the sights. One of the most scenic long-distance cycling routes is the *Radweg* (cycle track) along the Danube river.

## Taxis

Taxis throughout Austria are generally of a high standard and very safe. Thanks to the comprehensive public transport systems, however, taxis are generally used not for daily transport around town but for trips to airports or train stations. Fares to the airport are usually fixed, with a 10 per cent tip expected. A ride to the airport from central Vienna, for example, costs around €30. To estimate a fare in advance, check taxifarefinder.com/at.

In the centre of a city it is easier to get a taxi at one of the taxi ranks, rather than hailing it in the street. Taxi ranks can be found near railway stations and large hotels. Alternatively, you can book a taxi by phone.

Uber, and other app-based taxi services, operate in Vienna, Salzburg, Graz and Innsbruck, and are steadily expanding.

## Buses

Many city centres are served by hopper buses, while larger buses take visitors to the inner suburbs. Municipal bus lines are often extensions of tram lines. This is signalled by a letter in the number of the bus, thus bus No. 46A extends the route of tram No. 46, making it easy to find the correct line.

## Trams

Along with buses and the underground, trams are the most convenient form of transport in the cities. It is easy to track your progress as each stop is announced

A typical bicycle-sharing station

Tram on the Viennese tram network,
or Strassbahn

you press the button to signal your intention to get out, otherwise trams or buses may continue without stopping if no one is waiting at the stop.

## Tickets

Tickets can be bought at newsagents, in blocks of five or ten, or in suburban railway stations where blocks of two or four are also available. In Vienna you can also purchase tickets at subway stations. You should always buy a ticket before travelling, since it is not always possible to buy one from the driver or the ticket machine inside the vehicle. Having boarded the bus, tram or train, you need to stamp your ticket at the start of your

just before you arrive, and all carriages display the route map, indicating the stops.

The doors are released by pressing a button. Make sure

journey; you will not need to stamp it again if you change to a different line or different mode of transport.

The tickets are valid for travel on all forms of transport within a town, within varying time limits. Besides single tickets, visitors can also opt to buy a 24-hour, 48-hour and 72-hour pass, a *Streifenkarte* (strip of tickets) valid for three or eight days, a *Wochenkarte* valid for one week, a *Monatskarte*, valid for one month, or a *Jahreskarte*, which permits you to travel for one year.

There may be variations in how tickets are purchased and used on public transport between the provinces in Austria. The tourist offices and hotels in the area will be able to advise you.

## Making a Journey by Underground

1 To determine which line to take, travellers should look for their destination on a U-Bahn map. The five lines are distinguished by colour and number (U1, U2, U3, U4 & U5). Simply trace the line to your destination, making a note of where you need to change lines. Connections to other forms of transport are also shown.

2 Tickets can be bought from newsagents, ticket vending machines or ticket offices. To get to the trains, insert your ticket into the ticket-stamping machine in the direction of the arrow. Wait for the ping indicating that it is validated, and pass through the barrier. Follow the signs (with the number and colour of the line) to your platform.

3 Once you are on the platform, check the direction and destination of the train on an electronic destination indicator.

4 Stops along the line are shown on a plan. A red arrow in the corner shows the direction in which the train enters the station.

5 At your destination follow the *Ausgang* signs to reach street level.

Pull handle to open door

The door opens out to the side

Sign showing stops on line 3 of the U-Bahn, including the connecting stops

6 At stations with more than one exit, use the map of the city to check which street or square you will come out at.

# General Index

# Acknowledgments

Dorling Kindersley would like to thank the following people whose contributions and assistance have made the preparation of this book possible.

**Consultant**
Gerhard Bruschke

**Additional Contributors**
Helen Harrison, Darrel Joseph, Doug Sager, Leslie Woit

**Additional Photography**
Maciej Bronarski, Dip. Ing. Walter Hildebrand, Renata and Marek Kosiński, Piotr Kiedrowski, Ian O'Leary, Peter Wilson, Paweł Wroński

**Cartography**
An Bundesamt Eich- und Vermessungwesen, Lundesaufnahme (BEV), Uma Bhattacharya, Mohammad Hassan, Jasneet Kaur

**DTP**
Vinod Harish, Vincent Kurien, Azeem Siddiqui

**Reader**
Judith Meddick

**Fact-Checkers**
Martina Bauer, Melanie Nicholson-Hartzell

**Proofreaders**
Emily Hatchwell, Christine Stroyan

**Indexer**
Helen Peters

**Senior Editor**
Jacky Jackson/Wordwise Associates Ltd.

**Managing Art Editors**
Kate Poole, Ian Midson

**Publishing Manager**
Helen Townsend

**Revisions and Relaunch Team**
Namrata Adhwaryu, Asad Ali, Hansa Babra, Subhashree Bharti, Jo Cowen, Conrad Van Dyk, Mariana Evmolpidou, Karen Fitzpatrick, Anna Freiberger, Rhiannon Furbear, Rupanki Kaushik, Juliet Kenny, Sumita Khatwani, Rahul Kumar, Kathryn Lane, Leena Lane, Carly Madden, Hayley Maher, Alison McGill, Sam Merrell, Deepak Mittal, Kate Molan, Rakesh Kumar Pal, Sangita Patel, Marianne Petrou, Rada Radojicic, Marisa Renzullo, Doug Sager, Beverly Smart, Sadie Smith, Susana Smith, Rachel Symons, Hollie Teague, Ajay Verma

**Additional Picture Research**
Ellen Root

**Special Assistance**
Wiedza i Życie would like to thank Mr. Roman Skrzypczak of the Austrian Tourist Information Centre for his help in obtaining materials and for facilitating contacts with other Austrian institutions.

The publisher would also like to thank all the people and institutions who allowed photographs belonging to them to be reproduced, as well as granting permission to use photographs from their archives:

Agencja Forum (Krzysztof Wójcik); Artothek (Susanne Vierthaler and Holger Gehrmann); Basilika Mariazell, Benediktiner-Superiorat (P. Karl Schauer OSB, Superior); Brahms Museum, Mürzzuschlag; Burgenländisches Landesmuseum, Eisenstadt (Julia Raab and Gerard Schlag); Corbis (Gabriela Ściborska); Chorherrenstift Klosterneuburg-Stiftsmuseum (Mag. Wolfgang Huber); Die Österreich Werbung, Bildarchiv (Dr. Dietmar Jungreithmair); DK Library; FIS Wintersportmuseum, Mürzzuschlag (Mag. Hannes Nothnagl); Festung Hochensalzburg; Heeresgeschichtliches Museum in Arsenal (Peter Enne); Kunsthistorisches Museum, Wien (Elisabeth Reicher); Lurgrotte Peggau; Museum Schloss Greillenstein (Elisabeth Kuefstein); Museumsverein Schloss Rosenau, Österreichisches Freimaurermuseum; Naturpark Grebenzen Büro St. Lambrecht (Frater Gerwig Romirer); Österreichischen Freilichtmuseum, Stübing bei Graz (Egbert Pöttler); Rathaus w St. Pölten (Andrea Jäger); Salzburger Burgen und Schlösser, Betriebsführung; Stadtmarketing Eisenstadt, Schloss Esterházy (Guenter Schumich); Stift Melk, Kultur and Tourismus (Maria Prüller); Wien-Tourismus (Waltraud Wolf); Zefa (Ewa Kozłowska)

**Picture Credits**

Key: a = above; b = below/bottom; c = centre; f = far; l = left; r = right; t = top.

akg-images: 42ca, 99cr; **Alamy Stock Photo:** 354bl; Peter Barritt 258b; Pat Behnke 332tl; Radim Beznoska 346cla; Caro 214; Cephas Picture Library 68tr; Colinspics 331tc; Denis Cox 22b; Rob Crandall 102bl; Danita Delimont/ Walter Bibikow 333tc; F1online digitale Bildagentur GmbH 194tl; Thierry Grun – Aero 266br; Paul Grove 347clb; Hackenberg-Photo-Cologne 116bl; Rainer Hackenberg 137cl; imageBROKER/Martin Siepmann 316tl; incamerstock 351bc; LOOK Die Bildagentur der Fotografen GmbH/Franz Marc Frei 321bc; Raquel Mogado 291tl; David Noble Photography 305tl; FAN travelstock/Michael Schindel 306cla; imagebroker 12tc, 319bl, 320b; imagebroker/Christian Handl 303tl; INSADCO Photography/Martin Bobrovsky 303c; Scott Kemper 160; LOOK Die Bildagentur 286-7; Barry Mason 305cb; mediacolor's 304cla; nagelstock.com 190; Pictures Colour Library 331br; Charles Ridgway 330br; Robert Harding Picture Library Ltd/Richard Nebesky 302cla; Volkerpreusser 94bl; Westend 61/ GmbH 21t Hans Huber 332bl; Zoonar GmbH/Joerg Hemmer 155br; **Arcotel Hotels:** 297tr; **Artothek:** Chr. Brandstätter 33cla; Photobusiness 33tr; Ernst Reinhold 32br; **Augarten Art Hotel:** 288cra; **Austria Trend Hotels & Resorts:** 295tr. **Basilika Mariazell:** 188–9 all; **Hotel Beethoven GmbH & Co KG:** 293tr; **Hotel Berghof Crystal Spa & Sports:** 298tl; **Benediktinerstift St. Lambrecht** 178c; **Boutique Hotel Stadthalle:** Monika Haas 345tr;**Brahms Museum** (Mürzzuschlag) 172c; **The Bridgeman Art Library:** 83clb; **Hotel Bristol:** 289tr; 315bl; **Bronarski, Maciej** 329cr; **Bruno - brasserie.cafe.restaurant:** 318bl;

Burgenländisches Landesmuseum: (Eisenstadt) 28bl.
Café Pruckel: 306bc; Café Sacher: 311tr; Cook: 321tr;
Corbis: 50crb; AFP 51crb, 51tl, 51bc; Archivo Iconografico
44bl, 47crb, 49tl; Bettmann 47tl, 50br; Jonathan Blair 35tl;
Corbis Sygma 35br; EJW/Westend61 128–9; Wolfgang
Kaehler 147crb; Bob Krist 225bl, 225br; Massimo Listri
146tr, 246tr; Ali Meyer 33br, 45tc; José F. Poblete 13bc;
Leonard de Selva 50tl; James A. Sugar 164cla.
The Dining Room: 313t; Dreamstime.com:
Alessandro0770 199tl; Alexirina27000 101tr, Anskuw 2–3;
Artzzz 357bl; Richard Banary 182tr; Boris Breytman 76,
273b; Buurserstraat386 10cl; Chaoss 92; Neacsu Razvan
Chirnoaga 56; Chistyakovartyom 346br; Dieter Hawlan
194cl; Fritz Hiersche 154b; Hiro1775 218cl; Hkratky 35c;
Jedynakanna 26-7ca; Angela Jones 237tr; Kanaman789 15br;
Julius Kielaitis 206–7; Kisamarkiza 326cc; Peter Lovás 352cl;
Pavle Marjanovic 14tr; Meinzahn 290tl; Krisztian Miklosy
14bc; Lucian Milasan 347cla; Natureactiv 4crb; Mtdozier23
13tr; Caranica Nicolae 359tl; Grigore Gabriel Petre 52–3;
Piotnikov 10bc; Jerard Octav Preisler 267bl; Arseniy Rogov
347tl; Romasph 97tl; Sborisov 1c; Tomas Sereda 152–3;
Elena Schweitzer 101bc; Susazoom 239b; Alexander
Tolstykh 5cr; Travelpeter 251b; Tupungato358; Xantana
167br; Robert Zehetmayer 197tl; Minyun Zhou 5cl.
Eisriesenwelt GmbH: Michael Gruber 229br.
Festung Hohensalzburg (Salzburg): 227cra; Fotolia:
badahos 104; Zechal 69bl; Freilichtmuseum Stübing:
171tc, 171br.
Getty Images: AFP/Josch 330cla; DEA/A. DAGLI ORTI 8–9;
Werner Dieterich 238; Fly away with your imagination 12br;
Roy Jankowski 18, 268; Joe Klamar 332br; Zoran Milich 351tr.
Heeresgeschichtliches Museum, Wien: 43cr, 48br, 50bl;
Österreichische Galerie 48cla; Heurigenhof Bründlmayer:
317bl; Hollmann Beletage: 292bc; Hotel Sacher, Wien:
307tl, 322bc. iStockphoto.com: OlegAlbinsky 75br.
Josefstadt Theatre: 85tl.
Kiedrowski, Piotr: 329bc; Kosińscy, Renata and Marek:
21br, 26cla, 26bl, 27 all; Kunsthistorisches Museum, Wien:
44ca, 44cb, 46crb, 88–91.
Lurgrotte, Peggau: 172tl.
Restaurant Magnolia: 319tr; Motto: 301tl; 315t; Museum
Schloss Greillenstein: 145tl; Cafe Restaurant Mozart bei
der Oper GsmbH: 310bl; Restaurant Motto: 315bc;
Museumsverein Schloss Rosenau, Österreichisches
Freimaurermuseum: 145br.
Naturhistorisches Museum: 86tl.
ÖBB: Roman Bönsch 354tr; Andrea Klausner 354c; Oberlaa,
Neuer Markt: 311bl; Österreich Werbung: 20br; Ascher 23t;
Bald 21c; Bartl 55cra, 55ca, 96tl, 119tr, 136cla, 328clb; Bohnacker
166br, 201b, 210tr; Carniel 212tl; W. Daemon 85br; Diejun

42clb, 186cla, 187bl, 328br; Fankhauser 38cr, 253br 337br; H.
Graf 71cra; Gruenert 204cla, 237b, 257br; Haider 29b, 48bl,
80br; Haller 49cr; Herzberger 30–1, 118t, 225ca 329clb, 355tc;
Hinterndorfer Ch. 150bl; Imprima 138br; Jalain 39bl; Jellasitz
159tl; Jezierzański 144tr, 148tr, 179t, 183cr; Kalmar 81tc, 81br,
112tl, 328cla, 328bl; Kneidinger 23c, 185br,; Lamm 179bl, 182cl,
182bc, 183br; Landova 203tl; R. Liebing 290br; Mallaun 216cla,
256bc, 260tr, 261tl, 336b, 337bl; Markowitsch 36cra, 37br, 108tl,
131tl, 183tl, 195tl, 225cla, 245clb, 251tr, 329tc; Mayer 63tr, 250tl;
Nechansky 263tl; A. Niederstrasser 250bc; OEW-Bildarchiv
150tc, 328cra; Robert Pfeifer 78bl; Pigneter 195cr, 211tl; 186br,
338br; Porizka 197br, 211br, 213bl; Ramstorfer 46bc;
Salzburger Burgen/S/B 221tr; Schmeja 329tr; Simoner 28tr,
151bl; Storto 46br 209cl, 257cl; Trumler 28cla, 29c, 29cr, 29tl,
32cla, 40, 41br, 41bc, 43tl, 44cl, 46ca, 47bl, 69crb, 115b, 138c,
145bl, 149cra. 149cr, 149crb, 149bl, 187tc, 196bc, 198bl, 199br,
200tl, 200clb, 201tl, 203bl, 210b, 243cr, 244tr, 274br, 277tra.
328tr; W. Weinhaeupl 211cra, 217tr, 276tl; H. Wiesenhofer 23br,
28cb, 36bl, 37cl, 39cra, 45crb, 142tl, 149cla, 158br, 165tc, 166tl,
173t, 187br, 205tr, 274clb; Winderer 38bl.
Parkhotel Tristachersee: 325tc.
Rathaus (St. Pölten): 136br; Reuters 34bl, 34cr; The Ring,
Vienna's Casual Luxury Hotel: 294bc; Robert Harding
Picture Library: FB-Rose 185tl; Rosengarten: 324bc.
Schloss Dürnstein: 301br; Schloss Igls: 299bc; Schloss
Schönbrunn: 114–15 all; Stift Melk 146cla, 146clb, 147tl,
147bl, 147br; Cafe Speri: 313tc; Superstock: F1 Online
230–31, 254-5; Henry Georgi/Aurora Open 340–41;
imagebroker.net 180–1; LOOK-foto 196br.
T-Mobile Austria GmbH: 350c.
Universalmuseum Joanneum: N Lackner 168bl.
Restaurant Vestibül: Ingo Pertramer 300br; 312bl.
Nikolaihof Wachau: 317tr; Wiener Linien GmbH & Co KG:
359bc; Wroński, Paweł: 329bl, 329crb, 337tr, 342br, 343c,
348c; Wintersportmuseum (Mürzzuschlag): 172c; Wien
museum: 66bc; Wien-Tourismus 62tr, 63c, 68cla, 68bl;
Wirtshaus Zum Hirschenwirt: 323t.
Zefa: Weir 182tr.

Front endpapers: Alamy Images: Caro Lbl; Scot Kemper
Rbr; nagelestock.comRtl; Corbis: Walter Bibikow/JAI Ltl;
Pascal Deloche/Godong Rtr; Dreamstime.com: Chaoss Lftl;
Fotolia: badahos Lbl; Getty Images: Werner Dieterich Lca;
Roy Jankowski Lbr.

Map Cover: 4corners: Gräfenhain Günter/SIME

Jacket Front Cover and Spine: Alamy Stock Photo: Jan
Wlodarczyk
Back Cover : 123rf.com: lianem

All other images © Dorling Kindersley. For further
information: www.dkimages.com

# Phrase Book

## In Emergency

| | | |
|---|---|---|
| Help! | Hilfe! | hilf-er |
| Stop! | Halt! | hult |
| Call | Holen Sie | hole'n zee |
| …a doctor | …einen Arzt | …ine'n artst |
| …an ambulance | …einen Krankenwagen | …ine'n krank'n'varg'n |
| …the police | …die Polizei | …dee pol-its-eye |
| …the fire brigade | …die Feuerwehr | …dee foy-er-vair |
| Where is a telephone? | Wo finde ich ein Telefon? | voh fin-der ish ine tel-e-fone? |
| Where is the hospital? | Wo ist das Krankenhaus? | voh ist duss krunk'n-hows? |

## Communication Essentials

| | | |
|---|---|---|
| Yes | Ja | yah |
| No | Nein | nine |
| Please | Bitte | bitt-er |
| Thank you | Danke vielmals | dunk-er feel-malse |
| Excuse me | Gestatten | g'shtatt'n |
| Hello | Grüss Gott | groos got |
| Goodbye | Auf Wiedersehen | owf veed-er-zay-ern |
| morning | Vormittag | for-mit-targ |
| afternoon | Nachmittag | nakh-mit-targ |
| evening | Abend | ah'b'nt |
| yesterday | gestern | gest'n |
| today | heute | hoyt-er |
| tomorrow | morgen | morg'n |
| here | hier | hear |
| there | dort | dort |
| What? | Was? | vuss? |
| When? | Wann? | vunn? |
| Where? | Wo/Wohin? | voh/vo-hin? |

## Useful Phrases and Words

| | | |
|---|---|---|
| Where is…? | Wo befindet sich…? | voe b'find't zish…? |
| Where are…? | Wo befinden sich…? | voe b'find'n zish…? |
| How far is it to…? | Wie weit ist…? | vee vite ist…? |
| Do you speak English? | Sprechen Sie englisch? | shpresh'n zee eng-glish? |
| I don't understand | Ich verstehe nicht | es tut meer lyte |
| I'm sorry | Es tut mir leid | es toot meer lyte |
| big | gross | grohss |
| small | klein | kline |
| open | auf/offen | owf/off'n |
| closed | zu/geschlossen | tsoo/g'shloss'n |
| left | links | links |
| right | rechts | reshts |
| near | in der Nähe | in dair nay-er |
| far | weit | vyte |
| up | auf, oben | owf, obe'n |
| down | ab, unten | up, oont'n |
| early | früh | froo |
| late | spät | shpate |
| entrance | Eingang/Einfahrt | ine-gung/ine-fart |
| exit | Ausgang/Ausfahrt | ows-gung/ows-fart |
| toilet | WC/Toilette | vay-say/toy-lett-er |

## Making a Telephone Call

| | | |
|---|---|---|
| I'd like to place a long-distance call | Ich möchte ein Ferngespräch machen | ish mer-shter ine fairn-g'shpresh mukh'n |
| I'd like to call collect | Ich möchte ein Rückgespräch machen | ish mer-shter ine rook-g'shpresh mukh'n |
| local call | Ortsgespräch | orts-g'shpresh |
| Can I leave a message? | Kann ich etwas ausrichten? | kunn ish ett-vuss ows-rikht'n |

## Staying in a Hotel

| | | |
|---|---|---|
| Do you have a vacant room? | Haben Sie ein Zimmer frei? | harb'n zee ine tsimm-er fry? |
| double room | ein Doppelzimmer | ine dopp'l-tsimm-er |
| twin room | ein Doppelzimmer | ine dopp'l-tsimm-er |
| single room | ein Einzelzimmer | ine ine-ts'l-tsimm-er |
| with a bath/shower | mit Bad/Dusche | mitt bart/doosh-er |
| key | Schlüssel | shlooss'l |
| I have a reservation | Ich habe ein Zimmer reserviert | ish harb-er ine tsimm-er rezz-er-veert |

## Sightseeing

| | | |
|---|---|---|
| bus | der Bus | dair booss |
| tram | die Strassenbahn | dee stra-sen-barn |
| train | der Zug | dair tsoog |
| art gallery | Galerie | gall-er-ee |
| bus station | Busbahnhof | booss-barn-hofe |
| bus (tram) stop | die Haltestelle | dee hal-te-shtel-er |
| castle | Schloss, Burg | shloss, boorg |
| palace | Schloss, Palais | shloss, pall-ay |
| post office | das Postamt | dee pohs-taamt |
| cathedral | Dom | dome |
| church | Kirche | keersh-er |
| garden | Garten, Park | gart'n, park |
| museum | Museum | moo-zay-oom |
| information (office) | Information | in-for-mut-see-on |

## Shopping

| | | |
|---|---|---|
| How much does this cost? | Wieviel kostet das? | vee-feel kost't duss? |
| I would like… | Ich hätte gern… | ish hett-er gairn… |
| Do you have…? | Haben Sie…? | harb'n zee…? |
| expensive | teuer | toy-er |
| cheap | billig | bill-igg |
| bank | Bank | bunk |
| book shop | Buchladen | bookh-lard'n |
| chemist/pharmacy | Apotheke | App-o-tay-ker |
| hairdresser | Friseur/Frisör | freezz-er/freezz-er |
| market | Markt | markt |
| newsagent | Tabak Trafik | tab-ack tra-feek |
| travel agent | Reisebüro | rye-zer-boo-roe |

## Eating Out

| | | |
|---|---|---|
| Have you got a table for… people? | Haben Sie einen Tisch für… Personen? | harb'n zee ine'n tish foor… pair-sohn'n? |
| The bill please | Zahlen, bitte | tsarl'n bitt-er |
| I am a vegetarian | Ich bin Vegetarier | ish bin vegg-er-tah-ree-er |
| Waitress/waiter | Fräulein/Herr Ober | froy-line/hair oh-bare |
| menu | die Speisekarte | dee shpize-er-kart-er |
| wine list | Weinkarte | vine-kart-er |
| breakfast | Frühstück | froo-shtook |
| lunch | Mittagessen | mit-targ-ess'n |
| dinner | Abendessen | arb'nt-ess'n |

## Menu Decoder

| | | |
|---|---|---|
| Ei | eye | egg |
| Eis | ice | ice cream |
| Fisch | fish | fish |
| Fleisch | flysh | meat |
| Garnelen | gar-nayl'n | prawns |
| gebacken | g'buck'n | baked/fried |
| gebraten | g'brart'n | roast |
| gekocht | g'kokht | boiled |
| Gemüse | g'mooz-er | vegetables |
| vom Grill | fom grill | grilled |
| Hendl/Hahn/Huhn | hend'l/harn/hoon | chicken |
| Kaffee | kaf-fay | coffee |
| Kartoffel/Erdäpfel | kar-toff'l/air-dupf'l | potatoes |
| Käse | kayz-er | cheese |
| Knödel | k'nerd'l | dumpling |
| Lamm | lumm | lamb |
| Meeresfrüchte | mair-erz-froosh-ter | seafood |
| Milch | milhk | milk |
| Mineralwasser | minn-er-arl-vuss-er | mineral water |
| Obst | ohbst | fresh fruit |
| Pfeffer | pfeff-er | pepper |
| Pommes frites | pomm-fritt | chips |
| Reis | rice | rice |
| Rind | rint | beef |
| Rostbraten | rohst-brart'n | steak |
| Rotwein | roht-vine | red wine |
| Salz | zults | salt |
| Schinken/Speck | shink'n/shpeck | ham |
| Schlag | shlahgg | cream |
| Schokolade | shock-o-lard-er | chocolate |
| Schwein | shvine | pork |
| Tee | tay | tea |
| Wasser | vuss-er | water |
| Weisswein | vyce-vine | white wine |
| Wurst | voorst | sausage (fresh) |
| Zucker | tsook-er | sugar |